CONTEMPORARY
GERMANY

A Handbook

Derek Lewis

Senior Lecturer in German, School of Modern Languages,
University of Exeter, UK

with

Johannes Schwitalla

Professor of German Linguistics, Institute of German Philology,
University of Würzburg, Germany

Ulrike Zitzlsperger

Lecturer in German, School of Modern Languages,
University of Exeter, UK

ARNOLD

A member of the Hodder Headline Group
LONDON

First published in Great Britain in 2001 by
Arnold, a member of the Hodder Headline Group,
338 Euston Road, London NW1 3BH

http://www.arnoldpublishers.com

Co-published in the United States of America by
Oxford University Press Inc.,
198 Madison Avenue, New York, NY10016

British Library Cataloguing in Publication Data
A catalogue record for this book is available from the British Library

Library of Congress Cataloging-in-Publication Data
A catalog record for this book is available from the Library of Congress

ISBN 0 340 74039 6 (hb)
ISBN 0 340 74040 X (pb)

1 2 3 4 5 6 7 8 9 10

Production Editor: Anke Ueberberg
Production Controller: Martin Kerans
Cover Design: Terry Griffiths

Typeset in 10 pt Palatino by J&L Composition Ltd, Filey, North Yorkshire
Printed and bound in Great Britain by MPG Books Ltd, Bodmin, Cornwall

What do you think about this book? Or any other Arnold title?
Please send your comments to feedback.arnold@hodder.co.uk

CONTENTS

INTRODUCTION

Just before the 1998 national German election the title 'Herr Mittel Europa' appeared as a headline in a national British newspaper. Despite the defective German, the headline was making a clear point: the then Federal Chancellor, Helmut Kohl, had established for himself a place in history as the first leader of a powerful re-united Germany at the heart of central Europe (Traynor and Walker 1998). At the same time many were concerned over the continuing economic price of unification: this included large and continuing financial transfers to the former German Democratic Republic (GDR), high unemployment and a domestic tax system that threatened to stifle German enterprise. Indeed these factors contributed to Kohl losing the election, but Germany's new-found status was undeniable. Other nations were also experiencing the consequences of Germany's emergence as an international political heavyweight: the strain on the domestic budget prompted its leaders to question its role as the EU's paymaster, and it began to develop a more proactive policy towards eastern Europe, whose countries were rapidly adapting their institutions to the post-Soviet era and were anticipating closer economic and political links with the west. Since Germany will increasingly become the focus of attention in an evolving European Union (EU), now is a particularly interesting time to consider its recent past and current social, economic and political structures.

The object of this book is therefore to provide an informative and readable general introduction to aspects of life, society and culture in contemporary Germany. It is intended to be of use by A-level students, first- and second-year undergraduates and to anyone with a broad interest in German affairs. While giving as much up-to-date detail as possible, the book aims to present insights into the general structures of areas such as the economy, the education system and the media.

A timeline of Germany's history from earliest times (1800 BC) to the end of the Second World War (1945) places the country in the widest possible historical context. Key events in more recent times are: the division into small states between 1805 and 1871; the rise of Prussia and unification in 1871 (the Second Reich); the origins and course of the First World War (1914–18); Germany's first experiment with parliamentary democracy during the ill-fated Weimar Republic (1919–33); and the Third Reich (1933–45).

Taking up the theme of Germany's position in post-war Europe, Chapter 1 reviews contemporary German history from 1945 to the present day. Not until unification did Germany begin to resume the historical role that it played from the middle of the nineteenth century until the collapse of the Third Reich, when the incorporation of the GDR and the Federal Republic of Germany (FRG) into separate east–west power blocs effectively removed the German state as an independent political force at the heart of Europe.

Chapter 1 outlines the stages that led to the foundation of the two German states in 1949, the policies of West Germany's first Chancellor, Konrad Adenauer, who integrated the FRG into the western economic and political community, and the principal domestic and foreign policy directions taken by subsequent West German administrations up to unification in 1990. After unification the focus shifts to Germany's attitudes towards eastern Europe, with which it now maintains a direct frontier, and to the emergence of new foreign policy positions in the context of civil war in the former Yugoslavia. An important post-unification issue is Germany's role in the enlargement of the EU, in particular how it will influence the extension of the EU into an area where it has already become a leading investor.

Chapter 2 supplies an overview of the human and physical geography of Germany. There are sections on the structures of German industry, infra-structure, demographical developments and a brief description of each of the federal states or *Länder*. The chapter concludes with a discussion of the geographical legacy of the former GDR and of some of the problems that still confront the eastern *Länder*. Continuing the theme of the eastern states, Chapter 3 looks more closely at the former GDR, its history, political system and the background to its collapse. After considering economic, environ-mental, political and social aspects of the East German legacy, it discusses how Germany came to regard the GDR as a fundamentally criminal regime; what to do with the controversial material contained in the spy archives of the East German secret police, or *Stasi*, presented a particular problem for the authorities in post-unification Germany. Finally, the current living stan-dards of Germans in east and west are compared.

Moving on to political structures, Chapter 4 outlines the political and legal institutions of the Federal Republic of Germany and the mechanisms of national and regional government. One section considers how the legal systems of the former GDR have been integrated into those of the Federal Republic and there are brief descriptions of the main political parties. The economic development of post-war Germany is the subject of Chapter 5, which looks at how the traditional institutional structures of the economy have evolved and are responding to changing patterns of wealth production, employment and, of course, to integration within the EU.

Focusing on the concept of the 'social state' in Germany and patterns of living, Chapter 6 describes how Germany led the way in developing state welfare provision in Europe from the late nineteenth century onwards, although it now faces the problem of financing a social budget that has become unmanageable. Sections outline the main areas of welfare, notably pensions, medical and nursing care and unemployment. The chapter concludes with an account of the rise of the leisure industry in post-war Germany and a com-parison of leisure pursuits in the eastern and western states. Another area in which Germany has traditionally maintained a high reputation but faces new challenges is education. After outlining the origins of the German education system, Chapter 7 describes how the Federal Republic has responded to the growing demand for education at all levels; there are sections on the main school types, developments in the eastern states, university education and the dual system of vocational training, which is widely held to be a major factor in Germany's economic success.

The media is a particularly fast-changing area. After discussing the origins of press and broadcasting in Germany, Chapter 8 considers how the media landscape has evolved in a federally organised state and presents issues such as the relationship between public and private broadcasting, the regulatory framework, media concentration, the role of advertising and viewing patterns. The impact of computer technology and the globalisation of communication is assessed.

Chapter 9 is devoted to a range of social issues, many of which are relevant to the problems of overcoming the 'wall in the head' (*Mauer im Kopf*) mentality, or the continuing sense of alienation between east and west Germans that has survived the fall of the physical barrier embodied in the Berlin Wall. The chapter looks at 'value change' (*Wertewandel*), including attitudinal differences between citizens of the FRG and the former GDR who grew up under different social and political systems. It discusses the nature and possible origins of right-wing extremism, attitudes to foreigners and the fiercely debated issue of immigration policy. Related to the rise of neo-Nazism in the east is the question of how Germany has come to terms with its National Socialist past. Further sections consider the role of the family, the development of the women's movement, abortion and the position and function of the Church in German society.

Germany has been a pioneer of environmental protection in post-war Europe. Chapter 10 examines how German policy towards the environment has developed – in particular how it has been shaped by a strong citizen involvement – and looks at the main institutions and mechanisms of environmental protection. Specific topics such as the programme of pollution clearance in the former GDR and controversies over nuclear energy are also addressed.

A chapter on the German language will interest more than linguists. In Chapter 11 Johannes Schwitalla looks at problems of communication between east and west Germans. Although the analysis is conducted primarily from a linguistic point of view, it also reveals the extent to which living under opposing political and economic systems contributed to differences in attitude, values and social behaviour that were reflected in language usage (an earlier version of this chapter appeared in *Deutschunterricht in Japan* (1998 (3), 3–21)).

In Chapter 12, Ulrike Zitzlsperger focuses on Berlin as the cultural capital of united Germany. What emerges here is a picture of a uniquely vibrant metropolis that recovered from wartime destruction and political division during the Cold War to become a remarkable centre for cultural experimentation and innovation. After reviewing the history of the city, the author discusses the debate surrounding the movement of the seat of government to Berlin and the building opportunities afforded by the removal of the Wall, including 'architainment' – an intriguing blend of architecture and entertainment. Other topics covered include the ways in which Berlin is attempting to recall its history and the treatment of the fall of the GDR in art, literature and cinema.

By way of conclusion, the book tackles the notion of a distinctive German identity as exemplified in various aspects of language, life, customs and behaviour. A list of useful web addresses and internet resources is also provided.

As a rule the book uses the original German versions of proper names, cities and federal states in place of the traditional English forms. Examples include Hannover (for Hanover), Köln (for Cologne), München (for Munich) and Bayern (for Bavaria). The term 'billion' is used in the American sense (of one thousand million) and is equivalent to the German use of milliard.

The fully capitalised terms East Germany/East Germans and West Germany/West Germans are used as synonyms for the GDR and FRG or their citizens respectively, i.e. they refer to the seperate political states prior to unification. The forms with lower case (east/west Germany) refer to the new/old federal states as areas of the new united Germany after October 1990.

ACKNOWLEDGEMENTS

I would like to thank my wife Mary for her patience and practical support in the writing of this book. I am also indebted to colleagues at the University of Exeter and to Werner Wegstein at the University of Würzburg. Without these people and the resources of the University of Würzburg this volume would not have been possible.

Derek Lewis
March 2001

TIMELINE OF GERMAN HISTORY: 1800 BC TO AD 1945

1800–600 BC   Germanic tribes settle in southern Scandinavia, Jutland and the North German Plain; by 600 BC they have reached the Lower Rhine.

From 50 BC   The tribes occupy the land from the North Sea to the boundary of the Roman Empire (the *limes*).

AD 200–250   Formation of the West Germanic tribes (Alemannic, Franks and Saxons) who cross the Rhine and the *limes*.

375   The Germanic tribes begin a great migration (*Völkerwanderung*): Slavs move westwards to the Rivers Elbe and Saale; West Germanic tribes establish themselves between the North Sea and the Alps.

400–476   The Roman Empire disintegrates.

481–511   Clovis (Chlodwig) unites the Franks to establish a Christian empire including most of present-day France, the Rhineland and territory between the Alps and the *Mittelgebirge*.

800   The Pope crowns Charles the Great, King of the Franks (742–814), as Holy Roman Emperor. The Carolingian Empire encompasses France, Germany, Italy and part of central Europe.

843   The Empire is divided into a western, middle and eastern kingdom; the eastern kingdom covers most of present-day Germany.

962   The Saxon Otto I is crowned Holy Roman Emperor, beginning a tradition of German Emperors which lasts until 1806. The Empire includes the German dukedoms and northern Italy; from the fifteenth century it is known as the Holy Roman Empire of the German Nation (*Heiliges Römisches Reich Deutscher Nation*).

1122   *The Worms Concordat*: imperial control over the Papacy is broken
                when the Pope is acknowledged as the Church's universal
                head. Nation-states emerge in Europe, but Germany remains
                a loose collection of kingdoms and bishoprics with the
                Emperor as titular head.

1125–1350   The German Empire expands eastwards: many cities are
                founded and the German language is spoken as far as the
                River Oder. The Hanseatic League (*Hanse*) of north German
                trading cities reaches the height of its power in the fourteenth
                century.

1156   Under the Staufer King Friedrich Barbarossa Austria breaks
                away from Bayern.

1254–74   Interregnum. There is no Emperor as the princes (*Fürsten*) try
                to undermine central authority. Lawlessness and insecurity
                prevail until Rudolf of Habsburg is elected German King
                (1273).

1495   The Imperial Diet (the *Reichstag*, representing the princes, free
                cities and prelates) meets at various locations to regulate laws,
                taxes and military movements; its decisions are ratified by the
                Emperor, who is elected by a college of electoral princes (the
                Kurfürsten). The *Reichstag* fails to halt inter-state feuding, levy
                a common tax or establish an imperial army.

1517   Martin Luther sparks off the Reformation in Germany by pub-
                licising 95 theses criticising the sale of indulgences by the
                Roman Catholic Church.

1522   Luther translates the New Testament; the Reformation
                spreads throughout Germany and northern Europe, further
                dividing the Empire.

1525   Inspired by the Reformation and driven by economic and
                social injustices, Swabian peasants rise up against their rulers.
                The revolt spreads but is ruthlessly suppressed. The peasants
                lose political rights and the authority of the nobility is
                strengthened.

1555   The *Augsburger Concordat*: the Empire acknowledges the equal
                status of the Catholic and Protestant Churches and allows the
                ruler of each state to determine his subjects' confession. This
                strengthens the princes' powers and cements religious divi-
                sions.

1618–48   The Thirty Years War. Much of the Empire is devastated as the
                Emperor and the princes, aided by European powers, battle
                for authority. Austria, Brandenburg-Prussia, Sachsen, Bayern
                and Hannover emerge as the strongest of the 360 states.

1663	By now the *Reichstag* is a standing council of ambassadors with little executive authority; the Emperor has no powers over foreign policy.
1650–1789	The Age of Absolutism. Prussia expands, wrestling Silesia from Austria in 1742; part of Poland becomes Prussian in 1772.
1756–63	The Seven Years War. Prussia successfully defends its gains against Austria, which is supported by France and Russia.
1789	The French Revolution.
1792–94	French armies invade the Empire, occupying the area west of the Rhine.
1803–14	Napoleon Bonaparte, French Emperor from 1804, defeats a series of coalitions to conquer most of western Europe. In 1795 he concludes a peace with Prussia to counter France's traditional enemy, Austria. The peace lasts ten years and gives central Europe a period of stability.
1806	Napoleon creates the Rheinish Confederation (*Rheinbund*) of 16 German states in the west and south. The Holy Roman Empire ceases to exist.
1807	Napoleon defeats a renewed challenge by Austria and Prussia; Prussia loses territory and survives as a state only through Russian intervention.
1815	At the Battle of Waterloo Napoleon is defeated by a European coalition which includes Prussia.
1814–15	The Congress of Vienna restores the pre-Napoleonic European order. It reinforces the fragmentation of Germany by setting up the German Confederation (the *Deutscher Bund* of 38 states and 4 free cities) whose parliament (*Bundestag*) has little decision-making power. Prussia and Austria emerge as the dominant German states: Prussia expands in Germany and Poland, and Austria establishes a large empire in southern and eastern Europe.
1834	Prussia forms with other German states a single trade area, the German Customs Union (*Zollverein*); Austria is excluded.
1848–49	Revolutions in Switzerland and France trigger anti-monarchist uprisings in Vienna and Berlin. The Frankfurt Parliament agrees (March 1849) on a democratic framework for a 'small Germany' (including Prussia but not Austria) under a constitutional monarchy. When Prussia and Austria recover their authority the assembly is disbanded. Austria, France and Russia oppose a united Germany under Prussian leadership. Popular pressure for unification increases.

1848–63	Russia and Austria compete for power in the Balkans. Prussia's neutrality fuels hostility with Austria.
1862	Otto von Bismarck becomes Prime Minister of Prussia.
1864	Prussia defeats Denmark and annexes Schleswig-Holstein.
1866	Prussia defeats Austria at Königgratz, destroying the German Confederation and establishing its hegemony in the north.
1867	Prussia forms the North German Confederation (*Norddeutscher Bund*). Excluded, Austria consolidates its empire, renaming it the Austro-Hungarian Dual Monarchy (*Doppelmonarchie Österreich–Ungarn*). The 25-member Confederation has an elected parliament (*Reichstag*) and a federal parliament of state representatives (*Bundestag*). Real power lies with the King of Prussia and his Chancellor.
1870–71	The Franco-Prussian War. On a pretext France declares war on Prussia which invades and lays siege to Paris; France surrenders in January 1871. Prussia imposes a harsh peace settlement on France, which is forced to cede Alsace and Lorraine and pay reparations.
1871	A united German Empire is proclaimed, with the King of Prussia crowned Emperor (Wilhelm I) in Versailles.
1871–1918	The Second German Empire. Prussia dominates the Federal Assembly (*Bundestag*). Executive power lies more with the Imperial Chancellor (*Reichskanzler*) and the Emperor (*Kaiser*) than the national parliament (*Reichstag*).
1871–90	Chancellor Bismarck conducts campaigns against socialists and the Catholic Church (*Kulturkampf*) but introduces pioneering welfare legislation from 1883. He creates a network of treaties with European states in order to isolate France and maintain Germany at the centre of a delicate east–west power balance. Germany becomes an industrial power.
1881–87	The Three Emperors' Alliance of Germany, Austria and Russia.
1879	The Dual Alliance of Germany and Austria; expanded to the Triple Alliance with Italy in 1882.
1887	The (secret) Reinsurance Treaty with Russia (this is not renewed by Wilhelm II).
1888	Wilhelm II becomes Emperor.
1890	Bismarck resigns and his foreign policy is abandoned.
1894	France concludes a treaty with Russia.

1904	France concludes an Entente Cordiale with Great Britain.
1907	France, Britain and Russia conclude the Triple Entente.
1908	Austria annexes Bosnia-Herzegovina and competes with Russia for power in the Balkans.
1914	When a Serbian nationalist assassinates the heir to the Austrian throne, Austria threatens Serbia. Russia mobilises its army. Supporting Austria, Germany issues an ultimatum and enters Belgium in order to attack France; Britain declares war on Germany.
1914–18	The First World War. Germany fights Britain and France (and the USA from 1917) on its western front and Russia in the east. Russia overthrows its monarchy and concludes a separate peace with Germany in 1917 (Treaty of Brest-Litovsk).
1918–19	Germany sues for peace with the western powers. After the collapse of the monarchy and the abdication of William II various factions fight for control; a republic is declared with a new and democratic constitution. In a humiliating peace treaty (Treaty of Versailles) it loses territory and its colonies and must pay reparations. The Treaty includes a clause allocating guilt for the war to Germany (*Schuldklausel*).
1919–33	The Weimar Republic. The constitution gives more power to the elected *Reichstag* but establishes a strong Imperial President (*Reichspräsident*), which undermines the executive role of the Chancellor (*Reichskanzler*). The Republic is eventually destroyed through the inability of parties to form viable coalition governments at times of economic and political crisis.
1923	France occupies the Ruhr.
1924	After severe inflation the currency and economy are stabilised.
1922–28	Germany concludes treaties with Russia (Treaty of Berlin, 1926) and the western European powers (Pact of Locarno, 1925). It joins the League of Nations and the Kellogg-Briand Pact (1928) which are designed to promote world peace.
1929	The Young Plan sets levels of war reparations and is fiercly attacked by right-wing extremists. The plan is overtaken by a world economic crisis.
1931	Unemployment reaches 6 million. Against the background of a polarised and impotent *Reichstag*, the extreme right-wing National Socialist Party (NSDAP) led by Adolf Hitler gains seats.
1933	Hitler is appointed Chancellor. He exploits an arson attack on

the *Reichstag* to declare a state of emergency and forces through special powers allowing him to govern without parliament (*Ermächtigungsgesetz*).

1933–45   The Third Reich. Hitler removes all forms of democratic government. He exploits the weakness of western democracies to recover territory lost after 1918, extends Germany's frontiers and leads the country into global war; from 1942 genocidal racial policies are implemented to exterminate Jews.

1935   The Saarland votes to rejoin the Reich; Germany re-arms.

1936   Hitler occupies the demilitarised Rhineland.

1938   Hitler occupies Austria and German-speaking Czechoslovakia.

1939   Hitler occupies the rest of Czechoslovakia and concludes a secret non-aggression pact with the Soviet Union. When he attacks Poland, Britain and France declare war.

1939–45   The Second World War. After initial successes Hitler gains mastery of continental Europe and attacks Russia (June 1941); the USA enters the war (December 1941). The German defeat at Stalingrad (1943) marks a turning-point in the war. Allied forces land in France (June 1944) and liberate western Europe. Soviet troops take control of eastern Europe and surround Berlin; Hitler commits suicide (April 1945). The German Army surrenders unconditionally (May 1945).

1941   The Atlantic Charter. Britain and the USA declare their war aims.

1943   Casablanca Conference (January): British and US leaders demand the unconditional surrender of the axis powers (Germany, Italy and Japan). Teheran Conference (November): British, US and Soviet leaders meet for the first time to co-ordinate strategy.

1945   Meeting at Yalta (February) and Potsdam (July), allied leaders decide on the treatment of occupied Germany.

1

GERMANY AT THE CENTRE OF EUROPE

Many of contemporary Germany's traditions and institutions reflect its historical development at the political and geographical centre of Europe. The territorial fragmentation before unification in 1871, for example, was in large measure due to Germany's strategic importance to the stronger nation-states that surrounded it. Similarly, the descent of the Second German Reich (1871–1919) into European war reflected its leadership's failure to maintain a complex balance of interests between eastern and western powers. Germany's short-lived attempt at a parliamentary democracy during the Weimar Republic (1919–33), the aggressively totalitarian regime of the Third Reich (1933–45) and the post-war division into East and West Germany (from 1949 until unification in 1990) all reinforce the importance of a politically stable and democratic Germany at the heart of Europe. This chapter reviews the course of recent German history from after the Second World War (1939–45) to the present day. It ends with a look at aspects of foreign policy, including the proposed enlargement of the European Union, which once again places Germany at the pivot of an evolving Europe.

FROM OCCUPATION TO FOUNDING OF THE FRG: 1945–1949

Occupation

For the European continent the Second World War was a 'total war' in several ways. It involved numerous countries, many of which served as battlefields for foreign armies. It was fought with extreme ferocity on land, sea and air, and engaged servicemen, partisans and civilians alike. The number of human casualties was enormous – probably around 55 million – and the conflict left Germany in ruins, although the physical devastation and social breakdown were more apparent in the cities than the countryside. Between

2 and 3 million German soldiers were killed or missing, 2 million were invalided and 0.5 million civilians died in air raids. Sixteen million Germans either fled or were expelled from the east; of these over 4 million died or disappeared. In addition the Nazis engaged 10 million people in slave labour, while 6 million Jews perished in horrific circumstances in concentration camps as victims of the Third Reich's genocidal racial policies (Raff 1985: 310; Kettenacker 1997: 6, 35). In contrast to the end of the First World War (1914–18), Germans found themselves completely in the hands of the victors. The conflict exhausted Europe economically and created a political vacuum which was swiftly filled by the United States and the Soviet Union. Both countries emerged as global superpowers ready to mould the world in the image of their respective systems.

During the war the allies (the USA, Britain and the Soviet Union) met at various times to plan the shape of post-war Europe and to lay the foundations for a new world order. The most important conferences took place in 1941, when Britain and the USA concluded the Atlantic Charter, in 1943 in Casablanca and Teheran and early in 1945 at Yalta. The allies agreed to respect a people's right to self-determination, to oppose tyranny and oppression and to co-operate economically and politically. From these principles emerged the United Nations Organisation (UNO), which was founded in 1945. However, it was clear from the outset that the German people would not immediately be included within the new post-war democratic framework.

Although a war is normally concluded with a peace treaty, no such treaty was signed with Germany on its defeat. Britain, France and the Soviet Union were more concerned to rebuild their damaged economies and assert their political influence in Europe than to normalise relations with Germany, which anyhow lacked a legitimate government that the allies recognised. In 1944, when planning how to treat a defeated Germany, the allies agreed to administer separate zones of occupation through a central Allied Control Council located in Berlin. The occupation would be short-lived and Germany would retain its 1937 boundaries (i.e. before Hitler began enlarging the Reich). In the event, the advancing Russians simply took control of northern East Prussia, including the city of Königsberg, which they renamed Kaliningrad, and placed southern East Prussia and German territory east of the rivers Oder and Neiße under Polish administration. Coupled with the forcible expulsion of 9.5 million indigenous Germans, these actions amounted to annexation. At the post-war Potsdam Conference (July–August 1945), the western allies agreed only that the new boundaries were provisional. To settle this and other issues once and for all, allied foreign ministers held a succession of abortive post-war conferences. Germany's eastern border remained a contentious point even after unification in 1990.

At Potsdam the allies reaffirmed the division of Germany into zones (adding a zone for the French) and agreed that their sectors would deliver material reparations to war-damaged states. The Soviet Union in particular would receive additional reparations from the industrial western zones. Through the Allied Control Council the country would be treated as an economic and administrative unit, although authority would eventually be decentralised and industrial cartels broken up. Starting at local level and after a programme of denazification, democratic political parties would be encouraged and organs of administration established.

Disputes between the allies: first moves towards a divided Germany

Differences between the allies soon emerged, principally between the western allies (the USA, Britain and France) on the one hand and the Russians on the other. In particular the western occupiers saw little point in extracting reparations while at the same time having to import food and other essential supplies into their zones in order to sustain a population reduced to subsistence levels. It was clear that, in order to survive, Germany would have to rebuild its industry, internal markets and export capability. Moreover, the national currency (the *Reichsmark*) had become worthless as the Russians printed large quantities of banknotes in order to buy goods in the west. Aside from the mutual distrust between two power blocs representing fundamentally different political systems, it proved impossible to reconcile the Russians' insistence on reparations with the west's desire to make Germany economically self-sufficient. Finally in May 1946 the Americans halted reparations. To co-ordinate recovery the British and Americans merged their zones in early 1947. They established a mini-parliament with legislative powers (the Economic Council or *Wirtschaftsrat*), a co-ordinating Executive (*Exekutivausschuß*) and, to give the 11 regional states a voice, a Council of States (*Länderrat*). The creation of 'Bizonia', as it was known, represented the first step towards a separate West German state.

Formation of a West German government

The next stage in the division of Germany occurred at the London Conference of 1948 when the western allies and Benelux countries agreed to allow the formation of a West German government and to extend to Bizonia the Marshall Plan of American economic aid for countries recovering from the effects of the war. Immediately after the conference Britain, France and the USA instructed the leaders (Minister Presidents) of the regional states to convene a national assembly that would draft a constitution for a federally organised West German state. The assembly, or Parliamentary Council (*Parlamentarischer Rat*), met in September 1948 and comprised 65 delegates from the 11 states, many of whom felt that the western allies were pressurising them into endorsing the permanent division of Germany. Although the Soviet Union had been the first to permit political parties (from June 1945) with the object of firmly establishing the authority of the communists in any future unified German state, the western allies, distrustful of Germans' political maturity after the Nazi tyranny, had preferred to hand-pick their own zonal administrations before licensing parties, first at local and then at regional level (Kettenacker 1997: 19; Roberts 1997: 11). Political moves towards creating a West German state were paralleled by economic ones: in June 1948 Bizonia replaced the inflated *Reichsmark* with a new currency. Claiming that western policy breached the commitment made at Potsdam to treat Germany as a unit, the Russians had walked out of the Allied Control Council in Berlin (March 1948), thus ending the last remaining organ of four-power control. More drastically, they imposed a land blockade on West Berlin, intending to force the western allies from the city altogether. The blockade lasted from June 1948 until May 1949 and only a sustained airlift of essential supplies enabled West Berliners to survive.

The Soviet blockade and its failure not only hardened western resolve to establish a separate German state, it also fostered a new spirit of co-operation between the (west) Germans and their occupiers. Many Germans, fearful of Soviet encroachment, put aside their reservations about establishing a western state that would cement the east–west political division and postpone unification. In April 1949, during the blockade, the French occupation zone joined Bizonia and all three western powers handed over military authority to civilian high commissioners. A final effort by foreign ministers from the west and the Soviet Union to agree a peace treaty that would preserve German unity was abandoned in the same year. In May the Parliamentary Council approved a Basic Law (*Grundgesetz*) for the Federal Republic of Germany (Bundesrepublik Deutschland; the historical title of Reich was regarded as too tainted to retain) and chose the small provincial town of Bonn as capital in order to underline the provisional nature of the state. The FRG was born when the Basic Law came into force on 24 May 1949. The Law set out the basic rights of citizens, the role and composition of the Republic's parliamentary institutions (*Bundestag* and *Bundesrat*), its electoral law and its organisation into federal states (for an account of how the political institutions of the FRG were agreed see Kettenacker 1997: 37–46).

The FRG did not become a fully sovereign state in 1949. Through a so-called Occupation Statute, Britain, France and the USA retained control over external trade, relations with foreign states and industrial output. They also reserved the right to veto internal legislation if it affected their status as occupiers. In particular the western allies retained special rights over West Berlin whose independence from the Soviet Union they preserved through insisting on its post-war status as an occupied city under four-power control. Thus West Berlin was only partially integrated into the FRG. While the city adopted the latter's currency and laws and received financial aid from the west, its delegates to the *Bundestag* had no voting rights; when the FRG eventually adopted conscription, for instance, West Berliners were exempted.

Once the Soviet Union realised that it could not halt the establishment of an FRG within the western power bloc, it moved swiftly to set up a separate East German state within its own sphere of political and economic influence. In April 1949 it established the Council for Economic Co-operation (*Rat für Gegenseitige Wirtschaftshilfe*) to co-ordinate economic development in eastern Europe. The following month the Soviet Zone saw the establishment of a

People's Congress (*Volkskongress*) which appointed a People's Council (*Volksrat*) whose task it was formally to constitute an East German state. The German Democratic Republic (GDR) came into being on 7 October 1949. The Congresses were intended to be a counterpart to the Parliamentary Council of the western zone, but were never freely elected: their members were political appointees approved by the communists. Similarly, although the Soviet Union was the first occupying power to license political parties, it allowed national elections later than the western powers and never enjoyed genuine parliamentary approval for its measures (Kettenacker 1997: 25, 47).

ADENAUER ERA: 1949–1963

On 14 August 1949 the FRG held its first general election. The overriding issue for voters was what course the Republic should adopt in order to rebuild the economy. The result gave most seats (139) in the new *Bundestag* to the conservative Christian Democratic Party/Christian Social Union (CDU/CSU), which had campaigned to maintain the free enterprise system already introduced in the merged western zones. Despite the clear short-comings of the socialist planned economy being implemented in the Soviet zone, the Social Democratic Party (SPD) had argued for greater state involvement and central planning; it gained 131 seats. The third strongest party, the Free Democratic Party (FDP) (52 seats) represented middle-class voters and small businessmen and favoured a system of liberal capitalism. Lacking an overall majority, the CDU/CSU formed a coalition government with the FDP and elected the 73-year-old Konrad Adenauer as the first Federal Chancellor. A Rheinlander and member of the Catholic Centre Party during the Weimar period, Adenauer had been mayor of Köln from 1917 until Hitler's take-over in 1933. Imprisoned briefly by the Nazis during the war, he returned to political life to co-found the CDU in 1945; as the most senior politician, he chaired the Parliamentary Council that drafted the Basic Law.

. In view of his age and provincial background, Adenauer was not expected to remain in office for long, but his political acumen, air of sober reliability and unequivocal pursuit of western integration (see below) appealed strongly to an electorate seeking national stability after the turmoil of war, defeat and occupation. Adenauer led his party to victory in three more elections until 1963, when he resigned as Chancellor.

Adenauer was content to leave management of economic recovery to Ludwig Erhard, who had chaired the Economic Council of Bizonia and masterminded the currency reform of 1948. As the FRG's first Economics Minister (1949–69) Erhard played a leading role in persuading the CDU to adopt the model of a social market economy (*soziale Marktwirtschaft*) in the party's Düsseldorf Guidelines of 1947 (for an account of what came to be known as Germany's post-war 'economic miracle', see Chapter 5). This course, in Adenauer's view, would be the most likely to attract American support and retain the unity of his party. Increased prosperity also enabled Germany to make financial restitution to Israel for the Nazis' persecution of the Jews (Luxemburg Agreement, 1952) and to repay the foreign debts of the old German Reich (London Debt Agreement, 1953). Both gestures indicated West Germany's readiness to use its economic wealth to atone for the past and to adopt a responsible international role.

Adenauer's foreign policy

From its two attempts, in 1914 and 1939, to assert hegemony in Europe through military conquest, Germany had emerged geographically smaller and politically weakened. After 1945 Germany ceased altogether to be a practitioner of power politics in central Europe. So when the FRG eventually secured both internal stability and international recognition through western integration, the view gained ground that Germany's historical difficulties had arisen in the first place from its attempts to follow an independent German 'special way' (*Sonderweg*) at the centre of Europe; according to this interpretation Germany's troubles stemmed primarily from its failure to orientate itself earlier and unequivocally towards western cultural and political values (Zimmer 1997: 27–78). No political leader embodied this view more clearly than Konrad Adenauer. As Chancellor from 1949 and also as Foreign Minister between 1951 and 1955, Adenauer pursued a consistent pro-western policy. In his view, embedding the FRG into the western system of political, military and economic institutions while at the same time maintaining a 'policy of strength' towards the Soviet Union took precedence over making concessions to the communists in the hope that they might accept a framework for reuniting Germany. The SPD, led between 1946 and 1952 by the veteran Social Democrat and survivor of Nazi persecution Kurt Schumacher, vigorously opposed Adenauer's direction. Schumacher wished above all to avoid the mistake that his party had made during the Weimar Period, namely, to neglect the importance of nationalism in the German psyche.

Adenauer worked steadily to incorporate Germany into various post-war institutions of (western) Europe. These included the Organisation for European Economic Co-operation, which the FRG joined in 1949, the Council of Europe (1950) and the European Coal and Steel Community (1951), from which would emerge the European Economic Community (established 1957). When the USA, engaged in defending South Korea from a communist invasion from the north, insisted on a larger European defence contribution in order to counter a possible Soviet attack, the decision was made – after protracted and difficult negotiations – to allow the FRG to re-arm. With the Paris Treaties of 1955 the western allies allowed the Occupation Statute to expire and formally recognised West Germany as a sovereign state. With some restrictions (the Germans could not, for example, possess nuclear weapons or maintain an independent military command structure) the FRG joined the North Atlantic Treaty Organisation (NATO) and the West European Union, an association of European defence forces. The allies also acknowledged the FRG's sole right to represent east Germans pending a formal peace treaty ending the Second World War, a right which Adenauer had been claiming since 1949 while also challenging the validity of the USSR's unilateral imposition of Germany's eastern border, the Oder–Neiße line. As the FRG was drawn into western military and economic structures, the Soviet Union responded by annulling its wartime alliance with Britain and France and founding the Warsaw Pact as the communist bloc's counterpart to NATO (1955).

Adenauer was singularly successful in turning West Germany into a key political and military ally of the western powers. At the same time, in an effort to overcome the legacy of historical conflict between France and Germany, he cultivated a close association with the French leader, Charles de Gaulle. De Gaulle's scepticism towards American hegemony in Europe and the FRG's alignment with France produced a certain deterioration in the relationship between Bonn and Washington, especially during the presidency of John F. Kennedy (1960–63).

Fall of Adenauer

Konrad Adenauer attained the peak of his political success in 1957 when the CDU/CSU became the first party in German history to gain an absolute majority in a general election. The CDU owed its success to its appeal as a 'people's party' representing all sections of the community. By contrast the SPD had campaigned as a party primarily for the working classes. It continued to reject the successful social market model and, despite the evident disadvantages of life under Soviet socialism, maintained an anti-western stance. But by 1959 the SPD signalled its determination to broaden its electoral appeal by adopting a package of internal reforms, the so-called Godesberg Programme. The party now endorsed private enterprise and accepted re-armament and integration in NATO; it also abandoned its Marxist-based hostility to the churches. As a result, the SPD's fortunes changed rapidly. Led by Willy Brandt, the youthful and charismatic mayor of West Berlin (1957–66), the party won significant gains in the election of 1961 at the expense of the CDU, which lost its overall majority. The FDP agreed to form a coalition with the CDU/CSU only on the understanding that Adenauer would retire during the life of the parliament.

Between 1957 and his resignation in 1963 Adenauer's personal popularity declined swiftly as a result of his increasingly authoritarian style of leadership and disregard of cabinet and coalition colleagues. He discredited himself in 1959 by attempting to engineer his personal appointment as Federal President and again in 1962 through his involvement in the arrest of journalists of *Der Spiegel* magazine who had questioned the capabilities of the *Bundeswehr* and criticised the CSU Minister of Defence, Franz Josef Strauß. The perception also grew that Adenauer's inflexible policy towards the communist east was isolating West Germany and might actually reinforce, not redefine, the contested eastern borders. In particular the so-called Hallstein doctrine, in force since 1955 and binding West Germany to break off diplomatic and economic relations with any country (except the USSR) that recognised the GDR, looked increasingly outdated. Calculated to deny the GDR legitimacy as a state, the doctrine in fact made the FRG appear intransigent, opened it to extortion by developing countries seeking economic aid and reduced its influence by preventing it cultivating links with more independent eastern bloc states such as Yugoslavia. Especially after the erection of the Berlin Wall in 1961, relations with the East appeared logjammed and the prospect of reunification seemed less likely than ever.

ERHARD GOVERNMENT: 1963–1966

When Ludwig Erhard succeeded Adenauer in 1963, the CDU/CSU–FDP coalition made tentative moves towards greater flexibility in foreign affairs. Without formally abandoning the Hallstein doctrine, West Germany developed trade links with Poland and other east European countries. It also improved relations with the United States by contributing towards the costs of stationing American forces in the FRG. But despite his success as architect of the economic miracle, Erhard was unable to steer his coalition through West Germany's first recession. Unwilling to cut public and welfare spending, he proposed raising taxes in order to balance the budget (a legal requirement under the Basic Law). This prompted the FDP to abandon the coalition, leaving the CDU/CSU without an overall majority in the *Bundestag*. Erhard resigned as West Germany's second Chancellor in December 1966.

GRAND COALITION: 1966–1969

Erhard's resignation gave the SPD its first opportunity to participate in government. The Social Democrats chose to form a 'Grand Coalition' with the CDU/CSU instead of a 'Small Coalition' with the FDP. Kurt Georg Kiesinger (CDU) was appointed Chancellor and Willy Brandt (SPD) Vice-Chancellor and Foreign Minister. Despite its two-thirds majority in parliament, the cross-party coalition faced considerable challenges: to balance the budget and rescue the economy without undermining social welfare provisions and to move foreign policy beyond the stalemate of the Adenauer era. An electorate spoilt by the benefits of the economic miracle expected a rapid return to prosperity and stability. The coalition also had to cope with a period of unprecedented social unrest.

By modifying Erhard's social market model (see Chapter 5) the coalition regained control over the economy. As growth resumed, the government adjusted welfare provision to recipients' incomes, raised disability and illness benefits and introduced further savings incentives. Other domestic measures included a law providing state funding for political parties in order to reduce their dependency on pressure groups (1967), an extension of the time limit for the prosecution of crimes committed during the Nazi period (1969) and the adoption by parliament of special laws to handle national emergencies (*Notstandsgesetze*, 1968). Because of the misuse of such powers during the Weimar Period and the restrictions they imposed on civil freedoms, the emergency laws generated fierce controversy. They did, however, enable the western allies to relinquish their remaining powers over West Germany, whose national sovereignty was thus further enhanced.

Protests against expanding the state's emergency powers took place against a wider background of social disturbance which reached its climax during the student demonstrations of 1967–68. The protests originated in the American civil rights movement and in opposition to the Vietnam War, but in France and Germany they extended to attacking what were perceived as outdated and undemocratic political structures and a culture of materialism. The existence of a cross-party coalition in Germany fuelled the notion that only 'opposition outside parliament' (*außerparlamentarische Opposition*) could force any change. In practice this opposition took the form mainly of left-wing radicals preaching Marxism and permanent revolution, although a small number of fanatical groups went on to commit sustained acts of terror against the establishment, including bombing, kidnapping and murder (the Baader-Meinhof Group, also known as the *Rote Armee Fraktion*, murdered 27 people between 1971 and 1993, when it dissolved itself). Students, disenchanted with an inefficient and autocratic university system unable to handle the growing demand for education, demonstrated for more democracy and for social and political reform. Left-wing extremism was paralleled by the temporary rise of the neo-Nazi National Democratic Party (NPD). Campaigning at the height of the recession against the presence of foreign guestworkers and adopting a strongly nationalistic platform, the party gained seats in some regional parliaments but lost them after failing to enter the *Bundestag* in the 1969 general election. Although the Grand Coalition maintained its moderate stance against political extremism, German society appeared disturbingly polarised.

Foreign policy under the Grand Coalition

The coalition made little progress in foreign policy. Abandoning the Hallstein doctrine, it established diplomatic relations with Romania, Yugoslavia and other states. International relations worsened again, however, when in 1968 the USSR (along with East German troops) invaded Czechoslovakia in order to depose a reformist government. West Germany's efforts to prevent the spread of nuclear weapons in Europe and to conclude a non-aggression treaty with the USSR and its allies failed over its continuing refusal to recognise the GDR. The lack of progress was also partly due to tensions between the coalition partners, with the SPD more willing than the CDU to compromise on the recognition issue.

SOCIAL–LIBERAL COALITION: 1969–1982

In the election of 1969 the SPD gained enough seats (over 40 per cent) to form a ruling coalition with the FDP. With Willy Brandt as Chancellor, the SPD headed a government for the first time since 1930. Committed to an ambitious programme of domestic reforms, the coalition was hampered by its thin majority, the distrust of right-wing members of the FDP and the CDU/CSU's domination of the *Bundesrat*. Nevertheless, as part of its pledge to introduce 'more democracy' in German society, the government lowered the voting age in an effort to overcome the alienation many young people felt towards the state. Politicians became more closely involved in citizens' initiatives, sowing the seeds of the Green movement's eventual participation in parliamentary politics. The SPD also planned to extend co-determination in industry, but this was blocked by the FDP. They did, however, draw up plans to expand, broaden and modernise the education system (1973), and they greatly extended welfare provision, opening up health care and pensions to large sections of the population. Some measures were highly controversial and were delayed by CDU opposition. Thus laws to liberalise abortion and to make divorce dependent on irretrievable breakdown rather than on allocating 'guilt' did not come into force until 1976. Brandt also planned major improvements in infrastructure, administration and the environment, but the combined cost of expanding social welfare (on which spending increased from 22 per cent in 1960 to 33 per cent in 1975) coupled with a worsening economic situation drove national and regional budgets heavily into debt. Brandt's inability to manage the economic crisis was a major factor in his resignation in May 1974.

Ostpolitik

Undoubtedly the main achievement of the SPD–FDP coalition was détente with the east, known as *Ostpolitik*. The notion of entering into dialogue with East Berlin as a contribution to world peace and as a way of improving the practical living conditions of fellow East Germans without formally recognising the GDR originated in a famous lecture delivered in 1963 by Egon Bahr, adviser to Willy Brandt. The lecture introduced the concept of 'change through *rapprochement*' (*Wandel durch Annäherung*). After his election Brandt moved swiftly to prepare the ground for this new policy by improving relations with the Soviet Union and its allies. The Sino–Soviet rift and the Russians' keenness to access western technology provided a helpful background for *rapprochement*. Historic, if rather inconclusive, meetings between Brandt and the leader of the East German Council of Ministers, Willi Stoph, took place in 1970 in Erfurt (GDR) and Kassel (FRG). West Germany concluded a non-aggression pact with the USSR (Treaty of Moscow, 1970), and agreed with Poland to respect its western border, the Oder–Neiße line (Treaty of Warsaw, 1970). At the same time the FRG insisted that the *Bundestag*'s ratification of the treaties depended on the four allies regulating the status of West Berlin, which the East Germans had long wished to incorporate into the GDR. On 3 September 1971 a complex accord (the Four Power Agreement on Berlin) was reached which gave West Germany unhindered access to West Berlin and the right to represent West Berliners. The accord largely removed the threat of international conflict over the city's status.

Despite bitter opposition from the CDU/CSU, who regarded the agreements as a sell-out that effectively conceded the recognition issue, the *Bundestag* ratified the treaties in May 1972. In the event CDU members abstained, realising that voting down ratification would severely damage the FRG's international position. A further treaty, the Treaty of Prague, was concluded with Czechoslovakia in December 1973. Both countries agreed to regard the 1938 Munich Agreement, which ceded the Czech *Sudetenland* to Germany, as void, while leaving open the awkward question of whether the *Sudetenland* Germans residing in West Germany had German or Czech nationality.

The specific task of regulating intra-German relations lay with the governments of the FRG and the GDR. This became much easier after the Soviets forced the East German leader Walter Ulbricht, who had opposed the entire reconciliation process, to resign in late 1970. Both countries agreed a Treaty on Traffic (*Verkehrsvertrag*, May 1972) which provided a legal basis for Germans to travel between the FRG and GDR. In the Basic Treaty (*Grundlagenvertrag*) of December 1972, East and West Germany agreed to maintain good relations, to respect each other's independence and to exchange permanent representatives (though not ambassadors, which would have implied official recognition of the GDR as a sovereign state by West Germany). The treaty established a positive basis for inter-German relations; practical and humanitarian issues would be settled through individual treaties. However, conservative politicians in the FRG continued to resist the agreement with the GDR. An attempt by the Bavarian state government to have the Basic Treaty thrown out as unconstitutional on the grounds that it violated the Basic Law's commitment to reunification was rejected by the Federal Constitutional Court. Not until the general election of 19 November 1972, triggered partly by the ruling coalition's loss of its majority through defections by *Bundestag* members hostile to *Ostpolitik*, was the electorate able to endorse Brandt's policy, returning the SPD with a comfortable majority.

From Willy Brandt to Helmut Schmidt

When Willy Brandt resigned in 1974 it was ostensibly because of the discovery of an East German spy in his circle of advisers. The real reason was his inability to overcome divisions within the SPD at a time of economic difficulty. Although he did not have the historic opportunities available to Adenauer and Brandt, Schmidt proved a capable leader and crisis manager. Nevertheless his chancellorship remained dogged by intractable economic problems, in particular budget deficits and high levels of unemployment. Despite the costs to the welfare budget, the government raised unemployment and child benefits; the relative value of pensions, on the other hand, fell slightly when they were indexed to net pay instead of gross income. (The economic background to this period is described more fully in Chapter 5.)

Possibly as a result of the protests of the 1960s and controversies over *Ostpolitik* and over the coalition's social policies, Germany became one of the most highly politicised societies in western Europe. Membership of the three mainstream parties reached unprecedented levels (the SPD registered over 1 million members in 1976), as did participation in general elections (around 90 per cent in 1972, 1976 and 1980). With the SPD, CDU/CSU and FDP commanding 99 per cent of votes between 1972 and 1976, party democracy appeared secure (see Pötzsch 1998: 185). At the same time the 1970s saw the rise of citizens' movements and protest groups. Preoccupied initially with local issues such as nursery care and traffic flows, these groups rapidly developed supra-regional organisations that were able to address national issues ranging from nuclear power to the building of proposed motorways and women's rights. Emerging from such groups, the Green Party entered the Bremen local parliament in 1976 and constituted a federal party organisation in 1980 (the Greens entered the *Bundestag* in 1983). In addition, the prospect of NATO stationing medium-range atomic weapons on German territory (projected for 1983 unless the Soviet Union withdrew similar weapons from Europe) stimulated a powerful anti-nuclear peace movement. In Bonn in October 1981 and June 1982 up to 300 000 mainly young people protested against deployment – the largest demonstrations hitherto seen in Germany.

CONSERVATIVE–LIBERAL COALITION: 1982–1998

The social–liberal coalition collapsed in September 1982 when the FDP withdrew its support. Since 1970 government borrowing had risen tenfold in order to finance public spending, but Chancellor Schmidt refused to accept the FDP's plan for cuts in welfare and business taxes in order to reduce the national deficit and stimulate the stagnating economy. Furthermore his own party, the SPD, was deeply divided over his endorsement of the deployment of nuclear weapons. Overriding several dissenting members, the FPD immediately formed a ruling coalition with the CDU/CSU. Helmut Kohl (CDU), Minister President of Rheinland-Pfalz from 1969 and chairman of the CDU/CSU parliamentary group since 1973, replaced Schmidt as Chancellor. The FDP's Hans-Dietrich Genscher continued as Vice-Chancellor and Foreign Minister. The coalition's parliamentary majority, however, was not secure. In a complicated and constitutionally questionable manoeuvre Kohl engineered the self-dissolution of the *Bundestag*, forcing a general election which took place in March 1983. Emerging with a clear popular mandate, Kohl went on to win the elections of 1987, 1990 and 1994 and to become the longest-serving Chancellor since Bismarck. Between 1982 and 1990 his government adopted a variety of measures to regain control over the economy (these are described more fully in Chapter 5).

Foreign policy under the conservative–liberal coalition

In foreign policy, the coalition maintained pragmatic relations with the GDR and other communist states against a fluctuating background of east–west relations and during the international tensions of the early 1980s. At the same time it refused to compromise on the issue of according formal recognition to the GDR and continued to draw attention to violations of human rights by the Socialist Unity Party of Germany (SED). In order to improve economic conditions for ordinary East Germans, however, Bonn transferred large sums to the east. These took the form of one-off bank loans, interest-free trade credits, payments for using the transit routes linking West Berlin with the FRG and ransoms for the release of political prisoners. In return the GDR removed the infamous automatic guns on the East–West German border. The high point in inter-German understanding came in September 1987 when the East German leader, Erich Honecker, paid an official visit to the FRG, where for all intents and purposes he was treated as the head of a sovereign state.

The Soviet Union had long regarded the FRG, its main trade partner, as the key power in western Europe, and both countries' leaders exchanged numerous visits between 1973 and 1981. In 1981 a brief ice age set in when the Soviet Union invaded Afghanistan, martial law was declared in Poland, and the newly elected US President, Ronald Reagan, announced a massive re-armaments programme. Two years later the *Bundestag* voted to station medium-range nuclear weapons in the FRG, despite fierce protests from the SPD, the Greens, the peace movement and many intellectuals. The thaw came after 1985, when the reform communist Mikhail Gorbachev became Soviet leader and the USSR began to relinquish its hegemony in eastern Europe.

Determined to reduce the crippling arms burden on the moribund Soviet economy, Gorbachev and his successor, Boris Yeltsin, concluded important treaties with the USA in 1987, 1991 and 1993 committing both powers to destroying two-thirds of all intercontinental missiles by 2003. Despite Chancellor Kohl's unfortunate comparison of Gorbachev with Hitler's propaganda minister, Josef Goebbels, the Russian leader soon affirmed his interest in resuming good relations with the FRG: Kohl visited Moscow in 1988 and in June the following year Gorbachev was enthusiastically received in West Germany. It was clear that Germany, as the strongest European economy and the second largest trading nation in the world, would play a key political role in post-Soviet Europe. In 1989 the US President acknowledged Germany's leadership position and its importance in ensuring the stability of former communist states in their transition to democracy.

Continuing Adenauer's policy of cultivating a special relationship with

France in order to secure the FRG's position in western Europe, Helmut Kohl established a personal friendship with the French President, François Mitterand. Under Kohl's influence the countries of the European Community continued the process of internal integration and also widened its membership. After the demise of Charles de Gaulle, the French leader from 1958 until 1969, the Community had already begun admitting new members: the UK, Denmark and Ireland joined in 1973, Greece in 1981 and Spain and Portugal in 1986. In 1987 a package of reforms, the Single European Act, came into force. Designed to enhance internal co-operation, the Act allowed for decisions in certain areas in the Council of Europe to be reached by majority voting, thus removing the ability of a single country to veto measures. The Act extended the powers of the European Parliament and provided for the creation of a single European internal market of goods, services and the movement of people and capital by 1992. In 1995 the Community was enlarged to 15 members to include Austria, Sweden and Finland (Norway negotiated entry but withdrew in 1994). Even more important than the Single European Act was the Treaty on the European Union, the so-called Maastricht Treaty (1992), which formally established the European Union on 1 November 1993. According to the Treaty, the Union would take the form of three pillars: full economic integration in the shape of a single currency managed by a European Central Bank; inter-governmental co-operation on foreign and security policy; and collaboration on justice and home affairs. The Maastricht provisions were revised by the Amsterdam Treaty of 1997. This laid down the rules for the single currency (the euro was launched on 1 January 1999 and the European Central Bank located in Frankfurt), permitted groups of states within the EU members to share certain powers (so-called 'differentiated integration') and introduced institutional and decision-making reforms to prepare the Union for future enlargement.

Helmut Kohl: Unity Chancellor

Despite presiding over a (comparatively) successful economy and playing a positive role in Europe, Helmut Kohl will largely be remembered as the 'Unity Chancellor' – the leader who, within weeks of the collapse of the SED regime in October 1989, saw the opportunity to reunite the two Germanies and pursued it to success. He expedited the treaties which transferred the political, social and economic system of the FRG to the former GDR and secured the international framework that incorporated the new Germany within NATO and the EU. On 3 October 1990 the GDR ceased to exist, its territory being incorporated into the Federal Republic. Germans in east and west promptly rewarded Kohl and his party with their electoral support. Regional parliaments for the new eastern states were elected on 14 October, with majorities for the CDU in most *Länder*. In the national election of December 1990 the CDU–FDP coalition gained 54.8 per cent of the vote, the SPD paying dearly for their half-hearted support of the unification programme. Helmut Kohl duly became the first Chancellor of the united Germany.

In Germany the rapid moves after 1990 towards European integration led both the government and the people to reassess what had hitherto been a national consensus on Europe. As long as post-war integration in western Europe and NATO had given Germany economic prosperity, military security and political respectability, ordinary Germans had consistently supported their leaders' commitment to the European ideal. After 1990, however, the picture changed: surveys showed public support declining from 70 per cent before unification to just 38 per cent in 1997. Germans were particularly concerned about sacrificing their strong currency for the untested euro. At the same time, without questioning the principle of European integration, the government began asserting national interests across a range of issues, such as Germany's contribution to the EU budget (the largest of all members) and proposals to reform agricultural policy that threatened to cut subsidies to German farmers. The prospect of an enlarged EU incorporating eastern European states that could expect to become net recipients of transfer payments made Germany even more aware of its role as the EU's paymaster, a role that it would no longer accept uncritically.

The 1994 national election saw the coalition returned with a narrow parliamentary majority. Kohl's personal popularity had declined with the unexpectedly high costs of unification: these placed what was widely regarded as an unacceptable burden on the citizens of the old *Länder* and exposed his failure to deliver on a promise made in 1990 to transform eastern Germany into 'flourishing landscapes' of prosperity. It was all too evident that the government had grossly underestimated the economic challenges of unification. Although the government initiated extensive programmes for improving infrastructure, buildings and the environment, east German industry lacked the productivity and competitiveness to support a swift economic recovery. The situation was made worse by the fact that the labour force expected wages and other benefits to match western levels. Moreover, the former GDR lost its traditional export markets in eastern Europe, while west German companies tended to bring goods into the east rather than invest there. As a result unemployment levels in the east rose from 10 per cent in 1991 to 16 per cent in 1994. For many east Germans disillusionment with the government was coupled with a broader perception of remaining second-class citizens in the new Germany. Nevertheless, in a year packed with regional elections alongside the national one, the CDU performed relatively well, even in eastern Germany.

Helmut Kohl's final term

During his fourth and final term of office Helmut Kohl continued to support closer economic integration with Europe, notably in the form of a single currency. At the same time – and as the 1998 election approached – he appeared to distance himself from political union (embracing the subsidiarity principle that aimed to protect the authority of member states), and argued for institutional and financial reform. But it was the central issue of unemployment that lost the CDU/CSU the national election of 1998. Levels exceeded 4 million in 1995 and rose to 12 per cent (20 per cent in the east) by the end of 1997 – a post-war record. Although electoral support for the CDU/CSU remained strong in prosperous Bayern and Baden-Württemberg, the eastern state of Sachsen and parts of the Rhineland, the party lost heavily in the east, where unemployment was highest, wage levels were lowest and many Germans continued to feel disillusioned with unification. During the election campaign Kohl admitted that east and west Germans 'have grown much further apart than I would have believed', leaving observers to dub him the 'chancellor of unification' (*Einheitskanzler*), not the 'chancellor of national unity' (Traynor 1998b).

Helmut Kohl's legacy

Throughout his 16-year tenure Chancellor Kohl had steadily pursued his vision of European integration and developed the relationship with the USA, who now regarded Germany as its most important European partner. At home he had maintained a consistently centre-right position, carefully nurturing the coalition with the FDP and resisting pressures from the more conservative CSU (he did, however, support moves to stem the influx of foreigners and had little sympathy for notions of a multicultural Germany). Although the economy registered an upswing during the 1980s, it declined owing to the fiscal demands of unification, a mounting national deficit, and its failure to respond to the challenges of globalisation: deregulation of industry proceeded slowly, and a much needed tax reform ran aground through lack of cross-party support. Kohl's post-election legacy to his own party was a leadership vacuum deriving from the system of personal patronage that he had developed over many years in order to maintain tight control of policy-making and to exclude potential rivals (Clemens and Paterson 1998).

Kohl's personal reputation was suddenly destroyed when in 2000 prosecutors began investigating his involvement in accepting secret donations to the CDU in return for political and commercial favours, including the sale of armoured vehicles to Saudi Arabia and of an east German oil refinery to the French company Elf Aquitaine. The disappearance of records from the chancellery days after Kohl lost the 1998 election and his refusal to reveal sources of anonymous donations to the CDU (amounting to 2 million DM) angered his party, which forced him to resign as its honorary chairperson.

RED–GREEN COALITION: 1998–

Under its charismatic leader, Gerhard Schröder, the SPD won a landslide victory in the national election of September 1998. With a combined majority of 21 seats in the *Bundestag*, the SPD and Green Party formed a historic coalition committed to left-wing and environmentally-based policies. Reducing unemployment was top of the agenda; taxes would be cut and the burden shifted from low and middle income families to the wealthy; German citizenship would be opened to around 3 million of the country's 7.5 million immigrants (almost all 160 000 Turks entitled to vote supported the SPD); all 19 nuclear power stations would be closed and 'green' taxes imposed on petrol, electricity and gas. The single European currency would also be used as a stepping stone to a deeper political union, with a strengthened role for elected politicians from member states and the European Parliament. The SPD's domestic base was strengthened by its control of the *Bundesrat*, where it ruled 11 of the 16 regional states.

   Within a year of the election, however, the red–green coalition experienced serious setbacks. In moves that alienated his party's left wing and were widely perceived as reneging on election pledges, Schröder introduced measures designed to reduce social costs and stimulate economic growth. He back-pedalled on the pledge to close down the nuclear industry swiftly and introduced a package of budget savings that decoupled pensions and other benefits from wage levels while relieving the tax burden on business. He also planned to shift the burden of expenditure to the federal states, but as unemployment continued at over 4 million, poor regional election results in Hessen, Brandenburg, the Saarland, Thüringen, Nordrhein-Westfalen and Sachsen removed the coalition's majority in the *Bundesrat*; while the Greens failed even to pass the 5 per cent barrier to enter a local parliament, the Party of Democratic Socialism (PDS) emerged as a strong voice of protest in the east.

FOREIGN POLICY AFTER UNIFICATION

With unification and the end of the bipolar system of east–west power blocs Germany resumed its traditional position as the dominant economic and political power in central Europe (*Mitteleuropa*). Speculation about the future evolution of the German state was often conducted with reference to the kind of foreign policy it would pursue, especially with its European neighbours (Davies and Dombrowski 1997). Various scenarios were proposed. Some observers argued that Germany would become a non-military 'civilian' state preoccupied exclusively with pursuing its economic and trading interests. Alternatively, a western-orientated 'Europeanised' Germany would subordinate its national and domestic concerns to the multilateral interests of the EU. By contrast, a 'revisionist' Germany would exploit its economic strength to bind its neighbours into self-serving alliances, as it had done during the Wilhelmine era and before the Second World War. It was also suggested that a 'normalised' Germany would maintain fairly conventional relations with other nations, balancing a degree of healthy self-assertiveness with a commitment to meet global responsibilities. The disparity of such views reflected uncertainty over whether a united Germany, now free of the power blocs of the Cold War, had genuinely overcome its legacy of militaristic nationalism.

Germany's first opportunity to undertake a foreign policy initiative arose when Slovenia and Croatia declared independence from Serbian-dominated Yugoslavia in 1991. Upholding the principle that Yugoslavia could not maintain its unity through force, the federal government led a reluctant EU and USA in officially recognising the fledgling states. The initiative was not entirely successful. When the civil war spread to Bosnia, Germany was overwhelmed with refugees and faced criticism that its intervention – together with outspoken criticism of the Serbs – had made a political solution to the conflict harder to achieve.

Despite the pros and cons of its action over Bosnia it was clear that the German government saw itself as adopting a leadership role in eastern Europe. Direct military intervention in the region was, however, another matter entirely. The Germans had long debated whether their soldiers could engage in military operations outside the NATO-area ('out-of-area' activities) without violating the Basic Law. It was precisely in order to avoid direct participation in the Gulf War of 1991, when an Arab–NATO coalition attacked Iraq in order to defend Kuwait, that Germany made a large financial contribution to NATO. In June 1994 the Federal Constitutional Court ruled that humanitarian and military out-of-area operations were not unconstitutional. Parliament subsequently approved *Bundeswehr* participation in the UN embargo against Yugoslavia, and in 1995 4000 German ground troops assisted NATO in Bosnia and Croatia.

Aside from the civil war in Yugoslavia, German policy towards eastern Europe after unification was at first informed more by the need to provide economic aid than by political issues. Germany took the lead in channelling aid to the countries of central Europe that were undergoing the transition from communism to western economic and political systems. The German government not only agreed to transfer large sums to the Soviet Union in return for assent to unification, it also assisted in an airlift of food and other supplies for Russia during the crisis winter of 1990–91. Indeed the 'Aid for Russia' programme was the largest emergency aid effort ever undertaken by private donors and charities in the FRG. Aid to non-Soviet states, on the other hand, was initiated, not by the government, but by individual ministries and the *Länder*.

From 1993 assistance to central Europe was co-ordinated through the Economics Ministry and it became clear that economic aid would in future be linked to national political interests. Germany soon became the largest single provider of economic assistance to the east in terms of donor aid, trade and private investment. By 1995 its total volume of trade with the region exceeded that with the United States, and it remains the area's largest trading partner. Compared with the rest of western Europe and the USA, Germany has committed considerable resources, both private and governmental, to the east. Aid has gone mainly to well-populated countries with relatively well-developed economies, i.e. those offering the most promising return on investment and a potentially lucrative export market for German goods (over half the aid consisted of export and investment credits, with the government bearing a high proportion of the risk). Thus between 1990 and 1994, 80 per cent of official aid went to Poland, Hungary, the Czech Republic and Slovakia, followed by Romania and Yugoslavia. Poland (38 per cent of the total allocation) and the Czech Republic (20 per cent) benefited most of all, suggesting that Germany was giving priority to countries with which it shares a border and in whose political and economic stability it had a direct interest. Germany also persuaded the EU to fund programmes that directly benefitted itself (an example is the cross-border co-operation (CBC) programme to revitalise the border regions of member and non-member states).

Alongside providing aid for eastern Europe, Germany concluded a series of bilateral treaties agreeing economic, political and cultural co-operation (with Russia in 1990, Poland and Bulgaria in 1991, Hungary, the Czech-Slovak Republic and Romania in 1992). The government has also made a concerted effort to promote the German language in these countries. On the whole, however, the basis of Germany's relationship with Russia remains economic. The development of long-term political ties has been hampered by disagreements over Russia's use of military force to suppress the independence movement in Chechnya (from 1995), Russia's reservations about its former satellite states joining NATO and its support for Serbian attempts to retain control over a disintegrating Yugoslavia. But despite the focus on economic assistance and the clear linkage between aid and national self-interest, it would be wrong to regard Germany's policy towards eastern Europe as marking a re-emergence of the aggressive, revisionist and militaristic tendencies of the Third Reich. In fact Germany appears to be adopting a role somewhere between the 'civilian' and 'normal' states outlined above. The 'civilian powers' approach is further exemplified in the Stability Pact of 1999. The Pact was conceived by Germany as a multilateral, inclusive strategy involving the EU, the USA, Canada, Japan and numerous international organisations and was designed to pre-empt and resolve international conflicts through economic co-operation and the promotion of democratic values in the regions concerned. At the same time in 1998 Germany agreed without hesitation to participate in NATO air strikes against Serbia in order to protect the autonomy of Kosovo. The move, which was generally supported by the political parties and the electorate, marked an important step in the evolution of Germany's attitudes towards the use of force in foreign policy. The reluctance associated with the Gulf War (1991) and Bosnia (1995) had evidently been overcome, partly out of a sense of international responsibility and partly in order to avoid isolation from the western powers. Germany had become a full player on the global political scene (Maull 2000).

ENLARGEMENT OF THE EU

The issue of economic aid for the countries of eastern Europe is also at the centre of a debate about extending EU membership to the former satellite states of the USSR. Several nations sharing a border with Germany assumed that their years of oppression under communism would be rewarded by integration into western Europe. In particular they hoped for swift admission to the 'club' of economically prosperous states, the European Union. The EU began negotiating with the first group of applicants (Estonia, Poland, the Czech Republic, Hungary and Cyprus) in 1998 with a view to admitting them in 2003. In the meantime the EU leaders undertook to agree on institutional and structural reforms that would enable an enlarged EU to function effectively (the so-called Agenda 2000 action programme adopted in 1997). Talks with a second group (Latvia, Lithuania, Slovakia, Romania and Bulgaria) started in 2000, with Malta and Turkey also recognised as candidates. Despite the agreed timetable, fears of new demands on the EU budget, of competition from east European farmers and of a possible influx of migrant workers prompted some EU governments to back-pedal on this undertaking. Threats of special screening processes and transitional periods of up to twenty years alarmed countries hoping for rapid entry.

The need for institutional reforms to cope with EU enlargement was agreed at Amsterdam in 1997. The reforms would have to address a number of key questions. First was the future size and composition of the current 20-member European Commission (the main executive body of the Union) at which all 15 member states are represented. Simply enlarging the Commission to include a further 12 or more states was likely to make decision-making impossible. A further issue was the distribution of votes in the European Council (where prime ministers of member states develop and define general policy guidelines for the Union); in terms of its population Germany, for instance, merited more than its 10 of the total 87 votes allotted to the 15 member states. The most contentious issue of all was whether the EU should continue to allow individual member states to veto decisions on important areas of policy. An alternative to the veto would be to permit more flexible majority-based decision-making in defined areas, although EU states differ in their views on what such areas should be: Germany, for instance, currently favours harmonisation of tax policy throughout the EU but would wish to retain its national veto on asylum and immigration policy (a summit of EU leaders held at Nice in November 2000 began to identify policy areas in which qualified majority voting would be introduced). Finally, the size of the European Parliament, currently capped at 700 deputies, would require existing members to surrender seats in order to make room for representatives of more countries.

For Germany, wider EU anxiety about the effects of enlargement was complicated for a while by the re-emergence of issues left over from the Second World War. Conservative elements in the German CDU/CSU, for instance, argued that Poland and the Czech Republic should not be permitted to enter the EU until they had given Germans whom they had expelled in 1945 the right to re-settle and to be compensated for the loss of property and land. The strongest pressure for this came from the German Expellees' Association (*Bund der Vertriebenen*). The Association represented mainly expellees from Silesia and the *Sudetenland*, German territories ceded to Poland and Czechoslovakia at the end of the War. The predictably robust line adopted by right-wing exile organisations in Germany was partially endorsed by Chancellor Helmut Kohl. Playing to a conservative electorate in the election year of 1998, Kohl referred pointedly to the injustice of the expulsions and to 'outstanding bilateral issues', which the Poles and Czechs took to mean that the German government was not prepared to let the matter of the expulsions rest. A less significant but equally contentious issue was the German demand for the return of 'cultural goods', such as the 'Berlin Library' of manuscripts and art works which was taken from the defeated Reich and housed in Cracow, in Poland (the Poles agreed to return the treasures in December 1998). From such statements and demands it appeared for a time that Germany was prepared to make enlargement of the EU conditional on its own bilateral interests and to use the EU as an instrument of its foreign policy.

On balance Helmut Kohl's successor, Chancellor Gerhard Schröder, has continued the policy adhered to by previous German leaders of working closely with France, in particular on the issue of structural changes to the EU. It is true that on specific issues the relationship has come under strain, notably when France provoked outrage in Germany by carrying out nuclear tests in the Pacific Ocean in 1995, or when Germany openly objected to increasing its contribution to the EU budget under the Agenda 2000 programme. Nevertheless the post-war Franco–German consensus has been based on mutually agreed objectives and on political, if not economic, parity between the two countries. This parity could come under strain if Germany insisted, for example, on extended voting rights in EU institutions in order to reflect its much larger population. Germany's support on enlarging the EU is keenly sought by applicant states, especially in eastern Europe, and the pronouncements of its leading politicians are carefully noted. When Schröder visited Poland in September 1999, the latter pressed strongly for a firm date on admission to the EU, arguing that it would complete the process of reconciliation between the two countries. Although a timetable was agreed (see above), Günter Verheugen, former spokesman of the SPD and EU commissioner in charge of enlargement, raised some eyebrows by suggesting that Germany should hold a referendum on admitting new member states. Such a measure had never before been applied by EU states to applicants (such as Austria, Finland or Sweden, who joined in 1995) and was widely seen as reflecting rising domestic concerns within Germany about the implications of enlarging the community to include eastern Europe (Osborn 2000). Such concerns were picked up by the German Chancellor in December 2000, when he proposed denying east European workers free movement throughout the EU for up to seven years after their countries had joined the EU (Paterson 2000c).

Probably more representative of the general guidelines underpinning German government policy were statements made by the German foreign minister, Joschka Fischer, in November 2000. Fischer reinforced his country's willingness to pool more of its sovereignty within a federal Europe, to allow a core group of states (led by France and Germany) to pursue closer integration, to introduce greater democracy in EU institutions by giving more power to the European Parliament and by electing rather than appointing the President of the European Commission. Such statements confirm the pro-European, integrationist policy which Germany has consistently pursued since Konrad Adenauer. At the same time they suggest that Germany will take a more prominent role in the wider debate about the precise terms and direction of that integration (Black and White 2000). A landmark step in the adoption of such a role was Chancellor Schröder's presentation of a blueprint for integration in May 2000. Arousing more controversy with Germany's European partners than with the domestic political opposition, the plan envisaged a framework for European government, including a European president and a two-tier legislature comprising a Lower House with deputies elected by national electorates and an Upper House of senators appointed by governments of member states. Its chances of success within the wider EU notwithstanding, the plan left no doubt about Germany's intention to set a new agenda for integration (Hooper and Connelly 2001).

FURTHER READING

There is an abundance of histories of Germany. Concise and accessible overviews devoted to post-war Germany are Kettenacker (1997) and Pötztsch (1998). Larres and Panayi (1996) contain useful chapters on domestic affairs and international policy in the Federal Republic. The periodical *German History*, the journal of the German History Society, covers all periods of German history, while *German Politics* is worth watching for its wide range of studies of contemporary political issues. The German publication *Geschichte in Wissenschaft und Unterricht* contains useful state-of-the art reviews (*Literaturberichte*) on topics and periods in German historical studies. Materials on historical and political topics for educational use are available on request from the *Bundeszentrale für politische Bildung* (Berliner Freiheit 7, 53111 Bonn, *http://www.bpb.de*).

2

GEOGRAPHY AND REGIONS

In terms of area, Germany (356 974 sq km) is, after France (543 965 sq km) and Spain (505 992 sq km), the third largest country in western Europe. With 82 million inhabitants it is, however, by far the most populous, followed by the United Kingdom (almost 57 million) and France (over 55 million). Even before unification the former Federal Republic (FRG) had the highest population (61 million) of western European states, dwarfing the 16 million of the German Democratic Republic (GDR). The most heavily populated region is the state of Nordrhein-Westfalen, with the cities of the industrial Ruhr (Dortmund, Essen, Düsseldorf). By contrast, Mecklenburg-Vorpommern and Brandenburg in the east are largely rural and the least densely populated of the federal states. The capital, Berlin, the city-state of Hamburg, and München, the regional capital of Bayern, each have over 1 million inhabitants. This chapter provides an overview of the physical and human geography of this large and diverse country (*see* Fig. 2.1) and briefly characterises each of the 15 federal states; Berlin, the 16th state, is the subject of Chapter 12, which focuses on the city as the cultural capital of Germany; the city-state of Bremen is considered below in the section on Nidersachsen (see Fig. 2.2). The chapter concludes by looking at the extent to which regional structural differences persist between the former GDR and the western states some ten years after unification.

BORDERS

Germany shares borders with the Netherlands, Belgium, Luxemburg and France in the west, with Switzerland and Austria in the south and with the Czech Republic and Poland in the east. Denmark lies directly to the north of Schleswig-Holstein. Germany's borders have been largely determined by historical and political developments rather than its physical geography. The frontiers to the west follow natural features for a relatively short stretch of the River Rhine between Basel and Karlsruhe; the southern border is marked by the Swiss and Bavarian Alps. Further eastwards the mountain ranges of

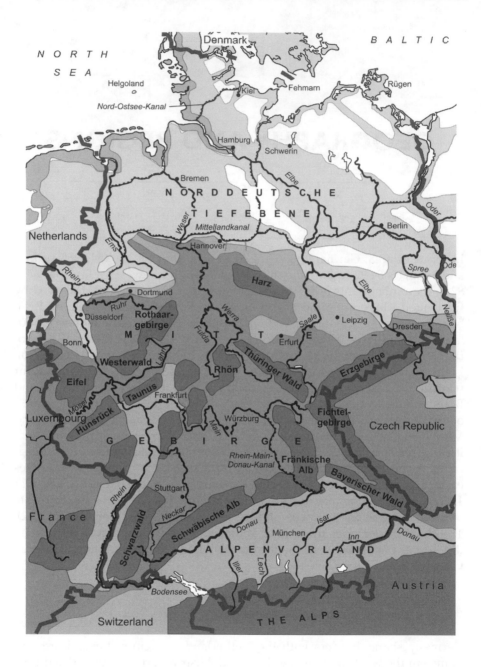

Figure 2.1   Overview of physical features

Figure 2.2 Overview of federal states. Bonn and East Berlin were the capitals of the FRG and the GDR respectively from 1949 until unification in 1990, when Berlin became the capital of united Germany. In August 1991 the *Bundestag* decided to move the seat of government and parliament to Berlin. In 1996 the *Bundesrat* also decided to move. By 2000 most central government and legislative offices had relocated to Berlin.

the Bohemian Forest and the *Erzgebirge* (literally 'ore mountains', an area traditionally rich in metals) divide southern and eastern Germany from the Czech Republic. Further north and east the rivers Oder and Neiße constitute the border with Poland. Before the Second World War German territory extended much further eastwards to include Silesia, the area south of the Baltic between the ports of Szczecin (formerly Stettin) and Gdansk (Danzig), and an enclave south of Königsberg. Germany's principal sea harbours are Hamburg at the mouth of the Elbe on the North Sea coast, and Rostock, which has direct access to the Baltic. Facing east and west and with borders to so many states, Germany truly lies at the heart of Europe, in both a political and geographical sense.

PHYSICAL FEATURES

Northern Germany forms part of the great North European Plain which stretches from France into Russia and has several major rivers, such as the Rhine, the Weser, the Elbe and the Oder, flowing across it into the North Sea. Covered with heathland or pine forests (especially in the east) the plain is mainly infertile; in the east are many smaller rivers and lakes. South of a line from Köln to Hannover and then to Leipzig, the landscape gives way to hills and woodland, interspersed with plateaux and fertile valleys. To the west are the *Eifel, Hunsrück* and *Taunus* mountains (cut through by the Rhine gorge around Koblenz) and further eastwards are the mountains of the Thuringian Forest and the *Erzgebirge*. This central mountain belt of medium-high uplands (*Mittelgebirge*, or mountains under 1000 m.) cuts Germany in two and represents a clear geographical barrier between the north and the south. Viewed from west to east and running from Belgium to the Polish/Czech border, the belt used to refer to 'central Germany' (*Mitteldeutschland*); however, during the twentieth century the term came to denote either all or part of what is now eastern Germany (Rother 1994). In the south-western corner of the central mountain belt lie the fertile plains straddling the upper Rhine; east of the Rhine (between Strasbourg and Basel) and running from north to south are the Black Forest (*Schwarzwald*) mountains, where the River Danube (*Donau*) rises. The Danube flows eastwards across southern Germany, through Austria and south-eastern Europe to the Black Sea, a distance of over 2800 km. South of the Danube the land rises gently towards the Swiss Alps in the west and the Bavarian Alps further east.

The North European Plain also covers most of eastern Germany. Directly south of the Baltic coastline the land, with some lakes and marshes, is low and rolling and rises gradually towards the Mecklenburg Lake Plateau, an area between 15 and 40 km. wide with low, steep hills, lakes and marshland. South of this plateau lies a belt of river valleys, notably of the Elbe, Havel and Spree, broken in the centre by the *Fläming*, an area of heathland. South of the river valley belt, in the west, are the *Harz* mountains (marking the beginning of the central mountain belt) and the fertile Thuringian Basin. The Basin, an area of early historical settlement, is bounded in the south by the Thuringian Forest, an 80 km long, narrow mountain ridge. East of this is the Saxon Basin. To the south, the rather inhospitable mountain chain of the *Erzgebirge* and the *Lausitz*, cut through by the Elbe, marks the border with the Czech Republic. At this point the Elbe valley, with its fertile floor and steep forested slopes reminiscent of a Swiss alpine landscape, is known as the Saxon Switzerland (*Sächsische Schweiz*).

CLIMATE AND AGRICULTURE

The climate of Germany varies from fairly mild, wet winters and cool summers on the northern coasts to the hot summers and very cold winters further inland typical of continental climates. Over 29 per cent of land in Germany is devoted to woodland and forest; the *Länder* of Rheinland-Pfalz and Hessen have the greatest proportion of these and pine, fir and spruce are the most common tree types. Around 55 per cent of the total land area is given over to agricultural activity, rising to over 60 per cent in the northern states (74 per cent in Schleswig-Holstein; Statistisches Bundesamt 1997: 274). Along the North Sea coast, Schleswig-Holstein and the lower meadows of the Alps, dairy farming predominates, while general farming is carried out in the fertile river valleys of the central belt, the upper Rhine and the Thuringian Basin; along the southern and middle Rhine, the Mosel and parts of the Main (notably Hessen and Franconia (Frankenland) in northern Bayern) vineyards are found. Germany's principal crops are, in order of tonnage: sugar beet, wheat, barley, potatoes and rye; wheat production rose sharply in the east after unification. For most German farmers meat production is the main source of income; in the north (Niedersachsen) and west (Nordrhein-Westfalen) pig-farming is widespread, followed by cattle (mainly in Bayern and Niedersachsen), sheep (mainly in the south) and poultry (also in the east). After France, Germany is the second largest beef producer in the EU.

As agriculture in the eastern states was radically restructured after unification and the large state-run collective farms were broken up, livestock holdings there fell dramatically (Statistisches Bundesamt 1997: 283–4). A legacy of the collective farms of the former GDR is that over 90 per cent of farmland in the east continues to be managed by concerns of 100 hectares or more. Compared with the west, farms also employ a relatively high proportion of the labour force, even though many agricultural workers in the east lost their jobs after unification (Schäfers 1998: 71). Although the soil was relatively poor, over 58 per cent of the surface area of the former GDR was given over to agriculture compared with 48 per cent in the west: the most fertile land lay in the south-west in the area bounded by Magdeburg, Erfurt and Leipzig. Combined with the inflexible planning structures of a command economy, the traditional pattern in the east of cultivating large arable areas for relatively low yields contributed to lower levels of productivity compared with western Germany. Since unification, however, productivity in the agricultural eastern states has risen sharply and the larger cereal farmers are considered by the EU to be globally competitive (Laabs and Meyer 2001: 32).

For Germany as a whole, agriculture meets around 80 per cent of national demand, the main imports being fish, butter, eggs, fruit and vegetables. The number of individual farming units has steadily fallen since unification (from 540 000 to 420 000 farms between 1990 and 1999). Germany still has over a quarter of a million small farms (under 10 hectares) but these account for a relatively small proportion of total farmland, most of which is managed by large concerns (over 100 hectares). Ecological and organic farming grew steadily in the final decade of the twentieth century and, in terms of area, is strongest in the eastern state of Mecklenburg-Vorpommern. Although Germany was a European pioneer in ecological farming, it has not made as much progress as, say, Austria or Switzlerland, where respectively over 10 per cent and 7 per cent of farmland is organic (compared with 2.6 per cent in Germany and an EU average of 1.9 per cent). Farms typically need considerable financial reserves to manage the two-year transition phase to organic methods, although these are likely to attract a new generation of well-educated, professionally minded farmers willing to invest in conquering new markets with high quality products (Laabs and Meyer 2001).

INDUSTRY

Traditional centres of industry are the coal mining, chemical and high quality steel producing areas in the Ruhr, with smaller coalfields in the Saar and near Aachen. Shipbuilding is located at the major ports, in particular Hamburg and Rostock. Until unification the former GDR had concentrated on exploiting its only significant mineral resource, the extensive opencast lignite (brown coal) fields located mainly at Cottbus in Brandenburg, which contributed up to 75 per cent of energy needs; chemical production and heavy industry were located in the south and east. High quality anthracite coal is mined only in the west. Although coal is still extensively mined in east and west, production steadily declined in the west after 1950 as the country became increasingly dependent on imported gas and oil and, to a lesser degree, nuclear energy. By 1995 coal accounted for 27 per cent of primary energy consumption, compared with 40 per cent for oil, 20 per cent for gas and 10 per cent for atomic power (Statistisches Bundesamt 1997: 370). Machinery, cars and electrical goods are manufactured in the south-west (Baden-Württemberg), parts of Bayern, in Sachsen (Leipzig, Chemnitz and Dresden) and around Magdeburg and Erfurt. Light industry and textiles are found principally in the Ruhr, throughout the south-west, northern Bayern and in the Rhein-Main area east of Frankfurt (Jones 1994: 98). Small to medium-sized concerns (the so-called *Mittelstand*), often family-owned, play an important role in the national economy.

On unification Germany was faced with major sectoral differences in the economies of its eastern and western states. In general the former GDR had concentrated on developing heavy industry and raw chemical production at the expense of value-added finished goods. Single sector industries and very large plants dominated towns and regions, and output levels were low by western standards. Plant and production processes were often outdated and environmentally unfriendly. Steel mills, for instance, used an obsolete open-hearth process to manufacture basic products, while the textile industry produced mass market wares in pre-war factories, operating at only 55 per cent of the productivity of western concerns (Jones 1994: 100). Since unification far-reaching structural changes have been underway in the east with the closure of most of the former GDR's traditional heavy industries, the abandonment of the single sector principle, and the development of light industry. Restoring medium-sized businesses has been a major goal of economic planners, although the lack of local capital available to citizens of a former command economy has acted as a significant obstacle.

TRANSPORT AND INFRASTRUCTURE

Long before unification West Germany had established a network of high quality road and rail links connecting its regions and major towns. The FRG's transport infrastructure was originally founded on a railway system nationalised in 1919 and on a 3000-km. network of motorways constructed during the 1930s. The post-war FRG assigned a high priority to building and maintaining fast and efficient transport links between the north and south of the country, partly to promote regional economic development and partly to facilitate trade with the rest of Europe. Germany has more length of motorway than any other country except the USA.

Before its division in 1949, Germany's transport infrastructure was orientated to link raw material production in the west with finishing industries in the east. When this pattern was disrupted the GDR was faced with the challenge of establishing a new north–south transport system that would satisfy its national needs. Unfortunately the challenge was never met; spending on transport failed to rise above 2 per cent of gross national product compared with West Germany's 5 per cent. The main casualty was the road system, which fell into serious disrepair. By unification the FRG had built 9000 km. of national motorway, while the GDR had only 2000 km. The contrast was not quite so marked in the railway network; the density of the east German railway system compared favourably with the west, although under 20 per cent of track was electrified and the technical standard was low (Jones 1994: 142). As for telecommunications, the development of an efficient and widely available public telephone service was not a priority for a regime committed to centralised economic planning and obsessed with maintaining political and social control: in 1989 over 60 per cent of lines were shared, most equipment was 30 or more years old, and the waiting list for a connection stood at 1.2 million (Jones 1994: 145).

Two years after unification a major infrastructure renewal programme for the east was implemented. Called 'Transport Projects German Unity' (*Verkehrsprojekte Deutsche Einheit*) the programme agreed 17 major projects that would not only improve links within Germany and provide the infrastructure to enable the eastern states to recover economically, but also integrate united Germany into the transport network of western and eastern Europe. Behind the plan lay the realisation that Germany (and Berlin in particular) would become the communications hub between the European Union and the east. The programme provided for the construction of extensive new rail, motorway and canal links, running mainly east to west (for details see Jones 1994: 142–5), and by 1998 the total length of motorway constructed in the east amounted to 17.6 per cent of the national network (Statistisches Jahrbuch 1999). Air traffic between east and west German cities increased after unification, and the national telecommunications company (then *Deutsche Bundespost Telekom*), also began upgrading the telephone network.

To meet the needs of private and commercial road users during the post-war period of more or less uninterrupted economic growth (the number of lorries rose by 350 per cent between 1950 and 1990 and private car ownership by a factor of 50), the FRG had concentrated on expanding its road system rather than the rail network. Although maintained to high technical standards the total length of rail track actually contracted (from 38 000 km. to 30 000 km.) between 1950 and 1990 as lines, mainly in rural areas, were closed. When the network of the former GDR was added, the total track length rose to 44 000 km.

In the decade before unification planners had begun to realise the disadvantages of simply extending the road system in order to handle an ever-growing volume of traffic and the emphasis moved away from building major new roads and towards bypassing towns and widening existing motorways. Within towns and cities, too, the earlier trend to replace trams by diesel-operated buses was reversed: many German cities developed extensive underground rail or city rail (*Schnellbahn*) networks in order to reduce reliance on road transport. At the same time government invested heavily in the railways, which currently account for over half the allocations from the German Unity Fund. Throughout Germany more lines were electrified, new stations were built and old ones renovated. By 1997 a new, north–south network was largely in place, constructed for high-speed ICE (InterCityExpress) trains with speeds of up to 250 km. per hr. The proposed magnetically powered Transrapid train link between Hamburg and Berlin was due for completion by 2005, although doubts about its cost and effectiveness were raised before this date. Despite the new investment the national rail operator (Deutsche Bahn AG) was widely considered to be inefficient and an unacceptable burden on public finance. In 1992 the government outlined plans to overhaul the system (which employed 240 000 people in 2000) and reduce costs through privatisation. Proposals included reducing labour costs, slimming down management structures and, more controversially, cutting loss-making long distance (Interregio) trains, which are financed by the railway company, and moving passengers to slower, regional lines, which are subsidised by the federal states.

Apart from investment in the railways, the 1990s saw major improvements in air transport: a new airport opened in München (1992), Stuttgart was upgraded (1995) and the decision was made to expand Schönefeld south of Berlin as the capital's future principal airport. The opening of a canal linking the River Main with the Danube in 1992 completed the waterway link between the North Sea and the Black Sea; around 25 per cent of goods were transported by rivers and canals in the FRG before unification and improvements in the inland waterway system of the east formed a major part of the German Unity investment programme.

In 1992 the government approved the first all-German transport plan (*Bundesverkehrswegeplan*) for the following 20 years. Of the projected budget of 539 billion DM, most was allocated to the railways (39.7 per cent), closely followed by roads (38.9 per cent), with waterways attracting 5.6 per cent. Although the plan envisages increases in the volume of freight carried by all three modes of transport, a strategic goal is to shift a significant proportion away from roads: the projected rates of increase are long-distance road haulage 46 per cent, inland waterway 84 per cent and rail 126 per cent. Whether these targets are achieved remains to be seen. In 1980 more long-distance freight was moved by rail than by lorry, but since then road hauliers have seen their share of the market rise considerably. In 1995 German railways conveyed only 7.6 per cent of the total volume of freight, with 82.1 per cent carried by road (of this 18.8 per cent was long-distance traffic) and 5.5 per cent by inland waterway.

Germany's national transport plan runs in parallel with a major European Union programme to develop interstate road and rail links, especially between eastern and western Europe, where the greatest growth in traffic is anticipated. It is estimated that the TransEuropean Networks (TEN) programme will have cost around 770 billion DM by 2010 (Statistisches Bundesamt 1997: 348–60). Economic co-operation and infrastructural development at a European level are also leading to the emergence of so-called 'Euro-regions'. These are very large areas of industrial and economic activity which transcend national boundaries. A notable example is the Maas–Rhine Euro-region, an economic community of 3.7 million inhabitants extending from the industrial Ruhr and Aachen to German-speaking Belgium and part of the Netherlands. A similar Euro-region may eventually emerge based on Brandenburg and Poland.

POPULATION

Although the population of Germany as a whole has steadily increased since 1945, the apparent continuity of growth masks various phases and shifts in the country's demography. The end of the Second World War was accompanied by huge movements of refugees and displaced persons: between 1945 and 1950 around 8 million refugees from former territories of the German Reich settled in western Germany, increasing its population by 16 per cent. Another 4 million (22 per cent) moved to eastern Germany (where they were known as *Neubürger* or *Umsiedler*). After 1949 the populations of the FRG and GDR developed along quite different lines.

From 1950 until 1961, when the Berlin Wall closed the escape route to the west, the FRG welcomed 2.6 million east Germans (*Übersiedler*) fleeing political repression and economic collectivisation in the GDR. Thereafter until unification the numbers of *Übersiedler* depended on the willingness of the GDR authorities to grant exit visas. Between 1962 and 1995 around 3 million *Aussiedler* (people of German ethnic origin with a right to settle in the FRG) came to West Germany, mainly from Poland and the Soviet Union; the numbers of immigrants rose sharply after the Soviet bloc began to disintegrate from the mid-1980s. After 1961 the demographic profile of West Germany was heavily determined by inward and outward movements of foreigners, mainly male guestworkers (*Gastarbeiter*) recruited to work in industry. When the economy faltered the recruitment of guestworkers was halted (after 1974) and the government even introduced financial incentives for foreign workers and their families to leave Germany (*Rückkehrhilfegesetz* 1984–85). Nevertheless, the number of foreigners continued to rise, partly as family members of guestworkers joined relatives in Germany and partly because of an influx of asylum-seekers after 1970 (reaching 438 000 in 1992). Between 1961 and 1995, 22 million foreigners settled in Germany, while almost 16 million left. Foreigners, mainly from Turkey and the former Yugoslavia, currently make up around 8 per cent of the population. They are, however, unevenly distributed across the country: the highest concentrations are in urban areas of Baden-Württemberg, Nordrhein-Westfalen and Hessen (all over 10 per cent); very few (under 2.5 per cent) live in the eastern *Länder* (see Chapter 9 for an overview of the policy of the former GDR towards migrant workers).

The population of the GDR declined between 1948 and 1961 as east Germans, disillusioned with economic decline and political oppression, moved to the FRG. Although the building of the Berlin Wall brought a brief period of stabilisation, a falling birth-rate (east and west Germany had the lowest birth-rates in the world during the 1970s and 1980s) resulted in the population dropping below 17 million. By unification the figure had sunk to 16 million, partly as a result of massive migration to the west during the *Wende*. During the next five years a further half a million east Germans migrated to the western states and it was not until the mid-1990s that the outflow showed signs of abating.

Since the 1980s Germans have become remarkably mobile, especially within their own country, producing significant regional shifts in population. In 1995 around 1 million Germans, mainly younger people and for reasons of employment, moved from one federal state to another (Schäfers 1998: 97). Populations of western states, notably Bayern, have increased, while those of eastern *Länder* have declined. In the west, and increasingly in the east, people are moving away from city centres to the suburban outskirts and to rural areas. As a result of post-unification economic uncertainties, almost 1.7 million eastern Germans migrated westwards between 1990 and 1997, although improvements in the economy and a more difficult housing and job market in the west have since brought this to a halt.

LÄNDER

Schleswig-Holstein

Area: 15 739 sq km
Population: 2.7 million
State capital: Kiel

After the Saarland, Schleswig-Holstein is by area the second smallest of the *Länder* (not including city-states). It is also the most northerly, a 'state between two seas', with coastlines to the North Sea and the Baltic. Schleswig-Holstein shares its northern border with Denmark. The region belonged to the Danish crown until a war of liberation (1864) and Bismarck's policy of territorial expansion turned it into a province of Prussia. After a plebiscite in 1920 northern Schleswig-Holstein (163 000 inhabitants) elected to return to Danish sovereignty, although 50 000 Danes still live on German territory. To the south lie Niedersachsen, Hamburg and Mecklenburg-Vorpommern.

The land is low and flat, rising to only 168 m. above sea level. Off the west coast lie the *Wattenmeer*, a protected area of mudflats and channels rich in marine and bird life, and the chain of North Frisian Islands (*Nordfriesische Inseln*). The largest of the islands is Sylt, whose long sandy beaches are a popular tourist destination. The area, including the islands, is subject to a constant process of alternate erosion by wind and sea and sandbank deposition. On the western mainland the area is marshy and protected by dykes. Around 40 000 Frisians, with a distinctive culture and Low German dialect, live here and on the islands. Between the coasts the flat and sandy landscape is known as the *Geest*. Off the east coast lies the Baltic. The milder climate on the eastern side supports several seaside resorts, including the regional capital Kiel (population: 240 000) and the historic Hanseatic city of Lübeck (216 000). The land between Kiel and Lübeck is characterised by low hills, woodland and numerous lakes. Centres of population are the towns of the east and south and the area around Hamburg in the south-west. Other towns include Flensburg (88 000) and Neumünster (82 000). As a result of its historical development Schleswig-Holstein has a large number of small communities: over 40 per cent of the population live in districts and towns of under 10 000 inhabitants.

Tourism, which is centred on the coasts and the islands, is a significant industry, directly employing 7.5 per cent (80 000) of the workforce. With 13 million visitors every year, Schleswig-Holstein rivals Bayern as Germany's holiday state. Sailing is popular along the Baltic coast and Kiel, a historic naval port, holds an annual international regatta. Historically Schleswig-Holstein has always been a rural region, where inheritance laws favoured the creation of fairly large and economical farming units. Arable crops (cereals, oil seed rape) are grown on the low hills. A speciality of the area is white cabbage (used for *Sauerkraut*). Dairy cattle and horses are reared on the more fertile grassland and marshland and pigs and sheep inland. Many meat and dairy products are exported outside the state. Market gardening is pursued intensively around Hamburg, which provides a large and convenient outlet for agricultural products. Schleswig-Holstein's many harbours also support a small fishing fleet. In all, over 7 per cent of the workforce is engaged in agriculture and the food-processing industry.

With no raw materials to speak of and located on the periphery of Germany, Schleswig-Holstein has not developed a significant industrial base. After being designated the home of the imperial navy in 1871, Kiel became a centre of shipbuilding, although the industry declined during the 1980s and currently employs only 7000 compared to 17 000 in 1977; the 11 remaining yards are mainly engaged in the construction of naval and special purpose vessels. While traditional activities in shipbuilding and textiles have declined, more modern industries, such as electronics, chemicals, biotechnology, engineering and synthetics, have expanded, especially in the Hamburg area. Centres in medical technology and research into microcomputer chips have recently been established (for example, the Fraunhofer Centre for Silicon Technology (ISiT) in Itzehoe). With over 1000 installations for generating energy from wind power, the region is also a leader in the application of environmental technology. By far the largest and fast-growing sector is service industries, contributing most of the region's GNP and employing two-thirds of the workforce. The sector includes tourism and government administration, as well as, for example, software and communications. Since unification the existing north–south transport axis has been complemented by new road and rail links designed to handle the greatly increased traffic between east and west. The focus for freight and passenger traffic passing through the region, is, of course, Hamburg. The North-Sea–Baltic Canal, linking the mouth of the River Elbe with Kiel, is the busiest artificial waterway in the world, while a canal between Lübeck and the River Elbe east of Hamburg connects the Baltic with Germany's extensive inland waterway network.

Hamburg

Area: 755 sq km
Population: 1.7 million

Like Bremen, Hamburg is a city-state with a long tradition of political independence born of its origins as a free-trading member of the medieval Hanseatic League (the *Hanse*). The second largest German city after Berlin, it is the country's leading centre for trade and commerce. Situated 100 km. inland from the mouth of the River Elbe, Hamburg boasts a huge natural harbour (the largest in Germany) that is able to accommodate large ocean-going vessels, including tankers and container ships. Inland river and canal links connect the harbour to the Ruhr, Berlin and eastern Europe. The harbour is the second largest container port in Europe (after Rotterdam) and the sixth largest in the world; it is Europe's leading rail container handling terminal. In 1996 12 000 ships arrived in the port. With the opening up of the eastern German states after unification and the enlargement of the EU to include Sweden and Finland and, in future, eastern Europe, Hamburg sees itself as well placed to maintain its position as a leading trading centre.

Hamburg's population of 1.7 million rises to over 3 million when the surrounding districts, which belong to neighbouring Schleswig-Holstein and Nordrhein-Westfalen, are included. An estimated quarter of a million people commute daily between the outskirts of Hamburg and the city centre. Despite its size and commercial role, Hamburg, with its two lakes, tree-lined avenues, waterways and nearby nature reserves well served by an integrated public transport system, is a very 'green' city. With around 11 400 retailers and large but tasteful indoor malls, it is also a major shopping centre, attracting visitors from as far afield as Scandinavia: in 1995 the turnover of retail trade totalled 27 billion DM. Culturally Hamburg provides for a hinterland that extends far into surrounding north Germany: it has a university, an opera house, an international ballet, many museums and 35 theatres.

Hamburg is involved in the trade and transfer of a huge volume of goods (72 million tons in 1996), mainly with the rest of Europe (in particular EU countries) but also with Asia and North America. Raw materials (coal, iron ore, oil), chemicals and foodstuffs all pass through the port, which handles much of Germany's fresh food imports. Three-quarters of Hamburg's working population are engaged in service industries, in particular trade, finance (domestic and international banking and insurance) and transport, although 50 per cent are now involved in media, information technology, consultancies and catering.

Although Hamburg has always been a centre of media and publishing, the last few years have seen this sector expand even further to involve over 6000 concerns employing around 50 000 people. Five of Germany's largest publishing houses are based here and several leading advertising agencies maintain branches in Hamburg (in all, over 2000 agencies employ about 10 000 staff). A number of national newspapers (*Bild, Die Welt, Die Zeit*), news magazines (*Der Spiegel, Stern*) and also television/radio magazines (*TV Movie*) are published in Hamburg, which is the home of many leading journalists. Hamburg's media landscape also extends to broadcasting and cinema. Apart from the German Press Agency (dpa or *Deutsche Presse-Agentur*) and the *Nordeutscher Rundfunk* (NDR), the city is home to Germany's first pay-as-you-view television channel *(Kanal Premiere)* and is a centre of sports productions by the satellite station SAT1. Apart from the Ufa film and television company, there are numerous smaller media firms producing animations, cartoon films and advertising films. Music companies such as Warner and Polygram are also represented.

Traditional industries, many of which still depend on the harbour, comprise oil refining and processing and refining imported goods such as coffee, cocoa, vegetable oil and rubber. Shipbuilding is much reduced (structural problems contributed to higher than average unemployment rates during the 1980s) and now concentrates on refitting and on the construction of modern, special purpose vessels. Civil aviation remains an important activity: Daimler-Benz assembles the European Airbus for final delivery and Lufthansa maintains and repairs its fleet of aircraft here. Small to medium-sized businesses predominate in mechanical and electrical engineering, microelectronics and crafts. Other industries include environmental and medical technology and pharmaceuticals. Alongside being a venue for large international conferences, hosting around 300 conferences each year for 150 000 participants, Hamburg has more recently become a focus of specialist fairs and exhibitions for smaller firms involved in maritime activities, technology, sport and catering.

Niedersachsen

Area: 47 606 sq km
Population: 7841 million
State capital: Hannover

Formed in 1946 through a merger of smaller provinces and statelets, Niedersachsen is the second largest German state in terms of geographical area. The Hanseatic city of Bremen (population: 675 000) at the mouth of the River Weser retained its independence to become the smallest of the *Länder*. It merged with the port of Bremerhaven in 1947 but nevertheless remains economically closely integrated into surrounding Niedersachsen. Niedersachsen is Germany's leading agricultural producer, with the largest number of pigs, the highest milk production per cow and the biggest field area devoted to sugar beet production. Despite its size the farming industry employs relatively few people (less than 7 per cent) and it would be wrong to regard Niedersachsen as a predominantly agricultural state. Compared with other German *Länder* it ranks fourth in terms of population, although the density of habitation (164 persons per sq km) is below the national average (229). After the Second World War an influx of refugees swelled the population by over a third but many incomers subsequently moved to the industrial centres of West Germany. In common with the rest of the country, a low birth-rate has led to an overall fall in population, with older people predominating in rural areas and city centres as younger families move to the suburbs (Grünewalder and Manthey 1986).

Niedersachsen is geographically and scenically diverse. Just off the coast lies the chain of the East Frisian Islands (*Ostfriesische Inseln*), of which the largest is Nordeney. Between the islands and the mainland is a shallow area of shifting sandbanks and channels, the *Wattenmeer*, which is exposed at low tide. The coast is lined with marshes, salt meadows and protective dykes, and flooding is a constant danger. The islands and coast are a designated national park (the *Niedersächsisches Wattenmeer Nationalpark*) and provide habitats for birds, maritime life and seals; tourism is a major industry. Further inland lies East Friesland (*Ostfriesland*), with many attractive towns and villages built in the Dutch style. Tea is the traditional drink and there are numerous varieties of fish dishes.

Further inland, on the North German Plain, the countryside changes to low, undulating hills alternating between forest and farmland, less fertile sandy land (the *Geest*) and heathland (notably the Lüneburg Heath). More fertile areas are devoted to cereal crops, sugar beet and potatoes, while sheep are reared on the heath. The heath developed as a tourist attraction from the early twentieth century, was used extensively by NATO for military exercises during the Cold War and is now largely a nature reserve.

Moving south and eastwards, the landscape resembles the *Geest*, but the more fertile soil and the raw materials found here historically supported a denser population and industrial development. As the southern uplands (the *Bergland*) are approached, the landscape changes to a mixture of wooded hills and heavily populated valleys and basins. Of the major towns and cities, Hannover, the regional capital and seat of parliament, is famous for its international trade fairs and Wolfsburg is the home of the Volkswagen car company. While most towns date back to the Middle Ages, Wolfsburg (founded in 1938) and Salzgitter (1942) were created quite recently as industrial centres. To the east lie the *Harz*, a range of medium-height mountains rising steeply (to over 1000 m.) from the surrounding lowlands. Extending into neighbouring Sachsen-Anhalt, the largely flat-topped mountains are about 80 km. long and between 24 and 32 km. wide. Because of its striking appearance the *Harz* has played an important role in German folklore and has strong associations with the supernatural. The western section of the range is covered with coniferous forests, to the east are beech and spruce woods and agriculture. The mountains are a favourite destination for tourists and winter skiers. On the edge of the *Harz* lies the historic town of Goslar, famous for its palace built for the Holy Roman Emperors.

The principal coastal towns of Niedersachsen developed during the nineteenth century as harbours for commerce and warfare. Emden at the mouth of the River Ems became a trading and fishing port (although it lost its fishing fleet with the decline of the industry in the 1970s) and Wilhelmshaven a naval base. Bremen and Bremerhaven (which merged in 1947) constitute Germany's second largest port after Hamburg, handling 10 per cent of the country's international trade. Bremerhaven became a great whaling port and during the mid-nineteenth century many thousands of emigrants passed through it on their way to North America. Still a major passenger port, it also has a container handling depot, a car terminal and a storage centre for banana imports. Wilhelmshaven, with the construction in

1958 of tanker handling facilities and a pipeline to the industrial Ruhr, became a major oil terminal. East of the Weser lies Cuxhaven, a fishing port. The expansion of the inland waterway network during the first part of the twentieth century brought increased international trade to the ports: leaving the Rhine, the *Mittellandkanal* reached Hannover in 1916 and Madgeburg on the Elbe in 1939.

Niedersachen's traditional industries included mining, steel production, engineering and textiles (Lüneburg was a centre of salt production in the Middle Ages). Because of its favourable position as a centre of communications, its proximity to fertile agricultural land, forestry and raw materials, Hannover developed as an industrial centre for car production, rubber, engineering, food and textiles, although many of these industries declined during the 1970s and 1980s. During the 1960s some companies in the southern industrial belt of the region moved to the coast, partly because of increasing reliance on imported raw materials, partly to combat labour shortages inland and partly to take advantage of government subsidies promoting regional development. Volkswagen, for instance, built a factory in Emden in 1964. The movement did not, however, solve problems of structural unemployment: the main industries along the coast are power stations, oil refineries and chemical plants, which are all capital- but not labour-intensive. In 1995 Bremen had the highest unemployment rate of all the western *Länder* (14 per cent; Statistisches Bundesamt 1997: 95). In many respects the most secure industry for the coast has proved to be tourism.

When Germany was divided (1949–90) Niedersachsen lost its historical road and rail links with the east. Although the region's ports and cities became part of a new north–south orientation in the Federal Republic, this was generally at the expense of railway lines, one-third of which were closed down as the motorway network expanded. After unification work on re-establishing the east–west infrastructure began as part of the German Unity programme. Major projects included the restoration of the railway line between Uelzen and Berlin, the building of new motorway links with Magdeburg and Halle and the construction of a canal to connect Hannover and Berlin (Jones 1994: 143).

Nordrhein-Westfalen

Area: 34 072 sq km
Population: 18 million
State capital: Düsseldorf

Nordrhein-Westfalen was created after the Second World War through the merger of a number of smaller provinces, including Westfalen and Nordrhein (both formerly part of Prussia) and Lippe. Inward immigration in the form of post-war refugees and large numbers of guestworkers during the 1960s added to its geographical and social diversity. The fourth largest federal state in terms of area, Nordrhein-Westfalen has by far the most inhabitants: its population exceeds that of the Netherlands and Belgium. Alongside Baden-Württemberg and Hessen, Nordrhein-Westfalen has a relatively high proportion of foreigners in relation to the population as a whole (between 10 per cent and 12.5 per cent, compared to the national average of 8 per cent); in absolute terms more foreigners live here than anywhere else in Germany (1.4 million in 1987), almost entirely in the cities. Although not the largest city, Düsseldorf is the state capital: its population of 573 000 is lower than that of Köln (963 000), Essen (620 000) and Dortmund (602 000). Düsseldorf's relatively small size, its location on the western periphery of the region and the development of Bonn as the capital of the Federal Republic between 1949 and 1990, undermined its status as a regional capital within a multicentric state. Nevertheless Düsseldorf remains an important financial and cultural centre with many elegant buildings, parks and gardens.

Although the *Ruhrgebiet* is famous as the industrial centre of Germany (see below), much of Nordrhein-Westfalen is rural and attracts many tourists. To the south-east lies the *Sauerland*, a landscape of low hills, river valleys and lakes; to the south-west are the *Eifel* hills, including the *Nordeifel Naturpark*, with forests, deep valleys and reservoirs. North of the River Ruhr is the gently undulating landscape of the *Münsterland*. In the north-eastern corner of the state, around Bielefeld, is the forest of the *Teutoburger Wald* whose uplands command excellent views across the *Münsterland*.

The industrial heartland of Nordrhein-Westfalen is undoubtedly the *Ruhrgebiet* area around the River Ruhr a tributary of the Rhine, which cuts through the western half of the state. In fact the industrial area extends far beyond the Ruhr valley, reaching Aachen and Bonn. During the nineteenth century the largest iron, steel and heavy industry centre in Europe developed around the Ruhr, where rich deposits of bituminous coal were found; brown coal is still mined between Köln and Bonn. Immigrants, including many thousands of Poles, flocked to work in the new industries. Leading figures in the expansion were the industrialists Alfred Krupp, who manufactured railway locomotives and armaments, and Alfred Thyssen, who produced coal, steel and heavy machinery and pioneered the exploitation of gas and electricity. A major cost of the reliance on heavy industry was a heavily polluted environment which earned the *Ruhrgebiet* the image of a landscape of soot-covered smoke-stacks overladen with an atmosphere of smog. But by the 1960s the traditional industries of the Ruhr were experiencing severe structural problems which resulted in closures, mergers and unemployment. By the 1980s the region had moved away significantly from coal mining and basic steel production towards newer and more profitable industries. These concentrated on precision engineering, quality steel and alloy products, metal processing, electronics, synthetics and chemicals. During the early 1980s the proportion of the workforce of the *Ruhrgebiet* engaged directly in manufacturing fell below 50 per cent, while numbers in trade and service industries steadily increased. At the same time the *Ruhrgebiet* developed an integrated transport system incorporating buses, trams, underground and overground trains, helping Düsseldorf, Köln and Essen to become major centres for exhibitions and trade fairs. By the late 1990s the number of small to medium-sized enterprises had risen to 450 000, although many large companies, such as Opel and Siemens, were also located in the region. As a result Nordrhein-Westfalen has retained its role as Germany's foremost industrial state, contributing one-third of gross national product. Links between industry and research are assisted by the presence of 49 colleges and universities with over 400 000 students. Alongside a new-found industrial diversity, the region also promotes itself as a centre for culture and the arts: it has no less than 23 symphony orchestras, 72 theatres and around 200 museums.

Rheinland-Pfalz

Area: 19 845 sq km
Population: 4 million
State capital: Mainz

When constituted after the Second World War, Rheinland-Pfalz was dubbed the 'test-tube state' by sceptics who doubted the viability of a patchwork state thrown together from parts of provinces formerly administered by Prussia (the Rhineland and Nassau) to the north, Hessen to the east and the Bavarian Pfalz in the south; until as late as 1975 a separatist movement campaigned for the state's partial dissolution. The area has a rich and varied history shaped by its location as a bastion against neighbouring France.

The north of the region is dominated by the central German mountain belt (*Mittelgebirge*), which include the Rheinish slate mountains (*Rheinisches Schiefergebirge*). To the south lies the *Pfälzerwald*, one of the largest forests in Germany. The Rhine flows from south to north, its many tributaries cutting through the hills and mountains on either side. In the north between the River Ahr and the Mosel (Moselle) lie the forests and uplands of the *Eifel*. Between the Mosel and the Nahe are the wood-covered hills of the *Hunsrück*. In the north-eastern corner on the other side of the Rhine are the forests of the *Westerwald* and *Taunus*; these are divided by the River Lahn, which enters the Rhine at Koblenz. Where the Rhine breaks through the hills between the *Hunsrück* and *Taunus* is the famous Rhine Gorge: here the river twists and turns through a dramatically beautiful area of steep, vineyard-clad slopes topped by ruins of medieval fortresses. The main towns (and many smaller ones) are located along the Rhine, a communications artery since Roman times. They include the regional capital Mainz (population: 185 000), Ludwigshafen (168 000) and Koblenz (109 000). Rheinland-Pfalz has very few large towns (even the state capital is relatively small), but a plethora of small communities. The distribution of population is also uneven, with the greatest concentration in the towns and cities along the southern stretches of the Rhine. Unfortunately, this section of the Rhine valley, which is economically the most important, is on the periphery of the region. As a result most of its towns are orientated to the Rhine-Main and Rhine-Neckar centres and to Karlsruhe, all of which lie outside the state boundaries. Koblenz is in fact the only city located in the geographical centre of the region.

Agriculture is very important for Rheinland-Pfalz. Intensive stock rearing and dairy farming predominate on the higher and cooler land of the central mountains, while the warm lowlands of the Rhine valley favour crops and arable farming. Of Germany's wine, 70 per cent comes from Rheinland-Pfalz; its vineyards are cultivated mainly in the valleys of the Rhine, Mosel and Nahe, and in the *Weinstrasse*, a long, sheltered basin between the upper Rhine and the *Pfälzerwald*. Although white wine is the rule, red wine is a speciality of the Ahr valley in the north. The area around Ludwigshafen is Germany's leading vegetable producer, with crops grown both in the open and under glass.

Although Rheinland-Pfalz lacks the classic raw materials of coal, iron ore or oil, it is rich in volcanic stones such as pumice (found in the *Eifel* and the *Neuwied* basin north of Koblenz), clay (extracted and processed in the *Westerwald* region, well known for its ceramics), gravel and stone, roofing slate (in the *Hunsrück*) and other naturally occurring stones. Further upstream the Rhine is a centre of a large chemicals industry: BASF employs around 50 000 at its headquarters in Ludwigshafen while the pharmaceuticals concern Boehringer is based at Ingelheim near Mainz. Cars are produced at Kaiserslautern (Opel) and lorries in Wörth at the largest heavy vehicle factory in Europe (Daimler-Benz). Other industries include computers (IBM in Mainz), sewing machines (the Pfaff concern in Kaiserslautern), glass-making (in Mainz and Bad Kreuznach), shoes (Primasens) and wood products (flooring, boards and cardboard in the valleys of the *Pfälzerwald*).

Saarland

Area: 2570 sq km
Population: 1.1 million
State capital: Saarbrücken

Apart from the city-states, the Saarland in the far south-western corner of the country is the smallest of the German *Länder*. A look at the map suggests that it is really a province of Rheinland-Pfalz, but this is not so. It has just over 1 million inhabitants, 199 000 of whom live in the state capital, Saarbrücken, although the density of population is greater than any of the eastern *Länder* and many western ones, too.

The Saarland is probably best known for its history as an area hotly disputed by France and Germany, who wanted control of its rich industrial resources. During the French Revolution the ruling nobility were driven away and all territories west of the Rhine incorporated into France. After the defeat of Napoleon, the area currently making up the Saarland became German again, albeit fragmented between Prussia, Bayern and Oldenburg. With German unification in 1871 and the exploitation of the rich anthracite coal seams in the valley of the Saar, the region became the third largest centre of heavy industry in the Reich. Combined with the iron ore from neighbouring Lorraine, which Germany annexed from France after the war of unification, Saarland coal formed the basis of a thriving steel industry. The population increased as thousands of incomers came to work in the mines. After Germany's defeat in the First World War the Saarland was once again separated from the Reich and administered by the League of Nations. Although it failed to annexe the region outright, France gained ownership of the coal mines as part of post-war reparations, earning the hostility of the German workers and civilians. In 1935 the population voted overwhelmingly to be reincorporated into Germany, handing Adolf Hitler a considerable propaganda victory. After the end of the Second World War the area reverted to provisional French rule and in 1951 the coal and steel industries of France and Germany merged (the so-called *Montan-Union*), providing the foundation for the future European Union. However, it was not until 1956 that France and Germany agreed to incorporate the Saarland permanently into the Federal Republic; this came into effect the following year.

After the Franco–German agreement of 1956 the Saarland's legal, political and economic system was integrated into that of West Germany, and its infrastructure improved. During the 1960s, however, the coal industry entered crisis, followed in the next decade by a collapse in demand for iron and steel. Only slowly has the region begun to halt the demise of its heavy industry and to counter the decline with newer, more modern businesses. Unemployment (10.7 per cent in 2000) is now only slightly above the national average. Around 20 per cent of the workforce are still engaged in coal, steel and mining. Growth sectors include service industries (employing 65 per cent of workers) and, to a lesser extent, building, metal products, the processing of rubber and synthetic materials, and the construction of public transport vehicles. Industrial landscapes have been reclaimed so that, despite its industrial history, Saarland has a generally green landscape, comprising forests (rich in fungi), vineyards, fruit orchards and farmland.

Hessen

Area: 21 114 sq km
Population: 6 million
State capital: Wiesbaden

With Nordrhein-Westfalen to the north and Baden-Württemberg and Bayern to the south, Hessen lay at the geographical centre of the old Federal Republic. Unification has scarcely altered its pivotal location. Along its north-western border run the Rheinish slate mountains (*Rheinisches Schiefergebirge*), with the wooded hills of the *Taunus* in the west and south overlooking the regional capital of Wiesbaden. In the southern corner are the forests of the *Odenwald* and *Spessart*, the latter extending into neighbouring

Bayern. Further north, west of Fulda, lies the *Vogelsberg*, a range of hills rising to 773 m. and interspersed with moorland and forests. The main cities are Frankfurt (651 000), Wiesbaden (266 000), Kassel (201 000), Darmstadt (139 000) and Offenbach (116 000). All but Kassel are concentrated in a relatively small and densely populated area in the south around the Rhine and the Main (the so-called *Rhein-Main-Gebiet*).

As with other west German states, Hessen's boundaries were set after the Second World War. Notably the industrial city of Kassel, located on the north-eastern periphery and virtually destroyed during the war, lost its links with Thüringen as a result of the post-war division: traditionally a centre of locomotive engineering and textiles, it was slow to recover economically until Volkswagen built a factory there in 1958. After 1945 Hessen's population increased dramatically: almost 1 million refugees from the east settled there and in the mid-1960s its industries attracted large numbers of foreign guestworkers. Today the proportion of foreign workers at nearly 14 per cent is much higher than the national average of over 9 per cent, which is partly due to Frankfurt's role as a European and international finance centre: over 840 000 foreign residents were registered in 1998. Between 1961 and 1989 the population as a whole expanded by nearly 22 per cent, a figure that was exceeded only by Baden-Württemberg and was only slightly higher than Bayern. Recent demographic trends have been marked by suburbanisation (a movement away from city centres to the suburbs and surrounding areas) and, since the mid-1960s, an increase in the number of workers in the service industries, especially in finance and local government (notably in Frankfurt and Wiesbaden). Reflecting a national move away from employment in traditional manufacturing, 67 per cent of the region's workforce are engaged in the service sector and 32 per cent in industrial production. In common with national trends, agriculture now employs only a tiny part of the workforce (the proportion fell from 23 per cent in 1950 to under 2 per cent in 1999).

Hessen is one of the most prosperous of the German states, with lower than average unemployment rates (8 per cent compared with the national figure of 10.6 per cent). As mentioned earlier, Frankfurt is a major employer in financial services: it houses the German stock exchange, the European Central Bank and the headquarters of many insurance companies and advertising agencies. The city also hosts numerous international exhibitions. The largest single employer is Frankfurt International airport, with 60 000 staff (followed by Opel with 25 000 workers). The airport, which is the biggest freight air terminal in Europe and handles the second largest volume of passenger traffic, attracts foreign companies to the region and contributes significantly to its export-orientated economy. In other respects, too, Hessen has developed primarily as a result of its favourable position as a communications hub: road, rail and river links all converge within a relatively small area bound by the major towns and cities of the south. Like Bayern, the lack of raw materials and traditional heavy industries has spared Hessen the problems of economic restructuring: while phosphates and brown coal are still mined in small quantities; iron ore extraction ceased in 1983. The leading 'big four' industries are chemicals, electronics, mechanical engineering and motor vehicle manufacture. Of these, chemicals and pharmaceuticals companies such as Merck, Wella, Hoechst and Behring account for over 25 per cent of gross national product. Larger electronics and electrical engineering concerns are based in Frankfurt, although many smaller firms in this sector are scattered throughout the region. Motor vehicle manufacture is located in Rüsselsheim (Opel) and Baunatal near Kassel (Volkswagen). In 1843 the first steam locomotive in Germany was built at the Henschel works in Kassel; by 1987 the Thyssen corporation had built over 30 000 locomotives.

Although Hessen does not suffer from extremes of wealth and poverty, the concentration of economic activity in the Rhine-Main-Area has produced a divide between the populous, prosperous south and the more rural north. To some extent this has been countered by investment schemes and the location of regional government and administrative offices in Kassel, where, also, a comprehensive university (Gesamthochschule) was founded in 1971. Peripheral areas have been helped by tourism, which by 1985 had long overtaken agriculture as a producer of wealth. Spas and health resorts such as Wiesbaden, Bad Schwalbach and Bad Nauheim were already popular in the nineteenth century; Wiesbaden, for instance, has been celebrated since Roman times for its curative hot springs and mineral waters. Other tourist areas include the wine-growing areas of the Rheingau (Rüdesheim) and nature parks such as Hochtaunus and Bergstrasse–Odenwald. Hessen's generally poor soil and hilly terrain mean that agriculture is economically insignificant. Increasing areas of land lie fallow or are given over to forestry (40 per cent of Hessen is woodland). Although many farms are managed as part-time concerns, the trend is towards more profitable larger units managed full-time as family concerns. Speciality crops (Sonderkulturen) include wine, asparagus, fruit and roses.

Bavaria (Bayern)

Area: 70 547 sq km
Population: 12.1 million
State capital: München

A decisive date in Bavarian history was 1806, when the reformer Montgelas create a unified administration and judicial system for the state of Bayern – structures which remained largely unchanged until 1972. Even before this date, Bayern had enjoyed several centuries of political and social stability as an independent dukedom ruled by the Wittelsbachs. As a result and partly because of its cultural and historical ties with neighbouring Austria, Bavarians have developed a keen sense of regional identity that has not always been in harmony with the political centre in Bonn or Berlin.

Geographically the largest of the German states, its population of 12 million ranks second only to Nordrhein-Westfalen (18 million). The most densely populated area is the economic and administrative hub of München (over 1.25 million), including nearby Augsburg (264 000); the proximity of the Alps attracts many incomers. Other relatively populous areas include Nürnberg (498 000), the Rhein-Main area around Aschaffenburg (which is within commuting distance of the financial centre of Frankfurt), Würzburg (128 000) and Regensburg (125 000).

Emerging from the limestone mountains of the *Schwäbische Alb* in the west, the River Danube cuts Bayern into two main regions. To the north lies *Franken* (Franconia) and to the south *Niederbayern* (Lower Bayern) and *Oberbayern* (Upper Bayern). Just north of the Danube, the *Schwäbische Alb* continues eastwards across the centre of Bayern, before turning into the *Fränkische Alb* east of the River Wörnitz. The *Fränkische Alb* eventually veers northwards towards the *Fichtelgebirge*, an area of converging mountains and forests punctuated by river valleys and known as the 'roof of Germany'. *Franken* itself is made up *Mittelfranken* (a mainly lowland area around the city of Nürnberg), *Unterfranken* in the west (around Würzburg, a winemaking centre) and *Oberfranken* to the east (stretching from Bamberg to Bayreuth). The main river of the region is the Main. In the far north-west are the low hills of the *Spessart* (around Aschaffenburg) and the *Rhön* mountains. North-east of Regensburg on the Danube are the mountainous forests of the *Bayerischer Wald* and the *Oberpfälzer Wald*, which form part of the huge Bohemian Forest that borders with the Czech Republic. A designated national park, the *Bayerischer Wald* contains woodland, wetlands and bogs. South of the Danube the landscape of *Niederbayern* opens out to a broad and flat basin before rising towards the foothills of the Alps and the regional capital, München. The Alps form a natural boundary with Austria, extending from the *Bodensee* and *Allgäu* in the west to Berchtesgaden and the *Salzburger Alpen* in the east. Due south of München, in the so-called *Bayerische Alpen* (Bavarian Alps) Germany's highest peak, the *Zugspitze*, rises to 2962 m. Originally a hunting reserve for Bavarian kings, the Berchtesgaden National Park (designated in 1978) is a specially protected part of the larger Berchtesgaden Alpine Park (*Alpenpark*), a centre of tourism and recreation. The national park contains glaciers, woodland, meadows and a rich variety of alpine flora and animal life.

Bayern was never a centre of heavy industry. Toys were traditionally manufactured in Nürnberg, while München was a centre of food products, optical equipment and precision engineering items. However, the absence of smoke-stack industries such as coal and steel has proved to be an advantage in developing a flexible, modern and export-orientated economy. Post-war growth was assisted by an influx of 2 million refugees, many with industrial and technical skills, and by incomers fleeing the GDR, who re-founded their businesses in Bayern, where land was readily available. Even today the proportion of small and medium-sized businesses remains high. The region's reputation for adaptability, quality and innovation is helped by the presence of a highly educated workforce (Bayern boasts several universities).

The main activities are computers and information technology (especially around München), electronics (employing 40 per cent of the German workforce), publishing and media (there are around 950 publishing houses), aeronautics, motor vehicle manufacture (BMW), medical and control equipment, solar energy cells and biotechnology. The regional government is investing considerable funds in research and development projects and aims to establish international centres of technological excellence (mainly in life sciences, medicine and biology) at its various universities. A major project, *BayernOnline*, currently comprises 16 pilot projects in telecommunications hardware and software (including telemedicine). Tourism is another industry in which Bayern claims a national lead. Over 70 million overnight stays by German and foreign visitors are registered every year, more than any other federal state. Bayern's evident tourist attractions are supported by intensive marketing, state subsidies, and a sophisticated information and booking system. Alongside Baden-Württemburg and Hessen, Bayern is one of the most prosperous states in modern Germany, with low unemployment rates, expanding growth and a high proportion of self-employed workers; it also has one of the lowest proportions of welfare recipients.

Forestry and agriculture account for 90 per cent of Bayern's surface area. The main exports are beef, dairy products, sugar and cereals; imports include pork, lamb, poultry, eggs, wine, vegetables and fruit. Centres of beef and dairy production are the *Allgäu* and eastern *Oberbayern*. Many small farms are run as secondary businesses, mainly in the *Spessart*, *Rhön*, around Bamberg and the *Bayerischer Wald*, while larger farms predominate in the foothills of the Alps and around München. Agriculture has been hit both by environmental policies and by reductions in EU subsidies, leading to a significant drop in income for farmers, who constitute a powerful political lobby in Bayern. Although seen as broadly competitive, Bavarian farms are acknowledged to have deficiencies in production methods and management and there is also room for improvement in export and marketing. It is likely that farms will have to diversify their activities although a potential growth area is the processing of basic food products.

Baden-Württemberg

Area: 35 751 sq km
Population: 10.4 million
State capital: Stuttgart

Baden-Württemberg is Germany's third largest state. It is also the richest and, indeed, one of the wealthiest regions of the world. It owes its present boundaries to an amalgamation in 1952 of the provinces of Baden (bordering the Rhine), Württemberg (the centre) and Hohenzollern (in the south). An echo of the tradition of petty states (*Kleinstaaterei*) can still be seen in the relatively dense network of towns and cities (with a large commuting population), the numerous castles and noble residencies and the close juxtaposition of small Catholic and Protestant communities. Differences in inheritance laws also led to the formation of large estates in some areas and of small farms in others. Unlike some other states, Baden-Württemberg is a well-balanced region that does not display a sharp contrast between prosperous urban areas and an economically stagnant rural periphery.

The region's population was increased dramatically after the Second World War by refugees from the east, many bringing new skills and re-founding businesses that they had been forced to abandon. Thereafter, a fall in the birth-rate was more than compensated by inward immigration from other parts of Germany and by an influx of foreign workers and their families, especially during the 1960s. Between 1952 and 1999 the population grew by 4 million; 1.3 million (32.5 per cent) of these were foreigners. The proportion of foreigners is well above the national average (8.8 per cent) and in Stuttgart it rises to around 20 per cent.

The upper reaches of the River Rhine, from the *Bodensee* (Lake Constance, after Lake Geneva the second largest of the Alpine lakes) to Basel (on the Swiss side of the river), and then northwards to Mannheim constitute Baden-Württemberg's southern and western boundary. Since earliest times the lowland valley of the upper Rhine (*Oberrheinisches Tiefland*) has been a major trade route linking northern Europe with Switzerland and the Mediterranean. In the south-western corner, parallel with the Rhine, is the *Schwarzwald* (Black Forest), a popular tourist area. The landscape of the *Schwarzwald* is highly varied. The north is primarily woodland, heaths and moors, while larger forests, farms and high, wooded ridges are found in the more scenic south. Leading north-eastwards from the southern *Schwarzwald* are the mountains of the *Schwäbische Alb* (Swabian Jura), whose steep, rugged ridges are cut through by deep ravines. On the south-eastern side of the ridge lies the valley of the River Danube and beyond this the foothills of the Alps (*Alpenvorland*, also known as *Oberschwaben* or Upper Swabia), an area of high moors and lakes. Between the *Schwarzwald* and the *Schwäbische Alb* is the valley of the River Neckar which, fed by several tributaries, flows north into a wide, flat basin, through Stuttgart and Heidelberg, before entering the Rhine at Mannheim. This large, fertile landscape is known for its division into *Gäue* (singular: *Gau*), an old Germanic word for tribally inhabited areas. Around 20 per cent of Baden-Württemberg is under some form of environmental protection.

The lowland areas, the *Gäue* and the *Bodensee* enjoy almost Mediterranean summers. The upper Rhine is the only part of Germany where almond trees grow and other special crops (*Sonderkulturen*) include vines, hops, fruit and even tobacco. On the whole agriculture is dominated by animal stock (dairy and beef cattle, sheep and horses), followed by cereals (wheat, barley, sugar beet, potatoes and vegetable oil).

Although industrialisation came relatively late to the region (after 1880), the area has been traditionally strong in small, highly skilled trades. This applied especially to areas where inheritance laws had prevented an expanding population from living entirely off the land. Small textiles and metal-working concerns (toys, harmonicas, turbines, cutlery, precision instruments) grew up in the foothills of the *Schwäbische Alb* (the *Albvorland*). Larger industries were established in the cities, such as Mannheim, Karlsruhe, Pforzheim, Heilbronn and, notably, Stuttgart. In the *Schwarzwald* glass production gave way to clockmaking (the first cuckoo clock was made here in the eighteenth century), providing a skills basis for the production of medical, optical and photographic equipment. Today Baden-Württemberg's main industries, which are strongly export-orientated, include engineering and metal processing, motor manufacturing (Daimler-Benz and Porsche), electrical generation and distribution equipment, papermaking and printing, food and tobacco processing, precision instruments, chemicals, textiles and electronics. Tourism and leisure are important in the *Schwarzwald* (famous for its health spas, hotels, restaurants and its opportunities for walking and winter sports), the *Bodensee* (where there is some conflict between the interests of tourism and ecology), the *Allgäu* (west of the *Bodensee*) and, to a lesser extent, the *Schwäbische Alb*. The region's prosperity and the diversity of its industry are reflected in the low unemployment rate: at 5.9 per cent in 2000 this was the lowest in Germany (average: 10.6 per cent) and contrasted markedly, for instance, with Sachsen-Anhalt in the east (21.5 per cent).

Mecklenburg-Vorpommern

Area: 23 169 sq km
Population: 1.8 million
State capital: Schwerin

Present-day Mecklenburg-Vorpommern is what remains of the pre-war provinces of Mecklenburg, lying to the east of Schleswig-Holstein, and Pomerania, which formerly straddled the River Oder (territory east of the Oder and the port of Stettin were ceded to Poland after the Second World War). When Bismarck declared that everything in this north-eastern corner of the then German Empire happens a hundred years later, he meant that it was the most backward of the provinces. Even today, of all the federal states it is the least known and visited by western Germans. Compared with the rest of the country it has few raw materials, little industry, a poor infrastructure and, after Sachsen-Anhalt (21.5 per cent), the second highest unemployment rate (19.1 per cent in 2000). Away from the scenic coastline the countryside is flat and often marshy and the land is relatively infertile, the main crops being rye, potatoes and, on better soil, wheat and sugar beet. Schwerin is the state capital, and Rostock the main port and largest town; the GDR developed an industrial centre at Schwerin and shipbuilding in the coastal ports of Rostock, Wismar, Warnemünde, Stralsund and Wolgast; a nuclear power station at Greifswald was closed after unification.

Mecklenburg-Vorpommern is the most sparsely populated of the federal states (with 79 inhabitants per sq km; Brandenburg to the south has 86).

From at least the nineteenth century Pomerania suffered from its status as a border region on the periphery of western Europe and, despite the GDR's efforts to introduce new industry, it continued to be marginalised and neglected by district administrations based in Schwerin (until 1952) and in Rostock and Neubrandenburg (1952–90; Albrecht *et al.* 1996). In 1945 the region as a whole experienced considerable instability as refugees from the advancing Soviet Army arrived while others fled westwards. Periodic influxes included farmers from the west of Germany after the First World War and armaments workers during the Third Reich; the GDR encouraged migrants to work in new industrial centres in Schwerin and in the coastal ports and between 1975 and 1989 the population actually grew by 1.5 per cent. After the fall of the GDR, however, there was a dramatic outflow; in 1990 a record 50 000 people left the region, mostly the young and well qualified. Although this figure was exceptional, the economic uncertainties of the post-unification period and a falling birth-rate mean that the population continues to decline (by 7 per cent between 1990 and 1999). In common with all the eastern states only a tiny proportion of the population are foreigners (1.7 per cent, compared with 6.7 per cent for Niedersachsen and over 15 per cent for Hamburg), but the incidence of racially motivated attacks on non-Germans is second only to Sachsen-Anhalt (*Der Spiegel*, (34) 21 August 2000: 37–40).

The Baltic coastline is an area of outstanding natural beauty, with two national parks, the *Vorpommersche Boddenlandschaft* (*Bodden* are large, shallow, offshore lagoons) and Jasmund on Rügen, Germany's largest island. Rügen's landscape of chalk cliffs, sandy beaches, shallow bays, low grassy hills and beech woods behind the sand dunes has attracted many artists and painters. After unification the south-eastern part of the island, including one *Bodden*, was designated a biosphere reserve and the offshore islet of Vilm houses an academy for the protection of nature. Further east, the island of Usedom is noted for its wide sandy beaches and small tourist resorts. The mainland boasts numerous nature reserves (30 per cent of Mecklenburg-Vorpommern is under some form of environmental protection), and the Müritz National Park in the south has abundant lakes, moorland and forests. During the Cold War Mecklenburg-Vorpommern was a favourite area for military manoeuvres, which allowed animal and plant life to thrive undisturbed by the public (for descriptions of the islands and their natural features see Speakman and Speakman 1992: 81–91).

The GDR authorities made concerted efforts to industrialise this region; an industrial complex based on leather goods, engineering and plastics was established in the southern part of Schwerin, providing 7600 jobs (1989) and increasing the population by 60 000. None of the industries survived unification intact, although by 1994 over 300 smaller, private companies had emerged from the original state-run eight and the physical area of the complex actually increased. The number of employees, however, declined to 5100, with few signs of large-scale re-industrialisation. Half a decade after unification only 2.8 per cent of the population were engaged in industrial production compared with 4.5 per cent for the new *Länder* and 8.7 per cent for the west (Eich-Born 1996: 517–22).

In 1939 Mecklenburg-Vorpommern had contributed only 2 per cent of national shipbuilding capacity. After 1945 the industry repaired vessels for the Soviet Union but expanded significantly when the GDR decided to build a national fishing and merchant fleet; by 1989 six shipyards were operating along the coast (Boizenburg, Wismar, Warnemünde, Rostock, Stralsund and Wolgast). Between 1984 and 1989, 60 per cent of vessels were built for the Soviet Union and 13 per cent for the home fleet: the rest were sold at a loss to the west for valuable foreign currency. By 1989 shipbuilding and its suppliers accounted for around 40 per cent of Mecklenburg-Vorpommern's economic production and employed 41 per cent of the working population. However, agriculture, food production and, especially on the coast, tourism continued to be the region's mainstays.

After unification the shipyards faced a crisis. They could not compete with the more efficient west German yards which ranked as the third largest producers (behind Japan and Korea), even after cutting their workforce from 78 000 to around 30 000 and their output by a half in response to a downturn in international demand for ships and oil tankers. The last thing Germany (and the European Union) needed at this stage was more shipbuilding capacity. Nevertheless, a political decision was taken to retain and, with the help of massive state subsidies, to privatise and modernise the eastern yards. Production was set at 40 per cent of the pre-unification level. The yards at Stralsund (Volkswerft) and Rostock (Neptun) ceased to build ships altogether, undertaking only repair work or diversifying into other industries. German and Norwegian companies took over the remaining yards. A positive outcome of the restructuring was the emergence of a network of medium-sized companies dependent on the shipbuilding core, although western suppliers predominated over local ones. Many companies involved in shipbuilding closed down during the 1990s, and the total workforce declined from over 34 000 in 1990 to 9500 at the end of 1995. Nevertheless the region accounted for 33 per cent of the total national shipbuilding production, ranking second after Niedersachsen; over a third of the vessels are for export (Eich-Born 1996: 517–22).

The food industry weathered unification relatively well. Once the initial popularity of western goods had worn off, locally produced foodstuffs reappeared in the shops and a 'buy east' movement sustained increasing sales after 1992. The restructured dairy industry became the most modern in Europe, although many smaller dairies closed and there were massive job losses. Similarly, the number of concerns producing animal feed and processing fish and other foods fell by two-thirds. Of around 50 000 employed in the food industry before unification, only around 12 000 were left in 1995 (Eich-Born 1996: 522). Of 128 000 engaged directly in farming and agriculture in 1990, one-quarter lost their livelihood.

Apart from national and EU-supported assistance for shipbuilding and infrastructure, the regional government undertook many initiatives to regenerate the area after unification. One of the first was the Anchor Project to assist state-owned concerns adapt to privatisation by giving them time and resources to develop products and identify markets; restricted initially to 31 medium-sized companies employing between 50 and 500 staff, the programme was eventually extended to all businesses threatened by closure. Over a hundred green-field sites were built to attract new companies. Innovation centres designed to promote and exploit scientific research were founded in partnership with universities and business; they include a biology research unit in Greifswald and two centres for food research in Neubrandenburg. By 1996 the centres involved 233 businesses and employed over 1100 people. Such figures suggest that despite efforts at diversification and improvements in road and rail links designed to open the region up to the west and south, it will probably be many years before Mecklenburg-Vorpommern overcomes the problems of its peripheral status.

Sachsen-Anhalt

Area: 20 446 sq km
Population: 2.7 million
State capital: Magdeburg

The central German state of Sachsen-Anhalt has often been described as a state without an identity: its inhabitants feel much more part of their local area than the much larger unit of the federal state. This is partly due to the diversity of the region's physical geography. The rural north (the *Altmark*) is lightly populated, with picturesque medieval villages and towns; walking, cycling and watersports are favoured leisure activities. South of the *Altmark* the landscape turns to heath and grassland, rich in black earth and rare flora. In the south and east the region's main industrial belt stretches from Dessau to Bitterfeld and Halle. Wittenberg in the east and Eisleben further west are famous for their associations with the Protestant reformer, Martin Luther. The valleys of the Saale and the Unstrut near Halle support vineyards: after Sachsen, the area is Germany's second smallest wine producer. The main cities are Halle and the state capital of Magdeburg, each with populations of over 200 000. The *Harz* mountain area, which stretches from the border with Sachsen almost to Halle, contains some of the most unspoilt landscape in Germany, with characteristic half-timbered houses in small towns and villages.

Although historically a centre of copper and silver mining, forestry is now an important industry for the *Harz*, despite the scaling down of timber extraction after unification to preserve areas of woodland. In 1990 a section of the *Harz* was designated a national park. It contains north Germany's highest (and, for climbers, highly popular) peak, the *Brocken*, as well as coniferous and deciduous woodland, cliffs, moorland, alpine flora, and various species of bird and reptile. The invigorating climate and natural springs have given rise to numerous spa towns and health resorts for tourists. Easy accessibility by private car, however, increases the risk of environmental damage, which the authorities have taken measures to minimise. The *Harz 2000* project was set up in order to create a network of controlled public transport and recreational facilities for visitors; this network is based on the narrow gauge (and partly steam) railway lines built during GDR times to link areas to the north and south of the mountains. After unification a section of the River Elbe south of Magdeburg acquired the status of a biosphere reserve with the immediate objective of cutting pollution in the river and rescuing both the endangered beaver population and the stretch of ancient waterlogged woodland known as riverine (Speakman and Speakman 1992: 92–103).

After unification Sachsen-Anhalt experienced mass unemployment (the economy virtually collapsed and only recovered after 1992), the birth-rate plummeted (to the lowest in the world) and with outward migration the population declined markedly: the fall of 7.8 per cent between 1990 and 1999 is the steepest of all the eastern *Länder* (*Der Spiegel*, (34) 21 August 2000: 40). Ten years after unification Sachsen-Anhalt still had the highest regional unemployment level in Germany; at 21.5 per cent it was double the national average of 10.6 per cent. The region's traditional industries are chemicals and engineering, but their importance is declining in relation to food production, tourism and service industries. The historically important salt mining, however, remains significant. The industrial area around Halle is a centre for chemicals, vehicle manufacture, engineering (also in Magdeburg), biotechnology, mining and energy (power stations and oil refineries). Many new companies were founded after unification, although the number of people employed in industrial production declined rapidly after 1989. Before the *Wende* Sachsen-Anhalt's industrial belt suffered severe atmospheric and ground pollution, leaving a disastrous environmental legacy. However, despite the closure of environmentally harmful brown coal (lignite), copper and potash mines, the overall structure of industry in the region was preserved after unification. Problems of land ownership in urban areas initially led many businesses, often encouraged by ambitious municipal authorities, to circumvent normal planning procedures and to set themselves up outside the towns.

Although the great state-run farming collectives of the GDR were broken up after unification and the land returned to private ownership, 90 per cent of farmland is still worked by tenants. After restructuring, farming units were larger than before 1945 but smaller and more numerous than under socialism. Much land was lost to commercial use and housing, although the overall area of farmland expanded at the expense of grassland and fruit orchards with most farmland given over to cereals, especially wheat. Greater efficiency after unification brought increased milk yields and 1995 saw record cereal growth, but at the same time cattle rearing declined sharply and employment in agriculture and forestry also decreased.

The area around Halle and Dessau is part of a larger industrial region that extends into neighbouring Sachsen, where Leipzig is a major manufacturing and commercial centre. To co-ordinate economic planning Sachsen-Anhalt and Sachsen concluded an inter-state treaty in 1994. The treaty committed the states to co-operate over a five-year period on managing the future of brown coal mining and the new oil refining industries. The states would also consult on restoring the landscape around Bitterfeld that had been damaged by years of opencast mining during the GDR period. Finally the states agreed jointly to finance the development of a regional airport (Leipzig-Halle), a goods distribution centre near Leipzig and new road links.

Brandenburg

Area: 29 481 sq km
Population: 2.6 million
State capital: Potsdam

The largest of the new eastern states (and the fifth largest in Germany), Brandenburg is, after Mecklenburg-Vorpommern, the second most sparsely populated state. One-third of the population lives in the area around Berlin, which includes the state capital, Potsdam. Since 1995 Brandenburg has been the only eastern state to register a rise in population, which is entirely due to migration into the Berlin-Brandenburg area. A proposal to merge Berlin with the surrounding state was rejected by plebiscite in 1996, notably by the Brandenburgers who feared that they would be financially disadvantaged. In common with other eastern states, Brandenburg experienced high unemployment after unification: two-thirds of jobs in industry were lost between 1990 and 1995 and agricultural employment fell by 60 per cent. The region, especially Brandenburg-Berlin and Potsdam, have historical associations with the monarchs Friedrich-Wilhelm I (the 'soldier king') and Friedrich II, who laid the foundations of Prussian military and political power in the seventeenth and eighteenth centuries. In the south-east around Cottbus in the *Niederlausitz* area is a small Slav community, the Sorbs. The community, which numbers around 60 000 and whose language and cultural identity are constitutionally protected, extends to Bautzen (*Oberlausitz*) in neighbouring Sachsen.

Formed by ice-age glaciers, Brandenburg's landscape is mainly flat and sandy, with many rivers, lakes (over 3000) and marshy valleys which have been drained to support agriculture. Half the total land area is used for farming and a further 35 per cent is forested. The main crop of cereals reached record production levels after unification. Around Berlin, market gardening to supply the city is steadily increasing. Few cattle are reared for meat, although some pig farming takes place; the number of animal smallholdings is in sharp decline. A target of regional planners has been to develop an approach to agriculture – the 'Brandenburg Way' – encouraging farmers to co-operate in maintaining the natural environment, which is one of the state's key assets. The authorities have pledged to designate 40 per cent of the total land area under some form of environmental protection. The

'Brandenburg Way', however, has led to conflicts between farmers wishing, for instance, to exploit the rich land of the Lower Oder National Park (see below), and environmentalists arguing for its preservation from human activity (Steyer 2000).

Following the valley of the River Spree for some 75 km., the *Spreewald* is a unique landscape of ash and alder woodland, drained marshes and water meadows (grassland subject to flooding). The small farms and villages are linked by a network of rivers, canals, channels and dykes. Part of the *Spreewald* has been designated a biosphere reserve. Easily accessible from Berlin, it is a favourite beauty spot for visitors and requires careful management in order to balance the interests of ecology and tourism. Indeed, when Brandenburg reviewed its poorly developed infrastructure for tourism after unification, it decided to reject projects promoting mass tourism in favour of small-scale schemes that would appeal more to individuals (Hoffman 1995). Other conservation areas include the *Märkische Schweiz*, a nature park east of Berlin, and the floodplain of the valley of the lower Oder along the Polish border. Largely uninhabited, the Oder is an area of marshy reedland, water meadows and ancient woodland lining the valley slopes. North of Berlin, around Schorfheide and Chorin, is Germany's largest biosphere reserve, where archaeological remains of medieval farming can be found; the reserve's numerous lakes, streams and forests support abundant wildlife.

As for industry, some lignite mining continues around Cottbus, although production was cut by 80 per cent between 1989 and the end of the century, largely to preserve the environment. Growth industries include recycling, engineering (mining and agricultural machinery, printing presses, cranes and railway locomotives), instrumental controls, optical equipment, glass, ceramics and timber. Through Berlin's role as a European focus of music, film and entertainment, the area around the capital has attracted many small and medium-sized concerns working in multimedia. A major base for the development of new media technologies is the High-Tech-Center (HTC) in Potsdam-Babelsberg, where films have been produced since the Weimar period. Potsdam, with the customer service centre headquarters for German Telekom and the mobile phone company Mannesmann, is now the telecommunications hub of eastern Germany.

With its long border with Poland, Brandenburg is strategically located on the main route for freight transport between western Europe and the east (Warsaw, Kiev and Moscow) and carries considerable traffic between southern Europe and Scandinavia. As a consequence Brandenburg sees itself as a valuable commercial partner for eastern Europe, especially Poland, which along with other eastern European states is due to join the EU in or soon after 2003. After the USA, Poland is the second largest importer of goods made in Brandenburg. Improved transport facilities with the west will enhance the developing relationship with eastern Europe; links, fostered by a German–Polish centre based in Guben, already exist between around 2000 German and Polish concerns. Although a question mark hangs over the proposed Transrapid rail link between Hamburg and Berlin, a high-speed (230 km. per hr.) ICE connection planned for 2003 would reduce journey times to 90 minutes. The immediate benefits of closer commercial and infrastructural links are, however, likely to remain confined to the Berlin area, with peripheral regions such as the *Lausitz* and the area around Cottbus remaining relatively disadvantaged. In 2000 local unemployment in Cottbus, especially among older people, was at record levels (24 per cent), only 20 per cent of small businesses made use of new technology and the prospect of large numbers of Polish immigrants (estimated at up to 600 000 annually) nurtured social anxieties (Wilke 2000).

Thüringen

Area: 16 175 sq km
Population: 2.5 million
State capital: Erfurt

Thüringen lies at the very centre of Germany, sharing borders with five other *Länder*. The area's new centrality stands in marked contrast to its previous status as a marginalised region on the periphery of the GDR. In the south lies the Thuringian Forest (*Thüringer Wald*), a protected area with extensive woodland (20 km. at its widest point), grassland slopes, river valleys, ravines and mountain peaks rising to almost 1000 metres. Wartburg castle near Eisenach, on the north-western edge of the forest, is famous for its associations with Martin Luther, who translated the New Testament of the Bible there in 1521 and gave the Protestant Reformation its most powerful impetus. North of the forest lies the Thuringian Basin (*Thüringer Becken*), the geographical centre of the state. The basin's flat and highly fertile landscape, through which the River Unstrut passes in the north, supports intensive agriculture. The far north of Thüringen is rural and thinly populated: it extends from the *Harz* mountains in the north and west to forested uplands interspersed with cultivated valleys further eastwards. The easternmost district of Altenburg suffered severe environmental damage from lignite mining during the GDR period.

Erfurt lay on an important medieval trade route between west and east (the *via regiae*, or 'king's way', named after the Emperor Charlemagne, who established Erfurt as a border trading town with the Slavs). The small town of Weimar is known for its associations with the poets Wolfgang von Goethe and Friedrich Schiller and with the *Bauhaus* school of architecture and design (founded there in 1919). The town also gave its name to the Weimar Republic (1919–33), when the national constitution for Germany was drawn up there in 1919; Weimar was chosen in preference to Berlin, where street fighting between political factions made the atmosphere too dangerous.

Around half of Thüringen's population and much of its prosperity are concentrated in the so-called 'fat belt' (*Speckgürtel*) – an east–west axis of towns and cities straddling the centre of the state and of which the largest are Erfurt (population 204 000), Jena (99 000) and Gera (204 000). In common with the rest of eastern Germany, the population declined after unification, although the fall was rather lower than in other states; many in eastern Thürigen migration to the west. In the central urban belt and in the south unemployment has been less marked than in the rest of the region; in the south this is partly because firms which set up in the former border region between the FRG and the GDR received particularly generous subsidies and partly because many workers were able to commute to neighbouring Bayern and Hessen.

Owing to the absence of raw materials (in particular, coal) and the mountain-bounded region's late connection to the rail network in the nineteenth century, Thüringen's economy became renowned for its small, innovative and highly skilled businesses producing quality finished goods. The skills of French and Dutch Protestant immigrants during the seventeenth century provided the basis for weaving, textiles, carpet-making and clothes production. The manufacture of porcelain, which was mastered in Thüringen around 1760, became a major industry in the nineteenth and twentieth centuries. Well-known larger industries included car manufacturing (until 1945 all BMW's car production was based in Eisenach), optics in Jena (Carl Zeiss) and toys and dolls in Sonneberg (the famous *Friedelpuppen*). Industrial collectivisation during the GDR era undermined the business sector and many entrepreneurs moved to western Germany, although the basic range of production was preserved. The largest industrial production units (*Kombinate*) were the Carl Zeiss works in Jena (employing 27 000), textiles in the north-eastern towns of Apolda, Worbis and Greiz (25 000), potash extraction (24 000), glass and ceramics (22 000), office machines in Erfurt and Sömmerda (19 000) and microelectronics in Erfurt (11 000). The number of small businesses, however, plummeted from 57 000 in 1945 to around 14 000 by 1989. A sharp disparity emerged between relatively prosperous zones around the *Kombinate* and marginalised areas with low wages, poor facilities and inadequate housing. The banking sector, where Thüringen had historical strengths, virtually disappeared and 40 per cent of export goods went to the Soviet Union.

Restructuring after unification led to massive job losses in agriculture (from 142 000 in 1989 to 33 500 by 1993) and in industry (from 645 000 to 120 000 in 1994). The Trust Agency's policy of immediately closing down the *Kombinate* resulted in a sudden deindustrialisation, especially in potash mining (in the southern *Harz*), office equipment (Sömmerda) and car manufacturing (Eisenach). An exception to this was the decision in 1990 by the west German company Opel to start building one of Europe's most modern car producing plants in Eisenach. A more general recovery did not set in until 1993 and was led by a building boom as the government financed new housing and commercial premises. Despite the inauspicious start, Thüringen boasted the highest rate of recovery of all the eastern states (58.6 per cent over 1991–98) and by 1998 many traditional industries had been successfully re-established. Manufacturing and processing industries accounted for 26 per cent of gross production, followed by services (23 per cent), trade and transport (15 per cent) and building (13 per cent). Total numbers employed in industrial production had risen to 127 000. Expansion in production and employment was registered in office machinery and microelectronics (centred on Erfurt), cars (the Opel works at Eisenach), lorries, the food industry, engineering, chemicals, optical instruments (around Jena) and timber (in the Saale-Orla district in the south-east); after some difficulties producers of toys, glass and ceramics goods began to re-emerge. Nevertheless, Thüringen's unemployment rate was high at 17.5 per cent (1998), although this was the lowest in the eastern *Länder* (average: 19.3 per cent). The economy was still excessively dependent on local and regional markets, while the numbers of very large and small to medium-sized businesses remained low – a problem shared by other eastern states. Although road and rail links were being expanded, the region was pressing the federal government to speed up its plan to build a high-speed ICE connection between München and Berlin that would also benefit Thüringen (Schuster 2000; see also Bricks 1997; Bricks and Gans 1996).

Sachsen

Area: 18 409 sq km
Population: 4.5 million
State capital: Dresden

Sachsen borders with Poland to the east, the Czech Republic to the south, Brandenburg and Sachsen-Anhalt to the north and west, and, for about 25 km., Bayern to the south. After colonisation by German settlers in the twelfth century the area extended its frontiers over the next 600 years to become a powerful state incorporating present-day Thüringen and Schlesien (now part of Poland). Most of its western and northern territory was lost to Prussia after the Napoleonic wars; the area east of the River Neiße became part of Poland in 1945. After 1919, with the abdication of the Wettin ruling nobility, Sachsen called itself a Free State (*Freistaat Sachsen*) – a title it shares with Bayern (although Kettenacker (1997: 107) suggests that the epithet is imaginary, apparently because it was re-adopted in 1990; see Kowalke 1994).

Since the 1950s the population of the region has declined, with notable outflows, especially of younger people, to the FRG before the building of the Berlin Wall in 1961 and to western states after the *Wende* (400 000 left between 1989 and 1991). Coupled with a falling birth-rate, outward migration has resulted in an unusually high proportion of old people: in 1992, 22 per cent of people were aged over 60 (see Kowalke 1994).

Sachsen's northernmost landscape is flat, with some heathland; the centre is hilly, with a fertile, loess-based soil. Agriculture in the north is mainly arable, while stockfarming predominates to the south. The long southern border is dominated by the *Erzgebirge* (ore-mountains), where minerals, especially silver, were mined in the Middle Ages. To the east of the mountains lie the hills and forests of the *Lausitz*, home of Slav-speaking Sorbs since the sixth century. The main town of the area is Bautzen, a centre of Sorb culture. After persecution by the Nazis, the Sorbs enjoyed constitutional protection under the GDR, although their villages and traditional way of life were undermined by opencast mining and collectivisation of farms; since unification the community has continued to decline as the birth-rate falls and younger people move away to find work. Between the *Lausitz* and the *Erzgebirge* proper is the *Sächsische Schweiz* National Park, where the upper Elbe cuts through a dramatic landscape of steep, wooded slopes, chasms and river gorges. High quality sandstone, used for instance in the Brandenburg Gate (*Brandenburger Tor*) in Berlin, is exported throughout Europe, but commercial exploitation of the forests has led to considerable environmental damage. The area attracts 2 million tourists a year. Tourism is much less developed in the eastern section of the *Erzgebirge* around Freiberg, although this is also a protected area and contains many former mining and textile towns. The central and western *Erzgebirge*, which still has significant ore and mineral reserves, contain moorland and large commercial forests. In the far west, around the textile and lacemaking town of Plauen, is the *Vogtland*, a landscape of gentle green hills.

The centres of population are Leipzig (population 488 000) in the northwest, Chemnitz (279 000) in the south-west and Dresden (478 000), the regional capital, towards the east. Leipzig is famous for its musical associations (J.S. Bach lived there during the eighteenth century and it has a celebrated choir and music school), its trade fair and publishing industry. Like the historic city of Dresden, war damage and utilitarian building during the GDR period destroyed much of its architectural heritage. Downstream of Dresden along the River Elbe lies the town of Meissen, where fine porcelain has been manufactured since the eighteenth century.

Before the Second World War Sachsen was the most heavily industrialised region of Germany, with an excellent local infrastructure and good road and rail links with the rest of the country. As part of the GDR it remained an industrial centre, with 60 per cent of the workforce engaged in engineering and light industries by 1989. After unification disputes over property ownership and closures by the Trust Agency undermined the region's former pre-eminence, although its industry retained a certain diversity. In 2000 unemployment was relatively high at 18.7 per cent (German average: 10.6 per cent). The main employers are now engineering, motor vehicle and metalworking industries, followed by electronics, optical equipment and precision engineering; there is a significant light industry (such as glass-making, timber, leather and synthetic materials) and textiles sector. Mining and mineral processing now account for a relatively small proportion of the workforce. Tourists are attracted to the beauty spots of the *Erzgebirge* and to the historical and cultural centre of Dresden, although the tourism infrastructure remains relatively undeveloped. After unification the region began to recover from the extreme environmental damage resulting from the industrial and agricultural policies of the GDR. In 1992 up to 40 per cent of forests, especially in the *Erzgebirge*, had been harmed by industrial emissions from nearby factories and neighbouring Czechoslovakia. Brown coal extraction devastated entire landscapes south of Leipzig and around Hoyerswerda in the east, while soil and water supplies were contaminated by industrial pollutants and chemical fertilisers; uranium mining in the *Erzgebirge*, *Vogtland* and the *Sächsiche Schweiz* left large quantities of untreated and highly dangerous radioactive waste.

LEGACY OF THE GDR AND REGIONAL CHANGE IN EASTERN STATES

Unification produced an almost immediate disparity between the eastern and western states, which persists to the present day. The disparity has political, economic, social and cultural dimensions and has to a large extent displaced the traditional north–south division that existed in the old Federal Republic. This section will outline the particular problems faced by eastern Germany as a whole, many of which are mentioned in the context of the individual *Länder* described above.

The continuing structural weaknesses of the eastern states originate in the deficiencies of the command economy during the GDR era. These include outdated industrial and agricultural facilities, the dominance of large, single sector industries, overmanning and inflexibility of labour deployment and an export-import regime orientated to the eastern European economic bloc of communist states. The region's transport infrastructure was run-down and ineffective, and dynamic urban centres were largely absent. Even the much vaunted triumphs of the GDR proved illusory after unification. The supposed success of the homes-building programme, for instance, was based on falsified statistics, and the scheme neglected needy regions to focus on selected towns and cities only.

Eastern Germany's main problems after unification were economic downturn and unemployment. The region's economy all but collapsed as its goods proved unable to compete with western products on price or quality and its traditional export markets in the east evaporated. Between 1989 and 1991 production fell by 40 per cent and by 1995 over one-third (3.4 million) of former jobs had disappeared, mainly in agriculture and in the heavily industrialised regions; shipbuilding, motor manufacturing and electrical goods were especially badly hit. An increase in services (trade, transport, media and communications) could not offset such huge losses, the true extent of which was disguised by early retirements, part-time working and government-sponsored training and work creation schemes. These measures reached a high point in 1991, affecting over 2.8 million people, and continued to be a major feature of economic policy by the end of the decade.

Although 65 per cent of the east German workforce was engaged in the service sector by 1997 (a similar proportion to the west), unemployment remained consistently higher than in the western states, with twice the proportion of easterners receiving welfare benefit as in the old *Länder*.

Uncertainties in the economy and labour market also reduced firms' willingness to offer training places and apprenticeships, while the proportion of registered independent businesses remained much lower in the east (7 per cent compared with 10 per cent in the west in 1996). Since women in the GDR were more closely integrated in the workforce than in the west, they were harder hit by unemployment than men. It is also true that, while unemployment in the west is concentrated in areas converting from traditional to more modern industries (such as the Ruhr or the Saarland) and is relatively low in regions such as Baden-Württemberg and Bayern, it is widespread in the east, where most states suffer from structural economic weaknesses. At the same time the eastern response to transformation has not been uniform. Urban and industrial regions, which in many respects have undergone the most drastic changes, have coped better than rural areas, which are sparsely populated, have a poor infrastructure and where investment in service sector jobs is minimal; this applies particularly to the northern part of east Germany, notably Mecklenburg-Vorpommern and north Brandenburg. It is therefore possible that a new divide between the rural, undeveloped north and the urbanised, industrial south may open up, this time confined to the east. In the medium term there is little doubt that the east will remain financially and structurally dependent on western transfers – these rose steadily from 139 billion DM in 1991 to 199 billion DM in 1999 (*Der Spiegel* 15 January 2001: 52) – and will continue to show significant disparities in living conditions (Maretzke and Irmen 1999).

FURTHER READING

Readers wishing to keep abreast of geographical developments in Germany will find useful up-to-date material, often tailored and presented for schools, in the German periodicals *Geographische Rundschau* and *Praxis Geographie*. The English-language periodical *European Urban and Regional Studies* contains occasional and accessible articles on Germany. Jones (1994) focuses on the eastern states in the years immediately after unification, while Blacksell (1995) covers demographic and general geographic issues. Current information and basic data on the individual *Länder* are available from the internet home pages maintained by each state, although some sites are more extensive than others; the Federal Office of Statistics (*Statistisches Bundesamt*) also provides statistical reports on topics of geographical interest (an overview of useful internet addresses is given at the end of this book).

3

UNIFICATION AND AFTERMATH

This chapter takes a closer look at the former GDR, its history, political system and the background to its collapse. The legacy of the former GDR in present-day Germany is manifold. Various aspects of the legacy, such as the need for economic regeneration, the state of the environment, the political landscape and social attitudes, are considered elsewhere in this book. Of particular interest this chapter is how post-unification Germany has approached the notion of the GDR as a criminal regime and managed the contentious issue of the archives which the secret police or *Stasi* assembled over many years of spying on the East German population. Finally, material living standards of Germans living in the east and west are compared.

GDR: HISTORICAL OUTLINE AND CHARACTERISATION

Some have tried to relegate the German Democratic Republic (GDR) to a 'footnote of German history' (see Weber 1993: 19). The basis for such a view is that the GDR, which a few idealists conceived in the immediate post-war years as offering the prospect of a genuinely democratic, socialist alternative to the capitalist Federal Republic, was in reality a temporary and unpopular aberration in the course of German history. Those who dismiss the GDR in this way argue that the GDR regime failed its citizens economically and lacked political legitimacy, enduring only as long as it was able to rely on the patronage of the Soviet Union.

Soviet occupation: 1945–1949

Before the GDR was formally founded on 7 October 1949, the Soviet Union, as occupying power, had already begun to introduce features of a socialist state. While reforms in land ownership (1945) and education (1946) won support from all political quarters, changes in the judicial system and moves towards state ownership of private industry were less popular, being driven almost entirely by the minority communists. Acknowledging the pre-Nazi tradition of party pluralism, the Soviet Union admitted non-communist political parties from June 1945; in 1948 it also founded new parties, notably for agricultural workers and conservative-minded citizens, such as former Nazis or soldiers. However, along with mass organisations such as the trade unions, the parties came to be increasingly dominated by the communists. Ultimately they were allowed to function only as vehicles of social control and for the transmission of socialism to groups who did not necessarily support the regime. The mechanism for this control was the all-party 'national front' or so-called block system, which forced all parties to be elected and to function politically as a unitary block under communist control. In April 1946 the German Communist Party (DKP) merged with the Social Democratic Party (SPD) to form the Socialist Unity Party of Germany (*Sozialistische Einheitspartei Deutschlands* or SED). Opposed by many social democrats, the merger was officially propagated as uniting the two leading socialist parties. In reality it enabled the communists to neutralise moderate socialism and to assert their control over a single mass membership party. On its foundation in 1949 the GDR adopted an outwardly liberal and pluralistic constitution, although this, too, masked the SED's monopoly of power.

Political, economic and social transformation: 1949–1961

Led by Walter Ulbricht, an arch-Stalinist who had spent the Second World War in exile in Moscow, the SED transformed East German society between 1949 and 1960. The party consolidated its power by placing its members in key positions throughout the administrative and judicial apparatus of the state and by systematically removing domestic opponents. Partly through its secret police, the *Stasi* (established in 1950), it maintained a Stalinist system of social control and political repression. In particular the GDR pursued a model of state ownership of industry and agriculture pioneered in the Soviet Union during the 1930s. By 1955 all energy production and leading industries were in the hands of the state and many farms had been collectivised, the owners surrendering their land, stock and machinery to large agricultural co-operatives. The party apparatus grew to huge proportions. In 1955 over 100 000 were engaged as full-time party functionaries, with several thousand also in socialist organisations; the party-controlled state administration comprised around 317 000 employees; by 1989 it had grown to 400 000, or 3 per cent of the adult population (Weber 1991: 65; Schroeder 1998: 407). During this process of social transformation the regime weathered a number of economic and political crises, of which the first and arguably most serious was the uprising of 1953.

The 1953 uprising came just one year after the Second Party Conference of the SED, at which the party had proclaimed the 'Construction of Socialism'. In practice this meant a further centralisation of political and economic control and a worsening of conditions for the population. The historical

Länder with their traditions of regional identity were replaced by 15 districts (*Bezirke*) that were centrally run from Berlin (the 15th district). The government also forced the development of heavy industry at the expense of goods and supplies for consumers (Weber 1991: 67). Partly prompted by the death of Stalin (March 1953) and the prospect of a more liberal approach in the Soviet Union, the uprising began in Berlin as a local protest against economic conditions but rapidly developed into nation-wide calls for free elections and a change of government involving demonstrations of over 500 000 and many deaths (Kettenacker 1997: 52). Only Russian military intervention restored the authority of the East German leadership. Ironically Ulbricht was able to exploit the uprising to consolidate his position. He purged the SED of opponents and moderates and resumed his Stalinist policies. A more liberal 'New Course', which had been announced days before the uprising and promised price cuts and improvements in living conditions, was officially rescinded in March–April 1954. Despite the political upheaval the GDR economy reached the end of its first five-year economic plan in 1955 having achieved its target of doubling industrial production (over 1950). Nevertheless, the disproportionate emphasis on heavy industry and a failure to raise living standards kept the economy in permanent crisis and seriously undermined the stability and credibility of the regime.

After the Soviet Union granted full sovereignty to the GDR in 1954, East Germany built up a National People's Army (from 1956) and became a full member of the Warsaw Pact. Despite its closer integration in the political and economic bloc of the Soviet Union, at the end of the decade the GDR entered its most serious domestic crisis since the 1953 uprising. An enforced and hasty programme of agricultural collectivisation between 1957 and 1960 produced widespread food shortages, while owners of small businesses became targets for a new wave of expropriation. Industrial production fell and economic plans were abandoned, only to be replaced by new ones that became ever more unrealistic in their targets. At the same time international tensions rose over the divided city of Berlin, which growing numbers of dissatisfied East Germans used as an escape route to the west. Between 1949 and 1955, 1.4 million citizens fled to West Germany, with 300 000 alone leaving in the crisis year of 1953. After falling off in 1958, the rate of emigration rose dramatically as land collectivisation, a hardening political stance on the part of the SED and increasing Soviet bellicosity over Berlin generated fresh anxieties in the population. Many feared that the Soviets would seal off the escape route to West Berlin altogether. While emigration figures had seldom fallen below an annual 200 000, they swelled to an avalanche of 30 000 for the month of April 1961 and reached 47 000 in August. Doctors, professional people, young citizens and trained industrial workers figured prominently in a mass exodus that the East German economy could ill afford. Although the Russians stopped short of applying direct military pressure on West Berlin, they agreed with the GDR leadership to seal off the western sector completely: in the early hours of 13 August 1961 East German guards began erecting the Berlin Wall. From the end of the war until the building of the wall over 3 million people had used Berlin to escape from the east.

Period of consolidation: 1961–1971

After a brief period of internal terror following the building of the Berlin Wall, the GDR stabilised itself politically and economically. At its party conference of 1963 the SED announced the start of the 'Age of Socialism' and adopted the New Economic System (NES). Drawn up by an emerging élite of younger and technically qualified SED leaders, the NES aimed to overcome the economic ills of the GDR by giving factories greater freedom in buying materials, arranging credit and in structuring prices, wages and material incentives for workers. The NES represented a fundamental change in economic direction: between 1961 and 1970 industrial production increased, consumer goods became more readily available and the standard of living rose. Between 1966 and 1968 farming gradually recovered from the damage of collectivisation. Ideological and political control remained firm, however, and a new 'socialist constitution' formally acknowledged the leadership role of the SED. In 1968 East German troops joined those of other east European states in entering Prague in order to suppress attempts by a reformist Czech government to introduce greater individual freedoms and to democratise political institutions. Apart from evoking painful memories of Hitler's invasion of Czechoslovakia, this was a manifest sign of the GDR's new status as a trusted junior partner of the Soviet Union. Its participation in the suppression of the Prague Spring and the success of the NES gave the SED leadership a political confidence that it had never possessed before. From 1967 Ulbricht began to portray the GDR as a model of successful, modern socialism – a beacon for other states which brought it into direct conflict with the USSR's leadership role. However, despite successes in the production of steel and coal, petrochemicals and agricultural machinery, the economy remained unbalanced: the energy, building and supply sectors failed to achieve their targets, resulting in shortages of foodstuffs and consumer goods. By 1970 these disparities prompted the state once again to intervene more directly in the economy.

Ulbricht's ideological challenge to the Soviet Union and his resistance to *rapprochement* with the FRG after 1969 (see the section on *Ostpolitik* in Chapter 1) are widely assumed to be responsible for his downfall. He resigned from leadership in May 1971 and died in 1973, airbrushed from East German public life. Recent research into East German archives after unification, however, has suggested that Ulbricht became surprisingly flexible after the removal of opponents inside the SED and the stabilisation of the GDR after 1961. According to this view his demise was primarily a result of internal conspiracies in the SED *Politbüro* and of Russian suspicions that he might go-it-alone in reaching compromises with the FRG (Grieder 1999). Be that as it may, Ulbricht undoubtedly laid the foundations of the East German political and social system between 1949 and 1971.

The Honecker era: 1971–1989

Ulbricht's successor was the ideologically orthodox Erich Honecker, a veteran pre-war communist who had risen through the ranks of the SED as a functionary responsible for youth. Under his leadership the GDR moved away from bombastic rhetoric, unrealistic economic plans and from pretensions to represent a model socialism that challenged the role of the USSR. He undertook in particular to modernise industry and to improve material conditions for ordinary citizens through a policy that unified economic and social needs. Displacing Ulbricht's technocrats and economic experts from the party élite, he promoted career politicians like himself, well versed in ideology and party organisation. The influence of the SED and the party apparatus was strengthened at all levels. A new constitution of 1974 reinforced the notion of the GDR as a permanent and separate German state with its own national identity and stressed the bond with the USSR as 'eternal and irrevocable'. As commercial links and contacts with West Germany expanded in the wake of *Ostpolitik*, the regime, with mixed success, placed considerable emphasis on the policy of demarcation (*Abgrenzung*) and on the notion of a distinctive East German identity. At the same time, as splits emerged in European and global communism, the GDR re-affirmed its loyalty to Moscow (Weber 1991: 150).

Under Honecker's direction, living standards improved between 1971 and 1976 to become the highest in the eastern bloc, although the gap with West Germany, which for most citizens was the only meaningful benchmark of comparison, widened. While the rest of the world experienced an economic downturn, East German incomes rose, full employment was maintained and prices for basic foodstuffs remained stable. Official statistics showed a steady increase in industrial and agricultural production and in the availability of consumer items, especially household electrical goods (Weber 1991: 144). The unity of economic and social policy was reflected in a two-pronged approach. On the one hand the leadership hoped to boost industrial performance through improved production methods. On the other hand it promised to enhance the quality of life by raising pensions, reducing working hours and, in particular, by building or modernising up to 800 000 new homes by 1980 in order to resolve the GDR's chronic housing problem (although after unification it emerged that figures proclaiming the programme's success were falsified (Weber 1991: 201)).

The end of the decade saw a return to economic stagnation as industrial growth and incomes declined. The downturn was partly caused by a further round of increases in global energy prices, but these only exposed the underlying weaknesses and the structural fragility of the centrally controlled economy: by comparison with the FRG the GDR continued to experience deficiencies in the quality, production and supply of anything but basic items. Increased contacts with West Germans resulting from the inter-German treaties of the early 1970s reinforced the perception of a failing economy. Alarming levels of foreign debt in the early 1980s were overcome through choking off imports, increasing exports and accepting credits from

West Germany. Nevertheless at the SED party conference of 1986 Honecker continued to proclaim the superiority of the socialist economy and set strategic targets for the microcomputing sector, for significant savings in energy and raw materials and for providing high quality consumer goods. Although the true extent of the deficiencies of the GDR's economy emerged only after unification, it performed well by east European standards and its shortcomings were never so acute as to produce the extreme social and political instability of the early Ulbricht era.

The main fruit of internal political stability and *rapprochement* with West Germany after 1970 was acceptance of the GDR by the international community. East Germany was diplomatically recognised by over 130 states (although not by the Federal Republic) and signed about 500 international agreements. Honecker himself made several state visits to foreign countries. The inter-German understanding weathered a deterioration in relations between the USA and USSR during the early 1980s over the issue of the stationing of nuclear weapons in Europe. When the east–west climate improved after 1985, Honecker visited West Germany (1987), where he proved quite popular. During this period increasing numbers of GDR citizens were permitted to visit the FRG for family reasons, with several thousand more even allowed to emigrate (Weber 1991: 206–9). The SED enjoyed a large membership (one in six citizens), the regime appeared secure and at the eleventh party congress in 1986 (the last in the GDR's history) the leadership delivered self-confident addresses about the dynamic state of the economy, the extensive welfare provision, the range of educational opportunity and East Germany's contribution to international peace.

Between 1985 and 1988 a new leadership in the Soviet Union adopted policies of political openness and greater democracy in order to resolve the crisis produced by the demands of maintaining a vast military machine on the back of a moribund economy. The power-holders in the GDR, however, remained unmoved. While Honecker welcomed the Soviet Union's initiatives on disarmament and peace as also being in the GDR's interests, it was a different story when it came to following the USSR's lead in encouraging domestic reform and opening up discussion about the Stalinist past (including Stalin's pact with Hitler). In a famous interview in the West German magazine *Stern*, Pultibüro member Kurt Hager publicly rejected the need for the GDR to 're-paper its apartment' just because its neighbour was doing so (1987). The SED went even so far as to prohibit the import of a Soviet publication (*Sputnik*) which was airing awkward questions about socialist history (Weber 1991: 185–6). Abandoning its traditional rhetoric about the international community of socialist countries, the party fell back on a strictly national vision of 'socialism in the colours of the GDR'.

Political institutions of the GDR

Ostensibly the GDR was a multi-party state with all the institutions of a liberal democracy, including a constitution. A parliament (*Volkskammer*, or

People's Chamber) of 500 deputies elected a 44-strong Council of Ministers (*Ministerrat*) and a 20-member State Council (*Staatsrat*). The councils were responsible for running the GDR's internal economic and political affairs and for foreign policy. In practice the SED had a built-in majority in all these bodies, partly through direct representation and partly through its control of the parties and mass organisations which served on them. The People's Chamber, whose members were not full-time parliamentarians, met infrequently and then only to rubber-stamp SED directives. Behind the facade of the state's democratic institutions lay the organs and apparatus of the SED. It was here that the real policy decisions were made and their implementation monitored. At the apex of the SED stood the Pultibüro, which was appointed by a Central Committee (*Zentralkomite*) elected by the delegates of the Party Congress. All power lay in the hands of the Pultibüro, which comprised 21 full members and 5 candidate members in 1989: within the Pultibüro power was further concentrated in a tiny circle of veteran communists (Erich Mielke, Willi Stoph, Hermann Matern and Günter Mittag) around the party leader, Erich Honecker. The Central Committee (which in 1986 had 165 full members and 30 candidates) acted as an executive committee for the SED, monitoring the implementation of economic and social policy. The Central Committee maintained a large secretariat (2000 staff) which attended to the day-to-day running of the party and prepared policy reports for the Pultibüro. Party congresses, where around 2500 delegates met every five years, were carefully staged festivals at which the leadership proclaimed new directions in policy. In theory the party operated according to the principle of democratic centralism, although this allowed citizens and party members to discuss how rather than whether to implement centrally determined policy. Public positions and posts were allocated according to an individual's progress through the so-called *nomenclatura*, a largely secret and strictly hierarchical system of ranking SED members on the basis of ideological reliability; political criteria generally counted more than technical expertise (Schroeder 1998: 407–11).

COURSE OF UNIFICATION

Although the last years of the GDR saw little organised internal dissent and certainly no call for unification, a significant proportion of the population and even some members of the SED were deeply dissatisfied with domestic conditions in East Germany. The dissatisfaction grew significantly during the 1980s and was fed by reform movements in other east European states, especially in Poland and Hungary. Record numbers of people were applying for exit visas for West Germany: although 40 900 were allowed to leave during 1984, the tide of discontent continued to rise, so that by 1989 the backlog of emigration requests had reached 1.5 million, almost 10 per cent of the population. Despite such signs of disaffection the GDR's disintegration, or 'implosion' as it is often termed, was non-violent, unexpected and swift.

The following sections outline the main phases in the fall of the GDR and the movement towards unification.

Phase 1: public protest

The first phase – public protest – began on 7 May 1989. On this day opposition groups in the GDR organised themselves nationally to monitor elections and to protest publicly about the official results, which were falsified and claimed a 98·85 per cent victory for the SED-dominated National Front. In Berlin on 7 June 1989 120 protesters were arrested. This was the beginning of many public demonstrations, centred on Leipzig, which attracted increasing numbers of people and which lasted until November 1989.

During this difficult and potentially violent phase the protests turned the *Wende* into truly popular revolution driven by mass discontent. Although the opposition groups came to enjoy a high public profile and to play a vital role in maintaining dialogue between the authorities and the protest movement, they had never by themselves posed a serious challenge to the regime. Around 160 dissident groups, with around 2500 members, are known to have existed in 1988. Harassed and monitored by the secret police (*Stasi*), the groups remained small, isolated and informally organised. From this basis, several new groups rapidly formed during 1989 as the *Wende* unfolded. However, despite sharing core values and ideals, the groups failed to unite. Some saw themselves as activist bodies campaigning for citizens' rights, while others were prepared to organise themselves politically and participate in government. Initially the most important and broad-based of the groups was New Forum (*Neues Forum*). After publicly challenging the regime with a manifesto of reform on 11 September 1989 and attracting widespread support for its petitions and declarations, the Forum failed to draw up a clear programme or establish an effective organisation; refusing to develop into a political party, it lost popularity after the opening of the Berlin Wall. The smaller group Democratic Awakening (*Demokratischer Aufbruch*), on the other hand, was instrumental in setting up the Round Table (see Phase 2 below) and joined with other groups to form an electoral alliance, the Alliance 90 (*Bündnis 90*) (for a review of the groups, see Richter 1994).

While many citizens demonstrated against the regime, others showed their disaffection by trying to leave. During the summer of 1989 increasing numbers of East Germans left the country, ostensibly to holiday in Hungary where on 2 May guards had begun dismantling the frontier with the west, but in reality to attempt to cross the border and reach West Germany via Austria; 21 000 left in May and 33 000 in August. At the same time many thousands occupied West German embassies in eastern Europe, seeking papers and exit visas for the west (the GDR leadership permitted two trains of these would-be emigrants to pass back through the GDR on their way to the west). Hungary eventually opened its border with Austria on 11 September: 57 000 left the following month, rising to 133 000 in November.

The SED leadership, and in particular Erich Honecker, reacted to the crisis by ignoring it. Honecker pointedly disregarded the advice of the Soviet premier, Mikhail Gorbachev, who used the opportunity of a state visit to East Berlin on 6 and 7 October, commemorating the fortieth anniversary of the GDR, to urge its leaders to move with the times.

Peaceful mass protests began on 5 October in Magdeburg and Dresden and were brutally broken up by the police. However, they soon spread to other cities, reaching a climax on 9 October with a demonstration of 70 000 in Leipzig. This time the police did not intervene and it was clear that the regime was in the event not prepared to resort to the 'Chinese solution' of violent suppression (the GDR leadership had supported the Chinese government's massacre of dissident students in Beijing in early June). Against a backdrop of continuing mass demonstrations the Politbüro forced Honecker to resign (18 October), although his successor, Egon Krenz, failed to rescue the SED's lost credibility. On the 23 October 300 000 citizens at the now well-established Monday demonstration in Leipzig chanted 'We are the people' (Wir sind das Volk), defiantly rejecting the SED's continuing claim to represent the people. At a demonstration on 4 November in Berlin of over 1 million – the largest in German history – prominent intellectuals and reform-minded figures in the SED argued for a purge of the old regime and a renewal of socialism. This was the last mass demonstration at which reform rather than unification was on the agenda. When the authorities, responding to public pressure for freedom of travel, opened the Berlin Wall on 9 November and East Germans were able to compare for themselves the so-called achievements of socialism with economic conditions in the west, the popular mood changed rapidly to embrace demands for unification. Sensing the political opportunity, Chancellor Helmut Kohl announced a 10-point programme for unification (28 November). On 11 December demonstrators in Leipzig called for 'Germany as united fatherland' (Deutschland einig Vaterland) and on a visit to Dresden to discuss setting up a joint East–West German confederation, Kohl was mobbed by crowds clamouring for unification.

Phase 2: political movement

The second phase of the Wende – the political moves towards unification – began soon after the fall of the Berlin Wall. The entire Politbüro resigned (8 November) and the People's Chamber (the national parliament which hitherto functioned as a mouthpiece of the SED) formed a provisional cabinet under Hans Modrow, a reformist regional SED leader. Although 16 of the 28 ministers in Modrow's cabinet were SED members, the party rapidly lost its leadership role and all but disintegrated during December. The interim cabinet committed the country to free elections, which took place on 18 March 1990 and at which most parties campaigned for unification. Even before this election Kohl and Modrow had initiated preparations for monetary and economic union in order to rescue the foundering East

German economy and to halt the continuing exodus of people to the west (3000 each day).

The March election brought to power a Conservative Alliance for Germany, which had campaigned for monetary union and swift unification. An all-party non-communist coalition government was formed under Lothar de Maizière (GDR–CDU), a lawyer and senior Church official in the GDR. Economic and currency union with West Germany was enshrined in the State Treaty on the Creation of Monetary, Economic and Social Union (*Staatsvertrag*). Concluded in April and effective from 1 July the treaty replaced the entire economic system of the GDR by the mechanisms of the social market economy of West Germany: the West German *Deutsche Mark* replaced the GDR *Ostmark*, the socialist system of centralised economic planning gave way to a western-style free market economy and the FRG's welfare model based on employers' and workers' contributions supplanted a system that was almost entirely run and financed by the state (Zimmermann 1985: 1229–30).

At local elections held on 14 October the 15 *Bezirke* (regions) which the SED had established in 1952 to reinforce control from the political centre were dissolved and replaced by 5 provincial states or *Länder*. All-German elections were set for 2 December. After the March election the governments of the GDR and FRG began negotiating a treaty for full political union. Concluded on 31 August 1990, the Treaty of Unification (*Einigungsvertrag*) stated that the Basic Law of the FRG would apply to the 5 new east German *Länder*, which were thus able to accede to the federation under article 23. The treaty established Berlin as a city-state and eventual capital, and provided for the western take-over of the GDR's financial and administrative institutions and state-owned property. A trust agency (*Treuhand*) was empowered to privatise state-run businesses. Guidelines were laid down for the recognition of educational qualifications and for the organisation of culture, sport and the media. Transitional arrangements applied to abortion, while the victims of injustices committed by the SED would be rehabilitated. Private property confiscated by the East German state after 1949 would be restored. The treaty also established a Unity Fund to finance the needs of the new *Länder*. The date for unification was set for midnight 2–3 October 1990.

An institution which played an important role in the peaceful transition from public protest to political action between the autumn of 1989 and the spring of 1990 was the Round Table. The Round Table was a forum for informal dialogue between opposition groups and the government which had been successfully used in other east European states emerging from communist rule. Chaired by pastors of the Protestant Church, the main Round Table met from December 1989 to March 1990 in Berlin, although similar bodies met in the regions. Alongside the opposition groups, also present at the Round Table were representatives of the Block Parties (the non-communist parties which the SED permitted to function under strict control as long as they acknowledged its leadership role) and the mass organisations (notably the trade unions). The forum prised the SED from power, negotiated free and secret elections and forced the government to disband the *Stasi*. All the opposition groups participating in the forum joined Modrow's all-party 'government of national responsibility' on 28 January 1990 and helped prepare for the March elections. As these approached, however, the Round Table lost influence and disbanded, especially when the political parties saw greater advantage in electioneering and after it became clear that the people were unwilling to endorse its aim of preserving a reformed GDR. Free from SED control, most of the Block Parties reconstituted themselves and, aided if not effectively taken over by their more experienced and better resourced sister parties in the FRG, campaigned in the March elections.

Phase 3: international agreement

The third phase in the unification process ran concurrently with the second. It involved gaining the assent of the allied powers of the Second World War, who had never concluded a formal peace treaty with Germany after 1945. The process passed a crucial hurdle in January 1990 when Gorbachev agreed in principle to German unification. Between February and September, in a series of negotiations known as the Two-plus-Four Conferences, the four allies (the USA, USSR, the UK and France) settled with the two Germanies (FRG and GDR) all external and security aspects of unification. The outcome was the Treaty on the Final Settlement on Germany, which was concluded on 12 September and came into force on 3 October. The treaty, which took the place of a post-war peace treaty, returned full sovereignty to Germany and ended all residual allied rights over German territory, including Berlin. Germany undertook not to extend its existing borders and, in particular, formally to recognise its existing frontier with Poland (with whom it would also conclude a separate treaty). In addition Germany committed itself to international peace, to remain within NATO, to renounce atomic, biological and chemical weapons, and to limit its army to 370 000. Finally, Soviet troops would withdraw from German soil over a four-year period in return for German financial aid.

Despite strong pressure from a disintegrating GDR to hold all-German elections even earlier and to bring forward the date of unification, the agreed timetable for unification was maintained. At the December election Helmut Kohl was returned with a large majority, confirming his position as 'the Unity Chancellor' (*Einheitskanzler*).

WHY THE GDR COLLAPSED

The collapse of the GDR formed part of the overall demise of communist regimes that took place throughout eastern Europe during the 1980s. Where regimes were less rigid or less secure, as in Poland and Hungary, the process began earlier and took a gradual course. Where political control was more firmly entrenched, it occurred later and more abruptly, as in the GDR,

Czechoslovakia and Bulgaria; in Romania the transition took a particularly violent course. Of all the eastern bloc states East Germany was held to be the most stable: it boasted the highest productivity rates, a reasonable standard of living and there had been no organised national opposition since the uprising of 1953.

Although the GDR was the best performing of all the centrally planned, command economies, gradual and accelerating economic decline during the 1980s was a primary cause of its political failure. It was heavily in debt and relied extensively on western imports and financial credits from West Germany. Since the east–west detente of the 1970s the FRG had supported the GDR's economy in order to improve the civil rights and the material condition of fellow Germans there. Nevertheless, as a result of family contacts and of ready access to West German television with its seductive images of affluence and consumerism, East Germans measured their standard of living not by other socialist states but by the economic achievements of their more prosperous neighbour. Surveys of 'subjective factors' conducted in the GDR between 1977 and early 1989 (Gensicke 1992) reveal how, after a high point of identification with their homeland in the mid-1970s (Welsh 1994: 27), East Germans developed progressively more negative attitudes towards their life and social conditions, especially with regard to the environment and the shortages of consumer goods. Although the GDR had extensive welfare state provision, factors such as poor quality housing, a rather basic system of health care, an inadequate supply of services and consumer items and a visibly damaged environment contributed to a generally negative perception of the quality of material life.

As the economy declined, so did the regime's political legitimacy. Directly after the war the SED drew heavily on its credentials as a party whose members had been persecuted by the Nazis. In particular it promised to create a society of greater equality, educational opportunity and material prosperity. As time wore on, however, the SED was judged less on its historical role as the enemy of fascism and more and more on its ability to deliver the material benefits of socialism. The party compensated for failure in this regard by increasing propaganda offensives stressing ideology and the achievements of 'real existing socialism'. In fact this unconvincing and ambiguous formula came to represent in the minds of many citizens the failures rather than the successes of socialism.

The loss of popular political legitimacy went hand in hand with a decline in leadership authority. The ageing Honecker, at the helm of a geriatric Politbüro, refused to relinquish power or to acknowledge the need for change. His narrow vision of socialism, in which the people would be satisfied if they had full employment and enough to eat, failed to evolve beyond his personal experiences of the class struggle as perceived by a young communist in pre-war Germany. Moreover the party he controlled, the SED, degenerated into a self-contained and self-recruiting clique which, at its highest levels, increasingly alienated the wider population by cynically reserving for itself the social and material privileges more commonly associated with a capitalist élite (Welsh 1994). The alienation was compounded by a rigid bureaucracy, all-pervasive control by state organs, and by media that were obvious mouthpieces of the regime.

All the above factors – the role of the opposition groups, the economic decline, the loss of popular legitimacy and a fossilised leadership incapable of responding to demands for change – contributed to the regime's collapse. However, the key external factor that made a change of regime feasible was Mikhail Gorbachev's implicit encouragement of internal reform and the Soviet Union's refusal to support the SED (with force, if necessary) in the face of mounting street protests.

THE GDR AS A TOTALITARIAN REGIME

From at least the early 1950s the GDR had all the features of a totalitarian regime. The ruling élite underpinned its authority with an all-embracing ideology that claimed to deliver a social utopia; a single, hierarchically organised political party exerted absolute power over most aspects of social life; a secret police, unaccountable to any civil authority, employed terroristic methods of physical and psychological control; all media and communications were state controlled; most land, property and economic assets were in government hands; and the economy was centrally directed according to medium-term plans. Up until the 1960s the totalitarian nature of the GDR prompted direct comparisons with the Third Reich. Such comparisons were unfair since the SED neither committed mass genocide based on racialist policies nor embarked on wars of territorial aggrandisement. As the GDR stabilised during the 1960s and inter-German tensions lessened in the wake of *Ostpolitik*, West German historians began to accept East Germany as a fundamentally different form of society that needed to be studied objectively in terms of its own political and social structures (the 'system-immanent' approach adopted notably by Peter Ludz (Ludz and Kuppe 1975) and Hartmut Zimmermann (1985)). Not only did observers note that East Germans were beginning to identify more closely with the socialist republic, but as a developed industrial nation the GDR was even seen as capable of change and modernisation. The totalitarian state of the 1950s, in which the regime often resorted to physical terror, had evolved by the 1980s into a 'total state', where bureaucracy, indoctrination and paternalistic authoritarianism exerted more subtle forms of social control. For ordinary citizens the influence of the SED extended to work, school, youth, culture, even fashion and entertainment (see Wehling 1989). East Germans reacted to this by retreating increasingly into so-called 'niches' of private life. Although East Germans developed more negative perceptions of life in the GDR from the late 1970s onwards, it may be argued that the more sophisticated, bureaucratic variant of Stalinism was able to command a degree of personal loyalty to the state, a loyalty which goes some way to explaining the phenomenon of post-unification nostalgia (*Ostalgie*) for the pre-*Wende* days (Schroeder 1998: 621–48).

A number of controversies arose after unification, all rooted in the question of how Germans should come to terms with the GDR's totalitarian past. While West Germany did not engage in significant public debate about the National Socialist past until the 1960s or even later, the GDR was subjected to immediate and intensive analysis. Historians questioned whether, in a state whose regime controlled so many aspects of life, it was at all possible to analyse social life independently of politics. Others doubted the reliability of using official archives and personal experiences as sources of objective information. Some challenged the credibility of historians who had worked in the GDR before 1989 (for a review of the issues and directions in research see Kleßmann and Sabrow 1996). In 1992 the government set up a commission of investigation (the *Enquête-Kommission 'Geschichte und Folgen der SED-Diktatur'*) to promote understanding between east and west Germans, contribute to the rehabilitation of victims of persecution and advise the federal parliament on what measures and political initiatives should be taken to overcome the legacy of the SED years. The commission sponsored research projects and conducted public forum debates with ordinary citizens, historians and other experts. When the commission's final report appeared in June 1994, it had held 44 hearings on issues such as government criminality and the *Stasi*, the role of the Church in the GDR and the economy as an instrument of the SED.

Legacy of the *Stasi*

One of the most powerful and feared mechanisms of control by the SED was the *Stasi* (short for *Ministerium für Staatssicherheit* or Ministry of State Security). Uncovering the role of the *Stasi* and its methods was a key element of the strategy that united Germany adopted in coming to terms with the east German past.

The *Stasi* was established by vague legislation passed in the People's Chamber on 8 February 1950. The role and functions of the Ministry were never properly defined in GDR law. Its activities were regulated by secret internal directives emanating primarily from whichever SED Minister it answered to (there were about 600 such directives by 1989). As the 'shield and sword of the Party', the *Stasi* became the personal instrument of the SED to whose leadership it was alone accountable (for an account of the *Stasi*'s relationship to the SED see Fricke 1991: 11ff.). During the early years of the GDR the SED's leaders probably saw the *Stasi*'s role as confined to countering the (albeit exaggerated) activities of western agents and heading off a resurgence of Nazism (Henke 1993: 59). Eventual post-war economic prosperity – it was assumed – would demonstrate the superiority of the centrally planned economy and gain the loyalty of the working-class population, including those who remained stubbornly sceptical of communism. In keeping with this short-term, limited role, the *Stasi* in 1952 had little over 4000 staff. Nevertheless the organisation became notorious for a series of spectacular kidnappings, especially of prominent 'traitors' – members of the

SED, the GDR armed forces and officers of the *Stasi* itself – who had fled to the west. As soon as they been returned to the east these unfortunates faced imprisonment and execution. There were several hundred such incidents and they continued into the early 1960s. The readiness to use openly violent tactics faded after the erection of the Berlin Wall in 1961.

The uprising of 1953 not only revealed the gulf between the people and its rulers, deeply shaking the GDR's leadership, it also exposed the *Stasi's* manifest failure to warn the leadership of the scale of popular discontent at a time when Walter Ulbricht was proclaiming the era of 'socialist construction'. As a result the organisation was reconstituted and, in the late 1950s, began to develop the vast apparatus that eventually monitored factories and industries, schools, colleges and universities, churches, dissident groups, east–west contacts, artistic circles – indeed as much of the population as possible by whatever means possible (informants, telephone tapping, opening mail, electronic surveillance, and so on). Before Mielke took over in 1957, the Ministers responsible for the *Stasi* were Wilhelm Zaisser (1950–53) and Ernst Wollweber (1953–57). Both were driven from their positions through internal party purges and it was under Mielke that the organisation began its long period of expansion. By 1974 its complement of full-time staff stood at 55 700. In 1983 the figure reached 85 000, at which point a national labour shortage and economic difficulties prompted Mielke to issue a directive halting further enlargement (Gill and Schröter 1993: 34–5).

The *Stasi* had (and used) its own powers of arrest and detention and frequently predetermined the outcome of any trial or judicial process. The organisation was especially severe on members of its own ranks who took up contacts with the west (one such, Captain Werner Teske, was executed as late as 1981). The *Stasi* conducted industrial and political espionage in the west, especially in the FRG. It sheltered and supported terrorist organisations such as the Baader-Meinhof Group/*Rote Armee Fraktion*, which murdered 25 members of the West German political and business establishment between 1971 and 1989. It also maintained companies and front organisations in West Germany in order to generate hard currency for the beleaguered GDR economy. Although the *Stasi's* privileged position in GDR society was a matter of general knowledge, its true size and generous budget remained a state secret until 1990. Eventually devouring 400 million Marks a year, the organisation maintained over 1800 buildings, including sports and recreational facilities and holiday homes, over 18 000 apartments, and a fleet of nearly 19 000 vehicles; the headquarters in Berlin-Lichtenberg stretched over several square kilometers and comprised about 24 separate administrative blocks and 3000 rooms and offices. The *Stasi's* arsenal of weapons could have equipped a small army, and it had at its disposal an 11 000-strong regiment of élite soldiers based south-east of Berlin. The regiment, the *Feliks Dzierzynksi*, guarded key installations and SED leaders and was on constant alert to suppress internal uprising; it employed brutal tactics against anti-regime demonstrators on 7 and 8 October 1989 and was disbanded in February 1990 (Fricke 1991: 37f.).

The internal organisation of the *Stasi* reflected its size and range of activities. In a hierarchical system of centralised line management, Erich Mielke maintained personal control over all aspects of the organisation. Day-to-day operational management, however, lay in the hands of his four 'representatives' – all *Stasi* officers with the rank of general (*Generaloberst* or *Generalleutnant*). Mielke took a particular interest in the affairs of Department (*Hauptabteilung*) II, which monitored foreign diplomatic services and journalists. The Department paid especially close attention to the Office of the West Germany's Permanent Representative in East Berlin.

The *Stasi* was divided into over 29 separate departments, each with its own specialist function. These functions included: to conduct espionage abroad; to combat infiltration in the army; to counter foreign espionage in the GDR; to monitor the radio, telephone and post (especially links with the west); to control foreign travel and tourism; and to combat terrorism and economic sabotage. The job of Department XX was to monitor the population of the GDR. For this it used informants to report on state institutions, the judiciary, the health service, education, youth work, the media and the churches. The Department's main targets were opposition groups which were undermined in every conceivable way; methods ranged from passive surveillance to active infiltration. A similar departmental structure was replicated in each of the GDR's 15 regions (*Bezirke*). As an aside it may be noted that the intelligentsia were well represented in the *Stasi*. Half its permanent staff were educated to university or college level, which was a higher proportion than any other institution or industrial concern in the GDR, including the national Academy of Sciences. It is likely that many of the *Stasi*'s informants were also relatively highly educated, although this is hard to prove (Henke 1993: 61). Given the extent of the *Stasi*'s information-gathering network, the question arises as to how the GDR leadership could be so out of touch with the people just before the *Wende*. After unification it emerged that not only were Mielke and his circle unable to exploit the sheer volume of data collected; their political myopia led them to interpret any manifestation of dissent as evidence of an external enemy, notably the FRG.

The *Stasi* assembled a huge volume of personal dossiers on the citizens of East Germany. Alongside its apparatus of over 85 000 full-time staff (100 000 according to some sources; see Gill and Schröter 1993: 35; Henke 1993: 60), the *Stasi* maintained an estimated 180 000 amateur informants or IMs (*informelle Mitarbeiter*) for short. These informants were cajoled, bribed or blackmailed into reporting regularly on the activities and political attitudes of colleagues, fellow students, friends and even close relatives; the organisation went so far as to exploit around 10 000 children as informants (Behnke and Wolf 1998). The full extent of this network and the scale of the 'information' that was amassed over the years did not emerge until after the SED relinquished power. Manfred Sauer, acting on behalf of Hans Modrow's transitional government, divulged the first authoritative figures on the size of the *Stasi* to members of the Round Table on 15 January 1990. Before that, official western sources estimated the *Stasi* to have about 20 000 permanent staff and between 60 000 and 80 000 informants (this was the figure entered, for example, in the 1985 edition of the official handbook of the GDR produced by the Federal Ministry for Intra-German Relations; see Zimmermann 1985: 909).

Once the *Stasi* had been disbanded, it was the archive and the sensitivity of its contents that raised the most serious issues for the German people. How reliable, for instance, was the information in the dossiers, especially when it could be used to destroy the reputations of eastern German politicians striving to establish their credentials as born-again democrats? Inconclusive allegations of *Stasi* involvement were made, for example, against the former GDR premier, Lothar de Maizière, the SPD premier of Brandenburg, Manfred Stolpe, and the leader of the PDS, Gregor Gysi. A different question was whether complicity with the *Stasi* merited immediate condemnation and withdrawal from public life in post-unification Germany, or whether it was wiser to accept that working for the authorities was just one of many compromises that individuals had to make in order to survive in a totalitarian system. Apart from these issues, individuals had to reckon with the personal consequences of reading their own files: they could, for instance, discover that a trusted friend or a family member had been informing the *Stasi* for years about their every move, opinion and conversation.

After the fall of the SED and before unification the GDR engaged in an intense debate on the future of the archives. Some, including de Maizière's government, argued that they should be destroyed or at least made inaccessible. Citizens' groups on the other hand insisted that they should be opened to the public, claiming that this was the only way to render them harmless: victims would be able to identify their persecutors and responsibility for injustices could be allocated. On 24 August 1990 the People's Chamber passed a law regulating the archives' status, in particular how the personal data which they contained should be handled. Citizens' groups fiercely resisted proposals to move the material to west Germany. Under the terms of the Treaty of Unification the archives were eventually located in the east and administered by a special representative appointed by the *Bundestag*, the former priest and co-founder of the New Forum opposition group, Joachim Gauck. What came to be known as the Gauck-Office comprised over 3000 staff distributed between the central headquarters in Berlin and the 14 regional offices (mainly former *Stasi* premises) where about half of the total archive was located; the budget for the archive totalled 200 million DM. The archive comprised 180 km. of files, including films, videos, tapes and computerised data (much of which is still being decoded); especially painstaking work involved piecing together papers shredded by *Stasi* officers before their organisation was disbanded. The final law on the archives permitted individuals to access their personal files for purposes of rehabilitation and compensation. Files were also opened to members of parliament and to officials pursuing criminal charges against former SED members and *Stasi* personnel. Despite initial fears about journalists exploiting material for commercial gain, extensive access was granted to the media. By 1993 over 1.35 million people had applied for access to the archives (Geiger 1993). By 1999 the figure had risen to over 2.7 million, with around 15 000 fresh applications each month. Levels of interest in the archives were expected to decline gradually rather than fall away suddenly. Most applications related to the vetting of staff in public and private organisations, followed by cases involving rehabilitation and compensation.

Joachim Gauck administered the archives until October 2000 before being succeeded by Marianne Birthler, an activist in the East German Protestant Church during the 1980s and leading member of the Alliance 90/Green parliamentary group, first in Brandenburg and later in the *Bundestag*. During his period of office Gauck steadfastly upheld the principle of allowing controlled access to the archives, dismissing staff who had passed files into the public domain. Although most of the files concerned east Germans, Gauck refused to accept that easterners should be the sole objects of their revelations, a stance that earned him the disapproval of the west German political establishment. In particular, the former Chancellor Helmut Kohl was angered by Gauck's offer to make available tape recordings made by the *Stasi* and apparently providing evidence that Kohl had received illegal donations for CDU party funds. Despite the issue of the tapes, ten years after unification the great political debates about the value of the archives were largely over. By this time all former SED Politbüro members had been convicted or amnestied, and the files had served their purpose in the vetting of public service workers. In time they would be opened up to historians and academic researchers (Kopka 2000; Seils 2000).

The SED as a criminal regime

The notion of the SED as a criminal regime rapidly gained ground after unification. The legal basis for placing citizens of the former GDR on trial was the inter-German Treaty of Unification. The treaty extended FRG law to the east after 3 October 1990 but allowed the law of the GDR to apply to crimes committed there before this date. Between 1991 and 1999 a specially created legal department (*Staatsanwaltschaft II*) in Berlin co-ordinated prosecutions for shootings and violent acts at the east–west German border, miscarriages of justice, economic crimes and criminal activities of the *Stasi*. By the time it was wound up the department had initiated almost 23 000 proceedings, although most were eventually abandoned: under 3 per cent of cases actually reached a conclusion and only 335 individuals were convicted, of whom 32 were imprisoned. Most convictions concerned the Berlin Wall and the border (104), followed by perversion of the course of justice (27) and crimes by members of the *Stasi* (25); the remainder involved economic and commercial offences, including corruption and misappropriation of funds, assets and property during unification. The pursuit of criminal actions against former members of the SED and its agencies raised a number of practical and moral issues. What some saw as the justified, if belated, application of the rule of law, others dismissed as 'the justice of the victors' (*Siegerjustiz*). Erhart Körting, a member of the Berlin judiciary, defended the very low rate of conviction as demonstrating that the state was not staging a witch hunt but observing proper legal procedures.

At first attention focused on the trials of border guards who had shot and killed east Germans attempting to escape to the west. Prosecutions began in September 1991 when the Berlin judiciary accused four guards of killing 20-year-old Chris Gueffroy as he attempted to flee to West Berlin on 6 February 1989 (Gueffroy was the last of over 900 victims who died trying to flee from the GDR, around 255 of these at the Berlin Wall (*Der Tagesspiegel* 26 August 1997: 5)). Two guards found guilty were sentenced to up to three years' imprisonment. The judges decided that the shoot-to-kill policy infringed international standards of human rights and also East German law; apart from a law sanctioning the use of weapons at the border after 1982, there was never an open official directive supporting such a policy.

The sentences on the border guards were widely perceived as unfair at the time, partly because more powerful and more culpable figures seemed to be escaping the machinery of justice. In summer 1992, 6 people, including the 80-year-old Honecker, were accused of complicity in the killing or attempted killing of over 75 escapees. Eventually Honecker was charged with manslaughter and the number of charges reduced in view of his ill health. When the Federal Constitutional Court decided that his continued detention infringed basic human rights, he was released to die in asylum in Chile in 1994. Willi Stoph (chairman of the GDR Council of Ministers) and Erich Mielke (Security Minister and head of the *Stasi*) were likewise released on grounds of ill health. Mielke's trial was postponed so that he could be prosecuted for his involvement in the murder of two Berlin policeman during a communist street demonstration in 1931. Serving four months of a six-year sentence for this crime, he was judged too senile to be tried for his actions as a senior figure in the SED and released in 1998 (he died two years later). On the whole the courts accepted that SED leaders were not directly involved in the killings but found that they were links in the chain of command; their reluctance publicly to acknowledge the shoot-to-kill policy suggested that they were fully aware of its criminality. During the course of the 1990s younger members of the Politbüro who had attempted to reach a compromise with the forces of the *Wende* were also convicted. These included Egon Krenz, sentenced to six years, and Günter Schabowski (three years), who won considerable respect as the only senior SED figure to admit his guilt. Along with veteran communist Günther Kleiber, Schabowski became in October 2000 the first convicted SED leader to be granted an amnesty. Further trials involved that of Manfred Berghofer, the former Mayor of Dresden, in 1993 for falsifying election results and several prosecutions against judges and lawyers for perverting the course of justice. East

Germany's spymaster Markus Wolf was found guilty of treason in 1993, although the judgement was reversed by the Federal Constitutional Court.

Related to the criminality of the SED regime was the issue of the vast financial and material assets of the party and the numerous organisations that it controlled. It took a commission over eight years and 90 million DM to identify these assets, many of which the SED and its successor, the PDS, attempted to conceal abroad and in a complex network of companies set up during the *Wende*. The total value of the assets identified by 1999 amounted to over 3 billion DM. The government reached an agreement with the PDS in 1992 and 1995 by which the party would retain only those assets which had belonged to the German Communist Party (KPD) during the Weimar Republic. The remainder would be distributed for public causes to the eastern federal states according to the size of their population.

STANDARDS OF LIVING

After 1990 and freed from the constraints of the totalitarian policies of the SED, east Germans began to experience the positive and negative aspects of the transition to western conditions. Particular aspects of unification and its aftermath as they concern issues such as the economy, geography, education and the environment are considered in other chapters in this book. The following section provides a general comparison of economic and social conditions in the eastern and western *Länder* a decade after unification. Many surveys of such conditions in the east, including personal attitudes, were conducted after the fall of the GDR. The ramshackle state of the economy was particularly well illuminated. Rather less information, however, was available for a direct and reliable comparison of conditions and attitudes between east and west. As attention focused on the high financial transfers from west to east, the stereotype of the poor and ungrateful *Ossi*, heavily subsided by industrious and efficient western Germans, gained currency. At the same time public interest in achieving a genuine convergence of the two economic areas diminished.

Despite the persisting stereotypes, eastern Germany caught up with the west in a number of key areas during the decade after unification. By 2000 household incomes in the east had risen twice as fast as in the west and living standards had reached broadly similar levels. Indeed, the western states had greater numbers of poor people and recipients of welfare benefit. However, the picture was varied and depended on what exactly was being compared. More details, which are based on the survey by Oppermann (2000), are given below.

Measured in terms of average annual disposable income, inhabitants of Hamburg were the richest (36 159 DM) and citizens of Thüringen the poorest (20 177 DM). Of the western states, the Saarland was worst off (26 132 DM), although wealthier than Berlin (23 959 DM) or even Sachsen, which was top of the league in the east (20 570 DM). Between 1992 and 1997 incomes in the east rose dramatically: the rates of increase were 28 per cent in Sachsen, for example, compared with between 14.9 per cent in Hamburg and 10 per cent in Hessen. At the same time absolute income levels remained much lower in the east: in 1998 east Germans earned on average 30 per cent less than their western counterparts. Measured in terms of the possession of household goods (television, video recorder, refrigerator, freezer and washing machine) differences between east and west were actually very small; only in cars, mobile telephones, microwave ovens and dishwashers did easterners lag behind. The discrepancy between income and actual possessions was undoubtedly due to east Germans' determination to catch up with western levels of outward affluence.

East Germans' desire to match western patterns of consumerism on lower rates of income coupled with continuing high unemployment (in August 2000 this varied in the west between 5 per cent in Bayern and 12.9 per cent in Bremen and in the east between 15.6 per cent in Berlin and 19.9 per cent in Sachsen) resulted in their having markedly lower levels of certain types of assets. Such assets notably included high quality consumer goods, property, investment accounts and financial resources; savings, for instance, amounted to just one-third of those in the west. Buying stocks and shares was clearly a western rather than an eastern pastime. Similarly east Germans invested much less in property. A survey by the German Federal Bank in 1999 showed that, although the proportion of east Germans owning their own home or apartment rose from 19 per cent in 1990 to 26 per cent in 1997, they had a long way to go in order to reach the 44 per cent of property-owning westerners, who also tended to borrow more from banks and building societies. Such figures are not surprising since every second household in the east was run by a pensioner or an unemployed person with limited disposable income.

The high unemployment in the east widened the relative gap between rich and poor. While in 1998, 2 per cent of east Germans earned incomes that were twice the national average, the figure was 3.6 per cent in the west. A family with a child and a monthly income of 7200 DM could be considered wealthy in the east but would have to earn 8700 DM to be in the same category in the west. It must be remembered, however, that Germany as a whole is not a poor country and that poverty is generally defined in terms of relative income levels. A distinction must also be drawn between material (or real) poverty and subjective (or perceived) poverty. Citizens earning under 40 per cent of average national income are considered to be poor in the narrow material sense, those earning 50 per cent are held to be relatively poor, while those earning 60 per cent are considered needy. In the mid-1990s in west Germany 6 per cent were in the first category, between 10 per cent and 12 per cent in the second, and 22 per cent in the third. The figures for the east were, respectively, 3 per cent, 8 per cent and 13 per cent. Not only did west Germany appear to have more poor people, but these stayed on welfare benefit longer than in the east (56 per cent of recipients in the west continued on welfare for over one year, compared with 36 per cent in the east).

As a consequence western states paid out on average much more on welfare per head of population (521 DM) than the eastern *Länder* (338 DM). At the same time there were wide regional variations: while Bremen paid out 1204 DM, the figures for the wealthy southern states of Bayern and Baden-Württemberg were 359 DM and 341 DM respectively, which was still higher than Sachsen in the east (237 DM).

The statistics on welfare support provide only a partial picture. After unification large numbers of east Germans were removed from state benefit by extensive work creation and retraining schemes. Moreover, there was evidence that, for a number of reasons, easterners failed to apply for the welfare support to which they were entitled. Possibly because unemployment in the former GDR was virtually unknown, many feared the social stigma associated with state support; some were simply unaware of their legal entitlement to benefit, while others were put off by the legal and bureaucratic obstacles involved. Interestingly, a survey of attitudes shortly after unification (1992) revealed that twice as many east Germans (35 per cent) as westerners regarded themselves as poor. Such a marked difference in the subjective perception of poverty was probably a left-over of pre-unification attitudes: West Germany was known to be prosperous, while the inhabitants of the GDR assumed that their state was economically backward.

FURTHER READING

Standard histories of the GDR are Weber (1991) and Staritz (1996), although the most comprehensive study of GDR history, politics and society is Schroeder (1998). Fulbrook (1995) focuses on the mechanisms and social consequences of the GDR as a dictatorship; for studies of the *Stasi* see Fricke (1991) and Gill and Schröter (1993). Lewis (1995) provides a brief overview of the political structures of the GDR. For a lively and readable account of East Germany see McElvoy (1992). Directmedia Publishing GmbH of Berlin have also published a CD-ROM containing a wealth of information about the GDR (see Enzyklopädie der DDR 2000). Kettenacker (1997) includes a chapter on the *Wende*, while Hancock and Welsh (1994), Jarausch (1994) and Behrend (1995) analyse the process and aftermath of unification from a variety of perspectives. Published directly after unification, Weidenfeld and Korte (1991) is a helpful and informative compendium of articles about most aspects of East and West Germany. The German periodical *Deutschlandarchiv* is a useful source of articles on the eastern states and post-GDR issues.

4

POLITICAL STRUCTURES AND THE FEDERAL SYSTEM

This chapter describes the main political and legal institutions of the Federal Republic of Germany, including the origins of the notion of the *Rechtsstaat* (constitutional state), the function and mechanisms of national government and the operation of the federal system. One section describes how the legal systems of the former GDR have been integrated into those of the Federal Republic. The chapter concludes with short descriptions of the main political parties.

THE PRINCIPLE OF SEPARATION OF POWERS

A cornerstone of modern democracies, including the FRG after 1949, is the principle of the separation of powers. The powers are: the executive, i.e. the government of the day which formulates policy and proposes laws; the legislative, i.e. the elected parliament which debates and approves those laws; and the judiciary, i.e. the legal system which applies the laws impartially. The object of separation is to achieve a balanced system which on the one hand provides for a stable and effective executive and on the other hand avoids the danger of a government or party usurping power to the detriment of the common good (as occurred, for instance, between 1933 and 1945 when the Nazis relegated the *Reichstag* and the judiciary to extensions of its own political will). In practice the precise nature of the balance between the powers varies, but a feature common to all democratic systems is the presence of a freely elected legislative (parliament) that is not merely an instrument of the government of the day. Apart from free national elections, genuine separation of power is also associated with independent courts (judiciary) that interpret the laws and with impartial civil servants who administer them.

The process of the separation of powers began at least in Great Britain in the seventeenth century as a result of conflicts between a hereditary monarchy and parliament. In the eighteenth century the philosophers Montesquieu in France and Immanuel Kant in Germany advocated the separation of powers in order to protect the individual from the unfettered authority of the state: for them ideals of personal liberty and moderated government were paramount. The philosophers' ideas found practical expression in the constitutions of the United States (1788) and the French Revolution (1791). Two years later, as the Revolution took its course, the French rejected the principle of separation, preferring instead to assign total and undivided power to the people in the form of the national assembly. Much later, in 1917, the Russian revolutionaries invested total power in so-called 'people's councils'. The communist governments that emerged in the twentieth century, notably the Soviet Union after 1918 and its satellite states after 1945, were also unitary systems of power. Although they claimed at an ideological level to embody universal democracy, these regimes were repressive party dictatorships that only ostensibly held power in the name of the people.

During the nineteenth century the German states preserved the powers of the monarchy and government – the two often went hand in hand – at the expense of the constitution and parliament. At the time the centralisation of executive power appealed strongly to perceptions of national unity, which was finally achieved in 1871. The downside, however, was that parliament played only a peripheral role in political decision-making and in running the state; there was no genuine separation of powers. Not until the Weimar Constitution of 1919 and, more enduringly, the Basic Law of 1949 was an effective balance between legislative (a democratically elected parliament) and executive (the government of the day) achieved.

ORIGINS OF THE GERMAN PARLIAMENTARY SYSTEM

The German parliamentary system has its distant origins in post-medieval assemblies of estates, which comprised members or representatives of the political classes involved in government. The first of these was the *Reichstag* of the Holy Roman German Empire, which sat in Regensburg from 1663 until 1806. As part of the post-Napoleonic settlement in 1815 this assembly was replaced by a loose federation of 38 largely autonomous states making up the German Confederation (*Deutscher Bund*). Apart from four free cities, the states were all monarchies which enjoyed full sovereign powers. During the course of the century the states drew up their own constitutions which provided for elected parliaments with albeit limited influence on executive government. With a gradual extension of the franchise (to all males in 1871 and all adults in 1918) these assemblies became more representative and evolved into a national parliament. The first truly pan-German parliament was the Frankfurt National Assembly of 1848, followed by the *Reichstag* of Wilhelmine Germany (1871–1918) and the genuinely empowered but ill-fated assembly of the Weimar Republic (1919–33). Finally, the West German Federal Parliament (*Bundestag*) was constituted in 1949.

The imperial Wilhelmine parliament had only limited powers: it approved laws but exerted only partial control over budgets and could not appoint the nation's leading minister, the Chancellor. With the Weimar Republic came a genuine increase in the powers and responsibility of a parliament elected by universal franchise. However, the Weimar *Reichstag* was flawed in a number of ways. By adopting an electoral system which favoured small political parties and by creating the institution of President (*Reichspräsident*) as a *de facto* continuation of the monarchy with partial executive powers, it produced a system in which the parties proved unwilling or unable to take responsibility for effective government. Incapable of reaching the practical compromises necessary to constitute and maintain viable administrations, they failed to gain the trust of the people, especially when confronted by a series of economic and political crises: these included the loss of territory and demands for reparations after the 1914–18 war, acute inflation in 1923, the Great Depression 1929–32 and the resurgence of political extremism in the early 1930s. During the Third Reich (1933–45) the National Socialists preserved the *Reichstag* in form only, stripping it of its parliamentary function and exploiting it as a facade in order to give the regime legitimacy.

THE *RECHTSSTAAT*: ORIGINS AND DEVELOPMENT

Germans commonly refer to their state as a *Rechtsstaat*. The term, imperfectly translated as 'constitutional state' or the 'rule of law', was first used in 1809 by Adam Müller to imply a body politic in which individuals enjoyed rights in law (*Recht*) that protected them from abuses by the sovereign power of the state (*Staat*). This view of the relationship between the individual and the state owes much to the Enlightenment, a cultural movement which flourished in the eighteenth century and which saw human beings not as passive subjects of authority, but as rational, active citizens participating in and contributing to society. As written constitutions were introduced in the various German states during the nineteenth century (in 1818 in Bayern and Baden and in 1850 in Prussia), the notion of the *Rechtsstaat* was refined. Above all it came to imply control of the monarchy/government (which before unification in 1871 meant the local territorial ruler) through written legal statutes rather than (as in the United Kingdom) relying on a strong parliament to counterbalance the power of the executive.

Such was the primacy of so-called normative laws in Germany that senior civil servants underwent a rigorous legal training. A Prussian statute of 1879 laid down a programme of three years' legal study at university and two State Examinations interspersed with practical training – prerequisites which still apply to the upper echelons of the German civil administration. The impartial application of a legal codex (one of the separated powers described above) was intrinsic to the emerging notion of *Staat* in eighteenth- and nineteenth-century Germany. 'Enlightened' absolutist states such as Prussia (1794) established a corps of 'state servants' (*Staatsdiener*) – i.e. a civil service – whose job it was to apply the law even-handedly.

Despite its moral and ethical origins, the concept of the *Rechtsstaat* began to be seen more formalistically during the nineteenth century. In particular, the 'positivist' notion that written statutes differ from and are not necessarily limited by ethics undermined the crucial link between (formal) law and (moral) justice. The Nazis drove the dichotomy to an extreme when they introduced laws on racial purity that directly contradicted moral values. It was as a result of these historical experiences that the West German Basic Law of 1949 re-established the relationship between principles of justice and written law.

The modern *Rechtsstaat* presupposes various safeguards for human rights and political balance. These include a written constitution setting limits to the power of the state; a body of laws defining basic human rights and protecting the individual against abuses from state authorities; and an independent judiciary. The most important human rights are: freedom of religious belief and practice; freedom of speech and association; and the right to private property. All these were guaranteed in the Basic Law of 1949. By contrast, the constitution of Imperial Germany (1871–1918) made only passing reference to an independent judiciary and mentioned fundamental rights (*Grundrechte*) not at all. Nor did it provide for any form of Constitutional Court. Matters improved during the Weimar period (1919–33), which saw the establishment of a supreme Imperial Court (*Reichsgericht*) responsible for constitutional issues, an electoral court and special courts for handling labour issues (*Arbeitsgerichte*) (Plöhn 1997: 359). During the nineteenth century demands were made to invest ordinary civil courts with the power to protect the rights of the individual against the state, but neither France nor Germany went down this road. France established special 'administrative courts' for this purpose, while Germany after 1949 adopted, in the form of the Federal Constitutional Court (*Bundesverfassungsgericht*), a model which owed much to the American Supreme Court.

Since 1949 the perception of the *Rechtsstaat* in Germany has undergone significant changes. At first, the Basic Law was concerned to establish the political and legal institutions that would ensure the rule of law and protect individual human rights. This approach expresses the formal aspect of the constitutional state (*formelle Rechtsstaatsidee*). It has, however, been argued that the state is now also responsible for the material well-being of its citizens (*materielle Rechtsstaatsidee*). From this has emerged the notion of the 'social constitutional state' (*sozialer Rechtsstaat*) in which citizens have a general constitutional right to social and economic justice and to a minimum standard of living. This general right, however, is not usually interpreted to mean that an individual has a constitutional entitlement to, for instance, a certain level of welfare benefit.

BASIC LAW (GRUNDGESETZ)

The Basic Law (*Grundgesetz*) was drawn up between September 1948 and May 1949 by a Parliamentary Council of representatives of the post-war states of western Germany and west Berlin (see Chapter 1). The allies, with whom the Council consulted, insisted on a strong federalist structure for the new state. The Basic Law was intended as a provisional constitution for what was thought would be a provisional state (the Federal Republic of Germany) pending final unification; its title reflected the Law's status as something less than a permanent constitution for the whole of Germany. Despite its transitional status, the Basic Law in the event provided a constitutional foundation not only for the 'provisional' republic of western Germany, but for unification in 1990.

Much of the spirit of the Basic Law reflects a conscious effort to avoid the mistakes of German history and to build a viable, stable democracy with the necessary safeguards that ensure a balance of powers between the executive and the legislative and between the political centre and the states. The primacy of human rights is reflected in the first section, which catalogues the rights and freedoms of the individual (for example, the freedom of action, opinion, religion, assembly and movement, and the right to own property). There are sections on the relationship between *Bund* and *Länder*, the institutions and organs of government (*Bundestag, Bundesrat*, the Federal President, the Federal Government), the legislative process (*Gesetzgebung*), the legal system (*Rechtsprechung*) and finance within the federal framework (*Finanzwesen*). Aspects of the Basic Law are referred to in the following discussion of the various institutions of the FRG.

BUNDESTAG

The founders of the post-war *Bundestag* in 1949 drew on their experiences of Weimar and on the Economic Council which the western allies had established in 1947 as a parliamentary forum for their combined zones of occupation (Turner 1987: 20–1). Among other things the originators of the 1949 Basic Law wanted to ensure was that the post-war west German parliament could not evade the responsibility of forming a government (for instance, by prematurely dissolving itself or by voting out the Chancellor without also nominating a replacement). After fifty years the *Bundestag* has achieved popular acceptance and international respect. Two commissions, one in 1976 and another after unification, looked specifically at the Basic Law with an eye to reform, but both concluded that there was little need for fundamental change. At the same time, frequent recourse by members of parliament to the Federal Constitutional Court and repeated calls for referenda on key issues (such as the location of the capital after unification) have led some to question whether German parliamentarians are in danger of abdicating the responsibilities which the founders of the Basic Law laid on them. It is also true that the mechanisms of the *Bundestag* are not always transparent and many Germans, while supporting the institution in principle, have little understanding of how it works in practice (Patzelt 1997: 128).

Function of the *Bundestag*

Located in Berlin after 1999, the *Bundestag* is the supreme legislative organ of Germany. Its role and functions are laid down in the Basic Law (section III, articles 38–49): this states that its members are elected for four years by universal, free and secret elections; the assembly chooses a President, meets and debates in public, enacts laws by simple majority, has the right to summon the Chancellor and his government, and must allow the regional assembly (*Bundesrat*) access to its meetings and committees. Since 1990 the *Bundestag* has comprised 656 members. A voter in a German general election casts two votes: one for a person, the second for a party. After an election half the total of seats in parliament are allocated to the first vote winners (the simple majority or direct mandates); the other half are allocated proportionally to party candidates on regional lists (list mandates). A complicated mathematical system ensures overall proportionality (for a description of the electoral system see Paterson and Southern 1991: 181–4). A party must gain at least 5 per cent of votes nationally in order to enter parliament, a measure introduced to prevent the proliferation of small, often extremist parties that did so much to undermine continuity of government during the Weimar period.

To prevent parliament evading the direct responsibility of forming government and enacting laws, the Basic Law lays specific obligations on the *Bundestag*. Thus the *Bundestag* may not dissolve itself prematurely or use public referenda in place of its own powers; nor may it vote out the Chancellor without also electing a replacement. And although the President may dissolve parliament, he himself has limited executive powers, so that the onus to govern always returns to parliament, even if this means tolerating a Chancellor who lacks an overall majority. In addition the *Bundestag* elects the Federal President (*Bundespräsident*), appoints a proportion of the judiciary, approves the budget and ratifies international treaties. The *Bundestag* appoints a representative (*Wehrbeauftragter*) to ensure parliamentary control of the army and defence; the post was established with conscription in 1955 and, for the first time, a woman was appointed in 1995; the representative acts as the serviceman's ombudsman and reports annually to parliament. If a national emergency, such as war, prevents the *Bundestag* from convening, a 48-person General Committee (*Gemeinsamer Ausschuss*) meets as an emergency parliament; chaired by the President, the committee routinely meets twice yearly to scrutinise the government's defence plans. With an administrative apparatus of around 2300 support staff and secretarial, office and communications facilities for every member, the *Bundestag* is one of the best equipped parliaments in the world in terms of infrastructure.

The *Bundestag* elects a Parliamentary President (*Bundestagspräsident*; this is not the same as the Federal President or *Bundespräsident*). Since 1920 it is customary for the strongest party to supply the Parliamentary President, who must, however, be acceptable to other parties and is elected with at least 80 per cent of votes. Vice-Presidents are drawn from all major parties. Although they cannot technically be removed from office during a parliament's lifetime, in practice Presidents resign if they lose the assembly's support. The President acts as the official representative and public spokesman of the *Bundestag*, directs parliamentary business, chairs and controls plenary sessions and manages its 2300-strong administrative apparatus. The President and Vice-Presidents constitute the Presidium (*Präsidium*); lacking constitutional powers, this body has an overriding duty to manage the affairs of the *Bundestag* impartially and exerts considerable influence.

Alongside the Presidium, the Council of Elders (*Ältestenrat*; a more functional translation is perhaps Steering Committee) plays a key role in the procedures of the German parliament. Originating in the nineteenth-century imperial *Reichstag*, its members are the party managers (*Geschäftsführer*) of all groupings in the *Bundestag*. In strictly confidential meetings, its prime function is to agree the assembly's business agenda, its calendar, and the time allocated for debate. It also mediates between the parties if these fail to agree on procedural issues during a plenary session.

Because the extensive powers accorded to the President (*Reichspräsident*) of the pre-war Weimar Republic had fatally undermined the executive authority of the democratically elected Chancellor (*Reichskanzler*), the Basic Law confined the functions of the Federal President (*Bundespräsident*) to largely ceremonial, representative ones. Elected every five years (and for a maximum of ten years) by a specially convened Federal Assembly (*Bundesversammlung*) of members of the *Bundestag* and nominees of the regional parliaments (*Landtage*), the President, who must be over 40 years old, formally summons and dissolves the *Bundestag*, appoints the elected Federal Chancellor and his ministers and signs laws that have been agreed in parliament. The President also represents the FRG in international law, on whose behalf he or she signs treaties with foreign states and organisations. Although the President's actions must in practice be approved by the Chancellor or his ministers, he can, through his personality and his position above party politics, exert considerable moral authority. Notably the respected Richard von Weizsäcker (1984–94) used the office to draw attention to wider social and political issues: in 1985 (the 40th anniversary of Germany's unconditional surrender in 1945) he called for his countrymen to deal responsibly with the issue of its Nazi past; after unification he drew attention to the problems of bringing east and west Germans together; and in 1993 he accused the political parties of alienating the people through their obsession with power (Jeffery and Whittle 1997: 35, 228; Bedürftig 1998: 75–6, 435).

Plenary session

To regard the plenary session (*Plenum*) of the *Bundestag* as the focal point of political decision-making in Germany is to see only part of the picture. It is, of course, the forum at which the Chancellor is elected, votes of confidence are taken, laws are enacted, and the government is publicly called to account. But possibly more so than in other countries, decisions in the *Bundestag* are reached in committees (see below) and through inter-party agreements before they are formally approved by the assembly. Only rarely is the outcome of a parliamentary debate genuinely open. Plenary sessions are in fact relatively infrequent and debates tend to be strictly managed, rather sterile affairs. Members are allotted speech time according to the size of their party and use the brief period they have at their disposal to put over a pre-agreed point of view; there is little opportunity to present complex issues, although speeches may be enlivened by witty and trenchant interruptions. Most votes are taken with a handful of members physically present, a practice which attracts negative public attention but which the Federal Constitutional Court has sanctioned in view of the specialist nature of much parliamentary business and of the time it would waste to require all members to be present for all legislation. The *Bundestag* introduced question time sessions (*Fragestunden*) in 1952 after the UK model, but these are dull, formal affairs: members need the permission of their party group to submit a question to a minister, who seldom answers in person. Much more lively is the *Aktuelle Stunde*. Introduced in 1965 and now a popular form of plenary debate, this hour for questions can be called by 5 per cent of members and enables topical issues to be aired; members and ministers may speak for five minutes only. The main debate in the parliamentary calendar is the approval of the federal budget.

Committee system

Most parliamentary business is conducted by an extensive network of committees (*Ausschüsse*), a system originating in the regional parliaments of the nineteenth century. Currently 20 or so cross-party committees, each with 30–40 members and serviced by its own secretariat, do most of the groundwork for decisions formally reached in the *Bundestag*. There are several categories of committee, some of which are required under the Basic Law: the main committees are the standing committees on foreign affairs, defence and the national budget; there is also a standing committee for each government ministry. Since 1969 parliament has made use of temporary committees to act as commissions of enquiry (*Enquête-Kommissionen*) on important issues. Such a commission was set up in 1990 to make recommendations on how to handle the legacy of communism left by the former GDR; it reported in 1994. The atmosphere of standing parliamentary committees is highly business-like. Freed from the party-based profiling required in the *Bundestag*, members are able to apply their personal expertise and focus on issues on which they can reach inter-party agreement rather than rehearse their political differences.

Fraktionen

Members of the *Bundestag* (and also of *Landtage*) are organised not only by party but also by parliamentary group (*Fraktion*). Groups of members sharing similar political aims, *Fraktionen* are normally formed along party lines but are not necessarily identical to them. To be formally recognised (and hence be entitled to staff and resources) a *Fraktion* must comprise at least 5 per cent of all members of the assembly. Virtually all deputies in the *Bundestag* belong to a *Fraktion*, which the Federal Constitutional Court has acknowledged as central to effective parliamentary democracy (Zeh 1990: 172). As self-organising bodies within the assembly, *Fraktionen* initiate most parliamentary business and make or break a government. *Fraktionen* hold their own elections, the most important office being the chairperson of the group (*Fraktionsvorsitzender* or parliamentary party leader), followed by the parliamentary business manager or whip (*Geschäftsführer*). The chairperson of the government *Fraktion* attends cabinet meetings and exerts an influence that is greater than most ministers and second only to that of the Chancellor; his or her counterparts are the chairs of the various opposition *Fraktionen*. A *Fraktion* can be very large (up to 300 members) and conducts much of its business through committees and working groups (*Arbeitsgruppen*). *Fraktionen* enjoy generous finance from the federal budget, from which they maintain support staff and civil servants (numbering 730 in 1991).

Full meetings of a *Fraktion* are informal and open-ended: the chairperson gives account of him or herself and takes part in question and answer sessions. The perceived advantages of the system are that it engenders team spirit and affords the most able members the opportunity to display their expertise and to rise within the party hierarchy; equally, the *Fraktion* can be dismissive of time-wasters. *Fraktionen* and their *Bundestag* committees are complemented by networks of similar, formal or informal groupings at *Land* level. It is worth noting that *Fraktionen* are far from subservient to the parent party and, in cases of policy conflict, often maintain a more pragmatic strategy against the 'official' party line.

GOVERNMENT BY COALITION

In preparation for a general election, parties choose a candidate for the Chancellorship (the so-called *Kanzlerkandidat*); the candidate need not be the *Fraktion* leader. By tradition the parties also declare to the electorate their coalition preferences, i.e. the party or parties with which they plan to form a coalition in order to command an overall majority in the *Bundestag*. Despite such declarations, post-election negotiations between coalition partners can be difficult and protracted: agreement must be reached on a common policy and on the allocation of ministerial posts. The coalition is concluded with a formal agreement (*Koalitionsabkommen*). The Federal

President (*Bundespräsident*) presents to parliament the candidate Chancellor, who is elected (often with a thin majority) by secret ballot of the whole assembly.

Government by coalition, which is favoured by an electoral system that promotes the entry of smaller parties to parliament, is well established in Germany. Indeed most post-war governments have been coalitions, with the small, neo-liberal FDP in partnership with either the CDU/CSU (1949–66) or the SPD (1969–82); unusually, 1966–69 saw a 'Grand Coalition' between the two big parties. Up till now, coalitions have commanded overall, if occasionally narrow, majorities. In contrast to the Weimar period and thanks to the electoral strength of two parties (CDU/CSU and SPD), post-war Germany has not had to experiment with minority governments tolerated by a numerically stronger parliamentary opposition. By convention, coalition parties appoint and remove their own ministers, regardless of the views of the Chancellor. An unpopular Chancellor may come under pressure from within his or her own party to withdraw or resign, with the coalition partner being conveniently blamed in order to save public face (as occurred with Konrad Adenauer in 1961 and Helmut Schmidt in 1982).

The constitutional right to approve laws is divided between the *Bundestag* and the *Bundesrat*. The Basic Law (articles 70–5) distinguishes exclusive and concurrent legislative competence (*ausschließliche v. konkurrierende Gesetzgebung*). Exclusive competence refers to the *Bundestag*'s sole right to legislate in areas laid down in the Basic Law, such as foreign relations, national defence, the currency, railways, air traffic and post. The *Bund* also approves 'framework' or guideline legislation (*Rahmengesetze*), which regulates, for instance, the structure of higher education. Where the *Bund* chooses not to legislate, the *Bundesrat* is entitled to do so. Such areas of shared competence include civil, penal, property, commercial and industrial law. As an overarching principle, article 31 of the Basic Law states that federal law overrides regional law (*Bundesrecht bricht Landesrecht*).

Despite the formal division of competence, by far the most legislation is passed by the *Bund* and relates to the provision of social welfare. The majority of bills are initiated by the government (60 per cent on average since 1949), followed by the *Bundestag* (34 per cent) and *Bundesrat* (6 per cent); about 77 per cent of government bills become law, compared with 18 per cent of the *Bundestag* and 5 per cent of the *Bundesrat*. *Bundestag* bills are likely to be on controversial issues (such as abortion) that reflect divisions within a *Fraktion*; the chances of the opposition presenting and getting a bill approved are under 10 per cent.

A government bill passes through various stages in parliament. After being prepared by one of the ministries and agreed in cabinet, the draft (*Referentenentwurf*) is sent to the *Bundesrat* for an initial opinion before undergoing its first reading (*Lesung*) in the *Bundestag*. It is then passed to one or more committees for detailed examination. The committee stage may involve requests for information and technical reports, public hearings, and complex interactions between working groups and *Fraktionen*. Of all bills 60 per cent are altered during the committee stage, which invariably decides the fate of the bill. The second (often poorly attended) reading in parliament is reduced to a public airing of well-rehearsed arguments. If there are no changes, the bill immediately undergoes its third and final reading and is passed (*Gesetzesbeschluss*). From 1953 to 1983 between 51 per cent and 71 per cent of laws were passed unanimously, reflecting the great care taken to reach agreement between the *Fraktionen* at committee stage. Not until 1983, when the Greens entered the *Bundestag* with a radically new political agenda, did this figure fall dramatically to 16 per cent.

Passage through the *Bundestag* is not the end of the story. A second passage (*zweiter Durchgang*) requires consultation with the *Bundesrat* (as laid down in articles 76–8 of the Basic Law). Regardless of who initiates it, every law must be sent to the *Bundesrat*, although the latter assembly has an absolute veto only over 'consent laws' (*Zustimmungsgesetze*), which directly affect the *Länder*. Changes to the constitution require a two-thirds majority in both *Bundestag* and *Bundesrat*. For ordinary laws (*Einspruchsgesetze*, literally: 'objection laws'), the *Bundesrat* has a suspensive or delaying veto. In this case the assembly may summon a mediation committee (*Vermittlungsausschuss*) made up of 16 representatives from the *Bundesrat* and an equal number from the *Bundestag*. The committee attempts to broker a compromise, although at the end of the day the *Bundestag* may override objections if it can command a sufficient majority. To signal a conciliatory approach to the *Bundestag*, the *Bundesrat* may also convene the committee to consider consent laws. In every case the onus is on the assembly to argue that a law requires its consent.

In practice, consent laws are those that involve changes to the constitution and affect the rights of the *Länder* in finance, taxation and in their administration of federal laws. Disputes between the assemblies about whether or not a law requires consent are not uncommon and are referred to the Federal President. In certain cases the mediation committee may be invoked by the government or the *Bundestag* (although they do so less often than the *Bundesrat*). Over half of all bills are consent bills, primarily because the *Länder* are responsible for their implementation (this has led to conflict between the two assemblies, especially where rival political parties command majorities). Once a bill is accepted by both assemblies, the Federal President checks that it has passed through the proper procedures and conforms to the constitution; it is then officially published and becomes law 14 days later.

Currently there is concern in Germany over the effect on the parliamentary process of the pressure to pass an increasing volume of legislation. Of 6686 laws presented between 1949 and 1990, 4389 (65.6 per cent) were passed. The mediation committee was summoned 475 times by the *Bundesrat*, 35 times by the government and 10 times by the *Bundestag*. There were 53 bills that failed during mediation and 2235 (33.4 per cent) were abandoned. The average time taken for a bill's passage through parliament is 14 months, with most requiring little or no debate, depending on the nature of the bill. Apart from the sheer volume of laws, most legislation is welfare-related and so complex that only members with specialist knowledge fully understand it. One thing that has contributed to the deluge of legislation (*Gesetzesflut*) is the tendency within Germany to regulate more and more areas of life through the law. Moreover, given the relatively short period within a parliament's life that is available for processing bills, governments are either tempted to rush through laws or forced to abandon them altogether. Finally, there is a danger that, where different parties command majorities in each house, the *Bundesrat*'s use of its power to impede or block important legislation may discredit the parliamentary process and reinforce public cynicism towards politicians. The danger is far from theoretical: the CDU used their control of the *Bundesrat* to delay and modify legislation during the 1970s, and when the majorities were reversed after unification an SPD-dominated *Bundesrat* blocked government-sponsored anti-welfare measures (Duckenfield 1999: 112–13). In this respect the relationship between *Bundesrat* and *Bundestag* illustrates a much wider issue: the very powerful role of so-called veto-players in the German polity, which can seriously hinder central government's ability to enact reform. Thus the *Bundesrat* limits the legislative powers of the *Bundestag*; the electoral system forces parties to build coalitions; the Central Bank controls monetary policy; and since the Maastricht Treaty of 1992, national governments are subject to transfer of powers to the European Union (for a discussion see Zohlnhöfer 1999: 148ff.).

Although the plenary session is the *Bundestag*'s main public forum, it is not where most parliamentary work is done or even where decisions are actually reached. For example, between 1949 and 1990 the *Bundestag* held 2244 plenary sessions. By contrast, between 1976 and 1990 alone, there were 9806 meetings of *Fraktionen* and 27 609 committee meetings, not to mention countless working parties and other forums. The German parliamentary system not only gives the impression of 'working behind closed doors', it also, despite a high level of media coverage (including 77 hours of televised plenary debates every year), ranks far behind the Federal Constitutional Court in terms of public confidence (see Patzelt 1997: 170). Public criticism has focused on a number of issues. These include: whether professional parliamentarians under strong discipline imposed by their party are truly able to reflect the wishes of the people; the lack of spontaneity in plenary sessions; the high salaries of members; and excessive influence exerted by economic interests and state bureaucracies. There have also been calls to make greater use of referenda in order to consult the popular will more closely on particular issues.

FEDERAL GOVERNMENT (*BUNDESREGIERUNG*)

The most senior minister in the German parliamentary system is the Chancellor, an office which originated with Bismarck. Bismarck, however, was the only government minister in the Reich, engaging senior civil servants or so-called state secretaries (*Reichsstaatssekretäre*) to run individual ministries or departments. Not until the Weimar period did government by cabinet ministers emerge. Even then, although the Chancellor was empowered to provide policy guidelines (*Richtlinien der Politik*), in reality he was frequently undermined by the executive powers of the President, who could, for instance, dismiss the Chancellor without consulting parliament. The authority traditionally invested in the German Chancellorship is still embodied in the so-called 'Chancellor principle' (*Kanzlerprinzip*). Germans often also refer to their system as a 'Chancellor-based democracy' (*Kanzlerdemokratie*).

In defining the Chancellor's role the originators of the Basic Law wanted to create an office that combined the authority to govern with accountability to parliament. Responsible only to parliament, the Chancellor is elected by a majority of the assembly, which may dismiss him or her only if it at the same time also elects a successor (the so-called 'constructive vote of no confidence'). This arrangement invests the incumbent Chancellor with considerable power; it also forces the *Bundestag* to take responsibility for mandating an individual to assume that power. The Chancellor lays down the guidelines of government policy (*Richtlinienkompetenz*), which ministers must implement. In addition he or she chooses ministers without the assent of parliament and sets the number and responsibilities of the federal ministries (*Organisationsgewalt*). The 'Chancellor principle' includes an obligation to preserve the unity of government by overseeing and co-ordinating the policies of the various ministries. The largest ministries are finance, justice and defence, although the total number since 1949 has ranged from 13 to 21. The Chancellor's deputy is generally the leader of the partner party in the coalition.

Each minister is served by a senior civil servant or state secretary (*Staatssekretär*). State secretaries, who are political appointees, wield considerable power but may be retired when the minister to whom they owe their position loses office. A more public and overtly political role is that of the parliamentary state secretary (PSS, or *Staatsminister*), an office established in 1967 after the UK model. Selected on similar lines as ministers, PSSs are members of parliament and often represent ministers or the Chancellor in the plenary session. Second only to the minister, the role of PSS is often a prelude to cabinet office. Each ministry has at least one PSS, whose number and importance have grown in recent years (from 7 in 1967 to 33 in 1991).

Two further principles of ministerial government should be mentioned. The first is the departmental principle (*Ressortprinzip*), which gives each minister responsibility for running a department within the guidelines set by the Chancellor. The second is the cabinet principle (*Kabinettsprinzip*), which requires all ministers to agree and represent policy as a collegiate: in other words, once policy is agreed, no individual minister may undermine it. The Chancellor is supported by a mini-ministry, the Federal Chancellor's Office

(*Bundeskanzleramt*). With a staff of 500, many of whom rotate between ministries, the office co-ordinates the work of the departments, settles conflicts, and ensures that government policy guidelines are observed under the terms of the *Richtlinienkompetenz*; the office also liaises between the government and the two assemblies, the political parties and the *Länder*.

The day-to-day work of the federal government is regulated by a routine of weekly meetings and consultations. Ministers and members of parliament generally devote weekends to constituency affairs and other engagements. During the first part of the week the government consults with its party executive, parliamentary group, the committees and its coalition partners at national and regional level. The cabinet meets on Wednesday morning, after which the government is available to the *Bundestag* for question time and holds its weekly press conference (a further question time is held the following day). On Thursday and Friday the parliament convenes plenary and committee sessions which ministers may choose to attend or to which they may be summoned. The obligation to report to parliament is referred to as the 'right of citation' or *Zitierrecht*. The *Bundesrat* meets once a month on a Friday morning, after meetings of the regional governments on the previous Tuesday. The system is highly regarded for providing efficient communication between the government and the party machinery. It also enables the government to work closely with parliament and emphasises the practical linkages between national and regional politics. Such networks are particularly important in the FRG, where successful Chancellors, such as Konrad Adenauer and Helmut Kohl, have also been strong party leaders relying on support from their parliamentary group. Where such support was absent or was lost, as was the case with Ludwig Erhard and Helmut Schmidt, the Chancellor did not survive for long.

Bundesrat

The present-day *Bundesrat* has its historical origins in the independent states that made up Germany before unification in 1871. Its constitutional predecessors were the Federal Council of the North German Confederation (1867–71) and the Imperial Council (*Reichsrat*) of the Weimar Republic (1919–33). From this tradition of regional sovereignty derives the individual states' responsibility for administering laws passed at national level by the *Bundestag* (the national executive has its own administrative apparatus in only a small number of fields). Although a regional assembly, the *Bundesrat* is by constitution a federal (in the sense of national) organ. It participates in appointing members of the Federal Constitutional Court (see above) and its assent is normally required for the declaration of a state of national emergency. Alongside the *Bundestag* it also ratifies international treaties according to whether their content corresponds to consent or ordinary laws (see above). In practice this affects about one-third of such treaties. Examples have included the project to establish a European Defence Community in 1953 and the *Ostpolitik* treaties of the 1970s. The assembly applied its suspensory veto to the treaty to normalise relations with Czechoslovakia in 1974. It has also been the most active of all European regional assemblies where EU legislation is concerned. In 1988 the *Bundesrat* established a special committee or chamber for EU affairs. Comprising a representative from each federal state, the chamber functions as a mini-*Bundesrat* and has powers to reach plenary decisions on EU affairs in the name of the main chamber.

Each state or regional parliament (*Landtag*) sends delegates to the *Bundesrat* roughly in proportion to the size of its population: the most populous states, Nordrhein-Westfalen, Bayern, Baden-Württemberg and Niedersachsen, have six representatives each, while Hamburg, Bremen and the Saarland have three. Unlike the *Bundestag*, the *Bundesrat* does not consti-tute itself according to election periods. Its 69 members are appointed by the regional governments (*Landesregierungen*) and come and go as and when these are formed. A state will normally send its head of government, gener-ally the Minister President (*Ministerpräsident*), its minister for federal affairs (*Minister für Bundesangelegenheiten*) and finance minister; it will send more representatives if seats are available, but all delegates must be members of the *Land* government. Unlike their colleagues in the *Bundestag*, *Bundesrat* del-egates, who may not also be members of the *Bundestag*, are not considered to be members of parliament and do not have salaries or enjoy parliamentary immunity. They may, however, attend all sessions of the *Bundestag*, includ-ing its committees. Indeed, they make ample use of this right in order to rep-resent regional interests at national level. Members of the government, but not of the *Bundestag*, are entitled to attend *Bundesrat* committee meetings and have a duty to attend if required. All the states maintain offices or standing representations (*Ständige Vertretungen*) in the capital. The function of these agencies is to promote regular contact between the *Bundestag*, the *Bundesrat* and the federal government, and also between the member states themselves.

Each year the *Bundesrat* elects a President. Since 1950 the office has rotated among the states and is politically uncontroversial. Like the *Bundestag*, the *Bundesrat* conducts most of its business in committees. There are 17 standing committees, reflecting the functions of ministries (e.g. finance, agriculture, foreign affairs). The chairpersons of the committees are elected annually by the main assembly and are normally allocated among the states. Since each state has only a single seat on a committee, member-ship is not in proportion to the composition of the *Bundesrat*. The *Bundesrat*'s 180-strong secretariat plays a particularly important role in servicing the standing committees. The full assembly meets around 15 times a year at three-weekly intervals. Government ministers attend if the agenda requires but the Federal Chancellor appears only on rare occasions. As with the *Bundestag*, most of the issues debated by the assembly are settled beforehand in committee. Since its sessions are carefully planned and conducted in a low-key atmosphere without drama or political rheto-ric (applause or interruptions are rare and calls to order unknown), they attract little media attention.

The *Bundesrat*'s low public profile, coupled with its obligation to administer national laws, has led to suggestions that its role is more bureaucratic than political and that it functions rather as a 'second government' than as a genuine second assembly. Against this it is argued that a more strongly politicised profile for the *Bundesrat* would undermine its effectiveness as an institution. It is true that the assembly can become a voice of opposition to the national government and can delay or even block *Bundestag* legislation if the two chambers are controlled by different parliamentary majorities. Notably this occurred during the social–liberal coalition between 1969 and 1982 and during Helmut Kohl's administration of 1994–98. In general, however, the *Bundesrat* has not acted as an 'anti-parliament' obstructing legislation passed by the nationally elected assembly. Inter-*Länder* coalitions have tended to form across party lines with regional interests at the forefront. Likewise national governments have not been able to rely on a compliant *Bundesrat*, even when opposition parties have lacked a majority there.

The *Bundesrat* illustrates the operation of 'co-operative federalism' in Germany. The term refers partly to the way in which the federal states choose to work together and co-ordinate their activities through regular conferences and meetings of political leaders, ministers and civil servants. It also denotes the more or less institutionalised contacts between the national government and the states (for example, through meetings between the Federal Chancellor and the Minister Presidents). Formal accords between federal and regional institutions are embodied in 'state treaties' (*Staatsverträge*) or 'administrative agreements' (*Verwaltungsabkommen*). In addition hundreds of *Bund-Länder* committees staffed by civil servants, constitute the apparatus of 'administrative federalism' (*Verwaltungsföderalismus*).

In many respects the integration of regional institutions into a national framework enhances the political role of the *Bundesrat*. At the same time it has led some to label the assembly (and the regional executive governments) as a 'transmission belt' for an increasingly unitary state. Support for this view derives from the progressive transfer of legislative powers away from regional parliaments (*Landtage*) and towards the centre. Only where the *Landtage* retain such powers, as for instance in town and country planning, the police and cultural affairs (which include schools and broadcasting), do clear differences from government policy emerge (Kropp 1997: 248). These and other issues have prompted calls for reform of the German federal system.

FEDERALISM: STRUCTURAL REFORMS AFTER UNIFICATION

Although the Basic Law envisages a clear role for the *Länder* in framing legislation and in the passing of laws, the *Bund*, even before unification, extended its powers and competencies at the expense of the federal states. By claiming large areas of concurrent legislation for itself and amending the Basic Law in order to widen its catalogue of responsibilities, the *Bund* effectively reduced the *Länder* to organs of pure administration. Such developments were taken as signs of a 'decomposition' of the German federal state (H.P. Schneider 1999: 70). If anything, unification made the situation worse. Not only did the federal government barely involve the (western) *Länder* in the negotiations for the Treaty of Unification or in setting up the administrative structures of the new states, it also expropriated most of the state-owned industries and properties of the former GDR. Moreover, the four-year suspension of the system of financial equalisation and its replacement by the Unity Fund, while economically justifiable, increased the eastern states' dependence on the political centre. The *Länder* also saw many of their decision-making powers drift to the European Union.

Pressure to address these issues led to the formation of a joint *Bundestag–Bundesrat* commission, which sat from 1992 until 1994. The commission's task was to recommend changes to the Basic Law and reforms of the federal system that would allow it to retain its viability in an enlarged Germany within an evolving EU. The commission's recommendations provoked fierce controversy in both assemblies. By 1994, however, a series of reforms was in force that secured a very powerful role for the *Bundesrat* with regard to Europe. The assembly not only obtained a veto on any further transfer of both regional and central sovereign powers to the EU, but the federal government was also obliged to take the *Bundesrat*'s views into account on any EU measure affecting the exclusive competencies of the *Länder*. A European Chamber, comprising representatives of each *Land*, was set up with powers to act on behalf of the *Bundesrat* at EU level. Furthermore, the *Bundesrat* won the right for a *Land* minister to directly represent the German government at meetings of the EU Council of Ministers.

In non-EU matters the *Bundesrat* was less successful in recouping its lost competencies (Lehmann 1996: 458–60; Kropp 1997: 274–5). Although the *Bund* must make a stronger case (based on 'necessity') for extending its catalogue of concurrent powers, the *Länder* have not regained significant areas of responsibility. Deemed too difficult for the commission, especially in the light of the severe economic downturn in the east after unification, the question of a comprehensive reform of the financial equalisation system was shelved in favour of provisional solutions (H.P. Schneider 1999: 74–81).

The commission also considered the long-standing issue of territorial reform, in particular whether the number of *Länder* should be reduced in order to create larger and more effective units. In the event the Unification Treaty, by establishing the five new *Länder* in the east, pre-empted the issue and the commission opted for a modest proposal to merge Berlin and Brandenburg. The merger was designed to avoid Berlin being treated as a 'hole' in the middle of Brandenburg and would have created a powerful political and economic unit both in the *Bundesrat* and at a European level. In fact the proposal was rejected in May 1996 when only 36.6 per cent of Brandenburgers voted for merger (53.4 per cent Berliners, mostly in the western part of the city, voted in favour). Nevertheless the Basic Law was amended to make it easier for the *Länder* in general to restructure their boundaries by mutual agreement (subject also to approval by the *Bundestag* and by plebiscite in the *Länder* affected). This may have implications for *Länder* boundaries in the future.

FINANCE AND THE *LÄNDER*

At the heart of the division of power and responsibilities between the *Länder* and the centre lies the system for allocating budgets. The basic framework for this is laid down in the Basic Law (articles 104ff.). In practice the *Länder* have only limited tax-raising powers and during the immediate post-war years the *Bund* used financial aid to the states to ensure compliance with its policies. The financial reform of 1960 and rulings by the Federal Constitutional Court placed legal limits on the extent to which the *Bund* could undermine the financial independence of the *Länder*. The system of financial equalisation (*Finanzausgleich*) now in place allocates tax revenues between *Bund* and the states (vertical equalisation) and among the states themselves (horizontal equalisation).

Horizontal equalisation is designed to ensure equality of living standards throughout Germany by transferring revenues from the richer to the poorer *Länder*. In practice the mechanisms of equalisation have proved complex and often controversial. The *Bund* (through *Bundesergänzungszuweisungen*) may allocate funds to financially weak *Länder*; the centre may also provide support for joint federal projects (*Gemeinschaftsaufgaben*). By 1985 the instrument of central allocations, originally intended for fine-tuning only, involved very large sums of money and was being manipulated by the CDU/CSU administration to exclude the SPD-controlled *Länder*. In 1986 the Federal Constitutional Court ruled such behaviour unfair and, notably after unification, pressed the *Bund* and states to establish a more equitable system (for details see Kropp 1997: 271–3). In a second ruling in 1992 the Court ruled that equalisation and central allocations could not be used to make recipient *Länder* financially better off than the donor states.

Before unification the donor states within the system of horizontal equalisation were: Nordrhein-Westfalen, Bayern, Baden-Württemberg, Hessen and Hamburg. Recipients were: Niedersachsen, Rheinland-Pfalz, Schleswig-Holstein, the Saarland and Bremen. Simply including the eastern *Länder* in the existing system in 1990 would have turned all the western states except Bremen into net donors. To avoid a politically unacceptable imbalance, the government and the western states agreed to establish the German Unity Fund, a jointly financed, four-year interim package of special transfers to the east (these had to be topped up in 1993 and 1994). After complex negotiations between the *Bund* and the *Länder*, during which the states were able to maintain a cross-party front against the government's strategy of shifting the burden of costs to the regions (which would have disadvantaged the SPD *Länder* in the west), a new system of equalisation was agreed in 1993. Replacing the now defunct Unity Fund, the so-called Federal Consolidation Programme came into force in 1995. It fully incorporated the eastern *Länder* and Berlin into the equalisation programme, retained the instrument of central allocations and re-affirmed the national, reviewable 'solidarity tax' of 7.5 per cent (first introduced in July 1991). These measures, it was planned, would enable the eastern states eventually to reach parity with the west. At the end of the first year of the programme the eastern *Länder* were net beneficiaries to the tune of 57 billion DM, the *Bund* contributing 53 and the western *Länder* over 4 billion DM respectively (for details see Lehmann 1996: 505–7). Although the new *Länder* were thus eventually incorporated into the existing structures of equalisation, they entered requiring extremely high levels of subsidy. At the same time the centre had been unable to exploit their economic dependence on subsidy in order to undermine the political autonomy of the regions in the country as a whole.

The 1995 equalisation scheme soon attracted criticism, partly because of the continuing need for large transfers to the east where economic recovery was slow. In particular the donor states Bayern, Baden-Württemberg and Hessen challenged (through the Federal Constitutional Court) the fairness of the system used to re-distribute tax revenues. Claiming that the current system was too complex to monitor and justify to their citizens, they argued that automatic external transfers provided little motivation for donor states to generate additional internal revenue while the receiving states were under no pressure to reduce expenditure. In addition they maintained that the city-states of Berlin, Hamburg and Bremen benefited disproportionately through having the size of their populations artificially raised for the purposes of the allocation (this was done because many Germans worked in the cities but lived in the surrounding regions; for similar reasons Hamburg and Bremen received extra subsidy for their harbours). Finally, the three donor states believed that *Bundesergänzungszuweisungen*, which had reached record levels, were being misdirected by the centre to ensure political compliance of the *Länder* and were subsidising poorly managed regional budgets. Although they did not reject the constitutional principle of horizontal transfer, the donor states questioned the scale of their contributions and the mechanisms used to calculate them.

By 1998 the continuing pattern of the wealthier western states contributing to the poorer eastern states meant that, for example, each citizen of Hessen was contributing 569 DM to the transfer fund, while each citizen in Berlin and Sachsen was receiving 1427 DM and 1352 DM respectively; benefits for the other eastern states ranged from 405 to 485 DM per person. Only the Saarland, Rheinland-Pfalz and Niedersachsen were net beneficiaries in the west and then at relatively low levels (between 100 DM and 211 DM). Ruling on the dispute in 1999, the Federal Constitutional Court retained the existing model. At the same time it required the government to have in place by 2002 new guideline legislation (*Maßstäbegesetz*) that from 2005 would identify and fix volumes of necessary expenditure and ensure that transfers to beneficiary states would not exceed 95 per cent of the average level; the special status of the city-states would also be reviewed (Knapp 1999: 1).

LÄNDER PARLIAMENTS

The *Länder* are either 'area states' (*Flächenländer*) or 'city-states' (*Stadtstaaten*), the latter comprising Hamburg, Bremen and Berlin. The regional parliaments themselves vary considerably in size, electoral law and their constitutions. Nordrhein-Westfalen, for instance, has a parliament of over 200 members, while the Hamburg senate comprises only 12. Bayern alone maintains a second chamber, or senate, alongside a *Landtag* of around 95 members. The Bavarian senate is drawn from 60 representatives from various organisations and interest groups ranging from agriculture to universities, although it rarely exercises its political powers. As for elections, most regional assemblies have now adopted the proportional, two-vote system used for the *Bundestag*: voters cast one vote directly for an individual and another for a party list. Only Baden-Württemberg and Nordrhein-Westfalen still operate a direct, single-vote system for a named candidate. In a procedure which has been criticised for making political parties insufficiently accountable to the electorate, voters in Hamburg and Bremen choose only a party, which then supplies candidates from its own lists.

All *Länder*, except for Bremen, allow for plebiscites, an instrument which is not available to the *Bundestag* but is often advocated as promoting direct, grass-roots democracy. The new *Länder* in particular also allow for 'people's initiatives' (*Volksinitiativen*), in which citizens can petition the *Landtag* and compel it to consider regional issues. In some states (Bayern, Baden-Württemberg and Rheinland-Pfalz) the *Landtag* may even be dissolved by plebiscite, although this has occurred only once (in Baden-Württemberg). The threshold for implementing the result of a plebiscite varies widely, from 4 per cent of the total electorate in Schleswig-Holstein and Brandenburg to 20 per cent in Hessen, Rheinland-Pfalz and Nordrhein-Westfalen. In practice plebiscites are rare and tend to be engineered by political parties as an expression of 'extra-parliamentary opposition' to the *Land* government. Nor have they been employed evenly across Germany: between 1949 and 1997, 14 plebiscites were held in Bayern and only 5 in Nordrhein-Westfalen (Kropp 1997).

There are regional variations in the relationship between the *Land* government and assembly. As a rule the head of government is the Minister President (or in Berlin, for example, the mayor) who formally issues laws and represents the *Land* externally. In some *Länder*, however, the Minister President is solely responsible for appointing ministers. In others, parliament also approves cabinet members. Two *Länder*, Niedersachsen and the Rheinland-Pfalz, require parliamentary approval even for a change of minister during a government's period of office. In all of the eastern and in some of the western *Länder* the Minister President is subject to a constructive vote of no confidence (which means that the assembly may dismiss him or her only if it also elects a replacement). The Minister President of Bayern enjoys the greatest degree of independence from parliament, although the constitution states in general terms that he or she is obliged to resign if he or she loses the confidence of the assembly. In most *Länder*, the government (including the office of Minister President) changes with the election of a new assembly. There is no such requirement in Bayern and Rheinland-Pfalz, however, which is seen by some as giving too much power to the regional government at the expense of parliamentary accountability.

LOCAL GOVERNMENT

Alongside national (*Bund*) and regional (*Land*) levels of government, the Basic Law provides for a third level, that of local self-government (the *Kommunen*). The form of self-government is regulated by the *Land* constitution, but each regional state is generally divided into *Kreise* (districts) and municipalities (*Gemeinden*). The district may be either a rural (*Landkreis*) or an urban district (*Stadtkreis*). Rural districts are broken down into municipalities, ranging in size from a village to a town, which elects its own council (*Gemeinderat*) or, in the case of a city, a mayor (*Bürgermeister*). Rural districts also elect councils, headed by a chief councillor (*Landrat*). While municipalities are multi-purpose authorities, the district generally administers broader functions which are beyond the resources of the *Gemeinden*, such as hospitals, schools, highways, social welfare and utilities. From the late 1960s until unification the number of municipalities in the old FRG declined from around 24 000 to 8500; some municipalities merged to form larger administrative units (*Gemeindeverbände*), sometimes sharing responsibility for specialised services such as water supply or education. A few *Länder* have inserted an extra, non-elected tier of administration, the *Regierungsbezirk*, between region and district (Paterson and Southern 1991: 162–3; Jeffery and Whittle 1997: 114).

Elections to municipalities and districts are by direct, majority vote and for most Germans local government is the first and principal point of contact with authority. While the fundamental structures of national legislative institutions did not change with unification, the same was not true for local government, where opportunities for citizens to engage in 'direct democracy' were extended after 1990. Admittedly the process was slow as critics of direct democracy pointed to the dangers of undermining the powers of democratically elected institutions. By 1997, however, all the main *Länder* had introduced procedures for holding a plebiscite (*Bürgerentscheid*) or to enable citizens to petition the local authority (termed variously a *Petitionsrecht*, *Bürgerantrag*, or *Bürgerbegehren*). The extent to which citizens have made use of such mechanisms varies geographically and does not suggest that there is likely to be a revolution in participatory politics. In Baden-Württemberg, for example, petitions are least likely to be admitted by the authorities and are submitted on average five times a year, a third less than in Schleswig-Holstein or Hessen (Gabriel *et al.* 1997: 352–4).

JUDICIAL SYSTEM

German courts are organised according to five areas of jurisdiction. In terms of the volume of cases handled and the number of personnel employed (including judges), the criminal and civil courts (*ordentliche Gerichte*) are the most significant. Industrial tribunals or labour courts (*Arbeitsgerichte*) consider cases relating to working conditions, wages and other industrial disputes; they also rule on conflicts arising from the law on co-determination (*Arbeitsverfassungsrecht*). Unlike other areas of German law, industrial disputes are not governed by fundamental written norms, with the result that German labour courts play an important role in forming or creating law on the basis of cases that arise in practice; within the continental German tradition of preferring to apply law from written norms, this is often perceived as a failing. Administrative courts (*Allgemeine Verwaltungsgerichte*) handle conflicts involving regional law (*Landrecht*; examples are complaints against the police or schools) and disputes between federal states (*Länder*); citizens believing that the state or government have infringed their rights will normally have recourse to an administrative court; such courts will also ultimately consider disciplinary matters involving civil servants and soldiers. Social or welfare courts (*Sozialgerichte*) consider disputes over national insurance, pensions and social welfare legislation, while finance or revenue tribunals (*Finanzgerichte*) are responsible for resolving conflicts on taxation and customs.

The five branches are also organised in a vertical or hierarchical structure. At the apex are the national or federal courts (*Bundesgerichte*), below which lie the regional or federal state courts (*Landgerichte*). The Federal Law Court (*Bundesgerichtshof*) is the supreme civil and criminal court; there are parallel federal courts for industrial law (*Bundesarbeitsgericht*), administrative law (*Bundesverwaltungsericht*), welfare law (*Bundessozialgericht*) and financial law (*Bundesfinanzgericht*). Within a region or federal state courts are structured as follows: at the bottom is the local or district court (*Amtsgericht*), above this the provincial court (*Landgericht*) and finally the high court (*Oberlandesgericht*). The special role of the Federal Constitutional Court (*Bundesverfassungsgericht*) is considered below. Constitutional issues at regional level are handled by regional constitutional courts (*Landesverfassungsgerichte*). These courts might decide on the admissibility of a regional referendum or establish the validity of a local election; they are seldom convened in practice.

Statistics on the distribution of cases across the five types of court indicate that most legal problems arise in civil, social and economic areas of German life and do not reflect disputes between the individual and the state (which normally appear before the administrative courts; see Plöhn 1997: 364). However, a particular feature of the German legal system is that the vast majority of cases are settled by regional, not federal (national), courts. The reason for this is that in practice regional courts (*Landgerichte*) apply national as well as regional law and effectively pre-empt the federal courts, which are restricted to cases involving national law. As a consequence federal courts tend to hear appeals and act as a unifying influence in the application and interpretation of law in the lower courts. Since most cases are settled at regional level, it is not surprising that 97 per cent of judges are in the service of the *Land*, not the *Bund*.

Germany has an unusually high number of judges and it appears to be growing (from about 13 000 in 1971 to 18 000 in 1991; see Plöhn 1997: 367). Despite the increase in personnel, the system is overburdened, reflecting a national propensity to litigation and a rising crime rate (Jeffery and Whittle 1997: 81). Unsurprisingly the flood of litigation is not without consequences for both the legal system and society in general: while law is being constantly refined and interpreted, diffuse concepts (such as 'negative influence on the environment') are clarified and the German bureaucracy adapts its procedures in the light of legal judgements.

To reflect a balance between regional and national interests and to ensure political independence, judges are appointed by a board comprising 16 regional ministers and an equal number of nominees of the *Bundestag* (though not necessarily members of parliament). Judges are not intended to be entirely apolitical and are free to join political parties and trade unions. They may not, however, be members of a regional parliament (*Landtag*) or the *Bundestag*. German judges tend to be professional lawyers with expertise in specific areas; interest groups such as employers' organisations and trade unions are free to nominate candidates.

It should also be mentioned that, in common with other members of the European Union, German courts are integrated into the European Court of Justice (ECJ) and the European Court of Human Rights (ECHR). The ECJ settles disputes between the organs of the Union, between individual member states, and responds to requests from national courts on how to interpret Community law. During the 1990s the ECJ was involved in disputes over the issue of parity between men and women in public service jobs in Germany. The debate came to the fore in the 1980s when German courts had to determine whether the Basic Law's commitment to sexual equality (enshrined in article 3) meant that men and women should be assessed for public service positions on equal merit or whether employers, by applying positive discrimination, should meet a fixed quota of female staff in order to achieve actual parity within a department or organisation. In a judgment of 11 November 1997, the ECJ declared its support for quotas; it argued that positive discrimination in favour of women was justified in order to redress social disadvantages and continuing prejudices experienced by women (Müller-Heidelberg *et al.* 1998: 65–9). Since 1994 the ECHR has been open to individuals from member states who have exhausted their national courts in pursuing redress for violations of human rights and basic freedoms. In the view of human rights activists, crackdowns by the German government on asylum-seekers since unification are likely to bring it increasingly into conflict with the ECHR (Müller-Heidelberg *et al.* 1998: 169–80).

FEDERAL CONSTITUTIONAL COURT

Since 1951 the Federal Constitutional Court (*Bundersverfassungsgericht*) has functioned as Germany's highest court. Sitting in Karlsruhe, the FCC comprises two senates, with (since 1963) eight judges in each; it controls its own budget and organisation and appoints its own personnel. The judges are appointed for 12 years by a highly complex and not entirely transparent procedure based on equal representation from the *Bundesrat* and the *Bundestag* and on consultations with the political parties, who have in practice agreed to balance party-based with politically neutral appointees. Apart from the three federal court judges required by law to sit in each senate, members tend to be regional court judges, law professors, senior civil servants or government politicians; representatives of lay interest groups are seldom appointed.

The FCC's principal role is to act as 'guardian of the constitution' (*Hüter der Verfassung*; see also article 93 of the Basic Law). As such it can ban political parties whose aims undermine the Basic Law; on these grounds the KPD, the German Communist Party, was proscribed in 1956. In practice over 95 per cent of the court's work is concerned with constitutional complaints (*Verfassungsbeschwerden*), mainly from individuals who allege an infringement of their basic constitutional rights or who are using the court as a final avenue of appeal. Although this demonstrates a high level of popular trust in the court, very few complaints are upheld: only 2.8 per cent between 1951 and 1995. Nevertheless over 85 000 complaints were presented in 1996 and the court is chronically overburdened, despite the introduction of preliminary hearings by small chambers comprising three judges, who determine whether a case should proceed to the full senate (95.6 per cent of cases were settled in this way in 1996). Proposals giving the court powers to pre-empt individual complaints by setting its own agenda of issues requiring constitutional rulings have so far been rejected, and it is not certain the measure would have much effect anyhow.

German courts may also refer laws and measures to the FCC to decide whether they are compatible with the Basic Law. In view of the increasing number of referrals, a similar system of preliminary hearings as for individual complaints was established in 1993. Also entitled to refer legislation to the FCC are the national and regional governments and members of parliament (if supported by a two-thirds majority). Opposition parties in particular have used this provision to try to block legislation and specific measures. Examples include: the Bavarian state government's opposition to the Basic

Treaty between the FRG and GDR in 1973; the challenge by conservative politicians in 1992 to the revised abortion laws; and the SPD's objections to the government deploying German forces in international military missions in non-NATO areas without parliamentary consent (Rohlfs and Schäfer 1997: 305–6).

The FCC also adjudicates between state organs and institutions, such as the federal states and the national parliament, although such disputes rarely arise. In 1960 the court upheld a complaint by the states that Chancellor Adenauer's proposal to establish a government-controlled national television company (*Deutschland-Fernsehen-GmbH*) would diminish their constitutional rights and endanger freedom of speech.

The court tends to be invoked at times of political crisis and constitutional change. In January 1983 it gave qualified support to a controversial manoeuvre to exploit an artificial and collusive vote of no confidence in order to dissolve parliament prematurely and call fresh elections (for details see Paterson and Southern 1991: 87–9). The court was involved in at least two constitutional issues arising out of the Treaty of Unification in 1990: it ruled that the federal electoral requirement of a 5 per cent hurdle unfairly disadvantaged minority east German parties; and it rejected the claim by conservative politicians that the Treaty effectively recognised the Oder–Neiße line as a state border and was therefore unconstitutional.

The FCC has been drawn so deeply into political arguments that some maintain that it is in danger of turning into a 'surrogate legislator' (*Ersatzgesetzgeber*; Jeffery and Whittle 1997: 42) and of taking over the functions of a political machinery that is no longer able to reach decisions. It is true that the court tends to give highly detailed judgments and has, in recent years, suggested specific revisions or interpretations of laws and measures. However, it has not done this out of a desire to take political initiatives or to interfere in the democratic process. Rather it has tried to avoid acting as a vetoing authority and to ensure that measures that come before it that are proposed by a mandated government are actually implemented according to the spirit of the constitution. Another debate has centred on whether decisions by the court are valid for all time. Since both judges and circumstances change, it has been argued that parliament should be able to have judgments reviewed if it considers them obsolete (Plöhn 1997: 373–4). Despite such controversies the FCC remains a highly respected institution and is frequently invoked.

INTEGRATION OF THE LEGAL SYSTEMS OF THE FRG AND THE FORMER GDR

The reunification of Germany in 1990 was a transaction in law in so far as the fundamental conditions of unification were set out in a series of legally binding treaties. These treaties were the Two-plus-Four Treaty between Germany and the former allies of 1945 (concluded 12 September 1990) and two intra-German treaties. Of the latter, the *Staatsvertrag* set out the terms of the Legal, Economic and Social Union (1 July 1990), while the Treaty of Unification (*Einigungsvertrag*, 31 August 1990) finalised the political framework of the new Germany.

As with virtually all their institutions, the east Germans retained little or nothing of their legal system: the judiciary and the framework of legal administration in the old GDR were displaced by West German models. The need for this was beyond question, since the East German legal system was irretrievably politicised. GDR lawyers and administrators had first and foremost to be ideologically committed and loyal to the SED. The West German model of the professional judge or technically competent civil servant interpreting and applying abstract law impartially to all citizens – a tradition which goes back to the Prussian civil service of the nineteenth century – had not existed in the east since at least 1949. As a result of unification the new east German states needed legal personnel who were experienced in western political, economic and social institutions. Imported from the west, these individuals suddenly became responsible for administering what was (for east Germans) new law in all areas of life, including criminal justice, land and property ownership, public finance and commerce.

During the first five years of unification, western Germany provided assistance in building up a modern, democratic, and impartial legal system in the east. In many cases this assistance was based on individual partnerships between old and new *Länder*, with the western partner helping its eastern counterpart (thus, for example, Bayern assisted Thüringen, Baden-Württemberg supported Sachsen and Schleswig-Holstein, Mecklenburg-Vorpommern). Up to 20 000 civil servants transferred from the old to the new *Länder*, leading to a majority of westerners occupying leading positions in the east; for instance, in 1991 over 70 per cent of officials in Brandenburg's justice ministry and over 60 per cent of civil servants in the finance ministry were west Germans. Statistics like these contributed to the widespread perception by east Germans that they were being colonised by westerners.

From the very beginning western civil servants were heavily involved in reorganising the administrative and political structures of the east. Before unification there was no such thing as autonomous local government in the GDR. By west German standards, the units of administration that did exist were too small and too numerous to support any form of viable autonomy at their level. Indeed, under the communist system of 'democratic centralism', these units existed, not to foster any sense of local political identity but to act as efficient implementers of central government policy; the system was often called 'government by telephone' as local officials gave priority over written law to telephone directives received directly from central party organs. By 1994 the new *Länder* had succeeded in establishing 87 viable administrative districts (*Kreise*) of between 100 000 and 150 000 residents along west German lines. Creating smaller local parishes (*Gemeinden*) proved much harder. The authorities were unwilling to displace the small units that already existed in the GDR for fear of alienating citizens already suffering from the shock of rapid westernisation; such units were, however, given the right to merge voluntarily.

The task of replacing communist party administrators by impartial civil servants well versed in local government law could not be accomplished overnight. Predictably, there was considerable popular dissatisfaction with the new bureaucracy (three years after unification up to 43 per cent of east Germans were expressing unhappiness with their local government machinery; Hettlage 1995: 44). The problems were due largely to the sheer scale and speed of the reorganisation. For example, during the 1950s and 1960s, civil servants and politicians in the old FRG focused on building up housing provision and transport, shifting their priorities to town planning and environment during the 1970s and 1980s. By comparison, in post-unification east Germany issues which had taken the FRG four decades to resolve had to be addressed almost instantly by imported personnel with enthusiasm and expertise but little knowledge of local conditions. The example of property ownership illustrates the problem. The Unification Treaty placed 2.7 million homes, formerly state property, in the hands of local government. From 1990 courts and officials were faced with processing over 2 million applications from individuals for restitution of land and property confiscated by the socialist state (in east Berlin two-thirds of property claims were settled by 1998; Mönch 1998); schools had to be built or reorganised; the extensive network of theatres and cultural institutions maintained; in particular, new roads, rail links and housing had to be financed, and decisions on investments, town planning and jobs reached.

Changes in the criminal justice system in the east were equally far-reaching. In the former GDR the judiciary was a political instrument of the SED, most judges being party members. GDR law distinguished only two types of crime: political contrarevolution, which meant opposition to the socialist state, and ordinary criminality, which was (at least in theory) seen as a relic of exploitative capitalism. Inevitably, many legitimate activities were criminalised. Throughout the history of the GDR its courts were used at various times to stage show trials of dissidents and political opponents (including some party functionaries), to convict 'leaders' of the 1953 uprising, to persecute Jehovah's Witnesses and to expel cultural figures who were critical of the regime (notably the singer Wolf Biermann in 1976). It was a criminal offence to attempt to leave the country without official permission. Even when trials took place, proper legal procedures were not observed: many trials took place in secret; charges and judgments were not made public; and defence lawyers were unfairly disadvantaged. Significantly, law was not a particularly prestigious profession in the GDR: the country boasted only about 600 practising lawyers as against 13 000 in the west German state of Nordrhein-Westfalen alone (Hettlage 1995: 52).

Between the fall of the Berlin Wall and unification, the interim government of the GDR began the long process of reviewing past legal injustices. Over 100 judges and state lawyers were immediately dismissed for misuse of office, and criminal proceedings were instituted against members of the

GDR's political élite (with, as explained below, mixed results). With unification it would have been feasible to dismiss all legal personnel and replace them with westerners (there was no shortage of lawyers in the Federal Republic). However, the authors of the Unification Treaty drew back from this radical measure. Instead, they passed responsibility for assessing the competence of individual judges and state lawyers to the new *Länder*, who were initially obliged to complete the task within a year (in the event they needed more time). The *Länder* showed themselves not to be consistent in the criteria that they applied (these included willingness to conform to political demands, harshness of judgments, and the degree of involvement with the SED). Possibly because of the relatively small numbers involved, many GDR lawyers were retained in the hope that they could be integrated into the western system. Given the introduction of west German programmes of training and qualification, a new generation of lawyers will inevitably emerge. The wider issue of the GDR as a criminal regime and the pursuit of crimes committed by its leadership is considered in Chapter 3.

POLITICAL PARTIES

Traditionally parties have been associated with the ideologies of conservatism, liberalism and socialism, which crystallised into political movements during the nineteenth century. The allocation of a party to the right, the centre or to the left originated in the seating order of the revolutionary assemblies of 1848–49, including the ill-fated Frankfurt Parliament. Today most democratic mainstream parties in Germany share similar organisational structures. The supreme forum for the party is the party congress (*Parteitag*), a national meeting of delegates which is held annually and whose business is managed by an executive (*Parteivorstand*). Party policy is shaped by the will and views of members expressed through internal democratic mechanisms (a process termed *Willensbildung* in German). German parties are financed by members' and parlamentarians' contributions, donations, income from assets and by public funds (the latter contributing up to 50 per cent). Apart from financial support for staff and civil servants in the *Bundestag*, parties receive annual subsidies calculated in proportion to the number of votes gained at general elections. To qualify for support a party must gain at least 0.5 per cent of votes. German political parties have also been involved in periodic scandals over tax evasion and undeclared or illegal private donations, the most recent and possibly most damaging affair involving former Chancellor Helmut Kohl.

The Basic Law gives parties constitutional rights, in particular the freedom to constitute themselves and to play a part in 'forming the will of the people' (*politische Willensbildung des Volks*). In return they are financially accountable and must observe the principles of the Basic Law as interpreted by the Federal Constitutional Court; the court banned the extreme right-wing SRP party in 1952 and the German Communist Party in 1956 (a brief review of the neo-Nazi parties is given in Chapter 9). Parties are normally organised at the national or federal level (*Bundesverband*), at the level of *Land* (*Landesverband*), district or municipality (*Kreisverband*) and at local level (*Ortsverein*).

Since 1949 the political landscape of West Germany has been dominated by the two main 'people's parties', the Social Democratic Party (SPD) and the Christian Democratic Party (CDU). For most of the period the FDP has acted as a more or less permanent junior coalition partner, although the situation became more complicated during the 1980s with the emergence of the Greens as a political force in the west and after unification with the unexpected resilience of the PDS in the east. As a result the western states operate with four parties and the east with three. Voter participation has also been a factor for change. From the early 1970s turnouts for regional and national elections in western Germany began to decline. Probable reasons for this include financial scandals involving politicians, party political patronage for jobs in the public services, high salaries for parliamentarians at times of economic recession and a lack of clear policy differences between the two main parties. When extreme right-wing parties enjoyed a resurgence during the late 1980s some observers argued that voters were becoming disillusioned with the established democratic institutions (the German term for this was *Politikverdrossenheit*). In the east, where voters had weaker party ties than the former FRG, patterns of voter participation proved erratic: they never reached the record 93.4 per cent that was recorded for the March 1990 election, the first fully democratic election there since 1933.

The parties differ in terms of size and the nature of their membership. The combined membership of the CDU (636 000) and the CSU (180 000) exceeds that of the SPD. While both SPD and CDU/CSU claim to be 'people's parties' in the sense that they are not class-based but aim to appeal to a broad electorate, the SPD's membership contains a significantly higher proportion of workers, pensioners and young people engaged in training and education. The CDU, on the other hand, recruits more self-employed people. The CSU in particular faces the problem of an ageing membership. In the 1998 election campaign most of the FDP's election candidates were lawyers, with the Greens fielding mainly teachers, academics and scientists; workers in the service sector and administration predominated in the SPD and CDU/CSU (Schäfers 1998: 82; Schwehn 1998). Despite a certain disillusionment with the established political parties, there is no evident shortage of candidates for general elections: a record 5062 presented themselves at the 1998 election, although in some parties (notably the FDP) female candidates were underrepresented (Schwehn 1998). General levels of interest and participation in political issues in Germany appear to remain high.

Social Democratic Party (*Sozialdemokratische Partei Deutschlands*, SPD)

The SPD regards its founding date as 23 May 1863, when Ferdinand Lasalle created the General German Workers' Association (*Allegemeiner Deutscher Arbeiterverein*). The party represented moderate socialism throughout the Bismarck era and played an important role in the foundation and political life of the Weimar Republic (1919–33), opposing the rise of Adolf Hitler and seeing its leaders and activists persecuted by the National Socialists. Under the leadership of Kurt Schumacher between 1946 and 1952, the SPD advocated state control of key industries, banks and land in order to overcome Germany's post-war economic problems and to prevent a resurgence of National Socialism. Although it supported the expansion of the welfare state and the establishment of democratic trade unionism, the party's anti-capitalist stance and hostility to western integration limited its appeal and it effectively condemned itself to permanent opposition during the foundation years of the Federal Republic. Not until the Godesberger Programme of 1959 did the SPD abandon its historical Marxist orientation and begin to attract a wider electorate. Under its popular leader Willy Brandt it joined a national coalition government in 1966. Finally, in 1969, the party formed a ruling coalition with the FDP, enabling it to embark on a programme of social reform and greater democracy; its policy of détente with the GDR (*Ostpolitik*) was internationally acclaimed. Following the discovery of an East German spy in the government, Brandt was replaced by Helmut Schmidt as leader in 1974. After economic difficulties contributed to the decision by the FDP to switch allegiance to the CDU, the SPD re-entered a long period of opposition in 1982 which lasted until 1998 and was marked by internal dissent and changes in leadership.

During the *Wende* the party lost popularity when it argued against swift unification and criticised the government's policy of rapid privatisation of the east German economy. Further tensions arose over changes to the asylum law and the use of German armed forces in peace missions outside the NATO area. Between 1991 and 1997 membership fell from 950 000 to 780 000.

With the emergence of the charismatic Gerhard Schröder as chancellor candidate, the SPD's fortunes recovered when in 1998 it was re-elected to government in coalition with the Greens. The coalition promised to improve the ecology, reduce unemployment, increase welfare benefits and reform the tax and pension system. Tensions between the moderate Schröder and his left-wing finance minister, Oskar Lafontaine, eased when the latter resigned in 1999 and Schröder also became party chairperson.

Christian Democratic Party (*Christlich-Demokratische Partei, CDU*)

The origins of the CDU lie in the conservative Catholic Centre Party (*Zentrumspartei*) of the nineteenth century and the Weimar Republic. Nazi persecution of Christians during the Third Reich led the CDU, which was founded in 1945, to embrace both Protestant and Catholic confessions, although the conservative Catholic tradition is strongly maintained by its Bavarian sister party, the Christian Social Union (CSU). At first the party was loosely organised and lacked a common political direction but under the influence of the Rhineland politician Konrad Adenauer, in 1949 the CDU committed itself to capitalism and western integration (the Düsseldorf Guidelines). As leader and Federal Chancellor from 1949 to 1963 Adenauer dominated the party and post-war German politics. The CDU presided over the economic miracle of the 1950s and 1960s and pursued a consistent policy of integration in NATO and western Europe. Adenauer cultivated the Franco–German relationship and worked hard to rehabilitate Germany as a responsible European power and member of what is now the European Union. In 1957 the CDU gained an absolute majority in the *Bundestag*, a feat which has never been repeated. Internal party tensions and Adenauer's reluctance to go along with the USA's wish to improve relationships with the Soviet bloc led in 1963 to his replacement by the economics minister, Ludwig Erhard. Despite his popularity as architect of the economic miracle, Erhard failed to unite his party or to overcome problems of economic recession. After a further change in leadership, in 1966 the CDU entered into a Grand Coalition with the SPD. By now widely perceived as a party of post-war conservatism at a time when Germany needed political and social change, the CDU lost the election of 1969 and remained in opposition until 1982.

Under Helmut Kohl, the CDU regained power in 1982, forming a coalition government with the FDP that lasted until 1998. The party's election campaigns reflected the core conservative values of freedom, family, state and church; in office it also embarked on reductions in government spending in order to control a spiralling budget deficit. Kohl's personal achievement in securing swift unification generated a long-term 'chancellor bonus' which was reflected in a strong electoral position in the eastern and western states that endured until 1994. Failure to control unemployment and the unexpected costs of unification led to national electoral defeat in 1998, when Kohl made way for the east German Angela Merkel. Kohl's success as leader was due to his acute sense of populism and to the system of personal patronage through which he maintained strict control of the party machine (see Clemens and Paterson 1998). In 1999, however, Germany was plunged into its biggest political scandal since the war when Kohl faced allegations of accepting secret donations for the party in return for political and commercial favours. The affair centred on the government's decision to sell tanks to Saudi Arabia in 1990 and on the purchase in 1993 of the east German Leuna oil refinery by the French petrochemical company Elf-Aquitaine. Kohl's unrepentant stance, his refusal to divulge the names of donors and his fierce attacks on his two successors, Wolfgang Schäuble and Angela Merkel, ruined his political and personal reputation and did great harm to the party.

The CDU's sister party, the CSU, has dominated Bavarian politics since 1946, ruling the regional parliament virtually without interruption. The

CDU and CSU form a joint parliamentary grouping (*Fraktion*) in the *Bundestag* and do not compete with each other in federal elections, the CSU standing only in Bayern. The CSU maintains a conservative stance on social issues and has close links with the Roman Catholic Church. Its co-founder, and possibly most famous leader, Franz Josef Strauß, made a reputation for himself as an outspoken critic of social reform and *Ostpolitik* during the social–liberal coalition (1969–82). For a brief period (1980) Strauß was the CDU/CSU's candidate for Federal Chancellor before making way for the more electable Helmut Kohl. Strauß never held office under Kohl, preferring to remain a right-wing critic of government policy and, somewhat surprisingly, pursuing contacts with leading figures in the GDR until his death in 1988. The leadership is currently split between Theo Waigel, the party chairperson, and the Minister President, Edmund Stoiber.

Free Democratic Party (*Freie Demokratische Partei*, FDP)

The FDP (or F.D.P. as the party has referred to itself since 1968) was formed in 1948 from a merger of regional liberal groups in the western zones of occupation. Almost immediately it committed itself to western integration and the social market economy and formed coalitions with the post-war CDU/CSU government (1949–56 and 1961–66). From 1960 until 1968 the party was led by Erich Mende, but under Walter Scheel (1964–74) it embraced more socialist notions of workers' rights, the public obligations of property-ownership and included environmental concerns in its programme (formulated in the Freiburg Theses of 1972). After a long period of coalition government alongside the SPD (1969–82) it switched allegiance to the CDU/CSU. Party leader Hans-Dietrich Genscher (1974–85) served for many years as foreign minister under Helmut Kohl, promoting *Ostpolitik* and playing a prominent role in the negotiations for German unity. Subsequent leaders Klaus Kinkel (1993–95) and Wolfgang Gerhardt (1995–) have had to confront the problem of the party's steadily declining popularity.

A small party, the FDP sees itself as a 'third force' in German politics acting as a builder of coalitions and as a moderating or corrective influence on the two large mainstream parties, especially in national elections (for this reason the party is less attractive to voters at regional level). The party's main supporters are the self-employed and professional middle classes, although it has traditionally depended on private donations from companies, which has reduced its electoral appeal and political independence. Towards the end of the Kohl era the FDP found it increasingly hard to maintain a distinctive liberal profile and was increasingly seen as a junior partner to the CDU. Party membership declined catastrophically after unification, falling from 170 000 in 1991 to 71 000 in 1997. The FDP lost ground in the 1998 elections and has notably failed to establish a following in the eastern states.

Green Party (Die Grünen)

The Green Party, or Greens, emerged from informal opposition and citizens groups campaigning during the 1970s against atomic energy, the deployment of nuclear weapons, and the destruction of the environment. In 1980 the groups organised themselves to form a national party which in 1983 entered the *Bundestag* with 27 seats, rising in 1987 to 42. The Greens lost seats in the all-German election of 1990, partly because east Germans had little interest in ecological issues and partly because of internal party conflicts between left-wing fundamentalists, who wished to continue campaigning from opposition, and realists, who were prepared to work with the political establishment. Under the moderating leadership of Joschka Fischer the conflict was resolved in favour of the realists. After the Greens joined up with former east German opposition groups to form the Alliance 90/Greens (a painful and acrimonious process that took three years), it returned 49 members to the *Bundestag* in 1994. In the election four years later, it became the third strongest party in the *Bundestag* and was able to form a national coalition government with the SDP, displacing the FDP as the 'third force' in German politics. The alliance stands under various names at regional elections and has a membership of around 49 000.

Since the early 1980s the mainstream parties have adopted many of the Greens' positions on ecological issues. The party's electoral strongholds are the towns and cities (especially in the western states) and it has entered into various, mainly 'red–green' coalitions with the SPD in regional parliaments (the first of these was established in Hessen between 1985 and 1987). After the Greens entered government, left-wing activists pressed hard for a relaxation of Germany's strict nationality laws and for a much faster withdrawal from nuclear energy. They also strongly resisted efforts by the moderate leadership to revise traditional 'green' principles of grass-roots democracy such as the prohibition on members simultaneously holding a party office and a ministerial post.

Party of Democratic Socialism (Partei des Demokratischen Sozialismus, PDS)

During a series of emergency congresses during 1989 and 1990 the SED expelled the former communist leadership, abolished the structures of the old socialist party (*Politbüro* and Central Committee) and renamed itself the PDS. The PDS claimed to be a completely reformed democratic party to the left of the SPD, although in 2000 the federal agency responsible for the protection of the constitution (*Bundesverfassungsschutz*) still had the party under observation on account of its extreme left-wing elements that were considered hostile to Germany's parliamentary democracy (Germis 2000). Campaigning on a platform of social solidarity and arguing for the right to work and an ecologically-orientated economy, the PDS, against all initial predictions, has consistently maintained a strong electoral presence in the eastern states. In the 1998 national election it returned 36 seats, making it the third largest party in the east. From 1990 until 2000 the party was led by Gregor Gysi, who maintained his position despite his former membership of the SED and allegations of links with the *Stasi*.

Although it campaigned in western Germany, the PDS failed to establish a foothold there. However, in regional elections in the east it attracted enough votes to force the SPD and CDU into a grand coalition (in 1994 in Thüringen and Mecklenburg-Vorpommern) and tolerated a minority SPD/Alliance 90/Greens government in Sachsen-Anhalt (the so-called Magdeburg Model). After 1998 it became a full coalition partner with the SPD in Mecklenburg-Vorpommern. Although the PDS continues to attract opprobrium on account of its SED past, it appeals to many easterners who do not see their interests well represented by the mainstream parties and who have a nostalgic longing for the former GDR; former SED members and functionaries in the Berlin area have provided a valuable bedrock of support. Despite its strong presence in the east, the PDS has never succeeded in converting its support into influence at national level. In 2000 it elected Gabrielle Zimmer as leader to replace Gregor Gysi. Although an SED official before the fall of the GDR, Zimmer claimed never to have been a dogmatic communist; she pledged to direct the party into the political mainstream and to open it up to German society as a whole.

FURTHER READING

Studies in German politics are legion. While somewhat dated, Smith *et al.* (1989), Derbyshire (1991) and Paterson and Southern (1991) still represent clear and readable accounts of the German political system. Examples of more recent studies include Jeffery (1999) on federalism and Roberts (1997) on the political parties. A standard reference work in German is Gabriel and Holtmann (1997), which covers national and federal political institutions and includes accounts of the workings of the German political system. The German periodical *Politik und Zeitgeschichte* (*Beilage zur Wochenzeitung Das Parlament*) contains a wealth of individual studies, as does the English-language journal *German Politics*. The German parliament maintains an excellent website; from here tutorial and archive material may be readily accessed and there are also links to the *Länder*, where the reader can readily ascertain the political composition of each regional parliament (see the section on the internet at the end of this book). Materials on historical and political topics for educational use are available on request from the *Bundeszentrale für politische Bildung* (Berliner Freiheit 7, 53111 Bonn, *http://www.bpb.de*).

5

ECONOMIC STRUCTURES: FROM MODEL TO MODERNISATION

West Germany's rapid economic recovery from the effects of the Second World War is widely attributed to its adoption of a 'social market economy', the theoretical principles of which were developed in the 1930s by German academics in Freiburg. As director of the Economic Council of Bizonia (1948–49) and the FRG's first Economics Minister (1949–69), Ludwig Erhard was able to put these principles into practice. For Erhard the social market economy was not simply a means of restoring prosperity to a war-damaged nation. It also represented a departure from many of the values and structures that had become established within the German economic tradition. The following section will outline this tradition and discuss its relationship with the new policies that Erhard advocated.

Economic tradition

During the Middle Ages the cities and statelets of the highly fragmented German Empire established economies based on local crafts practised by well-educated and highly skilled artisans; these activities often enjoyed monopoly status as each state protected its domestic production of goods for trade and export. The tradition of independent small-scale enterprises was strongest in the south, which had fewer natural resources and where land inheritance, unlike in the north, was not subject to primogeniture. Prussia, by contrast, built up its economic power during the eighteenth and nineteenth centuries through direct government involvement: here the state financed, managed and subsidised numerous enterprises, especially in transport, coal and steel, protecting them from foreign competition. The banks played a key role in financing and managing large businesses and in promoting the cartels that emerged during the rapid industrialisation of the second Empire (1871–1918). However, a financial crash in 1873 and speculation against the *Reichsmark* linked to the war indemnity to France nurtured long-standing hostility towards capitalism. Primogeniture also helped establish the very large estates and concerns that predominated in northern Germany. As Germans migrated to the cities and other industrial centres, agriculture attracted large numbers of foreign workers, mainly Poles seeking seasonal work on the Prussian estates. Agriculture remained the single largest sector of employment, occupying over 43 per cent of the workforce in 1882, compared with 34 per cent in industry, although by 1925 the proportions were reversed (Statistisches Bundesamt 1997: 82–3). Despite periods of depression the Wilhelmine era was marked by economic expansion and growing prosperity. With industrialisation and social change also came the first state-sponsored welfare programmes.

After the First World War Germany entered a period of acute economic instability, with periodic financial crises and high interest rates. Disputes over reparations culminated in the hyperinflation of 1923, when the value of the *Reichsmark* sank to over 4 billion dollars, inflicting enormous damage on families and businesses. Although the economy recovered, the respite was brief: in 1929 the global economy collapsed, this time with far-reaching political consequences for Germany. Mass unemployment and loss of confidence in financial and economic institutions did much to radicalise German society and undermine support for the parliamentary system. Exploiting popular frustration over economic conditions and disillusionment with the moderate political parties, Adolf Hitler seized power in 1933. Between 1939 and 1945 the Nazis established a highly centralised economic system dedicated primarily to the war effort. They imposed strict price controls that concealed the large volumes of paper money and heavy borrowing required to finance military spending. As a result Germany after the war was left with a high national debt and a heavily debased currency.

The German economic tradition before 1945 had positive and negative aspects. On the one hand Germany had established itself as a leading trading and mercantile power with a broad industrial base of small to large-scale enterprises manned by a highly skilled and motivated workforce. On the other hand the direct involvement of banks and of the state in businesses had fostered protectionism and promoted the formation of industrial cartels that were politically tainted through their close association with conservative, militaristic interests during the two World Wars. German banks and international finance were, in the minds of many, also linked with exploitatively high interest rates. Bitter experiences of hyperinflation and periodic economic collapses prompted Germans to value stable prices, a sound currency, and steady, long-term growth.

Model of the social market economy

In adopting the social market model Ludwig Erhard wanted to establish an economic environment that would combine prosperity with entrepreneurial opportunity and which could not be exploited by centrist political forces. Such a system would underpin a free, democratic and peaceful society, avoiding the ruinous conflicts between left and right that had fatally undermined the Weimar state. Although not everyone shared Erhard's enthusiasm about the ability of the social market system to meet these goals, all agreed on the need to move away from the old economic structures and to achieve political and social peace through economic consensus.

The social market model allowed entrepreneurs maximum possible freedom of enterprise, with the state setting a broad regulatory framework and intervening only to ensure fair competition and to protect vulnerable members of society. After the currency reform in June 1948, which saw the new *Deutsche Mark* (DM) replace the inflated *Reichsmark*, and the formal foundation of the FRG in May 1949, Erhard implemented the model in various ways. To the dismay of the allies he removed the strict price controls and other economic restrictions which they had introduced during the occupation. He lowered taxation to encourage investment, stimulated competition by discouraging cartels and monopolistic practices, and worked to reduce international trade barriers. At the same time as providing more freedom for business activities, he extended welfare provision for the unemployed, the elderly, the disabled, veterans and other victims of the war, and introduced a national system of medical care based on private insurance. He also embarked on a rapid programme of reconstruction and social housing to replace properties destroyed during the war. In a measure which reflected the state's commitment to achieving a balanced society, undamaged properties were subject to a one-off tax used to compensate the homeless (*Lastenausgleichsgesetz* 1952). This measure did much to integrate the large numbers of eastern refugees and displaced persons into west German society.

Economic miracle

The social market economy was not an immediate success. At first unemployment remained high (reaching 2 million or 12 per cent in 1950) and poverty increased as goods became more expensive after the currency reform. The outbreak of the Korean War (1950–53) drove up the price of raw materials and widened the balance of payments deficit, making it harder for Germany to finance recovery from profits. But by 1951 the world was witnessing what came to be known as the German economic miracle (*Wirtschaftswunder*). Alongside Erhard's policies, several factors aided recovery: the American Marshall Aid programme, which injected investment capital into the economy; a plentiful labour supply in the form of refugees; and trade unions prepared to work alongside employers in order to develop a non-confrontational framework of industrial relations. At this stage the war damage actually assisted recovery by making it easier to replace outdated plant and machinery and rationalise production methods. Production increased by 25 per cent in 1950. By 1960 it had risen by two and a half times the level of 1950, while unemployment plummeted from 10.3 per cent to 1.2 per cent (Smyser 1993: 16).

With full employment at the end of the decade Germany began recruiting foreign 'guestworkers' to bridge its labour shortage. Its currency remained one of the strongest and most stable in Europe until well into the 1970s. Growth was largely export-led, so that by 1960 Germany was the second largest trading nation after the United States. Cities and transport systems were rebuilt, the standard of living rose sharply and the government had sufficient revenue to expand its social welfare programme. In 1957 the German Federal Bank (*Deutsche Bundesbank*) was established with extensive powers over monetary policy. In the same year the Federal Cartel Office (*Bundeskartellamt*) was set up to prevent the re-emergence of the pre-war industrial monopolies. In 1964 the five-member Council of Experts (*Sachverständigenrat*) met for the first time to provide objective, annual assessments of the state of the economy. In line with Erhard's concept of a free economy functioning with minimal state interference, both the Federal Bank and the Council of Experts were independent of government.

Although Erhard succeeded in establishing a dynamic and balanced economy in which employers, workers and trade unions operated for the most part in a spirit of consensus, he failed to break up large monopolies or to change the fundamental structures of German industry. This and the climate of prosperity encouraged trade unions to focus on achieving a fairer distribution of wealth and in allowing workers a voice in decision-making at management level – so-called co-determination. By threatening a national strike, a well-organised and coherent trade union movement (a single union represented 16 trades) forced a reluctant government in 1951 to concede co-determination in the large coal, iron and steel industries. A weaker form of co-determination followed for smaller companies a year later. The Weimar system of tariff autonomy (*Tarifautonomie*), which empowered unions and employers to conclude legally binding wage agreements, was reinstated and extended in 1957. In the same year the government index-linked pensions to economic growth and wage levels. Such measures contributed to the harmonious industrial relations which characterised Germany during its economic miracle. They were an important element in what many later came to regard as the 'German model' (*Modell Deutschland*).

MAIN PERIODS OF ECONOMIC DEVELOPMENT IN THE FRG

The era of post-war reconstruction and dramatic growth known as the economic miracle lasted from 1950 until 1960. Thereafter growth in the Federal

Republic continued, with some exceptions and at a declining rate, until unification in 1990. We can distinguish various phases during this period.

1960–1973: consolidation and full employment

Between 1960 and 1973 the FRG consolidated its economy and enjoyed a long period of full employment. A minor recession in 1966, however, when growth fell to 2 per cent, prompted the government to modify Erhard's original concept of the social market model by introducing elements of government intervention – called 'medium-term financial planning' – to help it cope more effectively with fluctuations in the economic cycle. The instrument of intervention was the Stability and Growth Act (1967) which gave the government greater powers in the areas of economic and fiscal planning (so-called 'global control' or *Globalsteuerung*) while retaining the principles of the free market economy.

The government used the Stability and Growth Act to lower taxes, increase investment and to finance local and regional projects. It also established a programme of 'concerted action', bringing together leaders of industry, labour and finance to agree and recommend guidelines for national economic policy. Finally the government undertook to deliver annual statements on the state of the economy using 'orientation data' to underpin its rational approach. The object of medium-term planning was to achieve the 'magic rectangle' of a stable currency, economic growth, high employment and a healthy trade balance. The policy of 'global control' was successful: productivity rose again in 1968 and unemployment fell. The recovery reinforced Germany's reputation as a model economy in which private enterprise, the state and labour co-operated to maintain prosperity and social balance. The term 'corporatism' is often used to describe this partnership of economic forces.

1973–1982: emergence of structural problems

Although the strategy of 'global control' was effective in overcoming Germany's first recession, its limitations soon emerged. Spending by governments and regions, largely on social welfare, could not be easily co-ordinated: deficits mounted and budgets ran out of control. The 'concerted action' formally broke down in 1977 when labour leaders abandoned the forum. It also became clear that domestic policy could not insulate Germany from international economic turbulence. In 1973 a global downturn triggered by steep rises in oil prices began to reveal structural problems in the economy which continued into the 1980s.

Although the oil crisis of 1973 was gradually overcome through energy-saving measures, industrial growth slowed, with unemployment exceeding 0.5 million in 1974 and hovering around 1 million in subsequent years. The underlying problem, which Germany shared with other western countries, was how to cope with structural weaknesses that were more clearly emerging after the post-war boom. The traditional coal and steel industries were in decline, while others, such as optics, electronics and textiles, faced fierce competition from the Far East. The service sector was unable to compensate for the downturn, despite the creation of a million public service jobs during the 1970s. The social–liberal coalition under Helmut Schmidt continued to develop the country's infrastructure and introduced measures to create jobs and stimulate industrial investment, but success was limited. Both the national deficit and unemployment remained stubbornly high. A revolution in Iran in 1979 generated a second sudden rise in oil prices, which drove up unemployment even further and fuelled inflation. In 1982 the jobless total reached 1.8 million, placing additional strains on the welfare budget. In the same year productivity fell (by 1 per cent) and inflation reached a relatively high 4.4 per cent (Smyser 1993: 27).

Although the German economy fared better than its European competitors at the beginning of the 1980s, internal criticism focused on unmanageable budget deficits, welfare spending, excessive labour costs and high taxes. In 1982 the Economics Minister, Otto Lambsdorff, who was also leader of the government's partner coalition party, argued openly that the government had actually damaged the economy by abandoning the principles of the social market economy (Lehmann 1996: 227).

1982–1990: conservative *Wende*

From 1982 the conservative–liberal coalition under Helmut Kohl curtailed the role of the state in the economy, although it shied away from the radical and socially disruptive free market policies of Margaret Thatcher in the UK (for an assessment of the government's economic reforms before unification see Zohlnhöfer 1999). Welfare suffered moderate cuts, although some benefits were restored after 1984 once the budget was felt to be under control. To regenerate the economy the government abandoned the previous policy of increasing public spending in order to cushion the social effects of recession. Instead it reduced taxes (in three stages, in 1986, 1988 and 1990), facilitated industrial investment and reduced state intervention – a so-called 'supply-oriented' policy. The privatisation programme was implemented gradually in order to avoid sudden and severe shocks to the economy. It began with the government shedding its shareholdings in the VEBA energy concern between 1984 and 1987, and continued with Volkswagen (1988), Lufthansa (1987–89) and the railways (1991). In 1990 the Post Office and telecommunications utility was split into three enterprises, although Deutsche Telekom continued to enjoy a monopoly on its telephone service until it was fully privatised after unification, while Deutsche Post was not scheduled to lose its letter monopoly until the end of 2002 (for a review of privatisation see Sturm 1997a: 626–9). The volume of regulations on businesses, widely perceived as an obstacle to introducing more flexible working practices, was also reduced. Although a new employment act of 1985 did not make it easier for employers to dismiss workers, limited steps were taken to make the labour market more flexible: these included provision for part-time contracts and the lifting of restrictions on shopping hours.

Luckily, a fall in the value of the dollar and a collapse in oil prices stimulated an export-led boom which lasted well into the 1990s (exports fell only in 1993), generating record balance of payments surpluses. Growth rose slowly but steadily (by 1 per cent between 1980 and 1984 and by 2.8 per cent between 1985 and 1989) and inflation eased (averaging 1 per cent between 1985 and 1989; see Smyser 1993: 27). Unemployment, however, remained intractable: despite 1.75 million extra jobs created between 1982 and 1990, the jobless total remained high, passing the 2 million barrier in 1983, reaching 2.2 million in 1988 and falling only to 1.75 million in 1990 (Pötzsch 1998). Employers complained about state regulations preventing them from shedding labour and were reluctant to employ new staff in an uncertain global market. Nevertheless the German economy was seen to be in good overall shape on unification and well able to absorb the former GDR.

PROBLEMS OF UNIFICATION

The FRG's strategy to incorporate the former GDR envisaged a short, sharp transition period in which private enterprise and investment would regenerate the eastern states; there would be no long-term subsidies for inefficient enterprises in order to preserve jobs. At the same time the generous West German social welfare system would act as a safety net for the vulnerable. For political and social reasons currency union took place on terms that overvalued the much weaker East German mark (*Ostmark*). The approach was wholly in keeping with the confidence that Germany felt in its free market economy to revitalise the east while also meeting social concerns – a second 'economic miracle' in fact. Rashly, as it turned out, Chancellor Kohl promised 'flourishing landscapes' of prosperity. A Trust Agency (*Treuhand*) was set up to manage and privatise the state-run enterprises of the old GDR and the government established a national Unity Fund in order to subsidise public spending in the eastern states until these were able to join the equalisation process by which resources were transferred from the richer to the poorer states (see Chapter 4). The European Union also provided assistance (Smyser 1993: 156).

On unification many small firms, several large concerns (e.g. Volkswagen, Daimler-Benz, BASF, Siemens and Opel) and the West German banks established themselves in the east. In less than a year, however, the east German economy had slid into crisis: production fell by over 50 per cent; unemployment reached almost 1 million; and housing, health and food costs rose sharply. At the beginning of 1991 over 10 000 east German workers were moving to the west every month. Unemployment rose steadily every year, reaching 1.35 million (17.4 per cent) by 1997 or even 2.28 million (27 per cent) including the early retired and those on work creation and training schemes (Pötzsch 1998: 269).

There were several reasons for the slump in the east, none of which was anticipated during the euphoria of unification. Apart from the collapse of the GDR's traditional export markets in eastern Europe, many western companies regarded east Germany as a consumer, not an investment market, and preferred to sell to the east rather than produce there. As for the indigenous industries of the former GDR, many, such as steel and shipbuilding and the seawater port of Rostock, could not be economically justified; others were ill-equipped to survive in a western market and failed to produce quality goods at competitive prices. In addition, claims for restitution of private property that had been confiscated by the GDR authorities after 1949 deterred potential investors from buying up land and plant. A further obstacle was the cost of cleaning up an environment that had been dangerously polluted by industrial practices in the GDR (the communist regime kept environmental data a state secret). The immediate upshot of unification was two widely divergent economies: one in the west which experienced a boom and another in the east which threatened to collapse altogether.

To avoid wholesale economic and social breakdown in the east the government transferred large sums to the new *Länder*, despite concerns that this was merely adding to the volume of money rather than generating investment. To the 115 billion DM Unity Fund were added annual transfers of 84 billion DM or more from 1996 and projected to continue until 2004. The government and other interest groups also undertook a series of initiatives to create jobs and promote investment. These included the Solidarity Pact (1993), in which banks and employers promised investment and trade unions restraint on wage demands, the Alliance for Jobs (1995), the Common Initiative for More Employment in the East (1997), the Stimulus for More Jobs (1998) and the Work Promotion Law (1991 and 1997) (for details see Flockton 1998: 41–4).

Between 1990 and 1994 the *Treuhand*, as the *de facto* owner of all state-run businesses in the former GDR, sold, modernised or liquidated over 15 000 concerns and properties, including 8000 very large enterprises (Hettlage 1995: 268). Shortly after unification, however, the Agency's holdings were soon found to be grossly overvalued, forcing it to draw on large government subsidies in order to settle inherited debts and meet the costs of cleaning up industrial pollution. As a result many concerns were sold at a loss and the Agency was wound up with a sizeable deficit. Although it gave priority to buyers who guaranteed investment and employment, the Agency was heavily criticised for its centralist (i.e. anti-free market) role, for favouring German over foreign investors and for breaking up enterprises and shedding labour. After the intensive privatisation phase, the east German economy was characterised by a preponderance of small firms owned by outsiders, mainly west Germans (Carlin 1998). In 1999 the 100 largest companies in eastern Germany were all western-owned.

Despite continuing high unemployment, the east German economy started to recover in 1993. In particular it benefited from a construction boom between 1993 and 1996 (when tax reliefs for building investment ended). Productivity, although below west German levels, also began to rise.

Persisting problems centre on a relatively small manufacturing sector and low productivity in relation to high labour costs ensuing from the policy of matching wages with western levels. Concern is also expressed at the continuing reliance on western transfers, while some regard the excessive subsidisation and government intervention as contravening the spirit of the free market (Flockton and Kolinsky 1998: 7–9). At the same time some large companies, such as the Opel car plant in Eisenach, are among the most efficient in Europe, and industrial centres are emerging in Sachsen (around Dresden and Leipzig) and Thüringen (Erfurt, Gera and Jena). Regeneration has not taken place across the board, with investment favouring low-labour, technology-based industries. As a result islands of prosperity have emerged, such as the German equivalent of Silicon Valley around Dresden, where microchip production has attracted a number of computer and software companies. Small pockets of economic wealth contrast sharply with large areas of high unemployment, notably in Mecklenburg-Vorpommern and Sachsen-Anhalt. Personal affluence is also highly concentrated: only 260 east Germans earn over a million DM a year compared with 25 000 in the west. One bright spot has been the resurgence of agriculture: a number of collective farms of the communist era became highly efficient and profitable concerns, although many farmworkers lost their jobs in the process. Overall, in the decade after unification, the 'sharp shock' of sudden incorporation into the Federal Republic's economic system actually worsened east Germany's economic position compared to other, relatively prosperous states of central Europe (Wiesenthal 1998). As long as the well-subsidised branches of large western firms remain prominent as 'cathedrals of the desert' (Koch 1998: 59), the eastern economy is likely to remain unbalanced well into the twenty-first century.

STRUCTURE OF THE ECONOMY

A review of West Germany's economy just before unification shows that its main sector, measured by the proportion of the workforce employed, was manufacturing (39 per cent). This encompassed engineering (mechanical, electrical and optical), motor vehicles, chemicals, refining, forestry, paper, printing, and iron and steel. Other sectors included trade and commerce (14 per cent), construction (6 per cent), transport and communications (5 per cent), financial services (4 per cent) and agriculture and fisheries (over 3 per cent); the state probably employed around 16 per cent of the workforce. Despite much lower productivity levels, the GDR, before its collapse, displayed a similar profile for manufacturing and construction, although it engaged over twice as many people as the FRG in agriculture and maintained a huge non-productive sector, including the state bureaucracy (over 21 per cent of the working population; for basic data see Smyser 1993: 2–3; Jones 1994: 97; Statistisches Bundesamt 1997: 82–3).

Changing patterns of employment

In terms of employment patterns (western) Germany has experienced two main phases of economic development. The first phase, the two decades between 1950 and 1970, saw a small but steady rise in employment in industry and manufacturing (from 45 per cent to 49 per cent), while numbers engaged in agriculture declined sharply (from 22 per cent to just over 9 per cent). During the second phase, which set in after 1970, the service sector expanded dramatically to account for 61 per cent of employees by 1995 (42 per cent in 1970). At the same time manufacturing dropped to just 36 per cent, a level hardly seen since before the First World War. There are clear indications, therefore, that Germany, especially since unification, is moving away from a manufacturing economy in the traditional sense (e.g. where large numbers of workers are employed in directly producing goods in factories) to one based increasingly on services. Such services are typically delivered from offices and involve activities such as training, commerce, repair work, management, research and security. Taking into account the precise nature of employment reveals that a little over 17 per cent of the working population are directly engaged in some sort of production activity (including cultivation, animal raising, building and installation); the rest provide services in a wide sense. The structural shift in employment patterns is partly due to technical innovation and the advent of new, less labour-intensive production processes; indeed many services actually support the modernised manufacturing sector. Over 50 per cent of employees in the enlarged service sector are now female (Statistisches Bundesamt 1997: 82–5).

Role of exports

Exports played a major role in the economies of both East and West Germany, but this was especially true for the FRG, which between 1980 and 1995 annually exported between 23 per cent and 29 per cent of its gross national product. The value of imports, such as oil and raw materials, over the period varied between 18 per cent and 23 per cent. Compared with the USA (10 per cent) or Japan (14 per cent) such export levels are very high and illustrate Germany's dependence on imported goods and materials for reprocessing and export. Indeed, after the USA, Germany is the world's largest exporter, with over half of its exports in the core industries of engineering machinery, transport equipment, metals and chemicals (Smyser 1993: 9; for a list of Germany's largest companies see Rohlfs and Schäfer 1997: 125–6; also Schäfers 1998: 68).

GERMAN ECONOMIC INSTITUTIONS

Germany's economic success is often explained by the interplay of its economic institutions and interest groups and, in particular, by how these work together to achieve consensus within a framework of market competition. The following section outlines the principal institutions of the German economy, in particular the government, the Federal Bank, the Cartel Office, banks and interest groups, such as employers' associations and trade unions.

Federal government

A key player in the economy is, of course, the federal government (*Bundesregierung*). Economic policy is generally subject to negotiation between coalition parties, although its general thrust is determined by the dominant partner. In accordance with their political orientation the first conservative administrations under Konrad Adenauer (1949–63) and Ludwig Erhard (1963–66) established the social market economy, while the SPD-led administrations of 1969–82 adopted a more interventionist approach and expanded social welfare programmes. From 1972 the SPD transferred power away from the Economics Ministry to the Finance Ministry, reflecting the importance of the national budget, spending programmes and the money supply; Chancellor Schmidt took a direct and technical interest in economic affairs. With the conservative *Wende* of 1982 came a return to less state involvement and a more business-friendly approach, although Chancellor Kohl avoided a clear political responsibility for economic policy. Despite such changes in direction and emphasis, there have been few radical government-led shifts away from an economic model that has served the country well since 1949.

Central government's role in fashioning economic policy is partly constrained by the federal system. The states not only enjoy a degree of financial independence through financial equalisation; they have also pursued policies of economic development that are appropriate for their region. Thus Bayern and Baden-Württemberg have led the way in encouraging new, technology-based industries, while Nordrhein-Westfalen has been concerned to protect its traditional interests in coal and steel.

German Federal Bank

The German Federal Bank (*Deutsche Bundesbank*) was established by law in 1957 primarily to protect the value of the currency and secondarily to support government economic policy. The government may not dictate to the bank or issue it with instructions. The Federal Bank maintains monetary stability by controlling the money supply and setting interest rates. If necessary it also buys and sells currency, bonds, and stocks and shares on the open market. By setting the so-called minimum reserve – the percentage of their liabilities that ordinary banks must deposit interest-free with the Federal Bank – it exerts a powerful lever over the overall level of credit that these banks can issue. The bank's Directorate (*Direktorium*) is nominated by the government and appointed by the Federal President. Based in Frankfurt its six members include a President and Vice-President. The Directorate and the presidents of the regional central banks (*Landeszentralbanken*), which the Federal Bank maintains in the federal states, constitute the Central Bank Council (*Zentralbankrat*). The central directorate is thus in a minority on the council; all members are independent of government and *Land*.

The bank's legendary independence is illustrated by periodic disagreements with both central government and international economic interests, although its wishes do not always prevail. Concerned to control inflation at home, the bank experienced conflict with the French and the Americans, for example, over its refusal to lower interest rates in the late 1980s. During the negotiations for unification its objections to the inflationary one-to-one exchange rate for the East German currency were overruled for political reasons, and after 1990 it openly criticised the government for delaying tax increases and spending cuts in order to control the costs of unification. At the same time the bank conducted a lengthy internal debate about whether each state should have its own separate central bank, with conservative members (generally the bank presidents of the western states) concerned that the new east German state banks might pursue policies of growth at the risk of inflation (Smyser 1993: 50–1).

The bank's role changed with the adoption of the euro from 1999, when the new European Central Bank (ECB) assumed responsibility for the unified European currency (euro). In many respects the ECB was modelled on the German Federal Bank – the political price for Germany's support for the institution: it too comprised a central (six-person) executive outnumbered by governors of the central banks of the 11 member states. As such the ECB was criticised for having an over-large decision-making body, a structural weakness which will become more pronounced as more countries join the EU. The ECB was also seen as needing more democracy and openness in the way it reaches its decisions (Brummer and Elliott 1999). Although the German Federal Bank is one voice among the other central bank governors, it is likely to continue its leadership role.

Federal Cartel Office

The Federal Cartel Office (*Bundeskartellamt*) was founded in 1958 to ensure competition and prevent the formation of monopolies and cartels, although important sectors, such as banks, insurance companies, energy companies and agricultural concerns, were excluded from its jurisdiction. Its powers remained limited, despite the merger law of 1973 (*Fusionsgesetz*) which allowed it to recommend the blocking of monopolies before and not after they were formed. Companies may appeal against a ruling by the Office through the courts or even the Economics Minister, who has not always backed the Cartel Office. The Office, whose 252 staff (in 1992) comprise mainly economists and lawyers, prefers to negotiate with prospective merger partners, avoiding confrontation and litigation. Its restrained approach has attracted criticism and has certainly not halted the trend of German industry towards concentration. Between 1973 and 1992 the Office prevented 224 (1.4 per cent) out of 16 146 proposed mergers through informal consultation and vetoed 101

(0.6 per cent); of 15 appeals to the Economics Minister, 6 were successful. On the other hand it faces considerable problems in assessing the size of a concern and its potential threat to market competition. In particular the Office must decide whether the market is a regional, national, European or even global one. It must also take employment into account and has in practice favoured mergers which aim to preserve jobs.

After unification the Office, which investigated 600 proposed mergers in 1990, was concerned primarily to prevent former GDR concerns from maintaining the sector monopolies left over from the state-run economy. It criticised the Trust Agency (*Treuhand*, see above) for excluding foreign investors, favouring large investors over small and medium-sized enterprises and for allowing concerns to dump goods on the market in order to remain competitive. More recently it has seen its powers curtailed by the transfer of anti-trust legislation to the European Union and is concerned at the lack of neutrality in reaching decisions on mergers (Sturm 1997a: 662–7).

Banks

Partly because of Germans' propensity to save (in which they are encouraged by government), banks (of which there are over 4000 in Germany) have large capital holdings and exert considerable influence as corporate financiers. Measured in terms of volume of business, 25 per cent of German banks are commercial and investment banks (*Kreditbanken*); these are joint stock companies (*Aktiengesellschaften*) in which management and ownership are separate. Best known are the three large national universal banks with branches throughout Germany: the Deutsche Bank, Dresdner Bank and Commerzbank. Alongside the national banks, a number of regional banks (*Landesbanken* or *Girozentralen*) also have very large holdings; part-owned by the federal state or *Land*, they are key players in financing industrial and commercial development within their region (for example, in Nordrhein-Westfalen and Bayern). Over 71 per cent of business by volume is handled by regional or trades-based co-operative banks (*Genossenschaften*), while municipalities (*Gemeinden*) operate local savings banks (*Sparkassen*).

From the industrial revolution onwards German banks have traditionally invested capital in domestic industry, although they tended to prefer large firms to small ones, favouring coal, steel, heavy industry and electrical engineering over textiles, machine tools or chemicals (Lütz 2000: 153). As a result many firms are owned by banks or have bank directors on their executive boards. The advantages of the banks' involvement with German industry are held to be that it enables them to develop close links with individual firms (including sub-contractors, suppliers, clients and employees) and to plan long-term investments in their activities. The 'house-bank' (*Hausbank*) relationship has been described as 'compassionate corporate lending' and been seen as a key feature of the social market model (Story 1996: 392). Others have argued that it gives banks undue influence over a company's affairs, amounts to a monopoly and stifles innovation, especially if a bank is reluctant to finance a company's competitors. The widespread practice of proxy voting, whereby shareholders authorise banks to vote for them at AGMs, enhances even further the banks' influence on decision-making.

Banks, insurance companies and corporations make up a powerful network of cross-directorships and mutual ownership of shares. Shareholders in Germany also tend to retain their holdings over long periods, discouraging company take-overs in the Anglo-Saxon style. Indeed, for reasons of national pride and out of a concern to protect manufacturing strength, German companies and governments have historically resisted foreign take-overs, with their implicit threat of sell-off and asset stripping (Story 1996: 377). After 1994 political moves were made to review bank participation in industry and recent data suggest that, for various reasons, banks have already reduced their holdings in German corporations, preferring to diversify their capital across more sectors and even outside Germany: whereas many holdings exceeded 25 per cent of a company in 1977, most were limited to 10 per cent by the mid-1990s. Large companies also appear to be more prepared to seek finance beyond the home banking sector. At the same time German banks currently face a number of challenges. These include pressure from the European Union to protect investors by making capital market transactions more transparent, moves to replace the traditional informal system of self-regulation by external government authority and objections to the legality of the regional state governments providing subsidies to their own *Landesbanken* (for reviews of the issues see Paterson and Southern 1991: 246–50; Smyser 1993: 83–90; Schröder 1996; Lütz 2000).

INTEREST GROUPS

Interest groups (*Verbände*), in particular employers' associations and trade unions are well established in German economic and business life. They are constitutionally empowered to regulate conditions (including training and wage levels) for whole sectors of the economy, not just their own members. Moreover, they have the right to lobby parliament (usually parties rather than individual *Bundestag* members), which maintains an official list of such organisations and actively seeks their views. This system of formal consultation underpins the consensual German approach to industrial relations and also plays a part in the process by which national economic policy is formulated (Busch *et al.* 1990: 108–10).

Employers' associations

The main employers' organisations are: the BDI (*Bundesverband der Deutschen Industrie* or Federation of German Industry), representing about 80 000 concerns; the DIHT (*Deutscher Industrie- und Handelstag* or German Industry and Trade Association), which organises the chambers of commerce and represents small businesses in particular; and the BDA (*Bundesvereinigung der Deutschen Arbeitgeberverbände* or Federation of German Employers' Associations), which represents 80 per cent of employers. The DBV (*Deutscher Bauernverband* or German Farmers' Association) embraces 90 per cent of concerns in farming, forestry and related activities. On unification the employers' organisations resisted attempts to set up independent east German associations and, through partnerships, simply extended the existing and well-resourced western network eastwards (Koch 1998: 59–60).

Trade unions

In contrast to the divided and fragmented trade unions of the Weimar period, the main umbrella organisation for trade unions, the DGB (*Deutscher Gewerkschaftsbund*), comprised 16 individual unions (in 1995, but see below) with a total of 9.4 million members. DGB members include the metal workers' union, IG Metall, which is the biggest trade union in the world with 2.9 million members (1995) and the public transport workers' union, ÖTV (1.8 million members). Alongside the DGB are the civil servants' union (*Deutscher Beamtenbund*: over 1 million members), the union for salaried employees (*Deutsche Angestelltengewerkschaft*: over 500 000 members) and the Christian Trade Union Federation (*Christlicher Gewerkschaftsbund*: over 300 000 members). German trade unions do not just negotiate pay and working conditions: working closely with businesses and chambers of commerce to organise training programmes, they consult with employers at state and regional level and have actively integrated their members in the social market economy. For most of the history of the Federal Republic German trade unions have pursued the twin goals of co-determination (*Mitbestimmung*) and improved working conditions, in particular a shorter working week, greater holiday entitlement and equal pay for men and women.

Industrial relations

Although a relatively low proportion of the German workforce is unionised (the figure actually declined from 35 per cent in 1995 to 29 per cent in 1998), the high concentration of German employers' organisations alongside a unitary trade union structure has produced stable industrial relations over a very long period. Without state involvement employers and generally non-militant unions have been able to hammer out collective agreements that are sector-wide and legally binding.

Industrial relations in Germany operate as a 'dual' system: at the level of the plant or factory (*Betrieb*) and of the company or enterprise (*Unternehmen*, which may comprise several plants). The co-determination system is governed by the Works Constitution Law (*Betriebsverfassungsgesetz*) of 1972. In contrast to its predecessor of 1952, which was severely limited in provision, this law gave the unions the right to represent workers collectively and extended the functions of works councillors to include participation in appointing and dismissing staff and in vocational training. Every company with five or more employees must elect a Works Council (*Betriebsrat*). The councils mediate with the management of an individual plant or factory while unions and employers' associations agree wages and conditions at industry and sector level; although the councils are formally independent of the unions, there is close linkage between the two.

At company level co-determination is regulated by laws passed in 1951 and 1976 (the so-called *Mitbestimmungsgesetze*). The first introduced co-determination to the iron and steel-producing industries employing over 1000; the second law extended it to all other companies with over 2000 staff. Employees have minority representation (5 of the 11 seats) on the powerful supervisory board (*Aufsichtsrat*) of a company, which appoints (and can dismiss) the management or executive board (*Vorstand*) and has an input into the firm's strategic policy. The executive board must include a personnel director who is responsible for staff issues and working conditions. The dual system guarantees employee representation, clearly defines agencies and responsibilities, promotes consultation over conflict, and is supported by a legal framework.

On unification the west German framework of interest groups and industrial relations was rapidly extended to the east, leaving little opportunity for alternative structures to evolve (for accounts see Koch 1995, 1998). The rapid and unexpected economic downturn, however, produced problems for employers and unions alike. Although DGB membership rose dramatically from 8 million in 1990 to 12 million in 1991 as the organisation acquired new members in the east, unemployment in both east and west led to an overall loss of 2.4 million members by 1996; easterners were especially disillusioned with the unions, although recruitment was also affected by an ageing population. During the late 1990s a number of unions merged, bringing the 16 members of the DGB down to 11 in 1997; further amalgamations in the pipeline were set to reduce numbers even further. Employers' associations also lost members as east German businesses demanded freedom to negotiate lower wages below the agreed level for their sector. The sector-wide collective bargaining system came under particular strain as employers in the east cancelled a 1991 agreement to raise wages incrementally to western levels by 1994 (the so-called *Stufentarifvertrag*).

By the end of the 1990s a more flexible structure of industrial relations was emerging in which variations of the broad, industry-based collective agreements were being negotiated at local and plant level, with smaller firms exempted from paying wages at the sector rate. As a result, works councils grew much more powerful as bargaining agents. At the same time, evidence from the textile and motor vehicle industries suggested that the councils remained willing to co-operate with management and to maintain the traditional consensus-based approach to industrial relations. Despite the undermining of centralised, sector-based agreements neither employers nor unions appeared to desire a fundamental shift towards local bargaining. The final outcome may be a 'collective agreement pyramid' with broad collective agreements between unions and industry at the apex and minimum but flexible conditions negotiated between works councils and individual firms at the base (Koch 1998: 64). Moreover, unification has not undermined the fundamentally unitary structure of the economic interest groups involved in setting wage levels and working conditions.

STANDORT DEUTSCHLAND

From the 1980s a critical debate began within Germany about the need for structural changes in the economy. Entitled *Standort Deutschland* (literally 'location Germany' but possibly better rendered as 'Germany as an economic hub'), the debate raised a number of issues about Germany's ability to retain its status as a leading industrial nation (Sturm 1997b: 677–80). Much of the concern focused on whether Germany remained an attractive prospect for investors. Since the 1970s the volume of German capital invested abroad (mainly in western Europe and the USA) has progressively exceeded incoming foreign investment: in 1996 the ratio was about five to one (Story 1996: 374; Schäfers 1998: 68). The *Standort* debate may be seen as part of a potentially far-reaching reassessment of Germany's position in the new global economy in which a number of issues are at stake.

The first issue concerns the quality and attitudes of German management. Traditionally German senior managers have a high level of technical expertise and, unlike the UK for instance, are not appointed primarily for their financial aptitude. However, some observers argue that German managers have become more concerned with maintaining personal status and security in their companies than taking risks by converting scientific inventions into market products. They maintain that old-fashioned, hierarchical management structures and authoritarian leadership styles promote indecisiveness and stifle innovation. Symptomatic of such failings is the proliferation of external management consultants and advisers. In organisations in which decision-making is strongly centralised and pyramid structures predominate, individual initiative is not encouraged and the task of middle management is to implement policy determined from above, not to question it or to initiate new approaches. On the other hand, this allows leaders of German companies to take breath-taking initiatives without consultation. An example of this was the announcement by the chairman of Volkswagen very soon after the Berlin Wall came down that his company would build cars in east Germany as part of a joint venture (Flamini 1997: 40).

Companies are also unhappy with the relatively high tax burden that they bear in comparison with international competitors. At 45 per cent of profits in 1997, taxes were higher than the USA (35 per cent) or France (33 per cent). German firms, that have long demanded an end to taxes that are unrelated to actual returns, are alone in paying both a wealth tax (*Vermögenssteuer*) and a business tax (*Gewerbesteuer*), although these were reduced after 1993 (for a review of tax policy see Sturm 1997a: 632–5). Businesses feel especially disadvantaged by high labour costs (among the highest in Europe and inflated by medical care contributions and generous paid leave), complex restrictions on shedding employees with permanent contracts and by a tradition of fixed, inflexible and increasingly shorter working times; in the early 1990s German employees worked markedly less than their international competitors. There is also concern about the ability of overcrowded universities and of an unresponsive vocational training system to provide a labour force that will meet the challenges of new industries in a period of deep structural change.

Although some companies are able to exploit ecological concerns to their economic advantage, many complain that the cost of accommodating the numerous regulations on the environment reduces their competitiveness. They also maintain that technological innovation is hampered by bureaucratic obstacles, over-regulation and the lack of venture capital. Continuing subsidies (by both central government and the regions, partly in the form of direct financial assistance and partly through tax concessions) attract criticism, although the picture is distorted by the need for medium-term transfers to the underdeveloped eastern states. Subsidised industries include coal, steel, shipbuilding, transport and agriculture, with some sectors becoming heavily dependent on state support (for a discussion of the issues see Smyser 1993: 113–17).

THE GERMAN ECONOMY AND THE EU

The following section considers Germany's role within the changing European economy. Two main aspects are discussed: the degree and nature of Germany's integration within the EU, and the function of the German currency in the move towards European Monetary Union (EMU).

Germany's linkage with the economy of western Europe, a result of successive chancellors' support for European political and economic integration, was established long before unification, when it actually helped allay international fears about the restoration of an enlarged Germany at the centre of Europe. Germany's principal trading partner is the European Union, in particular France: in 1996 the EU accounted for 57 per cent of exports, followed by the USA (7.7 per cent), Switzerland, Japan and the countries of eastern Europe. Indeed so closely enmeshed is the Federal Republic in the European and the wider global economy that one in four German jobs depends on international trade. At the same time, Germany is not so heavily reliant on the EU as other members: most other states, including the Benelux countries, Ireland, France, the Netherlands and Spain conduct larger proportions of their trade within the EU (Smyser 1993: 242), and it is likely that Germany's economic links with eastern Europe will increase as the latter's economies expand.

During the 1980s and 1990s Germany's commitment to global trade sat ill with trends within the EU towards greater protectionism and the creation of an economic 'fortress Europe'. Notably the EU and the USA were in dispute over high subsidies for European farmers and the exclusion of cheaper, imported produce. The issue dominated the series of negotiations (termed 'rounds') on reducing barriers to world trade conducted from the 1960s onwards through the forum of the General Agreement on Tariffs and Trade (GATT, renamed the World Trade Organisation in 1993). The instrument of the EU's subsidies was the Common Agricultural Policy (CAP). Agreed in 1967 and originally designed to protect Europe's many farmers and promote self-sufficiency in food production, CAP was consuming 70 per cent of the EU budget by the 1980s and generating huge surpluses of unwanted food. Germany supported CAP for external and internal political reasons: on the one hand it had traditionally backed France, whose farmers profited hugely from the policy, while on the other the conservative government was reluctant to alienate its constituency of small domestic farmers. Germany, by now contributing 25 per cent of the EU budget, upheld CAP until 1991, when it began reducing subventions for its agricultural sector (see Schäfers 1998: 70). Undoubtedly a factor in the shift in policy was Germany's recognition of the importance of its industrial and trading sector over agriculture: in 1996 trade and services contributed 65 per cent of GNP, manufacturing and processing 34 per cent and agriculture a mere 1 per cent (Schäfers 1998: 64).

Germany has promoted European economic (and political) integration at all stages. The process can be charted by various milestone treaties and agreements, most of which have resulted in a gradual convergence towards a common European currency. The Treaty on the European Economic Community (1957) affirmed the importance of co-ordinating currencies and exchange rates. The European Currency Agreement (1959) established a fund for countering short-term balance of payments problems between member states and set out the rules under which a central bank (the Bank for European Settlements, based in Basel) would co-ordinate and settle currency transfers. The 'snake' (1972) set broad limits for exchange rate variations. The European Currency Unit (ECU), comprising a 'basket' of currencies of the European states, was agreed in 1975 and was soon widely used for international loans and payments. Through the mechanism of the European Exchange Rate Mechanism (ERM), the European Monetary System (EMS) set narrow exchange rate limits for national currencies based on the ECU from 1979. The Single European Act (1986) formally recognised political union as an explicit aim of the community and set out rules for introducing a full currency union. Following a report by President of the European Commission, Jacques Delors (1989), European leaders, in the Treaty of Maastricht (1991), agreed the details and timetable for full economic integration, including a single currency (European Monetary Union or EMU) managed by an independent European Central Bank (ECB). The following decade was taken up with the implementation of Maastricht. The completed internal European market, with border-free movement of persons, goods and capital, came into force on 1 January 1993; in the same year the European Union, a term used after 1972 to denote the goal of advanced integration, was officially founded. The single European currency, the euro, was launched on 1 January 1999. From this moment 11 participating states, including France, Germany, Italy and the Benelux countries, began using the euro for cashless transactions: rates of exchange were fixed irrevocably, with euro notes and coins progressively replacing national currencies during 2002. Germany also supported the creation of the European Economic Area (1993), which included the EU and other states in a politically and economically looser organisation.

While the European currencies were moving towards convergence the German Mark (DM) acted as an anchor currency for the snake and the EMS, so much so that these became known as a 'D-Mark zone' (for an account of these monetary systems see Smyser 1993: 264–70). The Mark's pre-eminence was due to the consistently strong performance of the German economy and accumulated trade surpluses; international confidence in the value of the DM was such that by the early 1990s it had become the second global reserve currency after the US dollar. Despite the strain that the EMS placed on their economies, many EU countries preferred to remain within the system in the interests of long-term stability of exchange rates, while the Federal Bank, by intervening on the open money markets, showed itself willing to protect the principle of linked European currencies. At the same time the bank maintained an almost doctrinaire monetary discipline in order to protect the Mark's stability, refusing in particular to counter downturns in growth with moves that might fuel domestic inflation.

After Maastricht the Federal Bank placed strict conditions on its support for EMU, insisting that the euro should be as stable and strong as the DM and managed by a politically independent and powerful central bank. Anxieties over the unexpectedly high cost of unification, growing domestic deficits, German contributions to the Gulf War and popular concerns about surrendering the strong Mark led the bank to stress these conditions with increased stridency. It took a particularly strong position on the need for EU states to converge economically as well as politically before merging their currencies (i.e. to achieve low inflation, similar interest rates, controlled budget deficits and national debts, and a stable currency within ERM exchange rate bands). Throughout the move to EMU the Federal Bank demonstrated its traditional commitment to monetary stability, regarding the future euro as an extension of the DM and, in many respects, domestic German monetary policy.

In conclusion, the creation of a common European currency and the emergence of a more open financial market are likely to reduce the traditional culture of bank–industrial cross-ownership in Germany and change the corporate climate significantly (Story 1996: 391–2). Some observers argue that the German system will meet the challenges of globalisation without abandoning its fundamental internal relationships and networks. They point, for instance, to the fact that German banks began moving significantly into international markets after 1990 while retaining their core domestic business. Companies also purchased or established strategic alliances with overseas concerns, while research foundations such as the Fraunhofer Institute began as early as the 1980s to set up technology transfer centres in the USA and offices in South America and China (Harding 1999: 82–3).

FURTHER READING

For accounts of the social market economy in West Germany see Peacock and Willgerodt (1989) and Giersch *et al.* (1992); Graf (1992) assesses the implications of globalisation for the German economy. Smyser (1993) reviews economic developments both before and after unification, while Smith (1994) contains a detailed and comprehensive overview of individual sectors. As well as describing institutions and mechanisms for controlling competition, Sturm (1997b) provides useful detail on the *Standort* debate. Koch (1995) reviews the post-unification economic situation, with an emphasis on industrial relations. Up-to-date studies of particular aspects of the German economy, including the impact of unification on the eastern *Länder*, may be found in the periodicals *German Politics* and *Politik und Zeitgeschichte*. The journals *Die Weltwirtschaft* and *Wirtschaftswoche* monitor national and international economic developments, while the German Federal Bank (*Deutsche Bundesbank*) produces monthly economic reports. For the economy of the GDR see Jones (1994) and Schroeder (1998); Hitchens *et al.* (1993) present an early study on productivity and the problems of transition in the east.

6

SOCIAL STRUCTURES: THE 'SOCIAL STATE' AND PATTERNS OF LIVING

A helpful starting-point for the current debate in Germany about the responsibilities of the welfare state is a historical overview of the relationship between social justice, equality of opportunity and the distribution of wealth. This chapter describes the problems facing Germany in meeting the increasing demands of its social welfare budget, before outlining the main elements of welfare provision (pensions, medical and health care, unemployment and other forms of assistance). The chapter concludes with a description of patterns of living from the point of view of how the relationship between work and leisure has evolved and how Germans now spend their free time.

THE CONCEPT OF THE 'SOCIAL STATE'

Although the personal obligation to exercise Christian charity to the poor had existed since the Middle Ages, it was the French Revolution that advocated a special role for the state in guaranteeing a system of social and material equality. For the revolutionaries the role was based on the premise that no-one should possess too much and no-one too little. After the French Revolution had degenerated into violent persecution and then into nationalist conquest under Napoleon, European thought came under the influence of English liberalism, a social philosophy that defended every citizen's right to gain material prosperity through personal effort but at the same time rejected the notion that it was the state's primary role to protect the needy. Such a view persisted long into the nineteenth century but proved unable to meet the social challenges of the industrial revolution. Towards the end of the century the mass poverty that accompanied industrialisation prompted the birth of the modern social welfare state. Germany's system of social security has its historical roots during this period, when Bismarck's pioneering legislation of 1883 onwards gave the country one of Europe's first comprehensive systems of state-sponsored welfare provision.

The first half of the twentieth century saw the systematic extension of state welfare provision, which by the prosperous 1950s and 1960s was securely incorporated in the electoral platforms of most western governments, especially that of West Germany. By this time the notion of welfare meant more than a safety net for the poor. It was widely acknowledged that the state also had a duty to ensure that its citizens possessed the material basis for enjoying genuine equality of opportunity and enhanced quality of life, for instance in the form of access to higher education.

In post-war West Germany social welfare had a constitutional basis: the Basic Law defined the country as a 'social federal state' (*sozialer Bundesstaat*; see articles 20 and 28) and itemised public welfare, welfare insurance and hospitals as areas in which the *Bund* had legislative responsibility (article 74). Despite their vagueness, the articles are now interpreted to mean that the state must provide the necessary material and social framework for an individual to enjoy basic freedoms (although this is not the same thing as giving a citizen the automatic legal entitlement to a particular type or level of benefit). The term 'social security' (*soziale Sicherheit*) became a legal concept in Germany with its adoption in the 'codex of social law' (*Sozialgesetzbuch*) of 1976, which lays down goals, standards and guidelines for social welfare. For Germans 'social security' means more than simply welfare benefit. It connects to a historical and constitutional tradition in which the state has a duty to ensure social peace and to avoid the emergence of socially divisive economic disparities. This tradition prevents Germany from adopting, for instance, an American model of minimal state intervention in welfare provision. Indeed, despite growing budgetary deficits, SPD governments during the 1970s and early 1980s in Germany remained firmly committed to the constitutional ideals of social justice through welfare. With the added burden of unification, however, it became clear that Germany would have to find a new way to finance its welfare provision. By the mid-1990s, an intensive debate was underway on how to undertake structural reforms in government spending and revenue gathering.

THE PROBLEM OF THE SOCIAL BUDGET

German governments had undertaken various measures since the 1980s (in health and pensions; see below) in order to control the welfare budget. Nevertheless, since 1900 government spending on social welfare had increased from 1 per cent of the gross national product to 35 per cent. By the end of the twentieth century, 35 per cent of employee's gross earnings were being deducted for welfare, rising to 60 per cent when taxes were included. For an income of 120 000 DM this meant 19 500 DM for a pension, 14 000 DM for health insurance and 8000 DM for insurance against unemployment and nursing care. In 1996 government expenditure on social welfare costs swallowed up over 50 per cent of a total budget of almost 2 billion DM. This compared with 10.6 per cent for education and research, 5.3 per cent for security and defence, 4.1 per cent for health and sport, 4 per cent for economic development, 3.2 per cent for housing and 2.5 per cent for transport and communications; some 19 per cent went on servicing government borrowing (*Der Spiegel* (37), 1999: 97). The sheer size of the welfare budget was only part of the picture. A complex tax system and a labyrinthine network of welfare regulations favoured the middle classes and numerous professional interest groups to the detriment of those in genuine need.

The red–green coalition under Chancellor Schröder assigned welfare and budgetary reform a high priority. Apart from simplifying the tax system, it planned to reduce national insurance contributions from the unemployed while lowering the level of unemployment and housing benefits and shifting more of the financial burden to the *Länder*; pay rises for civil servants would be cut and pensions no longer automatically linked to pay levels; levels of basic income tax would also fall. At the same time, in order to stimulate the economy, the coalition lowered national insurance contributions from businesses. In a complex debate, trade unions and opponents within the SPD argued strongly against welfare cuts and for a redistribution of wealth through increased taxation of the rich. The government's plans to implement a package of savings and reforms by 2000 were also hampered by the loss of its parliamentary majority in the *Bundesrat*. Nevertheless, politicians in all parties acknowledged that the state alone could not support current pension levels: sooner or later the state would have to abandon financing pensions entirely through taxing the current working population (the so-called *Umlageverfahren*) and, in common with other west European countries, introduce a compulsory element of private insurance, the *Zwangsrente* (*Der Spiegel* (41), 1999: 130–2). The main areas of welfare provision are outlined below.

Pensions

Since 1969 the social budget has been based on the principle that the current working population, who are mainly men but include increasing numbers of women (for figures see Schäfers 1998: 18), would generate the income required to finance the needs of the young and the pensions of the retired. The pension reform of 1957 (which introduced a 'social plan for Germany') had already increased pensions and established the 'equivalence principle' linking pension level and previous income. Contributions were calculated as a percentage of gross wages and the 'standard pension' was reckoned to provide, after a 40-year working life, about two-thirds of the national average net income. Since linking pensions to previous income still disadvantaged the poorly paid, a second pension reform of 1972 aimed to correct this by setting pensions from a minimum wage level. Restrictions on the age of retirement were also lifted: men could apply to retire at 63 (since 1957 women had been able to retire at 60), while both men and women could increase their pension by staying in work until 67 (Nissen 1997: 685–7).

The third pension reform of 1993 aimed to act as a brake on rising costs (at current levels contributions would have risen to 38 per cent of wages by 2030) and harmonise pensions in western and eastern Germany (at unification pensions in the eastern *Länder* were only 40 per cent of western levels; by 1996 they had reached 80 per cent, a dramatic increase in eastern terms). The reform linked automatic annual pension increases to net wage levels instead of gross income (although this was put aside in 1994 after a fall in real income levels). The standard retirement age was raised to 65, with early retirement possible alongside a reduced pension of between one- and two-thirds the maximum rate. Contribution-free periods (due to unemployment, illness or education) were reassessed and three years allocated for raising a child (Nissen 1997: 687).

Over 70 per cent of Germans are compulsorily insured for retirement pension and for continuation of income in the event of accident, invalidity or the loss of a wage-earning spouse. This system of national insurance, which is partly financed by contributions from income, is administered at *Land* level (for workers) and nationally for miners (by so-called *Knappschaften*) and salaried employees. Separate provision is made for civil servants (*Beamte*, a much wider category of employees than in the UK), the self-employed and for victims of the Second World War. The level of pension is determined by how long the wage-earner has contributed to the fund (contributions must have been made for at least five years), the wage level on retirement and national income levels (i.e. it is index-linked). Housewives have no separate national insurance.

Health

The Federal Ministry of Health (*Bundesministerium für Gesundheit*) sets the legal framework for health care but has little control over costs, which are met through a system of compulsory health insurance. By the end of the century the costs were unusually high, even by European standards. In 1998 around 90 per cent of Germans were members of health insurance companies (*Krankenkassen*). Statutory contributions to insurance companies were paid by 50.6 million employees and their employers; 7.2 billion Germans subscribed to private schemes. Insurance companies and tax revenues financed a large national network of pharmacies, 2000 clinics, 112 700 doctors, 51 988 dentists and other health workers, including dieticians, masseurs and professionals in over 80 recognised health disciplines. The health sector was one of the nation's largest employers, accounting for 4.2 million employees, or 12 per cent of the working population. The system also maintained a large and fragmented bureaucracy: the 582 companies providing statutory insurance employed over 145 000 administrative staff. In total, health care cost 550 billion DM, or 10.7 per cent of the gross national product. This was more than in other high spending countries, such as France or Sweden.

By the end of the twentieth century standards of treatment and health care in Germany were exemplary: the ratio of 66 hospital beds per 10 000 inhabitants was among the highest in the world and even country practices were equipped with the latest medical technology. Life expectancy had risen steadily since 1950, while the feared pre-war diseases of scarlet fever, diphtheria and tuberculosis became rarities. Polio and most sexually transmitted illnesses were also brought under control. Most deaths were now due to heart and circulatory diseases (around 50 per cent) and cancer (25 per cent). Doubts, however, arose over whether the system genuinely provided value for money, especially when doctors were effectively rewarded for carrying out often unnecessary diagnostic procedures and treatments. Although Germans were X-rayed on average twice as much as the Dutch, visited the doctor three times more frequently than the Swedish and purchased twice the volume of medicines as Norwegians, they were neither necessarily healthier nor did they live longer; they topped the league for workdays missed through illness and cancer sufferers did not enjoy a higher than average life expectancy after treatment.

The model for Germany's health care system originated in 1883, when Bismarck introduced basic health insurance for manual workers suffering serious illness: contributions were set at 3 per cent of gross wages, the employer meeting one-third of costs. The system was soon extended to cover other categories of employee and their families. In 1933 the health insurance companies (*Krankenkassen*) formed a powerful umbrella organisation. From 1955 doctors, who had created their own lobby group, were entitled to automatic reimbursement for each aspect of patient treatment (*Einzelleistungsvergütung*). The result was a six-fold increase in costs between 1960 and 1975, a three-fold increase between 1975 and 1992 and a dramatic rise in the numbers of medical students attracted to a highly lucrative profession: between 1970 and 1995 the number of doctors doubled, from 615 patients per doctor to under 300. Efforts by various governments since the mid-1970s to reduce costs through legislation on matters such as the level of prescriptions or the apparatus used by general practitioners (about 50 laws and over 7000 regulations were passed between 1975 and 2000) had limited success. Apart from structural defects in the health system itself, the situation was exacerbated by the challenges of an ageing population and the emergence of costly new medical techniques, such as organ transplants.

On the whole German doctors have proved reluctant to countenance what they see as dangerous moves towards an unfair, tiered system of medical care. Discussion on reform has centred on making the system more transparent and accountable and on exposing it to market forces. Ideas have included moving the cost burden away from statutory contributions and towards an element of voluntary contribution for enhanced benefits, introducing standard block fees for whole courses of treatment and encouraging insurance companies to conclude contracts with lists of approved doctors who would apply agreed standards of treatment and be open to audit.

Medical and nursing care

Around 90 per cent of Germans, including family dependants, are compulsorily insured for medical treatment and loss of income through illness (the total in 1996 was 72.1 million). As a rule employers are also obliged to continue paying wages during the first six months of illness (*Lohnfortzahlungspflicht*). Medical costs are met by health insurance companies (*Krankenkassen*) who recompense doctors, pharmacists and others according to nationally agreed tariffs for each medical service that is delivered (*Einzelleistungsvergütung*). The number of *Krankenkassen* providing statutory health insurance fell dramatically from 1207 in 1993 to just 482 in 1998. Health insurance is compulsory for all wage-earners, farmers, pensioners, students and the disabled, although the wealthy may be exempted. Wholly private health insurers cater primarily for the latter, for the self-employed and for those willing to pay for additional benefits; around 8 million people are in private health schemes. Special arrangements apply to civil servants (*Beamte*), who are insured partly through their employers (the state) and partly through private companies. Premiums depend on company and health risk, but varied from 8 per cent to 16.8 per cent of income at the beginning of the 1990s. Like accident insurance, services and provision are based on individual need, not on the level or length of contributions. From January 1995 separate insurance arrangements applied to home nursing care (*Pflegeversicherung*): wage-earners were obliged to contribute 1 per cent of monthly gross income for home care (this rose to 1.7 per cent the following year). A number of difficulties arose with the new system, which was likely to prove expensive: in particular a large number of individuals who had received no support for minor nursing care under their old health insurance scheme applied for benefits under the new system (Nissen 1997: 691).

There were several obstacles to the reform of the health system. Up until 1998 the junior coalition partner of the conservative–liberal government, the FDP, which represented the medical profession and pharmaceuticals industry, exerted a powerful veto against change. Second, the division between the *Länder* (responsible for health care and hospitals) and the government (controlling social security) produced complex bargaining positions which hindered reform. Finally, the fact that pricing was in the hands of a large network of insurance companies that negotiated agreements with similarly well-organised providers prevented the operation of a true market regulating supply and demand (Blanke and Perschke-Hartmann 1994). Doctors' organisations exerted their monopoly powers to ensure that *Krankenkassen* could not invoice individual doctors for services, only the organisation as a whole: *Krankenkassen* could not therefore monitor which doctors treated which patients and how successfully (Neubacher 2000).

Nevertheless governments tried repeatedly to control the spiralling costs of health provision. From 1983 'luxury medicine', such as rest cures, was no longer freely financed by the state and prescription charges rose. From 1989 patients were required to contribute to services, which were subject to auditing and greater financial transparency; fixed prices were introduced for approved drugs. In the most comprehensive health reform since 1945, the Health Act (*Gesundheitsstrukturgesetz*) of 1992 set charging limits for providers (i.e. doctors, dentists, pharmacists, hospitals), lowered medical fees for certain services, restricted the admission of new doctors in over-provided regions and raised contributions required from patients. Approved lists of drugs were introduced in 1996 and from 1997 citizens were free to choose their health insurance company. The act, which was widely opposed by medical practitioners, produced short-term savings (Lehmann 1996: 339, 342, 508; Nissen 1997: 688–90). Further changes were instituted by the red–green coalition elected in 1998. The so-called *Reform 2000* programme obliged patients after 2000 to visit their general practitioner before a special-ist, allowing the former to co-ordinate treatment and avoid duplication of medical examinations (hitherto the patient could go directly to a specialist); *Krankenkassen* were empowered to negotiate competitive contracts with net-works of GPs and specialists, leading to reductions in patients' contribu-tions; the length of rest cures now depended on the severity of the illness; and controlled annual rises in the contributions of private patients in their younger years would replace the sudden and steep increases that they had hitherto faced as they approached old age or, in the case of women, when they became pregnant (Kowalski *et al.* 2000).

Unemployment

Unemployment benefit is administered via the Federal Ministry of Labour (*Bundesanstalt für Arbeit*) and its national network of 11 regional employ-ment offices and 184 local offices (*Arbeitsämter*), which also assist in finding work. Unemployment benefit comes in two forms: earnings-related benefit (*Arbeitslosengeld*) and unemployment assistance (*Arbeitslosenhilfe*). The former is calculated, for an adult with a dependent child, at 67 per cent of the level of wage during the last six months before unemployment and at 60 per cent if there is no child; how long the benefit is paid depends on previous contributions. Unemployment assistance, which is additional, is paid on the basis of need (*Bedürftigkeit*) and varies between 53 per cent and 57 per cent of previous net income. Only those who have worked and contributed (through compulsory insurance contributions) and are registered with the employment office for work are entitled to unemployment benefit. Employers also contribute to benefit, a measure designed to encourage them to pursue policies of full employment. The employer deducts insurance contributions directly from wages; the deduction is a percentage of the overall wage (6.5 per cent in 1994), up to a national maximum level (the *Beitragsbemessungsgrenze*), and includes pension, health and unemployment insurance (Nissen 1997: 688). Employer and employee contribute equally to national insurance (in 1988 the proportions were 9.35 per cent for pensions, 2.15 per cent for unemployment and between 5 per cent and 7 per cent for health). The state also finances benefits through taxation. Steadily increasing rates of unemployment (e.g. from 6.3 per cent in western Germany in 1991 (10 per cent in the east) to 11 per cent (20 per cent) in 1997) have placed a severe strain on the social budget.

Social welfare benefit

In its narrowest sense social welfare benefit (*Sozialhilfe*) is the 'net beneath all other nets', in other words, the benefit of last resort which is available to anyone resident in Germany who lacks recourse to other forms of assistance. There are two main categories of *Sozialhilfe*. Maintenance (*Hilfe zum Lebensunterhalt*) is means-tested and designed to meet basic needs of clothing, food, accommodation and other essentials. Assistance is also available for one-off emergencies (*Hilfe in besonderen Lebenslagen*); in practice this is mainly used to provide nursing or disability care. In 1994 over 1 million households received basic maintenance: almost half the recipients were single persons; most were women (57 per cent), with a high proportion (24 per cent) of single mothers (Statistisches Bundesamt 1997: 220). From November 1993 asylum-seekers were taken out of the general benefits system. Instead of *Sozialhilfe* they received vouchers for food and other necessities and a small 'pocket-money' cash allowance; they continued to be entitled to medical care (Lehmann 1996: 449). At the end of 1994, 447 000 asylum-seekers were registered for benefit, with an average age of 23 (Statistisches Bundesamt 1997: 221).

Characteristic of the German system of welfare is a highly fragmented network of private, semi-private and state insurers and providers, many of which cater for particular trades and professions; the type and level of benefit vary accordingly. Compulsory accident insurance, for instance, is in the hands of over 77 trades and local organisations, while 19 co-operatives specialise in insuring farmers and agricultural workers for pensions, accident and illness (for an overview see Weidenfeld and Zimmermann 1989: 314).

After the steep decline in the German birth-rate from 1975, it became clear that the number of people in work and contributing to the social welfare budget would decline while the demands on the budget would rise. These demands were exacerbated by a lengthening of the period which children and young people spent in full-time education, rises in pension levels, an increase in the number of retired people and, of course, growing unemployment after 1980. These developments threatened the ability of the traditional *Umlageverfahren* to continue to provide welfare at levels to which Germans had become accustomed. Solutions to the problem can be divided into at least three categories. Arguing from a free-market economic standpoint, some proposed stimulating the economy and restoring full employment by reducing the proportion of wages (and employers' contributions) currently devoted to the social budget. Others criticised the linkage of benefits and pensions with wage levels, which was a traditional aim of trade unions but which pushed up costs without necessarily helping the most needy. There were few signs that governments were prepared to take on vested interest groups by radically restructuring the present network of providers and suppliers. This left the third option of retaining the current, fragmented system while attempting to fine-tune its mechanisms, and it is the strategy which governments have pursued from the 1980s onwards.

LEISURE

The division between working and leisure time as we understand it today is a product of industrialisation, urbanisation and social progress. A major goal of workers' movements and trade unions from the mid-nineteenth century was a reduction of working hours and an increase in the time available for leisure. The eight-hour working day (over a six-day week) was introduced in Germany after the First World War and a 50-hour working week, including Saturdays, remained the norm until 1955. Trade union demands for a 40-hour week were not realised for 90 per cent of the workforce until 1974 (Müller-Schneider 1998: 224). Between 1960 and 1994 the average number of hours worked fell by 27 per cent, and by 1995 amounted to 38 hours a week. From 1963 employees in Germany were by law entitled to 18 working days' (three weeks') paid annual holiday, although agreements concluded between unions and employers in the early 1980s ensured that almost 80 per cent of employees received at least twice this. In the former GDR workers were entitled to between 18 and 24 days' basic holiday, with certain groups receiving an extra 10 days; just before unification the average holiday was 21 working days compared with 29 in the west. In the decade after unification the tradition of working more hours and having shorter holidays persisted in the east, although the gap has steadily narrowed (Statistisches Bundesamt 1997: 147–8).

Although the number of hours spent in employed work is a major factor governing the quality and nature of leisure time (*Freizeit*), it is not the only one. Until well into the 1960s leisure time was equated with simple physical and mental relaxation as people recovered from the twin demands of work and domestic chores: in predominantly multi-person households without modern labour-saving devices, doing the laundry alone was a full day's activity. Since most income went towards meeting basic needs (food, clothing and accommodation), leisure pursuits were simple; foreign travel, for instance, remained beyond the budget of many citizens until the early 1970s. Increasing material prosperity during the 1960s and the gradual extension of the five-day working week, however, spawned what is now commonly known as the 'leisure industry'. Leisure activities became more varied and differentiated, and also more commercialised as providers exploited the new and lucrative 'leisure market' (*Freizeitmarkt*) which capitalised on the rapid increase in the proportion of both time and personal income that became available for activities such as motoring, sport, television, hobbies and, above all, travel and tourism. A good example of how a leisure activity developed is television. German television began in 1955 as a single channel service broadcasting a limited number of programmes in black and white for only a few hours a day. By 1999 it had evolved into a complex mix of public and private (including pay-as-you-view) national and regional providers catering round the clock for a variety of audiences and interest groups.

Leisure activities during the post-war years in Germany were circumscribed on the one hand by the physical need to rest from work and on the other by social conventions demanding conformity in family life, sexual behaviour and fashion. By the end of the 1960s growing economic prosperity, a shift away from social conformity and a relaxation of social taboos (expressed through fashion, sexuality and popular youth culture) had led many Germans to regard the pursuit of pleasure as a primary goal in life. Leisure was now expected to provide fulfilling personal experiences (*Erlebnisse*). Such experiences were often associated with the consumption of goods and services and could make their own demands in terms of time or stress. Researchers moved away from studying the relationship between leisure and work to identifying individual 'life-styles' based on how individuals spent their free time. Typical life-styles involved out-of-house activities (going to the cinema, pub or sports club), high-brow cultural interests (theatre, concerts, music) and trivial, usually home-based pursuits (such as watching television quiz shows). In many respects adoption of a life-style milieu began to convey more about contemporary social structure than traditional class membership. A similar change of attitude towards leisure time occurred among Germans in the GDR, although there existed fewer opportunities in the east to indulge consumerism; organised, collective leisure pursuits were officially promoted at the expense of those geared towards individuals (Müller-Schneider 1998: 226).

While west Germans devoted progressively more of their personal income on consumer goods between 1965 and 1995, spending on leisure activities increased at a markedly higher rate. Surveys indicate that single most expensive item for all social groups is the annual holiday (*Urlaub*, often associated with travel), followed by motoring, television, sport and camping. There are, however, differences according to income and type of household. Retired couples and those on social security spend slightly more on electronic goods (television and radio) than on motoring, while higher income brackets favour sporting activities and motoring over electrical items. In the east pensioners and welfare recipients devote a significantly greater proportion of their income to leisure activities, especially holidays; this group also spends more on gardening and pets than on sport and camping. Overall, easterners attach considerable importance to acquiring electrical goods, even some years after unification (Statistisches Bundesamt 1997: 149). Other significant leisure activities include spending time with the family, reading, eating, hobbies and DIY, and going for walks (see Müller-Schneider 1998: 227). Well subsidised by the state and region, German opera houses attracted almost 7 million visitors in 1993–94, followed by theatre (5.5 million). Cinema in west Germany was most popular between 1954 and 1958, when each person went on average 15 times a year; cinema was also popular in the GDR, although it declined steadily in both Germanies after 1960 as more people acquired their own television sets.

In many respects income is less indicative of how Germans spend their leisure time than education and age. Those with a higher level of education are more likely to attend concerts, the theatre and to read in their spare time rather than watch television or *Heimatfilme* (a genre of sentimental film, usually in an idealised, rural setting). Unsurprisingly, people under 25 rate out-of-house sporting activities very highly, although these are also becoming increasingly popular among the under-40s, especially those who are single, live alone and have no children. The arrival of children produces a radical shift towards family-based pursuits, although younger Germans tend to assign a higher priority to leisure interests than setting up a family. Following the division into life-style milieus proposed by the sociologist Gerhard Schulze, we can distinguish an 'entertainment milieu', a 'self-fulfilment milieu', a 'status milieu' and a 'harmony milieu' (see Müller-Schneider 1998: 228–9). The entertainment milieu attracts less well-educated young people looking for external stimulation through action-oriented pastimes (going to discos, playing fruit machines, watching action films, riding a car or motorbike). The self-fulfilment milieu on the other hand comprises better educated young Germans who engage in culturally more demanding activities, such as the theatre and concerts, and are more likely to be involved in further training and self-improvement; this group also displays a particularly strong preoccupation with sporting activities and personal physical health. Well- educated persons over 40, often in well-paid professional positions, predominate in the 'status milieu': more likely to be members of country clubs, own yachts and to take expensive holidays, they are also keen readers, listeners to classical music and theatre-goers. By contrast, the 'harmony milieu' is dominated by less well-educated older people in manual jobs who consciously reject what they perceive as high-brow culture and seek peace, comfort and relaxation in the home environment, often through undemanding television programmes.

Leisure in east and west Germany

A comparison of the how east and west Germans use and regard leisure time a decade after unification reveals more similarities than differences. Easterners, who reported serious conversation, a quiet cup of tea or coffee, or writing letters as their relaxation activities during the GDR years, rapidly adapted to the western model, where leisure time is equated with more hedonistic product consumption. The shift to 'enjoying life', 'doing something for personal enjoyment' was one of the most striking attitudinal changes to take place after the fall of the GDR and is in line with the general convergence of behaviour and social values that has been observed since unification (for a fuller discussion of this topic see Chapter 9).

Despite rapid westernisation, east Germans retained different perceptions of leisure for some years after unification. Because easterners worked longer hours and had lower wages than westerners, they had less time and income to spend on leisure. They also derived less personal satisfaction from their leisure time. This was due partly to the closure of the numerous state-sponsored and works-based leisure facilities, but also to attitudes and patterns of behaviour left over from the communist period. As a reaction to the organised activities that characterised the socialist system, easterners were reluctant to join the many groups and clubs (*Vereine*) that were founded along western lines. East Germans also tended to favour trivial leisure activities over culturally more demanding ones, probably as a relic of traditional, working-class life and as part of a need to catch up on pursuits that were not available in the former GDR (Müller-Schneider 1998: 229–30).

FURTHER READING

Detailed accounts of Germany's social welfare system can be found in Weidenfeld and Zimmermann (1989; see in particular the contribution by Kaufmann) and Nissen (1997). Various aspects of the social state are touched on in the several contributions in Schäfers and Zapf (1998). The August 2000 edition of *Aus Politik und Zeitgeschichte* (*Beilage zur Wochenzeitung Das Parlament* B35–36/2000) reviews the position that Germany has reached in attempting to reform its system of social welfare, with articles on demographic change, pension provision and health care.

7

STRUCTURES OF EDUCATION: SCHOOLS AND HIGHER EDUCATION

Mindful of how the National Socialists exploited a centralised education system to disseminate their ideology, the Basic Law of 1949 allocated responsibility for educational and cultural policy to the federal states. Education thus became a key element of so-called 'cultural sovereignty' (*Kulturhoheit*) through which the *Länder* were able to exercise their independence from the political centre. Despite the regional variations that such sovereignty inevitably produces, the individual *Länder* co-ordinate and plan policy through several joint bodies. The most important of these is the Standing Conference of State Ministers of Education, or *Kultusministerkonferenz* (KMK). Originally founded in 1948, the KMK has become in all but name Germany's ministry of education. Other bodies include the Conference of University Rectors (*Hochschulrektorenkonferenz*, HRK), comprising the rectors or presidents of the universities, and the Research Council (*Wissenschaftsrat*, WR), a joint *Bund–Länder* body founded in 1957 and made up of academics, leading figures from public life and representatives of local and national government in order to make policy recommendations for higher education and research.

Whilst Soviet-controlled East Germany initiated a radical reform of the education system, the newly founded FRG turned the clock back and restored the school system of the pre-war Weimar Republic. This system owed much to the nineteenth-century Prussian statesman and humanist philosopher Wilhelm von Humboldt, whose models of secondary and university education, established in the form of the *Gymnasium* (1808) and the Humboldt University of Berlin (1810), have profoundly influenced thinking on educational policy in Germany to the present day. The *Gymnasium* provided a general, theoretical education for the minority of academically able children and aimed to develop a fully rounded personality within the classical and humanistic tradition. By the end of the nineteenth century the *Gymnasium* had expanded its curriculum to include classical and modern languages, sciences, economics and performing arts. The majority of children, who would be engaged in vocational work, were educated in the *Volksschule* (called *Hauptschule* after 1964). A third school type, the middle school (*Mittelschule*, or *Realschule* after 1964), was founded later in the nineteenth century in order to educate the technical and managerial personnel needed for Germany's growing commerce and industry. After the National Educational Plan of 1959 the *Volksschule* was divided into a primary school (*Grundschule*) and secondary school (*Volksschule/Hauptschule*). All children now attended the *Grundschule* before progressing to the *Gymnasium*, *Realschule* or *Hauptschule*.

After the restorative phase of the 1950s Germany became aware of the pressing need to overhaul its school and university provision in order to meet the needs of a modern economy. By European standards the numbers of school-leavers qualified to enter higher education were low, while children of manual, industrial and agricultural workers were grossly underrepresented in selective schools and higher education. Georg Picht (1964) warned of a 'catastrophe' in German education with dire consequences for the economy, while Ralf Dahrendorf (1966) argued for greater access to education for all citizens as a matter of human right. In response to such calls the government and *Länder* invested huge sums in expanding schools and, in particular, universities: between 1960 and 1970 numbers attending the *Gymnasium* and *Realschule* rose by 526 100 and 432 800 respectively, while university student numbers doubled. The expansion programme included preschool nurseries and adult education, although the *Hauptschule* and vocational education benefited less so.

Along with the expansion of the school infrastructure, the school attendance age was raised and reforms were undertaken in the structure of schooling and the curriculum. An important organisational change was the Hamburg Agreement (*Hamburger Abkommen*, HA) of 1964, an inter-state agreement which the eastern *Länder* also adopted after unification. The HA regulates school types (it introduced the terms *Hauptschule* and *Realschule*), the criteria for transfer between schools, the length of compulsory education, the school calendar and holidays, standards of assessment, the recognition of leaving certificates, and so on. The HA and KMK co-operated closely in the reforms of the 1960s and 1970s. In 1965 the government and *Länder* also set up a joint advisory body, the German Educational Council (*Deutscher Bildungsrat*), although this was disbanded in 1975 when Baden-Württemberg and Bayern refused to agree to its continuation.

In 1969 the German Educational Council recommended establishing a new school type, the *Gesamtschule* or comprehensive school, which was introduced in 1972. The idea was that pupils would no longer have to make a premature decision on their type of secondary school, would enjoy greater mobility between school types and would be offered a wider choice of subjects. After a prolonged and controversial experimental phase, the state education ministers finally agreed on the structures of *Gesamtschulen* in 1982. So-called 'additive' or 'co-operative' comprehensives retained the separate school types (*Gymnasium, Realschule* and *Hauptschule*) alongside each other on the same campus. The 'integrated comprehensive' (*integrierte Gesamtschule*), on the other hand, combined the two streams and employed 'setting' to constitute individual ability groups. Never popular with conservative *Länder*, comprehensive schools were not introduced uniformly throughout Germany and in no federal state did they completely replace the traditional three-phase school model. The KMK admitted them as a valid school form for all states in the 1980s. Most *Gesamtschulen* are now in Hessen and Nordrhein-Westfalen, while Bayern has none; in 1994 there were only 638 integrated comprehensives in western Germany (319 in the east) compared with 2504 (648) *Gymnasien* (Rohlfs and Schäfer 1997: 69).

Between 1970 and 1973 the FRG agreed a structural plan which set a national framework for education: school years 1 to 4 comprised the primary level (*Grundschule*), years 5 to 10 secondary stage I (*Gymnasium, Realschule, Gesamtschule* or *Hauptschule*) and years 11 to 13 secondary stage II (sixth form). An important recommendation was the introduction of a unified curriculum for years 5 and 6 which would act as an 'orientation stage' (*Orientierungsstufe* or *Förderstufe*) to assist the pupil's choice of secondary school. The proposal has since been adopted by all *Länder* except Bayern. A radical reform of the sixth form was undertaken in 1972 (see the section below on the *Gymnasium*). The plan also upgraded the status of vocational training to secondary stage II. The effectiveness of general education from primary to secondary stage I is widely acknowledged: at under 1 per cent, the rate of analphabetism in Germany is one of the lowest in the world (Gukenbiehl 1998: 86).

The reforms of the 1960s and 1970s came to a standstill in the 1980s. Unlike countries such as the UK, Sweden and Denmark, Germany has not replaced its traditional vertically-structured school system based on separate school types by a horizontal model where all pupils attend a unified comprehensive-type school. As a rule, on leaving primary school, pupils stay in their chosen secondary school until attaining a leaving certificate, so selection of school type is decisive. At the same time, the system is far from rigid. Although the vertical model discourages mobility between school types at secondary stage I, transfer at stage II has increased, with more pupils going on to seek further qualifications, often in conjunction with vocational training or at another type of school (a possible exception to this is in the east, where the linking of teaching posts with falling pupil numbers is discouraging already low rates of transfer between higher and lower school types; Pritchard 1998: 133). Thus in 1994 one-third of those leaving the *Realschule* went on to complete a certificate for admission to university (*Hochschulreife* or *Abitur*), while a similar proportion at the *Hauptschule* continued beyond the required ninth school year. The number of children from working-class families who completed the *Abitur* rose steadily until 1980, but has since begun to fall (Grammes and Riedel 1997: 741).

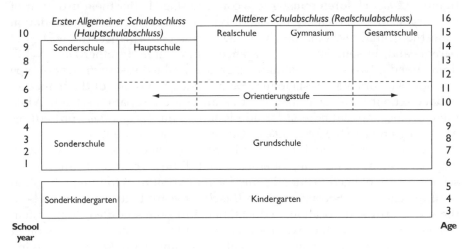

			Diplom, Magister, Staatsexamen	
			Universität	
			Technische Universität	
			Gesamthochschule	
			Pädagogische Hochschule	
			Fachhochschule	
		Allgemeine Hochschulreife	Kunsthochschule	
			Musikhochschule	
	Fachschule	Abendgymnasium/Kolleg	Verwaltungsfachhochschule	

					Allgemeine Hochschulreife	19
13	*Mittlerer Bildungsabschluss*		*Fachhochschulreife*		Gymnasiale Oberstufe	18
12	Berufsschule+Betrieb	Berufsfachschule	Fachoberschule		In: Gymnasium / Berufliches Gymnasium	17
11	Dual System				Fachgymnasium	16
10					Gesamtschule	15

	Erster Allgemeiner Schulabschluss		*Mittlerer Schulabschluss (Realschulabschluss)*			16
10	*(Hauptschulabschluss)*		Realschule	Gymnasium	Gesamtschule	15
9	Sonderschule	Hauptschule				14
8						13
7						12
6			— Orientierungsstufe →			11
5						10

						9
4						9
3	Sonderschule		Grundschule			8
2						7
1						6

				5
	Sonderkindergarten	Kindergarten		4
				3

School year   Age

Figure 7.1   Overview of the education system

PRIMARY SCHOOL (*GRUNDSCHULE*)

Children who have reached the age of six on 30 June must attend primary school until the age of ten. Entry to primary school is also open to able children whose sixth birthday falls between this date and the end of the year. Teaching is mainly in the morning and concentrates on basic skills (reading, writing and numeracy) and on areas of general interest. Progression from year to year depends (as at higher school levels) on performance, which is measured on a scale of 1 (very good) to 6 (unsatisfactory).

SPECIAL SCHOOLS (*SONDERSCHULEN*)

Special schools are designed for the 4 per cent of children with special needs. The special provision may begin at preschool level and continue into secondary education. More recently special schools have aimed to integrate children directly into the general school system. This is most readily achieved for children with learning and speech difficulties and, to a lesser extent, for those with physical and sensory disabilities. All types of schools in Germany are faced with the challenges of integrating children of foreign workers, asylum-seekers and, since unification, ethnic Germans from Russia and eastern Europe. Success rates, measured as the number of children gaining a school-leaving certificate, are highest with children who are born or have grown up in Germany (Gukenbiehl 1998).

SECONDARY SCHOOLS

In most *Länder* children transfer to secondary stage I after the fourth year of primary school. The choice of school type is based on a recommendation from the primary school, the child's academic performance, the wishes of parents and, in some cases, an entrance examination. In other *Länder* children attend a two-year orientation stage before the decision on school type is made. The orientation stage may be integrated into one of the main secondary school types or it may exist as an entirely separate school. While there are no national criteria for admission to the *Hauptschule*, procedures governing entry to the *Realschule* or *Gymnasium* vary widely.

After their tenth school year, pupils leaving school at secondary stage I may begin an apprenticeship or embark on full-time vocational education at school; all are obliged to attend some form of vocational training education until the age of 18. Secondary stage II (school years 11 to 13) includes both the sixth form and vocational education within the so-called dual system (see below). Entry to the sixth form is subject to satisfactory completion of year 10 at *Gymnasium* or the equivalent (for example, the *Realschule* leaving certificate).

Below are brief descriptions of the three main secondary school types. The *Gesamtschule* has been described above.

Hauptschule

This provides a general, practical education for pupils who will either go straight into work or, more commonly, take up vocational training on leaving. Pupils leaving at 15 (after the ninth year of compulsory schooling) obtain a general leaving certificate (the *erster allgemeinbildender Schulabschluss* or *Hauptschulabschluss* for short). Those leaving at 16 may obtain the *mittlerer Schulabschluss* or *Realschulabschluss*. Pupils may also opt for more demanding classes which will prepare them for transfer to

Realschule or *Fachoberschule*. This entitles them to a higher leaving certificate, the *qualifizierender Hauptschulabschluss*, which increases their chances of being accepted for an apprenticeship or vocational training. The range of subjects has also been widened. Despite such enhancements and although the *Hauptschule* was originally conceived as the standard school type for the majority of German children, its role has become increasingly unclear within the west German system and it has progressively lost popularity: 70 per cent of 13 year olds attended the *Hauptschule* compared with only 25 per cent at *Realschule* or *Gymnasium* in 1960; in 1995 the ratio for the whole of Germany was 23 per cent to 54 per cent (Statistisches Bundesamt 1997: 53). In the west the *Hauptschule* is widely regarded as a sink school. Better represented in the rural areas than in the city, it suffers from discipline problems and absenteeism; boys outnumber girls, leading to a gender imbalance. In the eastern *Länder* the position of the *Hauptschule* is even more precarious and it is possible that it will cease to exist altogether as a separate school type (Pritchard 1998: 132).

Realschule

Of all the school types the *Realschule* has enjoyed the most remarkable growth in post-war Germany. Accounting now for about 25 per cent of the secondary school population, it owes its popularity to the desire of middle-class parents to combine academic education with a vocational orientation. Children enter the *Realschule* on leaving the primary school or the sixth year of the *Hauptschule*, attending a total of six years in the former case and four years in the latter. The *Realschule* differs from the *Hauptschule* in its compulsory tenth year (age 15) and its wider range of subjects. These include foreign languages, mathematics and sciences, often with an applied or vocational accent (e.g. business English or accountancy). The leaving certificate (*Realschulabschluss*, formerly *mittlere Reife*) is the basis for entry to many technical professions and higher level jobs. It can also qualify for admittance to secondary level II (school types such as *Fachoberschule* and *Fachgymnasium*). The *Realschulabschluss* is achieved by 39 per cent of pupils making it the standard school-leaving qualification in Germany.

Gymnasium

Since 1955 the *Gymnasium* refers to all schools providing secondary education leading to the general university admission certificate (*Abitur*). For most pupils entry to the *Gymnasium* is directly after primary school or the sixth year of the *Hauptschule*. Completion of the tenth year of schooling is normally accompanied by the award of the *mittlerer Schulabschluss* (or *mittlere Reife*), which is equivalent to the *Realschulabschluss* and admits the holder to the sixth form (secondary stage II or *gymnasiale Oberstufe*). The sixth form, which lasts three years, underwent a radical reform in 1972. The class as the unit of teaching was replaced by a more flexible system of semester-based course modules grouped into two or three main subjects (*Grundkurse*) and four or five subsidiary options (*Leistungskurse*). The traditional school-leaving certificate (*allgemeine Hochschulreife* or *Abitur*) was retained, although the assessment scale of 1 to 6 was replaced by a more differentiated points-based system (0 to 15); an element of continuous assessment was also incorporated. The reforms were accompanied by far-reaching changes to curricula and syllabus content which continued well into the 1980s (Neather 1995: 149-50). Admission to the *Gymnasium* has increased from 10 per cent of children in a single year during the 1950s to around 25 per cent or even 30 per cent in some cities. While more children from all social classes attend the *Gymnasium*, the relative differences remain, with the middle and professional classes best represented; at the same time more girls now attend than boys (Gukenbiehl 1998). Since unification, the re-establishment of the *Gymnasium* in the east has greatly increased the proportion of young people qualified to enter higher education (rising from 16 per cent in 1990 to 35 per cent in 1995), although numbers actually going on to university have fallen, possibly as a result of continuing economic insecurity (Pritchard 1998: 137).

SCHOOL TYPES IN THE EASTERN STATES

In contrast to the FRG, the authorities in the GDR did not restore the pre-war school system, claiming that it unfairly disadvantaged working-class children in favour of those from bourgeois backgrounds. The GDR thus made a conscious effort to remould the education system into one that inculcated young people with socialist values and a sense of loyalty to the state. By 1959 the GDR had replaced the traditional German secondary schools by a standard type, the ten-year General Polytechnical Upper School (*Zehnjährige Allgemeine Polytechnische Oberschule*, POS). The POS provided a comprehensive education for all children from the age of 7 to 16 (school year 10) and comprised a primary stage (3 years) a lower secondary level (3 years), and an upper secondary level (4 years).

The traditionally accepted aims of school education, however, which included the development of a well-rounded, knowledgeable individual, were grossly distorted in the GDR by the overriding need for teachers to instil in their pupils a collective loyalty to the socialist state. Admission to the two-year sixth form in years 11 and 12 (the *Erweiterte Oberschule*, EOS, or Extended Upper School) ensured progression to university but was not open to all on grounds of ability alone: national economic plans regulated numbers and entrants had to demonstrate political conformity. Despite its commitment to the unitary POS, the GDR also maintained some special schools for exceptionally gifted pupils. A widely praised feature of the GDR system was the opportunity for continuing education while in work: by the end of the 1960s this was producing a much higher proportion of East Germans with *Abitur* than the FRG (Gukenbiehl 1998: 89).

Although many regarded aspects of the GDR's school system as worth retaining after unification, the POSs were dissolved and replaced by the west German school types (for a review of the debate see Neather 1995). This was part of the general process of dismantling the GDR education system after 1990: universities and higher education were remodelled along west German lines, works-based vocational schools were closed and the extensive preschool facilities drastically reduced. Nevertheless, most eastern *Länder* took advantage of the principle of cultural sovereignty to introduce their own variations of western school types. Only Mecklenburg-Vorpommern adopted the traditional tripartite model of post-primary entry into *Hauptschule*, *Gymnasium* and *Realschule*. Other states opted for a bipartite division into a selective *Gymnasium*, creaming off the most able pupils, and one other type, which went under a variety of names (*Gesamtschule* in Brandenburg, *Mittelschule* in Sachsen, *Sekundarschule* in Sachsen-Anhalt, *Regelschule* in Thüringen). The *Hauptschule*, perceived by parents as offering little in a competitive western economy, all but disappeared in name, although in many secondary schools it continued to exist as a stream alongside that of the *Realschule*. Due to its proximity to Berlin, Brandenburg retained a small number of *Realschulen* alongside the *Gesamtschule*. Proponents of the bipartite system argued that it preserved the best aspects of the POS, although in what form is uncertain (Grammes and Riedel 1997: 741). Bipartite school types combining *Hauptschule* and *Realschule* may also be found in the west, notably in Hessen (*Verbundene Haupt- und Realschule*), Hamburg (*Integrierte Haupt- und Realschule*) and Rheinland-Pfalz (*Regionale Schule*).

A sharply falling birth-rate in the east (between 35 per cent and 42 per cent between 1989 and 1993 and remaining at a low level after 1996) is likely to have a marked effect on planning for school provision. If the fall continues, by 2005 the newly established *Gymnasia* will be able to accommodate most entrants to all school types for the year. Many *Grundschulen* and other small schools may have to close, and secondary level classes may have to be integrated across different school types. Further options include teaching different year groups in the same class (multi-age classes) and restricting course options. The policy of introducing several different school types at the same time as school rolls are falling has proved questionable, especially for sparsely populated *Länder* such as Mecklenburg-Vorpommern. Arguably, the eastern states' enthusiasm for differentiation of school type along western lines has cost it the opportunity to promote a genuinely viable two-stream *Gesamtschule* (Pritchard 1998: 131–2). Although access to the *Gymnasium* in the east varies widely (current rates of transfer range from 5 per cent to 60 per cent), the prospect of an increasingly heterogeneous intake to the higher school type is likely to be a serious challenge for teachers (Pritchard 1998: 133–4).

The traditionally high value attached to the *Abitur* in German society contributed to a fierce debate after unification about the equivalence of the qualification in east and west: while the sixth form traditionally required three years in the FRG, all but Brandenburg retained the two-year model of the now defunct EOS of the former GDR. Proponents of the more rapid path to the *Abitur* pointed to the generally shorter sixth forms of other European countries and argued that it offered advantages to able pupils. The KMK finally worked out a compromise setting out a minimum number of teaching hours for the *Abitur* and allowing *Länder* to choose between a fast-track programme (12 school years in all, with 9 years at *Gymnasium*) and a slower, 13-year preparation period which included 8 years at *Gymnasium* and a three-year sixth form (*gymnasialer Aufbau*) that could also be combined with vocational training. The compromise illustrates the KMK's need to be pragmatic in accommodating regional pluralism in educational policy since unification. Teachers' organisations and trade unions criticised the fast-track *Abitur* for placing utilitarianism above education and promoting élitism within schools. Nevertheless, CDU-controlled *Länder* such as Baden-Württemberg and Bayern led the way in introducing pilot schemes for the shorter sixth form, with SPD *Länder* following. Ironically, within ten years of unification, eastern *Länder* had reverted to the traditional model, with only Sachsen and Thüringen offering the two-year sixth form (*Der Spiegel* (6), 2000: 64–5).

VOCATIONAL TRAINING

In the year before unification two-thirds of 16–18-year-old west Germans (1.8 million), mainly from *Hauptschulen*, *Realschulen* and *Gesamtschulen*, attended some form of vocational school (*Berufsschule*). Of these, 538 000 had an apprenticeship or training contract with a firm. By 1995 the figures for the whole of Germany had fallen to around 1.7 million (almost 40 per cent of these were female), due in part to a growth in numbers studying for a university entrance qualification which was seen as providing a competitive edge in a difficult job market. The number of apprenticeships also declined (456 000 in the western *Länder*, 122 000 in the east). The fall has been most noticeable in urban areas offering more attractive alternatives to vocational training. On a national level the number of available traineeships exceeds the annual demand by around 19 000, although there are wide regional variations and overall the number of firms offering apprenticeships has fallen. Despite these figures, attendance at a vocational school with or without an apprenticeship still plays a major role in the education of most young Germans and enjoys a high social status.

Full vocational training is based on the 'dual system' (*Dualsystem*), a combination of paid training at the workplace with part-time attendance until the age of 18 at a vocational school (*Berufsschule*). The school provides a mixture of general education and training in skills relevant to the chosen trade. The scheme is largely financed by employers and requires intensive co-operation between employers' organisations, trade unions and educational providers. Trainees sign a contract with a firm or company which lays down the length and type of training. The basis of the dual system was laid down in law in 1969 (*Berufsbildungsgesetz*) and in an inter-state agreement of 1975. Around 400 occupations are officially designated as eligible for vocational training, with young men opting mainly for manufacturing, engineering, crafts, electronics and building; young women prefer sales, purchasing, banking and office work, and the health sector. Rates of pay while on training contracts range from around 255 to 1200 DM a month, and many students go on to attend universities or technical colleges after the initial training period.

Although held in high regard abroad for the quality and flexibility of the training provided, the dual system has its critics within Germany. Trade unions argue that it does not promote the skills of participation and co-operation at the workplace, while employers point to its failure to meet the national need for skilled workers. The system (it is alleged) has not responded rapidly or flexibly enough to the broader range of skills now required, while unions and employers took the best part of the decade before unification in order to reduce the number of recognised job categories from 465 to 374 (Sturm 1997b: 679). Employers have also been criticised for exploiting trainees as cheap labour (Smyser 1993: 77). The dual system's increasing dependence on state funding is controversial: by the middle of the 1990s one-third of traineeships were subsidised by the state, partly in response to high unemployment. While some argue that deregulation of vocational training would provide more training places, others maintain that firms that do not take on trainees should pay for those that do, despite the risk of increasing the bureaucracy. Although the factory-based vocational schools (*Betriebsberufsschulen*) of the former GDR have survived only in some large concerns (notably Siemens and Schering), they could serve as a model for a more deregulated system. Another problem is that completion of a training contract does not guarantee employment. One in five who completed their training in 1995 could not get a job, rising to one in three in the eastern *Länder*. Many young people were unable to continue in the trade for which they qualified and were forced to re-train or become unemployed.

Despite such criticisms, the dual system has a long tradition in Germany and is considered an essential part of Germany's recipe for industrial success. Although expensive, it has resulted in a highly qualified, well-motivated and productive workforce in which skilled personnel can move fairly smoothly into management and the higher echelons of small to medium-sized firms (for the particular role such firms play in the German economy see Chapter 5).

Types of vocational school

There is a bewildering variety of vocational school types in Germany, mostly offering part-time or full-time education and normally for between one and three years. Vocational schools cater for a wide range of entry qualifications and offer both academic and vocationally-based leaving certificates. School titles vary according to region.

The *Berufsfachschule* provides full-time training (between one and two years) for school-leavers who have no previous experience of work. The *Berufsaufbauschule* is designed for trainees who are either attending or have completed the ordinary *Berufsschule*; studies (lasting up to three and a half years) are organised according to subject area or trade and lead to the award of the *Fachschulreife*, which is equivalent to the *Realschulabschluss*. The two-year full-time *Berufsoberschule* or *Technische Oberschule* enables those with *Realschulabschluss* and a vocational qualification to study for a university admission certificate (*Hochschulreife*). Likewise, *Fachoberschulen* are higher level vocational schools which prepare those with *Realschulabschluss* for study at a *Fachhochschule*, a diploma-awarding technical college (see below). The *Fachgymnasium* is similar, but prepares students for general university entrance over three years. The *Fachschule* allows students who have completed an apprenticeship to extend their professional qualifications or update their skills: courses last between six months and three years and are especially attractive to skilled individuals thinking of setting up their own business.

UNIVERSITIES AND HIGHER EDUCATION

Continuing a tradition established by Wilhelm von Humboldt in the early nineteenth century and confirmed in the Basic Law, German universities exercise autonomy in teaching and research and enjoy considerable managerial independence. In practice this means that the state cannot dictate the content of degree programmes and that universities have their own constitutions. As part of the educational reform debate of the 1960s, which saw a huge increase in demand for tertiary education, the Framework Law (*Hochschulrahmengesetz*) of 1976, which was reviewed in 1985 and on unification in 1990, set the first national guidelines regulating universities. The guidelines covered procedures on admissions, internal democracy, the recognition of degrees and laid down prescribed periods of study (*Regelstudienzeiten*). The *Länder*, which had regional responsibility for education, then implemented their own laws to conform with the national framework. As a result, the higher education sector in Germany is very diverse despite the national framework. The reforms of the early 1970s also opened up the management of universities to greater participation by students and other groups.

Higher education is financed jointly by the *Bund* and the *Länder* and subject to an annual inter-state transfer of funds (*Länderfinanzausgleich*) that is designed to ensure a balanced provision across the country; in practice the states contribute 90 per cent of the funding. The issue of funding was particularly important after unification, when eastern universities needed a large and rapid injection of resources in order to reach parity with the west and offer a full range of subjects to their students. However, the question of how to allocate scarce funds fairly and at the same time maintain quality of teaching and research remains controversial. While quality evaluation is well established in the UK and USA, no such system exists in Germany and would be held by some to contravene a university's autonomy. Questions over the principle of autonomy also arose after unification when the universities of the former GDR found that the (west German) state was prepared to intervene massively in their affairs in order to purge academics considered to be close to the communist regime and to reorganise them along western lines.

Despite the national framework and an expansion in the numbers of higher education institutions (totalling 346 in 2000), German universities proved unable to cope with the huge demand for tertiary education. Between 1960 and 1990 student numbers increased five-fold and, despite a levelling off of demand after 1995 due to demographic developments, were projected to exceed 2 million by 2000 (a particularly rapid expansion occurred in the eastern states after unification). Such rapid growth led the government and *Länder* to abandon the principle that the *Abitur* automatically entitled its holder to study the subject of choice. In 1974 the *Länder* established a central office in Dortmund (the *Zentralvermittlungsstelle*, ZVS) which allocated university places according to a complex formula based mainly on school-leaving certificate grades and on the period the applicant has been waiting for a university place. The ZVS and the *Länder* also imposed an admissions quota (*numerus clausus*) in popular subjects such as law and medicine. Many continue to regard the *numerus clausus* as violating the Basic Law, which guarantees universal access to education.

Conditions of study

At around 22 years old, German students enter university comparatively late and take on average six years to graduate. While difficulties in the job market tempt some students to prolong their studies (so-called *Parkstudium*), it is other factors that make for the relatively long study periods. German students attend school for a year longer (13 years) than in many other countries, while men spend a further year doing national service: in 1999 the average age of graduation was 28. Despite officially laid down lengths of courses (*Regelstudienzeiten*), students in Germany do not enrol for the fixed-term degree programmes that are found in, say, the UK or the USA; nor is their progress closely monitored by academic and administrative staff. They are likely to be taught in large groups at unfavourable staff–student ratios (1:13 in Germany as a whole, with more staff per students in the eastern *Länder*) and have considerable flexibility to take papers and tests when they choose. Moreover, most students (an estimated 60 per cent in 1995) work during the semester in order to finance their studies. They also have little chance of obtaining subsidised university accommodation (11 per cent in the west, 44 per cent in the east).

Around 13 per cent of students in the western *Länder* and 28 per cent in the east currently receive a state grant, named BAFöG after the law (the

Bundesausbildungsförderungsgesetz) which entitles students aged between 15 and 30 whose parents cannot support their studies to state funding. The grant, half of which comes as an interest-free loan repayable five years after graduation, is means-tested and index-linked to inflation. In 1999 the scheme provided a maximum 860 DM a month, some 300 DM less than needed for actual living expenses in the west (the average grant in 1998 was 618 DM). A 1995 survey by student unions pointed to significant differences for students in the eastern and western *Länder*: living costs in the east were markedly lower than in the west, while more eastern students were on a state grant. During the 1990s the number of students receiving BAFöG fell by almost a half. The reasons for the fall included government budget cuts and changes in the rules of entitlement: periods of study abroad or sabbaticals for student union work ceased to be automatically supported; the loan element was no longer necessarily held to be interest-free; and students changing subject more than once in the first two semesters forfeited BAFöG altogether. While the numbers of schoolchildren and those on vocational training programmes receiving BAFöG support actually rose, student leaders argued that the low level of grant discouraged members of low-income families from entering university (Jeffery and Whittle 1997: 16-17; Rohlfs and Schäfer 1997: 78; Hahlen 1999). For whatever reasons, the drop-out rate of German students remains high. Currently only 10 per cent of students graduate within the recommended period, while one in four leaves university with no qualification at all. Many students enrol and then leave, as shown by the high proportion of first-year over other students (90 per cent until 1975 and expected to continue at around 75-80 per cent).

Officially German universities are equal in status and are not subject to the league tables or rankings that are published in the UK or the USA. Since the 1990s, however, information published by the magazines *Stern, Der Spiegel* and *Focus*, and by the Gütersloh-based Centre for Higher Education Development (*Centrum für Hochschulentwicklung* or CHE) provides students with enough data to select universities according to the quality of teaching, research and other facilities. Despite the availability of such information, 80 per cent of students still choose to study at their local university. The main reasons for their reluctance to move away from home are the need to rely on parental financial support and the attractions of an established circle of friends (Schlicht 2000).

Fees

Despite fierce opposition from student unions, *Land* ministers have long debated introducing tuition fees in order to reduce student numbers and costs. Although the issue does not follow clear-cut party political lines, cultural ministers from SPD *Länder* and the east have tended to oppose fees on the grounds that they would discourage poorer students from entering higher education. However, at the same time as the SPD–Green coalition government elected in 1998 confirmed its rejection of compulsory fees, a number of ministers in SPD–*Länder* acknowledged that some form of fee-derived finance would become necessary in the long term. Meanwhile, the absence of a formal inter-state agreement means that some *Länder* currently levy fees while others do not. As a result students migrate to the 'cheaper' universities across state boundaries with little or no effect on enrolments nationally.

Tuition fees in Germany masquerade under different titles and are levied under varying circumstances. During the 1990s Berlin, Baden-Württemberg and Niedersachsen introduced registration fees (*Einschreibegebühren*) of 100 DM per semester. Bayern and Sachsen on the other hand levied fees for a second period of study (*Zweitstudium*) only. When in 1998 Baden-Württemberg required students continuing into their 14th semester to pay 1000 DM, enrolments in this category showed an immediate and dramatic fall (35 per cent). Compared with other countries, however, German fees are low and are likely to be pegged at a socially acceptable level. Leading North American universities, for example, require between 7000 and 30 000 dollars a year (between 15 000 and 66 000 DM, although food and accommodation may be included); figures for the UK are £1000 (2800 DM) and for Australia 2450 dollars (2950 DM). As in other countries, a state-sponsored loans scheme for students in Germany is on the political agenda (Schlicht and Törne 1999).

Subjects studied

Alongside medicine and dentistry, the most popular subjects have traditionally been economics, engineering and law, although German studies (*Germanistik*) tops the list for female students. A decline in enrolments in engineering and informatics, partly as a result of the depressed job market during the early 1990s, produced genuine fears of a national shortage of graduates in these areas, which are perceived as essential to Germany's economic future. In natural sciences and engineering Germany currently produces under half the number of graduates per 100 000 employees compared with other developed countries. Between 1975 and 1995 the proportion of students training to enter the teaching profession fell drastically (from 30 per cent to 12 per cent) in line with the decline in the number of teaching posts available (Statistisches Bundesamt 1997: 64). Many see German universities as producing 'too few students too slowly and in the wrong academic fields' (Buck 2000).

Proposed reforms

In September 2000 Germany's education minister, Edelgard Bulmann, announced plans for a radical reform of the higher education system. Her proposals for reducing basic salaries for university and college staff and introducing performance-related payments generated a predictable storm of protest from academics (Buck 2000). For students, one of the options under consideration is the extension of a more structured three- to four-year bachelor/masters degree following a model well established in the UK and the USA. Such programmes were introduced in 1998 in Germany for the first time: by 2000 they numbered over 400 and the figure was expected to rise, although most students continue to regard them as inferior and as inadequate preparation for the job market. Changes to degree structures may, however, be necessary in order to increase the proportion of graduates in Germany, which at 16 per cent of the population is low compared with the UK (35 per cent) and the USA (33 per cent). German employers have also criticised graduates for poor communication and business-related skills (Buck 2000). A major barrier to a comprehensive overhaul of the German higher education system on a national scale is the autonomy of the federal states, which have been unwilling to embrace swift reform. However, in March 1999 the regional educational ministers agreed on national guidelines (*Strukturvorgaben*) on degree programmes (at the level of bachelor and master) in order to standardise provision, make courses more transparent and to make it easier for students to move between levels and from one institution to another (both within Germany and the EU).

Types of universities

Historic universities such as Heidelberg, Köln, Leipzig and Erfurt date from the Middle Ages. While Humboldt's ideal of a university was a place of theoretical learning and research for a small number of students in the humanistic tradition, the growth of the natural and applied sciences in the nineteenth century saw the emergence of very large universities, such as Berlin, München, Hamburg and Bonn. The next wave of expansion occurred during the 1960s and 1970s, when many new institutions were founded, including Essen, Dortmund and Regensburg. Several technical colleges gained university status during the 1980s and 1990s and the number of institutions dedicated to teaching and vocational training (*Fachhochschulen*) increased. Many German universities, so-called 'mass universities' (*Massenuniversitäten*), are now very large indeed. Around 140 000 students, for instance, are registered for higher education in Berlin, which has three major universities. Other universities or cities with high student populations include Hamburg (62 000), Münster (52 000), Köln (31 000) and München (93 000). Even medium-sized universities such as Würzburg (25 000), Augsburg (18 000) and Siegen (12 500) are large by UK standards (Schäfers 1998: 33).

The so-called scientific or academic institutions of higher education (*wissenschaftliche Hochschulen*) in Germany consist of the universities proper (163 in number) and the higher technical colleges (183). A few small, private universities (38) account for just 1 per cent of students nationally (Hahlen 1999). Alongside teaching (usually through lectures and seminars) the universities engage in independent research and are the only institutions entitled to award doctorates. Undergraduate admission is via the *Abitur* or its equivalent. The recommended period of study (*Regelstudienzeit*) varies according to subject and level but is generally four or five years, although most students take longer. Students graduate with a diploma (*Diplom*), a masters degree (*Magister*) or a doctorate (*Promotion*); a second, post-doctoral dissertation (*Habilitation*) is normally required for a professorial or senior academic post. Students intending to be schoolteachers study for the so-called state examination (*Staatsexamen* or *Lehramtsprüfung*) at secondary stage I or, if teaching sixth formers, stage II. Around 66 per cent of all students in Germany are enrolled at universities.

Research at universities is financed by the state and by independent research foundations such as the German Research Association (*Deutsche Forschungsgemeinschaft*) which supports many short- and long-term projects. The Max Planck Institute (founded in 1948) conducts basic research in the natural and social sciences: it focuses on developing new or interdisciplinary areas beyond the means of individual universities and derives 95 per cent of its funds from central and regional government. The München-based Fraunhofer Society (founded in 1949) maintains 47 establishments throughout Germany and has branches in the USA and Asia: a leader in converting scientific research into commercial applications, it attracts considerable funding from small to medium-sized businesses. This is also true of the Hermann von Helmholtz Society, whose 16 centres conduct research in the earth sciences, energy, health, communications and transport. A number of industrial concerns such as Volkswagen, Fritz-Thyssen and Robert-Bosch have established foundations (*Stiftungen*) which support research in the arts and sciences.

Technical colleges (*Fachhochschulen*) expanded strongly in the FRG after 1975 and currently account for a quarter of all enrolled students (Rohlfs and Schäter 1997: 78). They focus on higher level vocational training, mainly in applied economics, social work, agriculture and engineering. Resources are directed towards teaching rather than research. Admission is normally by a technical school-leaving certificate (*Fachhochschulreife*) or *Abitur* with vocational training (although this can now be included in the study programme). Students study for three or four years and graduate with a diploma which will admit them to further study at university.

In 1973 the government planned establishing 'comprehensive universities' (*Gesamthochschulen*), which would combine under a single roof the functions of the traditional universities and technical colleges. The concept of the *Gesamthochschule* was never fully developed, however, and in 1995 only one was listed by the Federal Ministry of Education and Science, although a small number of institutions have adopted the title (Rohlfs and Schäfer 1997: 78). *Gesamthochschulen* account for only 8 per cent of the national student population (Statistisches Bundesamt 1997: 64). Apart from the institutions already mentioned it is worth noting the *Kunsthochschulen* (46), which train students in the fine arts, design, music, film, theatre and television, and a number of specialist *Hochschulen* for areas such as sport, administration and management.

CONCLUSION

In common with other European countries, the expansion of educational systems in post-war Germany widened access and increased opportunities for personal and professional development. The main improvement in Germany occurred from the 1970s onwards: whereas in 1934 only 2 per cent of the school population entered university, the figure had risen to 11 per cent in 1975 and to 37 per cent by 1998 (Statistisches Bundesamt 1997: 63; Hahlen 1999). The emergence of new disciplines, such as information processing, computer science, educational and social sciences, has in turn generated new jobs in industry and academia. Nevertheless several challenges remain. These include the continuing relatively low participation of working-class children, the 9 per cent of 15–17-year-olds who leave school every year without a qualification and the question of whether mass universities offering loosely structured degree programmes are capable of meeting the twin demands of providing a cost-effective and high quality education to increasing numbers of students. On the other hand there are also signs that the boom in university education that set in particularly in the east after unification was short-lived: while 80 per cent of school-leavers in the east registered as students in 1990, the figure fell to 60 per cent by 1996 (in the west, the fall was from 76 per cent to 67 per cent). Notably, while eastern women were overall better qualified to study, fewer actually did so. The reasons for the general trend away from higher education are unclear, but may have to do with a desire among young people to earn an income as quickly as possible by seeking out vocations that do not require university study. This is likely to contribute to the current skills deficit and also to a shortage of qualified academic personnel, especially in subjects such as information technology (*Der Tagesspiegel* 22 December 1999: 6).

FURTHER READING

For overviews of the development of the German educational system as a whole see Gukenbiehl (1998) and Grammes and Riedel (1997). Menze (1996) looks back at the history of the German university system since 1945. The periodical *Bildung und Wissenschaft* (available in English as *Education and Science*) is published monthly by Inter Nationes and provides a view on current issues. The websites of the *Länder* generally contain details of the school types and educational system of each state. Neather (1995) and Pritchard (1998) describe how the eastern states managed the transition to western schools, while Neuweiler (1994) and Schluchter (1994) focus on the transformation of east German universities and higher education.

8

STRUCTURES OF COMMUNICATION: THE MEDIA

Mass communication media have traditionally been divided into print or text-based media (daily and weekly newspapers, magazines and books), audio media (radio, audiotapes/CDs) and visual media (television, video, cable and teletext). With the advent of computer-based technologies and advances in digital processing the distinctions between media types are becoming increasingly blurred. The integration of text, audio (including speech) and picture on a single, often interactive platform (such as CD-ROM, personal computer or television) is well underway and is likely to change radically our traditional perceptions of separate channels of communication or 'media'. This chapter looks at the traditional forms of media (press and broadcasting) in Germany and traces how they have evolved to encompass changing patterns of ownership and new technologies.

THE PRESS

Germany was the birthplace of newspapers. By the end of the seventeenth century, when the first (weekly) newspapers appeared, the German-speaking area had more news publications (about 70) than the rest of Europe put together. This was largely due to religious and territorial divisions and an efficient postal service at the geographical crossroads of Europe. Academic journals appeared from the seventeenth century onwards and periodicals aimed at women from the early eighteenth century; literary publications were also popular, although titles were generally short-lived. Party political newspapers, family-orientated and humorous periodicals appeared in the mid-nineteenth century. The modern type of universal newspaper, with headlines, column layout, separate thematic sections (politics, opinion, culture, business and sport), advertising and a distinctive journalistic style began to take shape from the late eighteenth century onwards. Despite the growing importance of newspapers and periodicals, professional journalists in Germany were long regarded as failed academics. With advances in printing and papermaking technology it became possible towards the end of the nineteenth century to produce and distribute daily newspapers for mass markets. The first large publishing concerns, such as Mosse and Ullstein, were founded at this time (for details see Noelle-Neumann *et al.* 2000: 417–38).

Although it was argued as early as the eighteenth century that newspapers should be free to reflect and/or form public opinion, censorship prevailed throughout the German states until 1848. After unification the 1874 law on press freedom (*Reichspressefreiheit*) abolished censorship throughout the German Empire, although this did not prevent the government from using the courts and economic methods to try to control the press. Censorship was restored during the First World War and applied occasionally even during the Weimar Republic, especially during the turbulent 1930s (the Weimar constitution contained no specific guarantee of freedom for the press). The Weimar period saw a remarkable proliferation of politically-orientated, often subsidised newspapers: a record 4275 titles appeared in 1932. Newspaper publishing was dominated by two large concerns: the industrialist Alfred Hugenberg controlled the nationalist, conservative press and, from 1927, the leading German film studios UFA; communist newspapers were in the hands of the less diversified Münzenberg concern (Noelle-Neumann *et al.* 2000: 439–41). Up until 1933 the majority of mainstream newspapers were openly sceptical of the National Socialists, who maintained their own small but vociferous press. Once in power, however, the Nazis built up an extensive propaganda apparatus and applied various measures of censorship and control, although personal differences in the political leadership, the traditional diversity of the German regions and the regime's desire to preserve a vestige of international respectability provided some room for the occasional critical voice (Noelle-Neumann *et al.* 2000: 441–52).

After the war and mindful of the Nazis' exploitation of the press for propagandistic purposes, the western allies allowed newspapers to appear only under licence. While the British licensed newspapers that reflected the political interests of the individuals who produced them, the Americans favoured jointly produced, non-party 'group newspapers'. The Soviets allocated licences only to approved organisations. None of the allies granted a licence to any publisher who had produced a newspaper before 1945. When licences were removed in West Germany in 1949 (the Soviet-sponsored regime in East Germany effectively continued the licensing system until its collapse in 1989), the number of newspaper titles jumped from 150 to over 600. However, the market was unable to sustain so many titles and a process of concentration and consolidation set in which continued until reunification in 1990. Although the number of titles and publishers steadily dwindled in the post-war FRG, overall daily circulation figures rose steadily to reach 25 million by the late 1970s, remaining at a similar level thereafter (Kaase 1998: 454).

The concentration of titles in West Germany resulted in a proliferation of 'single newspaper districts' (*Ein-Zeitungs-Kreise*), which are areas served by only one local daily newspaper. While such areas applied to only 8.5 per cent of the population in 1954, by 1997 the figure had risen to 42 per cent (Noelle-Neumann *et al*. 2000: 386). A commission set up in 1964 to investigate competition in the media after newspaper proprietors had expressed concern over unfair competition from television identified various forms of co-operation between newspaper editors and publishers. Many local dailies, for example, carried different titles but shared political and current affairs sections (Noelle-Neumann *et al*. 2000: 124, 384). Press concentration, which resulted partly from mergers and take-overs and partly from market domination by successful titles, has progressed to such an extent that over half of all German dailies (including supra-regional titles) are produced by 3 per cent of publishers, the largest of which is the Hamburg- and Berlin-based Axel Springer Verlag (for a full list see Noelle-Neumann 2000: 390–1). In 1967 the government set up the Günther Commission to investigate the implications of this concentration for freedom of expression. The commission recommended restricting market shares of publishing concerns, although it was not until 1976 that a special press merger law (*Pressefusionskontrolle*) was incorporated into general legislation on monopolies and later used to block a number of proposed mergers. At the same time the government began to collect statistics on the press industry in order to monitor its development. However, these moves did not halt the overall trend towards concentration, and unification in 1990 actually accelerated the process. At first, with the lifting of the state monopoly on publishing, the number of newspaper titles in eastern Germany rose, reaching 158 in 1991. But by 1993 it had fallen to 137 after the Trust Agency, whose primary concern was to attract investors, maximise profits and protect jobs, sold off the popular district newspapers formerly run by the SED to west German publishing houses (Noelle-Neumann *et al*. 2000: 127–8).

Genuine competition in the German newspaper industry is found among the national quality dailies and the major regional titles with a national circulation – a sector which has remained remarkably stable over a long period. Well-known titles (with daily circulations) include: *Frankfurter Allgemeine Zeitung* (400 000), *Süddeutsche Zeitung* (413 000), *Die Welt* (218 000), *Frankfurter Rundschau* (200 000) and *Westdeutsche Allgemeine Zeitung* (605 000). These are all supra-regional publications: although based in a particular city or region, they are circulated nationally and even enjoy international status. A number of national dailies have a very limited readership. They include the left-wing *taz* (58 000) and *Neues Deutschland* (65 000), the organ of the PDS, the successor party to the SED. The strength of genuinely local or regional titles in Germany is illustrated by their circulations, which are often higher than the national or supra-regional newspapers. Examples include the *Sächsische*

Zeitung (published in Dresden and with a circulation of 494 000), the *Freie Press* (Chemnitz, 435 000), the *Mitteldeutsche Zeitung* (Halle, 435 000), and the *Rheinische Post* (Düsseldorf, 395 000).

In a class of its own is the *Bild-Zeitung*, which relies on street sales rather than subscriptions (*Abonnements*) and appears in several regional editions. With a circulation of around 4.5 million (which represents a slight fall from previous years but is still the highest in continental Europe), *Bild* is in many respects Germany's only truly national daily newspaper (*Tageszeitung*). First appearing in 1952, it soon became a favourite with the German public and is well known for its sensationalist presentation and journalistic style. Until his death in 1985, *Bild*'s founder, Axel Springer, used the paper as a platform for his right-wing political views. One of Springer's most contentious campaigns was directed against students during the social and political unrest of 1967–68, when *Bild* was widely held to have contributed indirectly to the attempted assassination of the student leader, Rudi Dutschke. This incident, alongside concern over the tabloid's journalistic methods, fuelled anxiety about the dangers of the concentration of the press and was an important factor in the government's decision to set up the Günther Commission (Sandford 1995: 204–5).

In contrast to the UK, Sunday newspapers (*Sonntagszeitungen*) are relatively new in Germany. *Sonntag Aktuell* (900 000) is widely distributed in the south-west, while many local and supra-regional daily papers now also include a Sunday edition. The main national Sunday papers are *Bild am Sonntag* (2.5 million) and *Welt am Sonntag* (400 000), both published by the Alex Springer concern but with separate editorial policies. A rather different genre is the weekly newspaper (*Wochenzeitung*) which aims to provide background information, opinion and analysis rather than pure news. Apart from politically affiliated publications such as the *Bayernkurier* (CSU) and those aimed at religious communities (such as the *Rheinischer Merkur*, circulation 108 000), the most successful and respected of such weeklies is the long-established and independent *Die Zeit* (490 000). Other, more recent publications include the *Wochenpost* (formerly published in the GDR and since 1992 throughout Germany by Gruner + Jahr) and *Die Woche* (circulation 100 000, published since 1993 by the Jahreszeiten Verlag), which is based on the format of *USA Today* and contains whole-page review articles on politics, culture and social affairs, often with colour graphics.

Modelled on the US *Time* magazine, the weekly political and cultural periodical *Der Spiegel* merits a special mention. Founded in 1947 and with a circulation of over 1 million, *Der Spiegel* has developed a reputation for aggressive, informed journalism, providing in-depth analyses of social issues, and for exposing political and financial scandals. Along with *Die Zeit*, it is widely regarded, not just as a news-reporting organ, but as a key shaper of public opinion and as part of the national cultural and political establishment. As a journalistic institution *Der Spiegel* remained unchallenged until 1993, when the Burda Verlag produced the rival magazine *Focus* (circulation 500 000). Containing shorter articles and making extensive use of colour illustrations and graphics, *Focus* has cultivated a more relaxed journalistic style than *Der Spiegel*.

While press concentration has reduced the number of daily newspaper titles, the same cannot be said of the 1600 or so weekly magazines (*Publikumszeitschriften*). These target mainly the huge leisure, sport and entertainment market that has emerged in contemporary Germany, but the sector is highly diverse, with numerous titles for social groups (such as women and young people) and readers with special interests (ranging from sex to computers). Compared with daily newspapers many of these magazines command huge circulations. The market leader is the motorists' weekly *ADAC Motorwelt*, which sells over 12.7 million copies (Noelle-Neumann *et al.* 2000: 404). The number of television and radio magazines has grown steadily since the launch of commercial and satellite stations during the 1980s: in 1998 eight titles achieved a combined circulation of 17 million, with *TV Movie* (2.9 million) leading the field. Magazines for women range from the fashion- and life-style-orientated *Bild der Frau* (1.77 million, first published in 1983) and *Brigitte* (941 000) to the feminist *Emma* (56 000, first published in 1977). To the category of *Publikumszeitschriften* also belong the so-called illustrated magazines (*Illustrierte*). Aimed at a general readership, these focus on human interest stories and well-known personalities rather than politics and current affairs. After a series of mergers and takeovers from the 1950s onwards, three major titles remain: *Stern* (1.1 million), *Bunte* (682 000) and, targeted at readers in eastern Germany, *Super Illu* (583 000). The most popular youth magazine is *Bravo* (970 000), followed by its companion *Bravo Girl* (563 000), both containing features on music, film, television and sports stars; the leading children's comic is *Micky Maus* (665 000).

The proliferation and, in some cases, transience of titles in the dynamic magazine market mask an actual decline in the number of publishing houses. Four major concerns, all located in western Germany, currently dominate the magazine scene: the Heinrich Bauer Verlag (Hamburg), the Axel Springer Verlag (Hamburg), Burda (Offenburg) and Bertelsmann/Gruner + Jahr (Gütersloh and Hamburg). Several new magazine titles appeared in eastern Germany immediately after unification. Their readership, however, remained confined to the east and most disappeared, a notable exception being the satirical magazine *Eulenspiegel*. Some western publishers initially brought out a separate eastern edition of their magazine (for example, the business- and finance-orientated *Wirtschaftswoche* and *Capital*), but with the convergence of conditions in the old and new states they have moved over simply to distributing the western version.

Advances in computer technology have affected the way in which the traditional newspapers are disseminated. During the 1980s newspapers, in particular the financial and business publications *Wirtschaftswoche* and *Handelsblatt*, offered access to their computer-based archives. The dailies soon followed, adding audio-text and fax facilities. Although complete editions of newspapers can be downloaded to a personal computer via a subscription to an on-line service, German publishers at first favoured the use of commercial computer mailboxes (or on-line services; see section on the impact of multimedia technology below). Between 1995 and 1996 the number of German dailies that could be accessed via computer or a modem leapt from just two to around 30, and all news publications now have a presence on the world wide web. Web-based material tends to be a digest of selected items and not the full paper edition, although some newspapers maintain extensive archives.

RADIO AND TELEVISION

Three years after the founding of the first regional radio broadcasting stations in 1923, Germany's first national long-wave radio transmitter, *Deutsche Welle*, began transmitting by agreement between the states of Bayern, Prussia and the national postal service (the *Reichspost*). Unlike the USA, radio in Germany was established as a state monopoly (in the hands of the *Reichspost*) with minimal private participation. Programme content was subject to official controls that were designed to ensure that broadcasting remained politically neutral and served the common good, i.e. not the interests of a particular government or political party. Partly because of technical limitations on reception, broadcasting was organised regionally, with nine states (*Länder*) responsible for their own stations. Exploiting the power of radio to reach and influence mass audiences, the Nazis centralised the system of broadcasting and exerted strict controls on staffing and programme content: after 1940 Propaganda Minister Josef Goebbels introduced a single channel (the *Großdeutscher Rundfunk*) for the whole of Germany. The Nazis also pioneered the world's first public television broadcasting, transmitting the 1936 Olympics to 28 public viewing areas in Berlin, Potsdam and Leipzig, although the war halted further development.

After 1945 the allies and western Germans reverted to the Weimar model of regional broadcasters operating within a legally enshrined framework that defined their responsibility to the general public. The model, which owed much to the BBC, was held to represent the most favourable framework for developing an independent and accountable public broadcasting service. While a fully commercial service funded through advertising was not considered viable in the shattered post-war economy, the allies refused to countenance a centralised, state-controlled service after the experiences of the Nazi era. Broadcasting in West Germany developed in three phases: the establishment and consolidation of a publicly accountable regional radio and television network (ARD) from 1950 onwards; the founding of a second, national television channel (ZDF) in 1961; and, finally, the era of the so-called dual system after 1984, when private radio operators were allowed alongside the public corporations. As radio broadcasters have moved into new media, the term *Rundfunk* (originally: radio) now refers to broadcasting in general, while *Hörfunk* denotes specifically radio.

The ARD radio network was set up in 1950 to enable the regional stations to produce and pool programmes and resources (ARD stands for *Arbeitsgemeinschaft der öffentlich-rechtlichen Rundfunkanstalten der Bundesrepublik Deutschland*). ARD inaugurated a television service in 1954, which, after a formal inter-state agreement, became fully operational in 1959. Protracted efforts by Konrad Adenauer's administration to establish a national commercial television company with the state as the major shareholder were rejected by the Federal Constitutional Court in 1961. The court ruled that the station, as planned, would violate the cultural sovereignty of the *Länder* and would be too much under the control of central government. After this setback the government withdrew from the scene, leaving broadcasting policy to the federal states. These agreed in 1961 to establish a second (national) television channel (*Zweites Deutsches Fernsehen* or ZDF) alongside the ARD. Centrally run from its base in Mainz, the ZDF was independent of the *Länder*, although it remained a public corporation and was partially financed by licence fees from the ARD; it began broadcasting in 1963. The two channels did not, however, operate entirely as rivals. They undertook to co-ordinate their schedules and to widen programme content without directly competing for audiences. In this way, it was hoped, viewers would be encouraged to watch more political and current affairs programmes. From 1963 onwards a number of regional stations launched a third television channel (*Drittes Fernsehprogramm*). Conceived originally to provide an alternative to the ARD and ZDF, the third channel focused on programmes for schools, culture and music. However, general entertainment, sport and films currently constitute 40 per cent of its output which also contains a high proportion of repeats compared with other channels.

Eleven regional stations comprise the ARD network. These are: *Bayerischer Rundfunk* (BR), *Hessischer Rundfunk* (HR), *Mitteldeutscher Rundfunk* (MDR, covering Sachsen, Sachsen-Anhalt and Thüringen), *Norddeutscher Rundfunk* (NDR, for Bremen, Hamburg, Mecklenburg-Vorpommern, Niedersachsen and Schleswig-Holstein), *Ostdeutscher Rundfunk Brandenburg* (ORB), *Radio Bremen* (RB), *Saarländischer Rundfunk* (SR), *Sender Freies Berlin* (SFB), *Süddeutscher Rundfunk* (SDR), *Südwestfunk* (SWF for Rheinland-Pfalz and part of Baden-Württemberg) and the *Westdeutscher Rundfunk* (WDR, for Nordrhein-Westfalen). The NDR contributes most to network programmes (16 per cent) and the ORB the least (0.7 per cent). The period between 5.30 p.m. and 8 p.m. is reserved for regional television programmes. The production and co-ordination of programmes are managed from a central ARD directorate in München.

Each of the 11 stations broadcasts two or three radio channels with a contrasting programming content. Of programmes, 54 per cent are devoted to (mainly light) music, but 3 per cent are aimed specifically at foreign residents and there is also a small advertising element (1 per cent). A particularly successful format that has opened up new audiences and turned radio into the most widely used of all the media is a mixture of popular music and short informative spoken contributions interspersed with hourly or half-hourly news items and traffic reports. Indeed, since its foundation the public broadcasting service in Germany has responded well to changing markets and technologies, despite losing audiences and advertising revenue to private operators after 1984 (see below). The ARD and ZDF began transmitting to the GDR in 1966 – well before unification. From 1992 they jointly produced a breakfast television programme (Noelle-Neumann *et al.* 2000: 497–8). In 1984 the ZDF combined with Austrian (ORF) and Swiss (SRG) corporations to provide an international German-speaking satellite channel, 3 SAT. In a similar joint venture with SRG, the ARD set up *Eins Plus* to broadcast mainly cultural programmes via satellite, although this ceased operation in 1993 when ARD joined the 3 SAT consortium.

The legal basis for German broadcasters is article 5 of the Basic Law, which guarantees freedom of the press, including broadcasting, and of journalistic reporting; the Basic Law categorically rules out censorship. At regional level these freedoms are reflected in individual state laws (*Landespressegesetze*) or, if more than one region is involved, an inter-state treaty (*Staatsvertrag*). Reflecting its special status as a world broadcasting service the *Deutsche Welle* was established by federal law in 1961; the station broadcasts in German and foreign languages and maintains a 24-hour television service. After unification all the *Länder* signed a special broadcasting treaty (*Rundfunkstaatsvertrag*, 1991) which regulated the rights and duties of public and private broadcasters throughout Germany. Subsequently these laws have been reinforced and clarified by numerous judgments of the Federal Constitutional Court (FCC). In particular, public corporation broadcasters are legally obliged to ensure a plurality of views and not to serve the interests of a particular group or party. In a landmark decision of 1961 the FCC effectively drew a distinction between external and internal pluralism. The former is exemplified in the press, where the plurality of competing titles is considered sufficient to prevent an interest group from gaining control of the medium. For financial and technical reasons radio and television are felt to be in a different category from the press. In particular they face stricter requirements to ensure an internal balance of views within a channel's overall range of programmes (internal pluralism). The laws also require the public corporations to transmit cultural and educational programmes.

The regional public corporation radio and television stations are organised and managed along similar lines. For each station a Broadcasting Council (*Rundfunkrat*) is appointed from representative sections of society, including politics, churches, trade unions, business, the arts, journalism and education. The size of the Broadcasting Council varies from 16 to 77, depending on the size of the station. Its role is to ensure that the station is meeting its public obligations, and, in particular, that programme content meets the criteria of plurality and balance. Although Broadcasting Council members are not bound to directives from their interest group and are supposed to act in the general public interest, they are in practice often susceptible to political influence and act along party lines. During the 1970s and early 1980s the CDU/CSU argued that broadcasters and journalists were applying a left-wing bias in their reporting and crucially influenced the outcome of the 1976 general election; in an effort to counter this perceived bias the Bavarian CSU attempted to pack the Broadcasting Council of the *Bayerischer Rundfunk* with its political allies. Members of the Council are also often overburdened by the task of personally monitoring a channel's entire output, relying on reports and committee papers rather than on first-hand experience of programmes they have no time to view for themselves. The Broadcasting Council elects the Administrative Council (*Verwaltungsrat*), whose seven to nine members are responsible for general management, financial planning and technical development. Finally, the Broadcasting Council elects the Director (*Intendant*) for a six-year period of office. The Director has global responsibility for the day-to-day running of the station, including programmes.

ARD stations are financed through advertising and licence fees. Until 1969 the annual licence fee was a mere 2 DM for radio and 5 DM for television; the low level of the fee was at first offset by rising audiences and revenue from advertising. In 1968 the FCC transferred responsibility for levying the licence fee from the national post office to the states, but it was not until 1992 that these agreed on a much higher, nation-wide fee of 23.80 DM. When the FCC expressed concern in 1994 that the states' monopoly of the fee level could be misused to influence programme content, the *Länder* had to submit their plans for setting and spending the fee to an independent monitoring committee. The corporations' increasing dependence on the licence fee is largely the result of a massive drop in advertising income since the advent of commercial satellite television, especially RTL and SAT 1. This is despite a marked overall increase in television advertising that set in at the end of the 1980s (Noelle-Neumann *et al.* 2000: 495–6, 514). The ARD's advertising revenue fell from 21 per cent of its total income in 1988 to just 9 per cent in 1992; the ZDF experienced a similar decline. In fact television advertising on the ARD and ZDF is restricted to just 20 minutes each day during the week (90 minutes for radio) and it is not permitted at all after 8 p.m., when audiences reach their peak. As a result the public channels are unable to fill even the restricted advertising slots that are available to them. Competition from private operators has forced the ARD and ZDF to take drastic cost-cutting measures and to explore private sponsorship (for instance, of sports programmes). Despite falling revenues, the public corporations face occasional but persistent demands from commercial interests to be divested of advertising income altogether. Restricted to transmitting cultural programmes, this would leave a heavily de-regulated private sector free to focus on entertainment and profit. Such naked commercialism does not, however, attract universal support in Germany (*Der Tagesspiegel* 19 November 1999).

Moves towards admitting private broadcasting operators in Germany began in the early 1980s with the advent of cable and satellite television. However, it was not until the conservative administration of Helmut Kohl (from 1982) that real progress was made towards privatisation, since the previous SPD government and SPD-governed *Länder* had resisted efforts to open up broadcasting to commercial interests. When the European satellite ECS1 came on-line in 1984, private broadcasters, led by a consortium of newspaper and magazine publishers, were granted a licence to transmit the first German commercial satellite channel, SAT 1. A second channel, RTL plus (later RTL), appeared the following year. During this initial phase of development, individual *Länder* passed often quite diverse laws regulating the private operators, leading to marked contrasts compared with the uniform structures that characterised the public sector.

In a series of landmark rulings between 1986 and 1991, the FCC established a constitutional basis for the co-existence of public and private broadcasting – the dual system – and clarified the different roles and responsibilities of the two sectors. The court affirmed the traditional function of public broadcasting: to offer a balanced and wide-ranging 'basic provision' (*Grundversorgung*) of programmes for information, culture, education and entertainment. At the same time the court emphasised the state's obligation to provide the public broadcasters with a secure financial basis. Somewhat less stringent requirements were placed on private operators, who have to meet a 'basic standard' (*Grundstandard*). Moreover, the federal states, which had to provide an adequate technical and financial framework for commercial stations, were afforded considerable leeway to frame their own media policies. These policies are embodied in the so-called state media laws (*Landesmediengesetze*) and the state media authorities (*Landesmedienanstalten*). In some states (Bremen, Hamburg, Nordrhein-Westfalen) the media laws favour internal pluralism, whereby each individual channel has to demonstrate a balance of views. Elsewhere (Bayern, Berlin, Rheinland-Pfalz) external pluralism is sufficient, with a balance required only across the totality of operators. Combinations of the two models are also found.

In practice the media laws, by distinguishing various categories of channels, have allowed one of the most diverse and dynamic private broadcasting markets in Europe to emerge. So-called full channels (*Vollprogramme*) offer a comprehensive range of programmes covering information, education, culture and entertainment. The first full channels were SAT 1 (1985) and RTL (1984), but these were soon followed by PRO 7 and Tele 5 (both 1989); RTL 2 began broadcasting in 1993. Niche channels (*Spartenprogramme*) are aimed at particular interest groups. The first niche channel, *Musicbox*, began transmitting in 1984, before turning into a full channel, Tele 5, which broadcast from 1989 until 1992. After 1992 a number of niche channels came online: n-tv (news), VOX (initially a news and information provider but now a full channel), Kabelkanal (providing films and entertainment via cable), VIVA (music and video), DSF (*Deutsches Sportfernsehen*, a sports channel which superseded Tele 5) and the digital pay-as-you-view entertainment channel Premiere (from 1991); tm3, a channel for women, appeared in 1995. So-called 'window channels' (*Fensterprogramme*) broadcast for limited periods on a purely regional basis and are usually part of a larger network. German operators also contribute to foreign channels such as Eurosport and

ARTE (a French–German cultural station). By the mid-1990s there were nine German television or cable channels financed through advertising and around 50 private regional stations, of which half provided window programmes for national operators. On occasion private and public stations work together to share programmes and resources (Noelle-Neumann *et al.* 2000: 517).

In terms of programme content the two largest private television channels, RTL and SAT 1, expanded significantly between 1986 and 1992. In 1987 they moved into breakfast television and now broadcast 24 hours a day. It has also been suggested that the private and public broadcasters have converged as a result of being in direct competition: while the ARD and ZDF increased the number of films and series in order to provide more pure entertainment, the commercial broadcasters imitated the more successful formats of the public stations. Nevertheless, the ARD and ZDF still broadcast significantly more news and information (about 40 per cent) than RTL or SAT 1 (18 per cent) and, within news programmes, devote more attention to politics. The main private channels tend to broadcast informative and current affairs programmes in the early part of the evening (Noelle-Neumann *et al.* 2000: 517).

Commercial radio in Germany has developed even faster than television, with around 200 providers broadcasting locally, regionally, and nationally. Combined with the public corporations, the total number of radio channels rose 20-fold between 1985 and the end of the century. Mention may also be made of the so-called 'open channels' (*offene Kanäle*). Operated mainly by hobbyists and special interest groups, these are small-scale radio and television channels run by private citizens with the media authorities providing technical support. Although initially conceived as a transitional phase in the move towards the dual system, the open channels now appeal principally to young people and do not command significant audiences among the general public (Noelle-Neumann *et al.* 2000: 510).

In 1984 the German *Länder* set up the state media authorities in order to allocate licences to private radio and television broadcasters and to regulate and monitor their operation. Since many regionally based private stations broadcast beyond state boundaries, the authorities established in 1987 a standing conference of station directors in order to co-ordinate policy at national level. In many respects the media authorities are structured like the regional radio and television stations. They are governed by Media Councils (*Medienräte*) on which, like the Broadcasting Councils of the public corporations, key social and political groups are represented, and they are financed from the general licence fee, which generates a sizeable income but also produces disparities between rich and poor states. The authorities' power to issue licences to competing operators who are located regionally but broadcast nationally has placed them at the very centre of media politics; as a result they have become the object of considerable attention by the regional governments and political parties. The dangers of concentration notwithstanding, the economic attractions of an international media giant located in a federal state are obvious, and it is largely as a result of political lobbying that SAT 1, for instance, is located in Rheinland-Pfalz, Hamburg and Berlin, while RTL is based in Nordrhein-Westfalen and Bayern.

To counter trends towards concentration of ownership in private broadcasting, the media authorities are obliged, by an inter-state broadcasting treaty (*Rundfunkstaatsvertrag* 1991), to commission an annual independent report on concentration and the plurality of views in broadcasting. To ensure competition and to prevent concentration of media power, German law before 1996 simply prohibited a single company from controlling more than one television station. This was refined by the broadcasting treaty of 1997, which declared that a company should not exceed 30 per cent of the total market share, calculated on audience ratings, if it also owned more than 25 per cent of shares in any individual broadcasting station. The media laws of individual *Länder* also specify restrictions on ownership of channels. In practice the patterns of cross-ownership are complex and the restrictions hard to enforce, especially if companies are involved in publishing, licensing and distribution alongside broadcasting. The laws have been criticised for targeting television alone and ignoring concerns, such as Springer, with relatively small television interests but large holdings in the press (Boothroyd 1998: 153–4; Noelle-Neumann *et al.* 2000: 508).

Two groups currently dominate private television. The Beta/Taurus Group led by Leo Kirch controls SAT 1, DSF and Premiere. Kirch also has holdings in the Alex Springer publishing concern, which in turn has a stake in SAT 1. Kirch's son, Thomas, has controlling interests in PRO 7 and the cable channel Kabel 1 (although Leo Kirch and his son claim that their interests are distinct, an inter-state monopolies commission set up in 1997 to investigate media concentration regarded them as a unit). After Leo Kirch made a strategic decision in the 1950s to buy up old movies, his KirchMedia group now either owns rights or enjoys access to a huge number of film and television programmes. As a result he has been ideally positioned to fill the air time of the new digital and private television channels. The main competitor to KirchMedia is Bertelsmann, whose broadcasting division is called UFA but which also controls RTL and has interests in Premiere, VOX, RTL 2 and Super RTL. Rupert Murdoch, the Australian media magnate, has significant investments in tm 3 and VOX. In April 2000 Bertelsmann merged its television and radio interests with the British Pearson group to become Europe's largest broadcaster (over 22 channels in 35 countries), although in the same year KirchMedia announced further mergers that would create Germany's largest single television company.

Generating half of Germany's total television advertising revenue (well above that of the state-owned ARD and ZDF) and with a turnover of over 10 000 million DM, the combined Kirch empire was in 1999 one of the 15 largest media concerns of the world and dominated German commercial television. The company controlled six satellite or cable stations: SAT 1, ProSieben, Kabel 1, DSF (*Deutsches Sportfernsehen*), N24 (a news channel to be launched in 2000 and controlling the leading German news agency

ADN/dpa) and the pay channel Premiere World. It was estimated that one in four German viewers tuned in to a Kirch-owned station. Programme content comprised mainly talkshows, football, comedy series, news and imported US films. In 1999 Kirch planned a formal take-over of ProSieben (owned by Thomas Kirch) and a wholesale co-ordination of programme provision. Broadcasting films and soaps, ProSieben would target teenagers and the younger generation. SAT 1 would provide general family viewing for the 29–49 age group, while Kabel 1 would broadcast films and special interest shows for the over-40s. With Bertelsmann-RTL as the only rival to the combined Kirch group, advertisers and independent film producers were apprehensive about the consequences of such a powerful duopoly on the German commercial television scene (Jakobs 1999).

Although the media authorities by no means adopt a uniform policy towards the private operators, they joined forces in 1993 to produce guidelines that reduced the extent to which programmes could be interrupted by commercial advertising, which, alongside subscriptions, provides the main source of revenue for the broadcasting companies; they also agreed guidelines on the protection of young persons (Noelle-Neumann *et al.* 2000: 127, 506). The measures on advertising resulted from requirements contained in the state treaties (*Rundfunkstaatsverträge*) of 1987 and 1991. In summary, total advertising time may not exceed 20 per cent of daily broadcasting, with commercial breaks (*Spotwerbung*) restricted to 15 per cent; the maximum hourly time for commercial breaks is 20 per cent. Advertising must be clearly distinguishable from normal programmes and be broadcast only in identifiable blocks. Longer features devoted to advertising (*Dauerwerbesendungen*) are permitted, as is the commercial sponsorship of standard programmes. The media authorities do not, however, intervene directly to dictate programme content. To ensure compliance with media laws, they sample programmes and follow up specific complaints. In practice the authorities have not had to resort to the ultimate sanctions of withdrawing a licence or prohibiting programmes.

As elsewhere, the viability of commercial broadcasting in Germany depends heavily on advertising revenue which in turn hinges on audience size (private operators derive no income from the licence fee). The ability of private stations to attract significant audiences has gone hand in hand with advances in communications technology. In the mid-1980s, when the first satellite stations appeared, signals could be picked up only by powerful receivers operated by the national communications authority (the post office) before being distributed to private subscribers via the terrestrial cable network. Audiences were small and operators suffered heavy losses. The situation improved towards the end of the decade, when the (West) German Telekom massively extended the cable network and domestic satellite receivers became readily available. After unification cable provision remained at a lower level in the eastern states, partly because the former GDR had never invested significantly in the technology and partly because of competition with satellite receivers. In 1995 the first digital satellite,

ASTRA 1 E, was launched; ASTRA 1 followed in April the following year. Under the auspices of the Luxemburg-based European consortium SES (*Société Européenne des Satellites*), ASTRA emerged as the market leader, although it soon found a competitor in the form of Eutelsat, a consortium of European telecommunication companies which launched the Hot Bird satellite shortly after ASTRA. While older satellites could handle around 50 different analogue channels, their digital counterparts could broadcast several hundred audio and television channels at a time (over 700 stereo radio channels is not unusual) and to a higher standard.

Broadcasting to widely available and affordable home satellite receivers, commercial television expanded rapidly in terms of both channels and audience size. The number of German households with a satellite receiver rose dramatically from a mere 135 000 in 1989 to over 10 million in 1999. In addition the private stations benefited from an expansion of the terrestrial network, especially in urban areas. Digital technology has greatly extended the potential of both television and radio to tap into new audiences. Digital Music Express (DMX) and Music Choice Express (MCX), for example, are two channels which provide 24-hour music to suit a number of tastes; with no advertising or audio commentary, they are accessed via a smart card which operates on a pay-as-you-listen basis. By 2000 almost all public and private television channels (including ARD, ZDF, *Drittes Fernsehprogramm*, RTL, SAT 1, Pro 7, and Kabel 1) could be received digitally.

As private television has grown, the public corporations have lost audiences. In 1988, ARD and ZDF commanded 77 per cent of television audiences, but within five years the figure had fallen to 35 per cent. By 1993, the market share of two main private satellite stations more or less equalled that of their public rivals: audiences were 19 per cent for RTL and 16 per cent for SAT 1, compared with 18 per cent for ZDF and 17 per cent for ARD. Radio, on the other hand, followed a rather different pattern, with the public corporations maintaining their domination of the market (similarly, the decline in advertising revenue has been less marked for the public radio stations than for television). In 1993 private radio accounted for 41 per cent of total audience time in the western states and only 19 per cent in the east, although the commercial operators are expected to increase their market share. The picture, however, is distorted by strong regional variations, with private radio commanding relatively large audiences in Berlin (72 per cent), Hamburg (56 per cent) and Schleswig-Holstein (45 per cent), compared with a mere 27 per cent in Baden-Württemberg and 23 per cent in Bremen (Noelle-Neumann *et al.* 2000: 513–16).

IMPACT OF MULTIMEDIA TECHNOLOGY

The rapid growth of computer technology from the early 1980s onwards eroded the traditional distinctions between electronic, broadcast and printed media and produced an explosion in the information, entertainment and communications market. In many cases the presentation of information ('news') is linked with commercial advertising or even on-line shopping. Apart from radio and television broadcasting (either via cable or satellite), we can distinguish various types of services.

In contrast to the internet and the world wide web, which allow any user with a personal computer to access a vast and largely unmanaged network of open services, so-called mailboxes or on-line services offer structured information to individual and corporate subscribers. CompuServe, which set up the first global information service in 1979, now offers a range of German-language facilities. One of the first German-based on-line service providers was the Federal Post Office (*Deutsche Bundespost*) whose initially rather primitive *Bildschirmtext* service (1984) developed into the more sophisticated Datex-J (*Data Exchange für Jedermann* from 1991) and Telekom-Online (T-Online from 1995). T-Online's great advantage is that it is an essentially German-language service giving electronic access to leading national daily newspapers and numerous databases. Competition between on-line service providers in Germany is stiff. In 1995 alone two new operators entered the scene: AOL Europa, a joint venture between America Online and Bertelsmann, and Europe Online (EOL), owned by Burda and a number of foreign concerns. The number of subscribers varies from around 100 000 (for AOL in 1996) to over 1 million (for T-Online). More recently, competition from the internet has forced many on-line service providers to make their information available via the web, so that the technical difference between web-based and on-line systems is disappearing (Wilke 1996: 8). Germany's first home-banking service BTX, started in 1983 and by 1986 had some 50 000 customers, although T-Online no longer enjoys a monopoly in this area.

Steadily growing areas are tele-working and tele-shopping. Estimates of the number of tele-workers in Germany vary, although it is clear that the figure is rising, from 30 000 in 1994 to anything between 80 000 and 150 000 in 2000 (this would represent around 0.5 per cent of the total working population). The computer company IBM pioneered tele-working in Germany, employing 2400 on this basis in the mid-1990s. Currently around 4.8 per cent of German companies engage tele-workers, compared with 2.2 per cent in Italy and 7.4 per cent in the UK. The home-based tele-worker typically uses a personal computer to access the national satellite and terrestrial telecommunications network and to send or receive work to/from a company. So-called telecentres or computels provide computer facilities at a central location for tele-workers who may be employed by more than one organisation. In the longer term the potential number of tele-workers in Germany may reach around 3 million, with significant implications for commerce and for patterns of working and social life (Wilke 1996: 8–9; Klimsa 1997: 365).

Tele-shopping in Germany refers to the use of television to promote consumer goods which viewers order via telephone or computer. For home-shopping a personal computer user browses a web-based catalogue of goods and places an order directly by a mouse-click. The commercial television station RTL experimented with a tele-shopping service (*Teleboutique*) in the late 1980s. A Bavarian tele-shopping channel, Home-Order-Television (H.O.T), started up in 1995 but ceased operation after objections from state media authorities in other *Länder* who argued that it constituted a normal broadcasting service and therefore required a licence (Wilke 1996: 9).

A major step in opening up the potentially vast new market of multimedia to commercial as well as public operators was the lifting in January 1998 of the German post office's monopoly of the national communications network (access had already been provided to private mobile phone and satellite companies). Well before this date providers had begun establishing strategic alliances with other European and US-based concerns. Thus Deutsche Telekom formed an association with France Télécom and the American company Sprint, while Bertelsmann joined forces with America Online. The Kirch group entered into an alliance with Vebacom and Metro to offer Germany's first digital television service, DF1 (on 28 July 1996). The public television corporation ZDF also agreed with Microsoft Network (MSN) to set up an on-line service.

The formation of commercial alliances designed to exploit multimedia technology and services has raised important issues of competition and public access. A potentially very powerful alliance proposed by Bertelsmann, the Kirch group and German Telekom was vetoed by the European Commission. By 1995 the communications market in Germany had polarised into two main rivals: on the one hand the Kirch concern, which controlled access to its digital television services by its own decoder, and on the other hand the multimedia consortium MMBG (*Multimedia-Betriebsgesellschaft*) comprising mainly Bertelsmann and RTL but also including the public corporations ARD and ZDF, Deutsche Telekom and the French pay-TV company Canal plus.

Regulation of services delivered by global land-based and satellite networks clearly requires international solutions. The dissemination of neo-Nazi propaganda, for example, is illegal in Germany but not in the USA or Canada. Nevertheless, the German government (*Bund*) and the states (*Länder*) agreed in 1996 on a multimedia law which attempted to allocate regulatory responsibilities at a national and regional level within Germany itself. In future the federal states would be responsible for all new media services aimed at the general public (such as video on demand or tele-shopping), while central government would regulate services for individual subscribers (such as on-line computer services). Many regulatory issues, however, remained unresolved. They include: the extent to which the traditional notion of broadcasting (*Rundfunk*) is still valid in the multimedia age; the question of which multimedia services require licensing and which do not; the control of copyright in an age of rapid and universal digital reproduction and distribution; the protection of individual privacy through adequate data protection laws; issues of security and consumer protection for on-line commercial transactions; and the control of pornographic, racist and other offensive material across open media. Although national German legislation ruled that internet providers had no duty of censorship, the state of Bayern adopted a firmer line and in 1998 mounted a test case against the former head of the German subsidiary of CompuServe, alleging that he allowed customers using his service to transmit illegal and pornographic material (Traynor 1998a).

FURTHER READING

See Sandford (1995) for a concise introduction in English to the constitutional background to the media, the regulatory framework, the press and broadcasting laws, types of media, the problems of concentration of ownership and developments since unification. Meyn (1992) remains a standard textbook on West German media before unification. A comprehensive reference work with extensive entries and statistical data on media-related topics is Noelle-Neumann *et al.* (2000). Current media information and issues are discussed in the journal *Media Perspektiven*, which has appeared monthly since 1963. Since 1969 the ARD has published a year-book (*ARD Jahrbuch*) which reviews developments in public service broadcasting. Occasional studies of the economic and political implications of media developments appear in *Aus Politik und Zeitgeschichte*. In such a fast-changing area the magazine *Der Spiegel* is also a useful source of information.

9

SOCIAL ISSUES

This chapter reviews some of the major social issues confronting contemporary Germany, in particular as they have been affected by unification. While the fall of the Berlin Wall was greeted as a symbol of the collapse of the physical and political division between East and West Germany, it soon became clear that the mental barrier, the 'wall in the head' (*Mauer im Kopf*) dividing easterners and westerners, would take much longer to dismantle. The reasons for the alienation of one section of German society from another lie only partly in the continuing economic disparities between the old and new *Länder* (see Chapter 3). Differences in attitudes and values that developed over forty years under quite different social, economic and political systems could not be easily overcome. This chapter therefore begins by looking at aspects of social and personal values which researchers have identified among east and west Germans. The notion of 'value change' (*Wertewandel*) is useful in this context.

The chapter also looks at a range of other issues that are relevant to German society. These include right-wing extremism, attitudes to foreigners and Germany's evolving policy towards immigration. How Germany has handled the question of *Vergangenheitsbewältigung* (coming to terms with the past) is also addressed. Finally, the role of the family, the development of the women's movement (including the controversial issue of abortion) and the position and role of the Church are reviewed. Many of these issues shed light on the continuing social challenges of unification and of the prospects of eventually overcoming the 'wall in the head'.

VALUES AND VALUE CHANGE

During the 1940s and 1950s sociologists developed the notion that personal values, which deeply influence individuals' goals and actions, are at least partly the product of cultural and social institutions. Values, they argued, can also change, either spontaneously or as a result of transformations in institutions; institutional changes may provoke, for instance, either greater social conformity or a sense of conflict which triggers a shift in individuals' values. The existence of quite different social and political institutions in East and West Germany after 1949 clearly has implications for the development of the personal values of the citizens of each state.

Research in the FRG conducted over forty years or more (between 1951 and 1995) showed that the greatest value shift occurred in the areas of 'obedience and subservience' (Gehorsam und Unterordnung) and 'independence and free will' (Selbständigkeit und freier Wille; see Klages 1998). When values of social conformity dramatically lost their significance during the late 1960s, West Germans began to rate individuality and freedom of personal action much more highly. The shift occurred at a time of intense social and political change in post-war Germany and it has persisted: it corresponded to the emergence of the student revolutionary movement and to a widespread perception that Germany needed to reform its society and take new political directions – embodied in Willy Brandt's Ostpolitik and his call to 'risk more democracy' (mehr Demokratie wagen). Interestingly, although the conventional and classically German values of 'love of order and industriousness' (Ordnungsliebe und Fleiß) declined at the same time as obedience and subservience, they had recovered by the mid-1970s to reach their former levels, before once again undergoing a slight fall in their appeal towards the end of the 1980s. This development shows that value change does not necessarily follow an all-embracing, clear-cut direction: elements of older, conservative attitudes can be retained if they are felt to meet individual needs. Nevertheless, a feature of value change in the FRG has been that it has applied to all generations and age-groups, although younger people have exhibited the most radical shifts in attitude, with the result that by the 1980s (or even earlier) the divergences in values between age-groups were much wider than in the 1950s. Finally, while men and women have been more or less equally affected by value change, such change has been much more likely to occur in individuals who have benefited from any form of education, regardless of gender or age.

Whether East Germans experienced similar shifts of values before 1989 is hard to ascertain. Some argue that industrialisation in the GDR stimulated a process of socio-economic modernisation that overrode the regime's efforts to mould its citizens into 'socialist personalities' through education and indoctrination. According to this view East Germans were thus able to develop areas of personal privacy at home and at work where value changes were able to take place, albeit about a decade later than in the FRG. Indeed, such changes probably contributed to the widespread dissatisfaction with the regime which surfaced in the peaceful revolution of 1989. Whether or not this was the case it is generally accepted that East Germans cultivated spheres of privacy, in particular the family, in order to escape the all-pervasive politicisation of life under the SED (Schroeder 1998: 585–6). This form of inner emigration was aptly termed the 'niche society' (Nischengesellschaft) by Günter Gaus, who represented the West German government in East Berlin from 1974 (Gaus 1983: 156). After unification personal values of east and west Germans appeared to converge rapidly. Easterners ranked independence and free will (also expressed in a desire to be creative, enjoy life and satisfy personal needs) equally as highly as westerners, although they also valued hard work, security and material standards of living rather more than their compatriots in the former FRG (Klages 1998: 704).

While it is possible to see evidence of a decline in social values (*Werteverfall*) in favour of greater individualism and personal egoism, it is also likely that human beings are merely adapting their values to suit the rapidly changing demands of a highly competitive and increasingly globalised society. Research published in western Germany in 1993, which categorised the population in terms of five types of personality, lends some support to this view. According to this typology the first category is the 'conventionalist' (17 per cent of the population of the western states) – someone who resists modernisation and seeks risk-free stable situations in which conformist behaviour is duly rewarded. A second type, described as resigned and lacking perspective (15 per cent) also avoids risks but goes further by retreating into private niches out of frustration or lack of success in life. Active realists (34 per cent), on the other hand, are success-orientated and able to react pragmatically and flexibly to challenges and to the demands of institutional change. Hedonistic materialists (17 per cent) are equally adaptive but are motivated more by the principle of personal pleasure. Non-conformist idealists (17 per cent) tend to be younger people (often journalists and teachers) who are modern, idealistic and egalitarian in outlook but easily frustrated or disappointed in their encounters with the new globalised society (Klages 1998: 706–7). If we accept the above characterisation, it appears that a significant proportion of Germans, notably the 'active realists', are responding positively to a changing society and are able to adapt their personal values accordingly to meet its challenges. At the same time, the widespread disillusionment with politics and political institutions (*Politikverdrossenheit*) that was noted from the late 1980s may be part of a general reorientation towards new and more highly individualised personal goals. This disillusionment may also be reinforced by a widespread perception that Germany's political institutions are essentially conservative, in need of reform and unable to respond to changing social needs (for an analysis of the issues see Winkel 1996).

It is worth noting that, although values of east and west Germans may be converging, observers have commented on certain differences in attitude, behaviour, consumerism and even patterns of thought. A comparison of television-viewing habits revealed that easterners watched television for longer and favoured private over public channels, partly because they lacked the traditional loyalty of west Germans to the ARD and ZDF. They also preferred light entertainment to serious programmes and valued channels and broadcasts with a local or regional (eastern) content that dealt with problems of everyday life. To some extent the tastes of east German viewers were informed by their sense of having a distinctive 'eastern' identity, a sense which was reinforced by feelings of alienation generated by constant criticism from the west of social and economic conditions in the new states (Frey-Vor 1999).

Studies were also made of the nature of romantic and sexual relationships between east and west Germans after the Wall came down. From these it emerged, for instance, that most relationships involved western men and eastern women, largely because many men came over from the FRG during the process of westernisation. While women tended to accept the guiding role of the man in the wider process of adapting to western conditions, they had a less romantic attitude to bearing children (most eastern women were mothers before reaching 30) and were attractive to their partners for their readiness to combine the roles of wife, mother and worker. Western men also found eastern women to be self-confident, independently minded and uncomplicated but also more open to compliments and to sexual relations than western women (Richter 1999).

Intriguingly, although general consumption patterns converged rapidly after unification, easterners and westerners tended to buy different products and brands, suggesting certain deep-seated and continuing divergences in outlook. For example, while wealthy westerners would buy a Mercedes Benz, easterners would still tend to regard this as socially unacceptable (a car for capitalists) and rank it below an Audi or BMW. To be successful in the east, advertising also had to appeal to values of normality, order, discipline and modesty and to stress the intrinsic quality of a product. While commonplace in the west, advertisements which were based on sheer superlatives ('our product is the best') or portrayed a certain life-style in order to convey a subliminal message would deter consumers in the east (Hooper 2000a). Finally, a research psychologist even found evidence of fundamentally different approaches to problem-solving between east and west Germans: while easterners adopted more thorough, analytical methods, westerners demonstrated less patience but greater intellectual creativity (Strohschneider 1997).

RIGHT-WING EXTREMISM

Right-wing extremism in Germany is a heterogeneous phenomenon with various ideological directions. In a general sense, neo-Nazi values can be seen to be based on a sense of racial superiority (Aryanism) and the simple notion of a state ruled by a strong leader (*Führerstaat*). For tactical reasons certain extremist groups attach less overt significance to race, stressing instead the importance of the nation-state and downgrading the value of parliament and the need to separate legislative and executive powers. Variations of this authoritarian, anti-democratic theme appear in visions of a new 'nation', 'state' or 'Reich' (with strong associations of the racial and political values of the Third Reich). While some extremists claim to support the free market economy, others argue for economic protectionism and adopt a socialist, anti-capitalist line. Family or even religious values (either Christian or pagan) are occasionally evoked. What all these directions have in common is an underlying contempt for democratic liberalism and for the institutions that protect cultural and political pluralism; they also reject any notion of Germany as a multi-ethnic society.

Post-war Germany has experienced three phases of right-wing political extremism, although they show little continuity either in terms of organisation or the behaviour of voters. The first phase came with the electoral successes of the SRP (*Sozialistische Reichspartei*) which attracted many ex-Nazis after the war and gained up to 11 per cent of seats in regional elections before it was banned in 1952. The second phase was marked by the emergence of the NPD (*Nationaldemokratische Partei Deutschlands*) during the second half of the 1960s. Adopting a less aggressive rhetoric and apparently accepting the democratic institutions of post-war Germany, the NPD refused to acknowledge that the NSDAP was responsible for the Second World War, denied the reality of the Holocaust and called for an end to trials of Nazi war criminals. The party also demanded the return of German territory in the east and priority for Germans over foreigners in allocating employment. Despite the party's outward commitment to democracy, many of its leaders came from other extremist groups and its internal structures remained authoritarian. The NPD's membership grew from 13 700 in 1965 to 28 000 by the end of the decade and it overcame the 5 per cent electoral hurdle to enter several regional parliaments. Failure to gain seats in the 1969 *Bundestag* election dealt the party a serious blow, after which it lost members and was racked by internal division.

The third phase is characterised by an unusually large number of competing right-wing parties. Its origins can be traced to the founding of the *Deutsche Volksunion* (DVU) in 1971. Remarkably, the DVU was not a political party with an organised leadership and activists but a loose and rather passive network of subscribers to a right-wing newspaper, *Deutsche National-Zeitung*, which was published by the DVU's founder, Gerhard Frey. On the basis of this network, membership of the DVU rose from 5000 (1976) to 22 000 (1990) before falling to around 15 000 by 1998. The DVU, which held annual rallies in Passau, demanded the re-establishment of a 'Greater Germany', indulged in anti-foreigner rhetoric (often associating foreigners with rising crime levels) and denied Germany's guilt over the Second World War. Supporters were urged to vote for the NPD.

With the rise of a rival neo-Nazi party, the Republicans (*Die Republikaner* or REP), in 1987 Frey founded the *Deutsche Volksunion – Liste D*. As a formally constituted party the *DVU-Liste D* worked closely with the NPD until 1990. Despite a rather diffuse ideological programme and no significant organisation – its pamphlets were delivered, not by party activists, but by an advertising firm – it achieved considerable electoral successes in north Germany. In 1998 in the eastern state of Sachsen-Anhalt it gained 12.9 per cent of votes, a record for an extreme right-wing party in the history of post-war Germany. At the same time the Republicans, who emerged in 1983 as a splinter group of the Bavarian CSU, entered regional parliaments in Baden-Württemberg (1992 and 1996) and Berlin (1989) and also the European Parliament. During the 1990s membership of the Republicans fluctuated between 20 000 and

15 000. While the Republicans and the DVU were establishing themselves as political representatives of right-wing extremism, the NPD, recovering from internal conflicts and leadership changes, succeeded during the second half of the decade in boosting its membership in the eastern states. By mixing traditional racial and nationalist rhetoric with criticism of social conditions, especially unemployment, it attracted many young, disaffected easterners to its ranks, but found it hard to convert public demonstrations into electoral successes.

Despite a high public profile and successes in regional elections, the extremist parties in Germany have consistently failed to achieve an electoral breakthrough at national level or to build up a solid voter base – in contrast, for instance, to the *Front National* in France, which can regularly count on around 15 per cent of votes. The German parties are highly fragmented, often presenting rival candidates at elections, and they lack the internal party organisation to wage effective electoral campaigns (Pfahl-Traughber 1999: 37).

Strictly speaking, the neo-Nazi scene in Germany has rather different origins and aims from the extremist political parties, although there are personal links between the two groupings. While parties such as the NPD tactically accept and work within the democratic establishment, the neo-Nazis work to destroy it through pamphlets, propaganda, street actions and often violent demonstrations. During the 1970s and 1980s a number of national and regional neo-Nazi groupings emerged. By drawing heavily on the ideology and imagery of the Third Reich, they appealed strongly to young, unemployed, working-class males. Individual groups counted their membership in the hundreds rather than the thousands; they were prone to internal rivalries although some had links with like-minded organisations abroad, for example in the USA. The combined membership of neo-Nazi groupings is probably under 10 000 (Kaufman 1998: 135).

Despite the official view of the GDR regime that socialism had overcome the 'capitalist' vices of racialism and fascism, a neo-Nazi sub-culture was also active in the east before 1989. It manifested itself through the daubing of swastikas, the distribution of Nazi propaganda and the abuse of Jews and foreign workers. Unsurprisingly, the opening up of eastern Germany after unification provided fertile ground for western activists. The Bremen-based *Deutsche Alternative* (DA) extended its operations to the eastern states and became the largest neo-Nazi group with some 350 members. Especially active in Cottbus (Brandenburg), the group attracted even schoolchildren and sixth-formers before it was banned in 1992. Until his death from AIDS in 1991, the DA was led by Michael Kühnen, a member of the NPD in the 1970s and an effective organiser and propagandist. Exploiting economic and social disaffection, eastern neo-Nazi groups, commonly known as 'skinheads', adopted an anti-capitalist rhetoric. They dominated youth clubs, streets and areas around railway stations in many parts of eastern Germany, claiming these as 'free spaces where we can practically take power and can administer punishment to deviants and enemies' (quoted in *The Guardian*, 2 September 2000: 21). Alarmed authorities reacted by banning neo-Nazi organisations and their demonstrations, while the courts imposed prison sentences for Nazi-related crimes. The groups responded by developing informal networks of communication throughout Germany. Using modern technology such as mobile phones, e-mail and the internet they shared information and co-ordinated activities and marches. Large public demonstrations, attracting between 2 000 and 4 000 neo-Nazis, were staged in München (1997), Passau, Leipzig and Rostock (1998). Monitoring units in the EU and in Germany reported a sharp proliferation of websites propagating racism and anti-Semitism; of more than 2 100 such sites in the world, 300 were registered in Germany at the beginning of 1999, rising to 800 by the end of 2000 (Black 2000; Jansen 2000a).

A key element of the neo-Nazi scene has been the sub-culture of violence associated with skinheads. Skinhead culture originated during the late 1960s among young unemployed in the East End of London and appeared a decade or so later in both East and West Germany. Skinheads draw heavily on the icons of National Socialism (Adolf Hitler, swastikas and uniforms), profess interest in Germanic and Viking culture, are aggressively racist and distribute songs and propaganda material with a violent and anti-Semitic content. Over half of Germany's skinheads are now active in the eastern states. However, direct violence, especially against immigrant foreigners but also against Jews, the disabled and the homeless, has appeared to be less a politically co-ordinated activity than to emanate from disparate groups of individuals. Skinheads have generally proved difficult to mobilise in any organised way for the right-wing cause, although the potential for this is clearly present. Parties such as the NPD, anxious to avoid an official prohibition, are also wary of becoming openly associated with street violence (Jansen 2000b).

In the decade after unification the youth wing of the NPD made a determined effort to recruit young easterners; by 2000 the party had gained a prominent following in the new federal states. Skinheads appear to be working-class unemployed males under 20, who drink heavily and cultivate an anti-female chauvinism. During the early 1990s, studies by a Trier-based research group attempted to shed more light on the skinheads' background and motives (Pfahl-Traughber 1999: 69–72). While violent acts were indeed committed by groups (not individuals) comprising mainly poorly educated males under 18, the majority of perpetrators were employed and came from both working- and middle-class backgrounds. Nevertheless, there was a clear link between unemployment and membership of skinhead groups. A follow-up study showed that the proportion of skinheads over 30 years old was rising and that this age-group was also more likely to be unemployed, criminally active, and politically organised (Pfahl-Traughber 1999: 65–71). The extreme right chalked up its first political success in the east in 1998 when the DVU entered the regional parliament of Sachsen-Anhalt, which has the lowest proportion of foreigners in Germany but the highest rate of joblessness.

Right-wing violence against foreigners escalated sharply after unification, rising from around 300 recorded incidents in 1990 to over 2 200 in 1993 and over 11 700 offences during the first ten months of 2000 (Jansen 2000c). A remarkable feature is that the scale of overt racism in the eastern states is not in proportion to the actual numbers of foreign residents: in 1993 in Brandenburg, for instance, where just over 1 per cent of the population were non-German, there were 77 attacks for every 10 000 foreigners, while Hamburg, with a foreign population of just under 14 per cent, experienced only 10 incidents. In the decade after unification the annual incidence of right-wing violence in the east was three or four times higher than in the west, measured in terms of the size of population (Bedürftig 1998: 161; Jansen 2000a/c). While attacks on immigrants are concentrated in the east, anti-Semitic incidents are more evenly distributed throughout Germany (Hooper 2000b).

The wave of violence against foreigners began with the murder of a 28-year-old Angolan in Eberswalde (Brandenburg) in 1990. It continued with attacks on refuges for asylum-seekers in Hoyerswerda (Sachsen) in September 1991 and notably Rostock (Mecklenburg-Vorpommern) in August 1992, where a hostel for Vietnamese was besieged for five days during race riots while sympathetic onlookers applauded and the police stood idly by. The violence reached a high point in western Germany when an immigrant Turkish grandmother and two children died in an arson attack in Mölln (November 1992); in a similar attack in Solingen (May 1993) two Turkish women and three girls died and two children were seriously injured. Chancellor Helmut Kohl's failure to visit the site of the atrocities suggested political indifference at the highest level and harmed Turkish–German relations. Germany's international standing was not helped by the fact that while most of the perpetrators were caught and sentenced to long prison sentences, others were treated with leniency. In the worst racist attack in Germany since the war, 10 immigrants and asylum-seekers died in an inferno in their homes in Lübeck in 1996. By 2000 the scale of violence, which included attacks on individuals and synagogues and a bombing in Düsseldorf, prompted the Chancellor (now Gerhard Schröder) to announce a crackdown on the far-right. The government was especially concerned that racism in the east was hampering Germany's integration in the global economy and would deter specialist foreign workers from moving to Germany. Several neo-Nazis were convicted and a ban on the NPD was considered. Bans are considered a last resort in Germany: apart from posing questions of civil liberties, they run the risk of driving far-right organisations underground, making surveillance harder and even increasing their attractiveness to young people on the fringes of society.

Shocked at the scale and ferocity of the atrocities, many Germans held processions, demonstrations and 'chains of light' (*Lichterketten*) to express their solidarity with the foreign population: 350 000 marched in Berlin on 8 November 1992 and similar events took place in other German cities. On 9 November 2000, the anniversary of the *Kristallnacht* when attacks on Jewish businesses, property and synagogues heralded the beginning of the Holocaust in 1938, Chancellor Gerhard Schröder led a rally of 200 000 in Berlin. The rally was designed to show the world that the current wave of racism was not the true face of modern Germany, which remained a humane, tolerant and open-minded country.

FOREIGNERS

Although Germany long refused to acknowledge itself as a land of immigration (*Einwanderungsland*), it has attracted many refugees and foreign workers and currently houses a sizeable proportion (8.8 per cent) of foreign residents, nearly half of whom have been living there for ten years or more (see Chapter 2 which outlines the economic and political conditions that have governed the country's principal population flows since 1945). Issues surrounding foreigners in Germany do not just derive from the size of the foreign population but also from official policy on citizenship and from social attitudes to integration.

Unlike the UK or the USA, Germany has, for most of the twentieth century, defined nationality not by place of birth, but by blood descent (James 1998: 9). The link between ethnicity and national identity, which goes back to a law of 1913, is therefore historically established in the German mind. However, the link has come under question as the birth-rate among Germans has declined at the same time as the number of foreign residents has increased. Indeed, if we include ethnic Germans from the former Soviet Union and south-eastern Europe, the volume of incomers is projected to rise by almost 5 million by 2010 (Bedürftig 1998: 128). These estimates may even be conservative: between 1991 and 1998 alone, 8.8 million people moved to Germany, including ethnic Germans, asylum-seekers, immigrant workers and refugees from civil wars. An important and controversial issue has been whether foreigners who have lived and worked in Germany for many years could acquire German nationality: only in 2000 did those born in Germany of foreign parents gain the automatic right to citizenship. In practice, each category of incomer, whether ethnic German or migrant worker, has been admitted to the Federal Republic under quite different laws and regulations.

In the decade after unification, naturalisation law in Germany was subject to a number of changes which were designed to improve the rights of long-standing foreign residents and to integrate children of migrants born in Germany. From 1 January 2000 adult applicants could apply for German citizenship if they had been resident in Germany for eight years (compared with 15 beforehand) and were able to satisfy a number of preconditions: they must have good mastery of the German language, swear loyalty to the Basic Law, have no criminal convictions and be able to support themselves and their families. They must also renounce their former nationality since dual citizenship is not permitted, although exceptions to this may be made. Naturalisation is subject to payment of a fee of 500 DM. Children born of a foreign parent who has been residing in Germany for eight years automatically gain citizenship, thus replacing the principle of nationality through ethnic descent (*Abstammungsprinzip*) by that of place of birth (*Prinzip des Geburtsorts*). Such children have until the age of 23 to decide on whether or not to take German nationality.

Despite measures designed to ease naturalisation, the end of the 1990s saw a continuing debate about the need for a modern, harmonised immigration law. Government plans to recruit 20 000 computer specialists from abroad in order to overcome an acute shortage of information technology professionals added fuel to the discussion. The so-called 'green card' scheme, which came into effect in 2000, allowed computer experts to live and work in Germany for up to five years provided they had a university degree or the offer of a job paying an annual salary of at least 100 000 DM. Although the scheme helped to remove public perceptions of foreigners as a burden to the state, it still assumed that its beneficiaries were essentially guestworkers who would be expected to return home after five years (Hooper 2000b). Germany's economic need for immigrants with specific skills must be seen against the background of a steadily declining ratio of wage-earners to pensioners. As a population study published by the United Nations in 2000 revealed, the annual number of immigrants needed in Germany to support pensioners at current levels was estimated at 3.6 million until 2050: this compared with 1.8 million for the UK and a staggering 13.5 million for the EU as a whole (Steele 2000).

While most political parties in Germany agreed that numbers of immigrants should be controlled, views on how this should be achieved varied widely. In 1998 the FDP proposed a fixed quota on numbers and categories of immigrants. The quota would be reviewed every two years by a commission of representatives from government, parliament, the churches and other interest groups. Openly stating that Germany currently admitted too many foreigners it did not need and too few it did, the FDP explicitly linked the quota to national economic requirements. Although the right to asylum would be retained, the number of refugees admitted would have to come out of the quota. Rejecting any notion of a quota (which might anyhow violate agreements with the European Union), the Greens argued that asylum-seekers, alongside spouses and children of foreigners already in Germany, had a legal right to citizenship under the Basic Law and under international agreements on refugees.

While the FDP and Greens at least adopted clear positions, the CDU was divided. The party's conservative wing (in particular the Bavarian CSU) insisted on strict controls for incomers and on subordinating an individual's right to asylum to a law on immigration. Ignoring warnings of inflaming xenophobia, they pressed for immigration to be a campaign issue and even introduced a racial element into the debate: this emerged, for example, in the CDU's controversial slogan 'children not Indians' (*Kinder statt Inder*) during a regional election in Nordrhein-Westfalen and in the call for immigration policy to be based on the 'centrality of German culture' (*deutsche Leitkultur*). Shortly after the new naturalisation law came into effect, CSU-controlled Bayern added a written language test for applicants which was not envisaged in the federal law and was widely seen as an administrative measure to exclude would-be immigrants. On the other hand, liberals in the CDU argued for a fair balance between admitting asylum-seekers on humanitarian grounds and recruiting specialist workers to meet shortfalls in skills. While the SPD appeared to regard an immigration law as unnecessary, it moved away from the historical (and increasingly untenable) position that Germany was not a land of immigration. No party committed itself to a specific figure for a ceiling on immigrants, although around 600 000 entered annually in 1997 and 1998, which as a percentage of the population was less than that for Luxemburg, Switzerland and Belgium but more than that for France or the UK (Krupa 2000).

Issue of asylum

After the persecutions of the Third Reich had forced many refugees from Germany to seek shelter abroad, the FRG incorporated the right to asylum in its Basic Law (article 16) and was fairly liberal in its implementation. In the period between 1972 and 1975, for example, between 22 per cent and 40 per cent of up to 9 600 applicants a year were granted asylum (Statistisches Bundesamt 1997: 43). Many were refugees from communist states in eastern Europe and were given refugee status more or less automatically. After 1975, however, sharply rising numbers of applicants from poor third world countries together with fears of an influx of 'economic refugees' at a time of economic recession prompted Germany to adopt a more restrictive approach to asylum policy and to change its admission procedures. Asylum-seekers were no longer allowed to work while their applications were being processed (the ban applied for one year to east Europeans and two years to others) and welfare benefit was issued as vouchers instead of cash payments; the application process was also accelerated. Nevertheless, the number of asylum-seekers rose to almost 440 000 in 1992, of whom 4.3 per cent were admitted. Although the increase was unconnected to German unification, it coincided with unprecedented numbers of eastern Germans migrating to the west. In 1993 the main political parties agreed a new asylum law which automatically turned away applicants from designated safe countries (these included all states sharing a border with Germany) and made special transitional arrangements for refugees fleeing the civil war in Yugoslavia. Thereafter the number of applicants fell dramatically (to 128 000 in 1995). Critics argued that these measures violated the fundamental and individual right to asylum under the Basic Law; in some cases church members sheltered asylum-seekers illegally with the tacit approval of the authorities.

Integration of foreigners

Four decades after the first guestworkers arrived in the FRG, mainly from Turkey, Italy, Greece, Spain and the former Yugoslavia, migrant workers still found themselves performing less well-paid or prestigious jobs compared with Germans. At first they encountered problems of social integration which were generally put down to language difficulties and prejudices on the part of the Germans. The second generation of children born of guestworker parents and educated and trained in Germany was expected both to enjoy greater access to the job market and to experience fewer difficulties of integration.

Expectations of a progressively well-integrated population of immigrant workers have in many respects been borne out, although significant structural differences between the social status of foreigners and Germans remain. Surveys carried out between 1984 and 1995 (Seifert 1997) show that the proportion of foreigners in unskilled and semi-skilled jobs fell from 70 per cent to 55 per cent (the proportions for Germans were 16 per cent and 11 per cent) while the number entering skilled or salaried positions or setting up their own business rose from 30 per cent to 45 per cent (the figures for Germans were 73 per cent and 80 per cent). Reflecting the broadly favourable trend in terms of quality of employment for foreigners, the differential between native Germans and foreign workers has narrowed slightly. For second generation foreigners the picture is even more positive, with 73 per cent gaining better positions in 1995 and climbing slowly up the job hierarchy, although relatively more Germans were still found in middle-ranking and senior salaried posts. Female foreign workers enjoyed a similar improvement, although a high percentage (65 per cent) were still engaged in menial and unskilled work; more foreign women than men were employed part-time and they tended to earn less, partly because they had lower qualifications. Turkish workers remain at the bottom of the scale but are steadily improving their prospects (the proportion in unskilled work fell from 78 per cent to 57 per cent). As for type of work, it is still the case that most foreigners (especially Turks) are employed in industry and manufacturing (50 per cent in 1995) while Germans predominate in the service sector, trade and commerce, welfare and the civil service (60 per cent). A similar pattern is found for second generation foreigners, although these are increasingly entering jobs in welfare and state services.

Difficulties with the German language, which have a profound effect on social integration, are largely a feature of first generation foreign workers, although second generation women and Turks continued to show a below average linguistic competence. Many German states provide voluntary tuition in the home language (mainly Turkish) for children of migrants, although some conservative politicians have demanded an end to the programme, claiming that foreign children would benefit more from exclusive teaching in German (Zurheide 2000). Somewhat worryingly, and despite the removal of the language barrier for foreigners born and educated in Germany, it appeared that after unification a rapid process of segregation set in, with all categories of foreigners reporting a decline in close social contacts with Germans. Inter-ethnic distance was particularly marked for Turks, of whom only one-third counted a German among their friends. Although Germany is the chosen home and focal centre for most of its resident foreigners, subjective attitudes to the host country are not necessarily what one might expect. While in 1984 less than one-third of migrants declared an intention to remain long-term in Germany, the figure had risen to 47 per cent by 1995; at the same time almost none had made concrete plans to return to their native country in the near future. Notably after 1991 the proportion of second generation foreigners claiming to wish to stay permanently in Germany fell slightly (from 59 per cent to 52 per cent in 1995). When asked to comment on whether they felt German, only 11 per cent of migrants reported that they did. As might be expected, significantly more second generation migrants identified with the host culture, although even here the proportion fell from 30 per cent to 21 per cent between 1991 and 1995. Surprisingly, relatively few foreigners have taken advantage of improved opportunities, especially for young people, to acquire German nationality: in 1994 around 86 per cent of migrants were entitled to claim citizenship, only 18 per cent considered doing so (Seifert 1997: 587–8). Progress on integration of the foreign community in terms of work and income thus contrasted with increasing social segregation and a lack of self-identification with the culture of the host country. The surge in right-wing extremism after 1990 must surely be at least partly responsible for this. Another factor may be a growing confidence and self-awareness within ethnic communities as they become economically more securely established.

Research into attitudes of native Germans towards foreigners also suggests that significant changes have occurred since unification (Böltken 1997). In the former FRG a large minority of Germans were positively disposed to closer integration (46 per cent), with most of the rest indifferent (35 per cent) and only relatively few hostile to the idea (19 per cent). Within two years of unification the proportion supporting integration fell and the percentage rejecting it rose (to 24 per cent). These shifts took place at a time when Germany's eastern borders were opening up to refugees and ethnic Germans who were widely perceived as placing an additional burden on an already strained housing and employment market; the public debate about economic migrants and misuse of the asylum law fuelled a popular climate of anxiety about the numbers of foreigners.

Nevertheless, levels of scepticism towards foreigners in western Germany never reached those of the eastern states, where in 1992 less than a quarter of Germans supported integration, while 35 per cent rejected it and 42 per cent were indifferent (Böltken 1997: 432). Moreover, easterners' attitudes remained constant while westerners began to regain their readiness for integration after 1993. At the same time, it appears that it is not so much subjective or psychological factors which determine attitudes towards foreigners as different social conditions in east and west – and these are likely to persist for some time. Important factors are the degree of contact with foreigners, the proportion of foreigners in the neighbourhood, and whether foreigners are recent incomers or are already established in the community. Easterners' unwillingness to support integration or at best their indifference to it can be explained largely by their historical lack of experience with foreigners, another legacy of the GDR years.

East Germans' inexperience of foreigners long pre-dates unification. In the former GDR the foreign population amounted to just 1.2 per cent (191 000 in 1989), compared to 10 per cent in the FRG. During the 1950s relatively small numbers of students from developing countries visited the GDR on scholarships. Towards the end of the 1960s the GDR began to recruit foreign labour from 'friendly' socialist countries. Despite official lip-service given to international solidarity, migrant workers were kept isolated from the population and endured often miserable conditions: ghettoised in compounds, they rarely received their full wages (payment was settled directly between the GDR authorities and the home country), were given only minimal language training and were sent home if they became ill, had an accident or became pregnant. Efforts by local churches to overcome their isolation were viewed with distrust by the authorities. In 1989, 70 per cent of foreign workers were males aged between 20 and 40 years. Most came from Vietnam (60 000) and Poland (52 000), followed by Mozambique (14 000) and Cuba (10 000). Soon after the *Wende* most of the unskilled workers were sent home, leaving around 50 000 with residence permits. Those who stayed faced a precarious existence in a faltering economy and encountered the full force of xenophobia and resentment from Germans competing for jobs. In contrast to western Germany, where NATO troops from foreign countries could fraternise freely with Germans, contact between east Germans and the 450 000 members of the Soviet armed forces had always been minimal: Russian soldiers were forbidden personal contacts with Germans and were rarely seen in public (Kettenacker 1997: 225; Schroeder 1998: 583).

Apart from the absence of contact with foreigners, other explanations for the general tolerance of relatively high levels of right-wing violence in the east have been advanced. They include: an authoritarian mentality nurtured from nursery days and reinforced throughout the school system; indoctrination to hate the 'class enemy' (*Klassenfeind*), in particular western countries; anti-Polish feelings fostered by the state in response to the 'Solidarity' reform movement in the early 1980s; and the culture of militarism promoted in the National People's Army (*Nationale Volksarmee*, NVA) and in the numerous socialist organisations of the old GDR. Despite the popular and spontaneous surge towards political freedom during the *Wende*, these factors no doubt helped to undermine a disillusioned population's capacity to embrace feelings of social tolerance and democracy when the promised 'blooming landscapes' of prosperity failed to materialise (Jansen 2000a).

VERGANGENHEITSBEWÄLTIGUNG

The term *Vergangenheitsbewältigung* ('overcoming the past') entered the post-war German vocabulary to denote the complex and often controversial process of how Germans dealt with the enormity of the crimes against humanity committed by the Nazis during the Third Reich. These crimes are widely equated with the Holocaust, or state-organised genocide of European Jews, but they also encompass forced labour, theft of goods and property, grievous bodily harm and the persecution of political opponents and other ethnic groups. The process of coming to terms with the past was conducted most thoroughly in West Germany. It was helped by the Federal Republic's claim on its foundation to be the sole legitimate successor of the Third Reich and its willingness to pay the latter's debts to foreign countries (Kettenacker 1997: 90). The GDR leadership, by contrast, eager to portray National Socialism as a purely western, capitalist phenomenon and its victims almost entirely as communists, pretended that East Germany rose out of a historical vacuum: their refusal to acknowledge any responsibility for the Nazi past or to permit an open public debate about it explains in part the resurgence of right-wing extremism in the eastern states. Austrians, too, found it convenient to portray themselves as victims of National Socialism rather than its accomplices, and it was not until the questionable wartime record of the Austrian President Kurt Waldheim was revealed in 1987 that a more open discussion began to take place there. *Vergangenheitsbewältigung* encompasses a number of issues: it means removing Nazi influences, punishing war criminals, accepting responsibility for the Nazi past and recompensing the survivors, and keeping younger generations informed about the past in order to ensure that history does not repeat itself (Kaufman 1998: 124). Some of these issues are addressed in the following section.

First, it is worth observing that the singular brutality of the Nazi regime and the scale of conflict that it unleashed continue to inspire debate on how Hitler as an individual was able to achieve and retain power in a modern industrial and well-educated European state like Germany. Hitler's immediate rise to power was no doubt due to the shortcomings of the Weimar system and the popular appeal of a 'strong leader' at a time of national crisis; the weakness and tolerance of the western powers also enhanced his domestic standing immediately after 1933. But such reasons are largely negative and fail to explain how Hitler was so successful in consolidating and retaining his position among the German people, despite the setbacks of the War.

It is possible to see Hitler as a product of wider historical and social movements within Europe, in particular as the final link in a historical chain of aggressive acts by Germany against its European neighbours. Arguing from an ideological point of view and partly to avoid accepting responsibility for undermining Germany's pre-1933 democratic order, the communists, on the other hand, simply linked the appearance of fascism with imperialistic capitalism. Some historians see Hitler, together with the German people, as victims of their own myth of the all-powerful leader, a 'messiah offering redemption to a fallen nation' (Cesarani 2000). They point to how Hitler was allowed to use power by those around him and to the fact that many initiatives and policies of the National Socialists originated lower down the ranks of his admirers (Kershaw 1999). As well as analysing how the regime selectively deployed its terror against unpopular groups, historians have also sought some explanation for the widespread indifference to the fate of the Jews on the part of the population as a whole and the conservative opposition to Hitler (Cesarani 2000). Although it may be possible fully to understand Hitler and his rise to power only in the wider context of German history and politics, the fascination with the individual and his exploitation of authority remains. The German historian Joachim Fest, for instance, perceives Hitler as a individual who passed through a number of stages during his political career but was finally motivated by a pathological desire to use the German people in order to wage war for its own sake in a constant, Darwinistic struggle of the species (Fest 1999).

For many Germans after the Second World War, any possible motivation to come to grips with the fact that National Socialism was a fundamentally criminal regime was hampered by the fact that the allies were determined to impose a programme of denazification and re-education agreed at the Potsdam Conference (see Chapter 1). In the first Nuremberg War Trials (November 1945–October 1946), 12 leading Nazis were sentenced to death and 3 to life imprisonment. Later trials, which ended in 1949, resulted in convictions for leaders of Nazi organisations, industrialists, members of the army, doctors and lawyers. In the western zones over 5 000 were tried and sentenced, including 806 to death and many more to terms of imprisonment. In the event 486 executions were carried out and most prisoners were amnestied as the Cold War set in. Three organisations (the Nazi leadership, the Gestapo and the SS) were judged to be criminal. The trials amassed a huge volume of evidence documenting the Third Reich's crimes against humanity (for an overview of the trials and the wider denazification process see Kettenacker 1997: 16–18).

At the time Germans tended to dismiss the trials as justice dispensed by the victors (*Siegerjustiz*): German judges played no role, certain crimes (such as 'crimes against peace') were retrospectively devised and atrocities committed by the allies were excluded. Preoccupied with economic reconstruction most ordinary Germans failed to see the Nuremberg trials as providing any impetus to get to grips with the past and to engage in personal or national *Vergangenheitsbewältigung.* According to some, the denazification process suffered from being a bureaucratic procedure which was conducted with different degrees of rigour in each occupation zone and which provoked resentment and reactions of self-defence rather than induced individuals to reflect on their attitude towards the Third Reich. At any rate the past became a taboo issue, allowing many former Nazis to reach leading positions in politics, business, medicine, academic life and the judiciary (for an alternative view see Kettenacker 1997: 18). The pattern was exemplified by the career of Hans Globke, an architect of anti-Jewish laws during the Third Reich and senior figure in Adenauer's government until he was exposed by the GDR in 1963. Membership of the Nazi Party did not, for example, prevent Kurt-Georg Kiesinger from becoming Federal Chancellor (1966–69). Although the Soviet Union conducted a more rigorous process of denazification than the western allies, many former Nazis also reached high positions in the GDR.

As part of a wider process of social and political change in West Germany, a significant shift in attitudes towards the Nazi past did not start to take place until the mid-1960s. The younger generation began to break down the wall of silence and to ask questions of the older generation. The process was helped by the first of a series of laws (1965) that eventually removed the statutory period of limitation (*Verjährung*) on murder, including genocide. These laws enabled the central office for war crimes at Ludwigsburg to pursue a number of ex-Nazis who had committed atrocities during the war, notably in concentration camps. So-called Auschwitz trials had taken place since 1958. The largest, which lasted from 1963 until 1965, involved prosecutions against 20 figures and resulted in several life sentences. The large body of evidence and the horrific nature of the crimes did much to lift the veil of ignorance about the past that was threatening to bury any prospect of *Vergangenheitsbewältigung*. A similar trial against the Auschwitz doctor Horst Fischer was held in 1966 in the GDR. Such trials did much to counter attempts by right-wing extremists to deny the reality and scale of Nazi genocide. Despite the overwhelming physical and documentary evidence of the Holocaust, apologists for the Third Reich would exploit inconsistencies in eye-witnesses' recollections of events or gaps in written records in order to cast doubt on the authenticity of the crimes. In 1994 the Federal Constitutional Court ruled that dissemination of the 'Auschwitz lie' was unlawful.

While not questioning the factual basis of the Holocaust, the ultra conservative German historian Ernst Nolte unleashed in 1986 a fierce controversy by arguing that the Nazi genocide was an aberration but not a unique crime in human history. According to Nolte, National Socialism was a reaction to Russian Bolshevism and its crimes should be viewed in the context of the mass murders that were also committed on a similar scale in the Soviet Union. Nolte appeared to be trying to lift the burden of a unique, almost racial guilt from the German people and to restore their national pride. In what came to be known as the 'historians' dispute' (*Historikerstreit*) opponents attacked him for making what they saw as an unnecessary and inappropriate effort to play down the nature and methods of the Hitler regime (for a discussion of the issues see Kaufman 1998: 130–1). In later claiming that Hitler had 'rational' reasons for attacking the Jews, denouncing the 'collective accusation' levelled at Germany since 1945 and in declaring that Germans should 'leave behind the view that the opposite of National Socialist views is always right', Nolte emphasised his proximity to the far-right and continued to attract criticism (Paterson 2000b). The debate about a collective German guilt – or at least a wider complicity in the crimes of the Nazis – was also fanned by a book by Daniel Goldhagen, *Hitler's Willing Executioners* (1996), in which he argued that many thousands of Germans assisted the Nazis either directly or indirectly through apathy, fear, indifference or even self-interest (Kaufman 1998: 136–7).

Since the Auschwitz trials of the 1960s, a succession of films, media events and publications have kept the issue of Nazi crimes against humanity (especially Jews) very much alive in the German mind. In 1979 German television broadcast the American serial *Holocaust*, a dramatisation of the lives and fates of Jewish victims of the persecution. In 1993 Steven Spielberg's film *Schindler's List* was released: based on true events during the Second World War, the film portrayed how the German businessman Oskar Schindler, motivated initially by profit, set up a factory to exploit cheap Jewish labour in Nazi-occupied Poland but ended up by rescuing over 1100 Jews from certain death in the gas chambers of Auschwitz. There are also numerous museums, exhibitions and sites of historical interest throughout Germany that are dedicated to keeping alive the memory of the Third Reich. To name but a few, these include the Jewish Museum in Berlin, the 'Topography of Terror' exhibition on the site of the former Gestapo headquarters uncovered after the fall of the Berlin Wall, and the concentration camps Buchenwald, Bergen-Belsen, Dachau, Sachsenhausen and Ravensbrück, all of which are preserved as memorials. To these may be added institutions such as the Centre for Research into Anti-Semitism at the Technical University of Berlin and the Moses Mendelssohn Centre in Potsdam. The provision and maintenance of these memorials and centres are largely in the hands of the federal states and there have been recent calls for a more co-ordinated and centralised approach to managing the legacy of the Third Reich in order to meet the need for ongoing education of forthcoming generations (Dittberner 2000). Although the Third Reich has been on schools' syllabuses since the 1960s, widespread ignorance of the Nazi genocide, especially but not exclusively in the eastern states, continues to generate concern (Salzen 2000).

An important element of *Vergangenheitsbewältigung* has been the readiness of (West) German governments to compensate victims of Nazi persecution. In the so-called Luxemburg agreement, concluded in 1952 with Israel, the FRG agreed to recompense European Jews for crimes suffered during the Hitler period. Thereafter it made large annual payments to Israel and also to the Jewish Claims Conference, which represents Jews outside Israel. Similar agreements with other states followed during the 1960s (Benz 1989: 49; Kettenacker 1997: 90). By making these agreements and by assuming responsibility for the crimes of the Third Reich, West Germany greatly enhanced its moral standing in the world and gained the sole right to represent German interests internationally. The policy was part and parcel of Konrad Adenauer's strategy of re-integrating Germany into the western world.

In late 1999 final agreement was reached on an outstanding issue of compensation: a framework of restitution for the million or so people, mainly from eastern and central Europe, who were forced to work as slave labour in German industry for the Nazi war machine. The fund was originally proposed by German companies wanting to expand in the USA but fearful of legal actions mounted against them by American lawyers acting on behalf of the victims of the forced labour policy. Approximately half of the proposed fund of 10 billion DM would be met by the companies and half by the German government. Negotiators faced particular difficulties in deciding how to allocate the compensation to the various categories of forced labour: around 240 000 Jewish 'slave labourers', for instance, worked under markedly harsher conditions than non-Jewish 'forced labourers'. Apart from international agreements and official programmes of compensation, individual Germans also participated in acts and schemes of reconciliation. An example is the *Aktion Sühnezeichen* (Operation Atonement) which began in the 1950s by sending young Germans to act as volunteers in Israel and promote understanding between the two nations (Kaufman 1998: 131).

Another form of compensation for past persecution is the liberal policy applied by the German government towards Jews wanting to settle in Germany. Jewish immigrants enjoy preferential treatment similar to incoming ethnic Germans. Many are settled in Berlin and the larger cities of eastern Germany, where they receive a six-month language course and enjoy full access to health and welfare benefits. As a result the Jewish population, which was virtually wiped out between 1933 and 1945, increased dramatically during the decade after unification. In this period over 60 000 Jews entered from the former Soviet Union, escaping poor economic conditions and anti-Semitism there and tripling the size of the Jewish community in Germany. After the USA and Israel, Germany became the most popular destination for Jewish immigrants, and Berlin in particular recovered its pre-war status as the centre of Jewish life and culture, with many Jewish cafes, clubs and shops opening in the east of the city. Before the war Berlin was home to around 140 000 Jews; of these 55 000 were deported and murdered, 80 000 fled Germany and 7000 survived to re-emerge in 1945. By 2000 the number had recovered to 11 000 affiliated Jews (registered members of the official Jewish Community) with possibly as many more who were non-affiliated. Liberal immigration policies and economic attractions are likely to ensure that Germany continues to act as a magnet for east European Jews, despite the rise of far-right activities throughout the country. Although anti-Semitic incidents attract considerable attention in Berlin, the volume of anti-Semitic acts in the capital is relatively low (for a history of Jewish Berlin see Roth and Frajman 1998).

ROLE OF THE FAMILY

The bourgeois image of the two-generation nuclear family, with the breadwinner husband away during the day and the mother caring for the children at home, emerged during the eighteenth century and remained an ideal of family life for the next two centuries. In practice the ideal was true for only some middle-class families: most working-class mothers were compelled to take jobs in order to supplement the family income. Nevertheless the ideal was strongly propagated, especially but not exclusively, by the church and politically conservative circles: workers' organisations also supported their campaign for higher wages for men on the grounds that this would allow their wives to devote more time to their families. During the Second World War, Nazi propaganda maintained the image of the ideal German mother and housewife, although many women worked in factories and other services as part of the war effort. After 1945 an acute shortage of employment helped to restore the traditional ideal, despite the well-known pictures of women clearing up the rubble of war-damaged cities (*Trümmerfrauen*). In 1950, 76 per cent of all mothers in the FRG were full-time housewives (Nave-Herz 1998: 202). From the late 1960s onwards, social, economic and cultural changes, including the rise of the women's movement and a widening of educational and vocational opportunities, heralded far-reaching changes for the structure and role of the family in west German society.

In different ways and for different reasons both East and West Germany propagated an ideal of the family and, in particular, the mother. As a matter of state policy the GDR promoted the 'socialist family', partly to expand the labour force and partly to integrate the family within an ideologically controlled society. Husband and wife in this ideal family were committed socialists and loyal to the state, while the children were brought up to respect socialist ideals and join the official youth organisations. Through financial incentives, access to better housing and extensive crèche facilities, East German mothers, unlike their western counterparts, were encouraged to work while also having a family. The fact that divorced women were not automatically entitled to financial state support increased the pressure to work outside the home. As a rule mothers in the east married and bore more children earlier than in the west; on average only 5 per cent of GDR women were childless compared with 23 per cent in the FRG (Nave-Herz 1998: 203). Families in both East and West Germany tended to form nuclear units inasmuch as they would cultivate close relations with selected individuals rather than the wider, extended circle of relatives. Before the *Wende* it was assumed that the family in the GDR represented an area of privacy and escape for people retreating from an intrusive state, but it later emerged that the secret police widely recruited individuals to spy on immediate family members.

Towards the end of the 1960s certain demographic trends set in that affected the nature and structure of family life. They were brought about partly by greater economic prosperity and partly by changing social attitudes. Among West Germans the number of formal marriages and the birthrate declined, while people married later in life, had fewer children, and divorced more readily (although marriages lasted longer on average than in the GDR). Longer periods spent in full-time education and changes in the role of women and in sexual behaviour led to more relationships being conducted outside marriage; the term *Lebensgemeinschaft* was coined to denote this mode of living, which achieved a legal and civil status. Single parenthood also became more common. As the number of multi-generation households declined, that of single-parent families rose (Nave-Herz 1998: 205–6). The process has been described in terms of a move towards greater individualisation in tune with modern needs. It was less marked in the FRG than in the former GDR inasmuch as life in East Germany was more closely organised by the state and afforded young people less opportunity to experiment with individual life-styles and to break away from planned paths of education and career.

Despite a decline in the status of marriage as an institution and variations in the form that the family unit can take, the family remains the most important social entity for many Germans. A comparison of families in east and west shows that about one-third of people over 16 live with a marriage partner and with one or more children under the same roof (Statistisches Bundesamt 1997: 468). Figures for the proportions of single (7 per cent) and divorced (4 per cent) Germans, of childless couples (25 per cent), of partnerships outside marriage (around 10 per cent), and single parents (6 per cent) are broadly similar. Notable, however, was the sudden fall in the birth-rate in the east immediately after the *Wende*. This produced a lower percentage of eastern families with children under six by 1995 (7 per cent; 11 per cent in the west) and can be put down to the social upheaval of unification and the economic insecurity that followed. A measure of the impact that unification had on easterners was that, between 1990 and 1992, the number of marriages, births and divorces more than halved before gradually returning to more normal levels (Geißler 1998: 648).

Despite the short-term regional distortions produced by unification, it is true to say that for Germany, as a whole, family-based relationships continue to thrive. Young people, for instance, maintain a close and positive relationship with their parents and, spending longer in education and training, depend on them longer than earlier generations for material support: around one-third of Germans remain financially dependent on their parents beyond the age of 21. The dependency often continues after the children marry and leave home. At the same time, parents reaching old age can expect to be looked after by their family: only 10 per cent of parents needing care are placed in homes. Adults also help their parents in times of emergency, illness or in routine activities (shopping, washing, looking after the garden, etc.). The picture was similar in the former GDR and was not appreciably affected by unification. Surveys show that over 80 per cent of east German children report a positive relationship with their parents, especially their mother, to whom they will turn for advice on diverse matters, including politics. West Germans, especially males, tend to remain rather longer in the parental home than easterners (Nave-Herz 1998: 206–7).

Not only is the family a dominant social form in Germany, it also continues to enjoy a high prestige. When asked what they most value in their lives, 90 per cent of Germans of both sexes, in east and west, and of all ages, rate a happy marriage or partnership as being important, even above success in work, owning their own house or travelling. Having children enjoys a slightly lower priority, although 75 per cent of west Germans and over 80 per cent of easterners regard this as at least important in their lives, with women assigning it a higher value than men. Subjective perceptions of happiness are also related to relationships with others and family situations: divorced, separated and widowed people are more likely to feel lonely and dissatisfied with life; the same appears to be true for 'singles' and those raising children on their own (Statistisches Bundesamt 1997: 477–8). Women throughout Germany increasingly refer to the 'double burden' of maintaining a job and family, especially in view of the lack of child-support facilities in the form of nurseries and flexible working hours; even though such facilities were much more extensive in the former GDR, the problem of combining work with family had always existed for East German women.

WOMEN'S MOVEMENT

In the late 1960s the women's movement began to challenge the traditional division of gender roles, where housewives stayed at home, often to look after the children, while the male functioned as the breadwinner. From the outset feminists identified the right to pursue a career and access to abortion on demand (see below) as the keys to economic and social independence. From its foundation in 1980, the Green Party pioneered the adoption of a quota system, whereby at least 50 per cent of offices and parliamentary seats were reserved for women. The other parties followed suit with less stringent quota requirements in 1988 (SPD) and 1996 (CDU) (Pogunkte 1997: 514; Young 1998: 145). During the 1980s women were also beginning to assume positions of political responsibility in key government departments (notably finance, economy and internal affairs) alongside their more traditional areas of family, youth and culture. In 1999 female ministers headed the departments of justice, education, family, health and overseas development aid. Similarly, the proportion of female members of the *Bundestag* rose from 9.8 per cent in 1983 to 15 per cent in 1990, attaining 26.3 per cent in 1994 (compared with 50 per cent in Sweden and 10 per cent in the USA).

Despite its achievements the women's movement fragmented and declined in influence during the 1980s. Radical feminists, often academics, retained their focus on social protest and on representing women as victims of patriarchal political and economic structures. It was widely felt that feminists failed, notably in Germany during the 'backlash' years of the conservative Kohl government, to establish the lobby groups that could have exerted more effective political influence. German feminists also failed to present a united front during the unification debate, when it might have just been possible to extend to the west the gains made in the GDR, which had a liberal policy on abortion and had integrated women into the workforce as part of state policy. Although the Basic Law was amended in 1993 to commit the state to achieving sexual equality and removing existing disadvantages (article 3), the commission charged with reviewing the constitution after unification refused to alter the favourable tax status accorded to marriage, which some feminists saw as penalising women and children (Young 1998: 145). In other respects, however, women's rights were significantly enhanced. From 1991 a woman was no longer legally required to take her husband's name; in 1992 women were no longer prevented from doing night work; in 1993 it became harder for male-dominated professions to discriminate against women; in May 1996, after a 20-year campaign, marital rape became illegal; and in 1999 the government announced proposals to protect women from domestic violence and even to legislate for chore-sharing in the home (Traynor 1999a).

For many years women could play only a limited role in the German armed forces. Although the *Bundeswehr* recruited its first soldiers in 1956, women were confined to performing administrative tasks since the Basic Law prohibited them from active combat. From 1975 the army admitted female doctors, dentists and paramedics, who could volunteer as officers, and from 1991 women could enlist in musical regiments; the following year top sportswomen were able to join units dedicated to promoting sporting activities (*Sportfördergruppen*). After a young woman electronics engineer in 1996 challenged in court the limitations on women serving in the armed forces, the European Court of Justice ruled (in 2000) that such restrictions were discriminatory and violated EU law. In October 2000 the *Bundestag* amended national law, after which over 1900 women applied to enlist in the *Bundeswehr* as commissioned or non-commissioned officers. In January 2001 a total of 244 female recruits joined combat units, mainly in the army but also in the air force and navy. In opening up the armed forces to women Germany went even further than some other NATO countries, where women remained barred from infantry combat forces or from serving in submarines (Wickel 2000: 32–3; Krechtig 2001).

Political and legislative gains notwithstanding, the practical obstacles to women combining work with motherhood remained formidable. Many fathers continued to regard the mother as primarily responsible for home and children and pursued their careers during the critical period after childbirth. Surveys suggested that over 70 per cent of married women did all the household chores and that the unequal sharing of housework was the main cause of marital rows (Traynor 1999a). At the same time mothers, rather than fathers, appeared to reinforce the traditional role model by choosing to make full use of their entitlement to three years post-maternity leave (*Erziehungsurlaub*) and paid maternity benefit (Statistisches Bundesamt 1997: 217). From 1999 every child in Germany over three years old became legally entitled to a nursery place, although the opening times were rarely geared to accommodate normal working hours (as they had been in the former GDR).

Despite such hindrances women succeeded in playing a more active role in business. By the end of the 1990s one-third of new enterprises in Germany were being founded by women, often as a response to continuing barriers to promotion (the so-called 'glass ceiling') in organisations dominated by men. More women were found in leading positions in the media, both as programme presenters and in management. Overall, 61.8 per cent of German women between 15 and 64 years old were in employment, 3.7 per cent of these in positions of seniority. These figures compared well with other west European countries, being lower, for instance, than Denmark at 74.2 per cent and 3.7 per cent respectively, but much higher than Italy at 43.6 per cent and 0.6 per cent. They also represented a considerable improvement over 1960 levels, when only 47 per cent of West German women were employed. Although women were finding it easier to enter employment, problems of lower pay and the 'glass ceiling' to advancement persisted. In the western states the average hourly pay in 1999 was still only 76.9 per cent of that for a male, although at 89.9 per cent it was considerably higher in the east, where during the GDR-era women had long formed part of the core workforce and where wage levels were, anyhow, lower.

In contrast to the pioneering campaigns of the 1960s and 1970s it was clear that the new generation of feminists was focusing less on protest and more on devising practical life-styles that attempted to integrate motherhood, family and work. The 1990s in particular saw a dramatic growth in the appearance of support networks for women, from around 75 at the beginning of the decade to over 300 by 1999. Many of these networks were aimed at businesswomen, professionals and academics; some also catered for the disadvantaged and fringe groups. Most networks were international, although several were organised regionally throughout Germany and offered forums for advice and mentoring, as well as support in education and job-hunting. With women representing one-third of internet users, web-based support groups also increased in popularity (for a survey see Weingarten and Wellershoff 1999). Compared to the early campaigners, the new feminists appeared more pragmatic and realistic in their approach. Feelings of sisterly solidarity had given way to practical forms of co-operation with existing structures. Now women seemed determined to concentrate on tactical, professional advancement rather than campaign for a better world through a utopian 'feminist revolution'. Although women were increasingly entering politics and the professions, the strategy of compromise enabled some feminists to continue to regard the state and corporate business as inherently 'exclusionary' for women (Young 1998: 140).

After the Second World War women made significant, if not exactly rapid, progress towards narrowing the educational gap. While in 1950 only 19 per cent of women attended university, the figure had risen to 42 per cent in 1996 (48 per cent of students in their first semester were female); postgraduate studies still appear, however, to be dominated by men, with women accounting for only between 24 per cent and 33 per cent of doctorates and master degrees. The proportion of 20–24 year olds with a university or college entrance certificate is now equally balanced in terms of gender, as are numbers of girls and boys attending the *Realschule*; rather more girls (54 per cent) than boys attend the grammar school or *Gymnasium*. Marked gender differences exist, however, in patterns of vocational education, with girls favouring colleges (e.g. in the health sector) and boys following works-based training programmes and apprenticeships (Statistisches Bundesamt 1997: 69–72). A pyramid effect has also been noted, whereby the higher the educational level, the lower the proportion of women engaged as educational professionals: thus while 70 per cent of primary school teachers are female, the figure for university professors is only 3 per cent (Sharp and Flinspach 1995: 182). It is clear that, while secondary and to a large extent tertiary education has become more accessible to women, differences persist at the higher levels of provision and in terms of how men and women are able or willing to translate their qualifications into working opportunities.

ABORTION DEBATE

Paragraph 218 of the German penal code of 1871 made abortion for any reason a criminal offence, punishable by up to five years imprisonment. After 1919 left-wing campaigners pressed for the removal of all restrictions on abortion or for legal termination within the first 12 weeks of pregnancy. Nevertheless, not until 1927 was abortion permitted on medical grounds, for instance to save the mother's life. In 1972 the GDR passed a law permitting termination on demand up to three months after conception (the law was the only one openly opposed by conservatives in the tightly controlled East German parliament). The Federal Republic, by contrast, retained the more restrictive law of the Weimar Republic but extended the medical grounds on which abortion was allowed and adopted a relaxed approach on enforcement: prosecutions for abortion fell from an annual 1800 in 1960 to about 150 a year between 1972 and 1988 (Prützel-Thomas 1993). Supported by the SPD and FDP and opposed by the Roman Catholic Church and the CDU/CSU, women's groups in West Germany continued to campaign vigorously for unrestricted abortion on demand: a landmark in the campaign occurred in 1971 when 374 women, including well-known actresses, openly declared in the magazine *Der Stern* that they had undergone an illegal abortion.

The pro-abortion campaign bore fruit in 1974 when, by a small parliamentary majority, the social-liberal coalition passed a law liberalising abortion along GDR lines. The following year, however, the Federal Constitutional Court (FCC) vetoed the legislation, ruling that the unborn child's right to life overrode a woman's entitlement to self-determination. At the same time, in a move which many regarded as an inappropriate entry into the political arena, the Court proposed ways in which abortion could be legalised. As a result the Abortion Reform Law of 1976 sanctioned termination if the mother was experiencing serious social hardship. Abortion was also allowed for medical or psychiatric reasons, or if the woman had been raped. By 1980 registered abortions rose to a record 87 000 in West Germany (14 per cent of the total births), 72 per cent of which were declared to be for reasons of social hardship. The actual figure was possibly twice as high, and in the GDR, whose population was barely 27 per cent of the FRG's, the figure was 92 000 or 37 per cent of births. In the FRG the number of abortions declined after 1982 with the return of a CDU/CSU-dominated government which, concerned about a falling birth-rate, introduced financial incentives to promote parenthood: in 1989 the official total was slightly over 75 000.

Unification re-ignited the abortion debate, especially in view of the fact that the quite different abortion laws of the FRG and the former GDR continued to apply in their respective territories. An all-German compromise emerged in 1992 which permitted termination during the first 12 weeks of pregnancy as long as the mother received prior counselling (provided by the state, the church or privately). The legislation, however, was again vetoed by the FCC, to which the CDU/CSU and the state of Bayern had appealed. In a curious decision the Court ruled that abortion, although not a punishable offence, remained contrary to law; the main consequence of this was that abortions undertaken for reasons of social hardship could not be paid for by the health service, which many saw as penalising the less well off. The Court also ruled that the aim of counselling should be the protection of the unborn, i.e. the mother should be persuaded to continue with the pregnancy. Modified to meet these conditions, the new legislation came into effect in 1996.

While east German women regarded the 1996 law as unduly restrictive (in the GDR abortion had been used virtually as a form of contraception), many in the west criticised what they regarded as intervention in the parliamentary process by a conservative and male-dominated FCC. Before the law came into force, registered abortions were running at around 74 000 a year in the old *Länder* and 24 000 (a marked reduction) in the east. Abortions in the west were also performed earlier during pregnancy than in the east; eastern women were also more likely to have already had a baby before termination (Statistisches Bundesamt 1997: 193–4).

After the 1996 ruling, a peace of sorts reigned over the abortion issue, disturbed abruptly in 1999 by the Vatican's controversial decision to disband the 270 counselling units maintained by the Catholic Church. Of the 1700 centres throughout Germany these advised more than 20 000 women every year, allegedly persuading around 5000 to continue their pregnancies. While the measure reflected the Vatican's consistent hostility to the 1996 abortion law and its provisions, the laity was unimpressed. A 'We Are the Church' movement had already emerged in 1995 to express opposition to the Church's conservatism on sexuality and birth control, and even leading clerics and prominent members of the Church supported private initiatives to continue the counselling service (Jeffery and Whittle 1997: 2; Traynor 1999b, Wensierski 2001).

THE CHURCH IN GERMANY

Religious life in Germany is dominated by the two major Christian churches. Over 28 million Germans are members of the Evangelical Church in Germany (*Evangelische Kirche in Deutschland* or EKD). Founded in 1948 as an umbrella organisation for Protestants throughout Germany (including the FRG and GDR), the EKD represents its members *vis-à-vis* the state and is governed by a synod (*Synode*) that is appointed by a council (*Rat*) and Conference of Churches (*Kirchenkonferenz*; Bedürftig 1998: 141). Some 27.5 million Germans belong to the Roman Catholic Church. A 72-member Conference of German Catholic Bishops (*Bischofskonferenz*) meets twice yearly (at different locations in the spring but always in Fulda in the autumn) to issue church laws and decrees, set up commissions and appoint representatives to Broadcasting Councils (*Rundfunkräte*) and other bodies. With origins dating back to 1848, the Bishops' Conference was officially recognised by the Vatican in 1966; it appoints a chairman every six years.

Despite the more or less equal numbers of Protestants and Catholics in the country as a whole, historical factors and the long anti-clerical tradition of the former GDR have produced major regional differences: while around 40 per cent of west Germans are Roman Catholic and an equal number Protestant, the ratio in the east is 5.3 per cent to 26 per cent. Between them the two churches account for 80 per cent of the population in the west but only around 30 per cent in the east. Although the constitution of the Weimar Republic (article 137) and the Basic Law of the FRG (article 1) eschewed the notion of an officially established state church, the two main Christian churches enjoy a privileged legal status as public institutions (*Körperschaften des öffentlichen Rechts*). This status entitles them, among other things, to tax revenue levied by the state. Other Christian churches in Germany include 13 orthodox denominations (1 million adherents) and numerous 'free' or non-conformist churches (*Freikirchen*; 400 000).

With 1.8 million members, Islam is the third largest religious community in Germany. Alongside the 60 000 or so Buddhists, organised Muslims are trying to gain a similar legal status as the main Christian churches. A small but growing Jewish community (80 000) represents a fraction of the number of Jews who lived in Germany before the Nazi persecution. A relatively recent phenomenon is the appearance in Germany of pantheistic or spiritually-orientated 'new age' movements outside the orthodox Christian tradition; often imported from the USA, they appeal primarily to younger adults. Alongside groupings such as Mormons and Jehovah Witnesses, such sects account for around 800 000 people. In the wake of public concern about fringe religious groups, a government commission of enquiry reported in 1998 on 'so-called sects and psycho-groups' (*Sogenannte Sekten und Psychogruppen*). The report commented critically on the small but active Scientology sect whose methods the Bavarian interior minister had vigorously denounced as hostile to the democratic state and which had been officially monitored by the federal agency responsible for the protection of the constitution. Members of sects could also be barred from state employment.

Christianity's long history in Germany is in part responsible for regional variations and national characteristics that persist to this day. For instance, the cultural differences between north and south Germany originate to some extent in the compulsory conversion of the northern tribes in the early Middle Ages compared with the generally peaceful adoption of Christianity further south. It has also been suggested that attitudes of political and civic sub-servience originated in the unity of temporal and spiritual power that was traditionally invested in the medieval feudal princes (Gabriel 1998: 373). Despite the forces for political change unleashed by the Reformation, Martin Luther, fearful of the threat to political and social order presented by the peasants' revolt, remained a strong supporter of the state. By establishing the principle that the ruler of a state automatically determined the religion of his subjects, the religious wars of the seventeenth century cemented the culture of subservience to state authority. The state-approved churches that emerged from this protracted conflict had quite different social constituencies. While Roman Catholicism remained influential in rural areas and small towns with long-standing folk traditions, Protestantism appealed to educated artisans and the rising middle classes in the larger cities.

The churches also responded differently to the social challenges of indus-trialisation during the nineteenth and twentieth centuries. Re-affirming its loyalty to Rome as the supreme religious authority, the Catholic Church established an organisation with hierarchical structures and a strong orienta-tion to the centre. Despite a firm sense of community as a faith, it singularly failed to appeal to an urban proletariat and bourgeoisie that was largely

indifferent to religion. It also remained hostile to the emerging socialist movement, preferring instead to support the forces of conservatism, although more
so in political than social matters. Protestantism identified more closely with
the newly unified national state and the monarchy than did the Catholic
Church and enhanced its political and economic status. At the same time the
Protestant churches were more regionally-orientated and maintained looser,
less formal structures than Roman Catholicism. They reacted to the social
challenges of industrialisation by developing notions of an 'inner mission'
and, along with the Catholic-orientated Centre Party in the *Reichstag*, supported Bismarck's pioneering programme of state-sponsored welfare.

Partly because of their traditional subservience to political authority
neither of the main churches was prepared for the progressive undermining
of this authority after the First World War or for its total usurpation by the
Nazis between 1933 and 1945 (Gabriel 1998: 373–4). Regarding Bolshevism as
a greater social danger than the Nazis, the Vatican concluded in 1933 a concordat with Adolf Hitler which guaranteed the religious rights of German
Catholics if the Church abstained from interference in politics. It soon became
clear, however, that Hitler wished to replace traditional Christianity and its
institutions by some Germanic form of religious worship within a state-
controlled National Socialist framework. When he continued to attack
Catholic institutions, the Vatican issued a general criticism of Nazi racial policies (1937), but its failure publicly and specifically to condemn the persecution of the Jews attracted censure after the War. The EKD's precursor, the
German Evangelical Church (*Deutsche Evangelische Kirche*) had been formed
in 1933 to bring together the various Protestant groups (Reformed, Lutheran
and United) that had remained divided for centuries, but the organisation
soon broke up after Hitler came to power. At first a strong pro-Nazi wing (the
Glaubensbewegung Deutscher Christen) allowed Hitler to gain control of the
Evangelical Church's leadership, although many Protestants increasingly
identified with the so-called 'witnessing church' (*bekennende Kirche*), an unofficial movement which from 1936 protested passively against the concentration camps and the murderous policies being pursued by the Nazis. Despite
their disapproval of National Socialism and acts of heroic resistance on the
part of individual clerics, neither of the two leading Christian churches
actively resisted the regime.

The aftermath of the Second World War profoundly affected the major
churches in East and West Germany. In the FRG, due to the loss of the mainly
Protestant areas in the east, Catholics and Protestants found themselves
numerically equal. Displacements of large sections of the population and
incoming refugees broke up many of the formerly close-knit religious communities. At this time the churches actually increased their congregations and
achieved a high official status in the newly founded Federal Republic. After
the moral bankruptcy of the Third Reich and the physical destruction of the
nation, the churches represented continuity and a return to civilised values:
of all the institutions which had survived the war the churches were seen to
have been the least compromised by association with the Nazis. Accorded

special status in the Basic Law (see above), they benefited financially as the state levied taxes on their behalf (the so-called church tax or *Kirchensteuer*; currently between 8 per cent and 9 per cent of total income tax, depending on the federal state). They assumed direct responsibility for compulsory religious education in schools and became major providers of social services alongside the state (the so-called dual system of welfare care). Propagating conservative social values based on service to society and the traditional family unit, the churches maintained their popularity and status until well into the 1960s. Few people formally left the church and many young people were closely integrated into religious life.

As part of a general move away from conservative, community-based social values and towards more individual, materially-orientated life-styles, the churches began to lose members towards the end of the 1960s. By 1973 congregations had fallen by one-third, with young people in particular deserting the church in record numbers. At the same time reforms in education reduced the role of religion in schools and the churches' influence on the major political parties weakened. The decline affected the Roman Catholic Church more than the Protestant, partly due to the relatively greater effect on the Catholic population of better education and a greatly expanded state welfare system. Towards the end of the 1970s the numbers leaving the churches rose less sharply than before, only to rise again at the end of the decade. Congregations declined steadily after the mid-1970s (although not so dramatically as before 1973–74) and increased in average age. Church attendance among the general population now appears to be highest for the key events in life, such as confirmation, first communion, baptism, marriage, death in the family, or a personal crisis. This suggests that individuals, while continuing to see religion as important, have become selective about what features of the established churches and their rituals they are prepared to integrate into their personal life-styles.

The Church in the GDR

In the GDR between 1949 and 1990 the churches developed under very different conditions from those in the west. Directly after the war relations between church and the Soviet occupiers were amicable. Confrontation came when the SED, which had no experience of exercising political power or working with churches, assumed leadership (Nowak 1995). Church taxes were abolished in 1956 and religious education banished from schools from 1958. The founding of the pan-German EKD in 1948 created particular difficulties for the SED, which pressurised church leaders into setting up a separate umbrella organisation for the GDR in 1968. The immediate trigger for this move was the churches' wish to provide pastoral care for the army (in the so-called *Militärseelsorgevertrag* of 1957 the West German government undertook to provide the framework and the finance for such care for the *Bundeswehr*).

After an initial period of tolerance the GDR regime from 1954 conducted a vigorous campaign against church confirmation of young people, who were encouraged to attend instead its state-approved substitute, the *Jugendweihe*, which marked the transition from adolescence to adulthood and involved making a public commitment to the values of socialism. A curious ceremony in which socialist ritual replaced religious form and content, the *Jugendweihe* proved highly popular and eventually encompassed over 90 per cent of GDR youth. Surprisingly the ceremony has undergone a minor revival in the post-unification eastern states, partly because it symbolises a rejection of west German values without involving a commitment to a church (Paterson 2000a).

By the mid-1970s the Protestant Church in the GDR – functioning according to the formula a 'church within socialism' (*Kirche im Sozialismus*) – reached a strained but stable accommodation with the regime, which tolerated its limited activities in return for not encouraging outright dissidence. The authorities also allowed western financial aid to reach the Church. After talks between the East German leader Erich Honecker and the Church in 1978, the latter was allocated television broadcasting time, although censorship continued to apply (as with the Church press) and strict limits remained on the Church's involvement in issues such as the environment, religious education and freedom of travel outside the GDR.

During the 40 years of the GDR, Protestant congregations fell most drastically of all (from over 14 to barely 5 million). Membership of the Roman Catholic Church – historically much smaller in the north and east – dropped only slightly (from 1.4 to 1.1 million). Protestants, who had traditionally identified themselves with the political élites and institutions of pre-Nazi Germany, failed in particular to maintain their cohesion as a religious community in the face of state-sponsored atheism. The Catholic community, on the other hand, accepted from the beginning its exclusion from public life and as a result remained relatively immune from repression, albeit at the cost of social isolation. One factor which helped the Protestant Church to adapt to the situation in the GDR was the emergence of a new generation of pastors who had grown up exclusively under socialism and who had no personal experience of church life during the Third Reich or before. The Protestant Church lost most of its adherents between 1955 and 1960, when hopes for reunification finally faded, and between 1967 and 1975, when dialogue with the regime replaced all notion of opposition (Nowak 1995: 151). For both churches the ratio of baptisms to births in the GDR fell from 90 per cent (1950) to 30 per cent (1965).

During the GDR's final decade, as the socialist leadership became increasingly isolated in eastern Europe, the Protestant Church became the focus of more vocal dissidence, especially among younger people. In the last days of the regime and the period immediately afterwards it played a key role as a moderator in discussions between the political leaders; it provided venues for them to meet and was especially respected for contributing to the non-violent course of the revolution. However, the church's function here was part of a general dissatisfaction with a moribund political system and did not represent any resurgence of religious feeling among the people. Acting as intermediaries between the outgoing leadership and the citizens' groups, Protestant pastors took a leading part in the GDR's peaceful transition to democracy. After the *Wende*, however, its heroic profile was dimmed somewhat by a debate about the extent to which it had engaged in dialogue with the regime and had maintained 'unofficial contacts' with the SED and the *Stasi* (Schroeder 1998: 483–4).

The Church after 1990

In post-unification Germany the population is divided equally between Catholics, Protestants and non-religious. Historical factors, including the 40 years' division, contribute to persisting differences between the old FRG and the eastern states. Although non-Christians are a minority in western Germany a greater proportion of them (26 per cent) have a higher school-leaving certificate than either Catholics (16 per cent) or Protestants (18 per cent); to some extent, therefore, atheism is more closely associated with a higher level of education in the west. In the generally more atheistic east, the proportions are more evenly distributed, being lower for Christians and non-Christians alike (between 10 per cent and 15 per cent). The great majority of eastern Germans (two-thirds) are not church members and do not take part in any church activity; nevertheless, in a 1996 survey by the organisation ALLBUS (*Allgemeine Bevölkerungsumfrage der Sozialwissenschaften*) almost half of easterners expressed an intention to baptise their children. This figure rose to 86 per cent in the west, where one-fifth of the population go to church at least once a month and up to two-thirds attend only occasionally. Catholics in both east (31 per cent) and west (33 per cent) are more regular churchgoers than Protestants (10–11 per cent). Surprisingly, perhaps, in view of the way in which the east German authorities targeted the youth for ideological indoc-trination, relatively more young people in the east are involved in church life than in the west. While most western Germans maintain some sort of rela-tionship with the church, the situation is the reverse in the east, where the majority explicitly reject any form of religious practice.

Despite falling congregations and a diminished influence over political parties, the two main churches in Germany continue to enjoy a considerable status. Financed from a percentage of general income tax, they are also among the richest in the world. Although an individual must formally quit the church in order to avoid paying this tax, it is likely that the churches will in the future experience declining revenues as increasing numbers of Germans opt to leave. Despite greater control of schools by the state, religious educa-tion remains compulsory by law, with a strong church involvement. The indi-vidual school constitutions of many federal states reflect ethical and moral values derived from mainstream Christianity. Moreover, the assertion of reli-gious values can still attract considerable support among the population, as illustrated in the so-called crucifix judgement (*Kruzifixurteil*) of 1995. In this case, triggered by a parent's objection to the hitherto compulsory display of the crucifix in Bavarian schools, the Federal Constitutional Court ruled that the display violated the state's commitment to religious neutrality and contravened a family's right to exercise religious freedom. In response the Bavarian federal parliament felt that it had enough public support to re-affirm its right to display the crucifix while at the same time acknowledging the right of parents to object. Finally, the churches' practical contribution to social welfare – in the form of the Catholic Caritas organisation and the Protestant *Diakonisches Werk* – may be said to outweigh its clerical and pastoral role in German society: between them the organisations employ over 700 000 people and are likely to continue as a major provider of welfare, despite moves to privatise parts of the system.

FURTHER READING

Social issues are wide-ranging and the material for this chapter has been drawn from a variety of sources. The volume by Schäfers and Zapf (1998) contains a number of review articles that summarise many aspects of contemporary German society. Relevant material also appears in the journals *Politik und Zeitgeschichte* and *Deutschland Archiv*. For more detailed studies of the German churches in east and west see chapters by Henkys, Höllen, Maier and Wilkens in Weidenfeld and Zimmerman (1989); Schroeder (1998) focuses on the relationship between Church and state in the former GDR.

10

ENVIRONMENTAL ISSUES

THE ENVIRONMENT AS A GLOBAL ISSUE

When Willy Brandt coined the slogan 'The sky over the Ruhr must become blue again' in the election campaign of 1961, he reflected popular concern about an urban environment that had become dangerously polluted as a result of the focus on unrestricted expansion during the post-war economic German 'miracle'. Within a decade Germany would become a world leader in advocating and pursuing environmentally friendly policies. The shift in attitude and policy took place in the context of a growing international awareness of the threat to the global natural environment as a result of uncontrolled industrial development over several decades and the exploitation of non-renewable natural resources. The main concerns focused on climate change brought about by industrial emissions, the encroachment of deserts on previously fertile land, the extinction of entire species of plants and animals and the chemical pollution of water, air and natural landscapes.

In 1972 a United Nations Conference on the Human Environment (UNCHE) took place in Stockholm under the motto 'Only One Earth'. The same year saw a report by the Club of Rome, a respected group of scientists, industrialists and intellectuals from over 50 nations, which highlighted the need to place limits on industrial growth. The oil crisis of 1973–74 forced industrial nations to look more seriously at ways of saving energy and using non-renewable fuels more efficiently. In 1980 the *Global 2000* report commissioned by the United States attracted world-wide attention as the most comprehensive and authoritative review of environmental issues so far. Following the Stockholm conference, the United Nations initiated an Environmental Programme (UNEP) whose small secretariat and regional offices prepared the groundwork for a number of international agreements. These included the regulation of trade in endangered species (1973), the protection of the ozone layer (1985) and restrictions on the export of poisonous waste to developing countries (1991). In 1988 UNEP founded the Intergovernmental Panel on Climate Change (IPCC), which produces technical and scientific reports on climate-related issues. The IPCC, whose bureau includes a German scientist, is a possibly unique attempt to establish a global scientific consensus on the environment. An important agreement was reached in Montevideo (1982) on the areas in which action to protect the environment was most urgently needed. Germany called repeatedly for UNEP to be upgraded to a more powerful world environmental organisation, albeit to no immediate effect. Nevertheless, in June 1992 a United Nations conference in Rio de Janeiro agreed a framework for achieving global climate change and set further targets for industrial nations, including Germany (the so-called Agenda 21). In 1995 the signatories undertook to work out a mechanism for reducing harmful emissions (the Berlin Mandate), which was finally hammered out at a conference in Kyoto (Japan) in 1997.

The Kyoto protocol was seen as a first step in committing the industrial nations to reducing emissions by 30 per cent by 2010 (taking 1990 as the base year). For Germany this meant a reduction of 8 per cent. International agreement on environmental change has proved to be a gradual and ongoing process, and many dismissed the Kyoto targets as inadequate. A convention held in November 2000 at the Hague (Netherlands) in order to finalise the implementation of Kyoto had to confront the fact that targets were not being met and that global emissions were continuing to grow at a rate of 1.3 per cent a year (Bunting 2000). A fundamental difference has emerged between the market-orientated approach to solving global warming, favoured by the USA, Japan and Australia, and the Europeans. While the USA in particular has sought to evade making real cutbacks in industrial pollution by 'selling' its emissions to other countries and by planting forests that in theory are able to act as sinks for carbon dioxide, the experience of European countries, including Germany, is that pollution is best reduced by direct regulation. There is also the fear that the western nuclear industry, subject to domestic pressure for closure, may relaunch itself in countries such as China and India.

A number of organisations campaigned and worked on ecological issues. Among the first were the International Union for the Conservation of Nature (IUCN, founded 1948) and the World Wide Fund for Nature (WWF, 1961). Starting off as a collection of informal groups in the early 1970s, Greenpeace evolved into an international foundation (1979) which undertook often spectacular actions against big business and governments. Greenpeace's scientists, often at risk to themselves, gathered information on environmental issues and alerted the public to the need for urgent action. Co-ordinated from Amsterdam, Friends of the Earth is a much looser federation of national partner organisations, including many in the third world. German members take an active role in all these organisations. As a leading member of the European Union, Germany has kept the environment at the forefront of the organisation's concerns. In 1972 the EU adopted the protection of the environment as a main objective; various guidelines and items of legalisation followed, including the establishment of a General Directorate (GD XI) to formulate and recommend environmental policy and the setting up of the European Environment Agency (EEA) in 1994. At the same time organisations from member states in the EU combined to open an office in Brussels, the European Environment Bureau (EEB), to lobby the commission and influence EU policy on ecological matters.

PHASES OF ENVIRONMENTAL POLICY

In the early 1950s most West Germans were more concerned with rebuilding the post-war economy than protecting the environment. Nevertheless, in 1953 a cross-party group of federal and regional parliamentarians set up a working party (the Inter-parliamentary Working Group for an Ecological Economy) which drew up a manifesto of environmental objectives that was remarkable for its far-sightedness. Their programme called for the careful husbandry of non-renewable fossil-based resources and the setting up of a holistic and ecologically-orientated economy that would retain the balance of nature while meeting the challenges of an expanding world population. Failure to achieve these aims, it was argued, could de-stabilise whole societies and endanger world peace (in Fritzler 1997: 40). Although the manifesto went to the very root of the problems that the contemporary industrial economy was sowing, it was a decade or more before its time and it had little effect on business or the government. The emergence of an effective German policy on the environment is described below, as are its subsequent phases and developments.

1969–1973: emergence of environmental policy

The political sea change in environmental policy came in late 1969 when a coalition government of the SPD and FDP included the environment in its reform programme. The move was surprising since ecological issues had barely figured in the preceding election campaign, despite media coverage of incidents such as the massive oil spillage in the North Sea in March 1967, when the tanker *Torrey Canyon* foundered on a reef off the British coast. Within weeks of becoming Chancellor, Willy Brandt made the government – through the interior ministry – responsible for water purity, waste disposal and combating noise pollution. In November 1969 ministry staff first coined the word *Umweltschutz* in German, a translation of the English term 'environment protection'. Progress was at first hindered by inter-ministry squabbles, notably with a minister of agriculture reluctant to share power. However, in 1970 a special 'environment cabinet' was set up at government level and in the same year Bayern established the very first regional ministry for environmental affairs. With the support of the opposition CDU (a political consensus which has rarely been repeated since), a national action programme was agreed. In 1971 the *Bundestag* passed its first environmental law on controlling aircraft noise near airports. At first, however, the government found its room for manoeuvre limited as the action programme impinged on the powers of the federal states. It was not until 1972 that the *Bundesrat* agreed to a change in the Basic Law, surrendering some of its competencies to the centre.

During the late 1960s local citizens formed hundreds of action groups to protest against aircraft noise, the construction of new roads and atomic power stations. In June 1972 these disparate groups came together under an umbrella organisation, the Federation for Environmental Citizens Groups (*Bundesverband Bürgerinitiativen Umweltschutz* or BBU). Through its vigorous and well-informed campaigns the BBU proved a highly effective body. Its activism and sense of urgency contrasted with the conservative approach of the traditional environmental organisations represented by the German Nature Protection Consortium (*Deutscher Naturschutz Ring* or DNR, founded in 1950).

In July 1972 the BBU published a hard-hitting Ecological Manifesto remarkable for its pessimistic and uncompromising assessment of the state of the environment. The manifesto declared that overpopulation was in danger of leading humanity to mass hunger, hatred, misery, violence and eventually suicidal self-extermination. It attacked the culture of unlimited industrial expansion and of the unbridled plundering and poisoning of the land and its resources. It also highlighted the transformation of healthy natural landscapes into monocultures or 'plant factories' producing poor quality food riddled with dangerous chemicals. Finally, the manifesto called for society to focus less on the economic profit motive and to stop paying mere lip service to environmental concerns (reproduced in full in Fritzler 1997: 43–4).

Welcoming the new groups, the German government assisted them financially and incorporated them into the political process. Alongside scientists and government administrators it included them on newly established advisory councils. A 1971 plan to set up a Federal Office for Environmental Protection in West Berlin, attached to the interior ministry, was delayed by a diplomatic wrangle with the Soviet Union, which saw the location of a West German government body in the city as a violation of the post-war Four Power Agreement on Berlin. The issue dragged on until 1974, when the office started work under a slightly different name (the *Umweltbundesamt* or UBA), which apparently satisfied political sensitivities. Unfortunately, the first oil crisis, a downturn in the economy and a wave of attacks by the radical left-wing terror group *Rote Armee Fraktion* (RAF) pushed environmental issues off the national agenda.

1973–1978: stagnation

The oil crisis in the autumn of 1973, when Middle East oil-producing countries drastically reduced output and increased prices, came as a mixed blessing to environmentalists. On the one hand the government appeared to propagate energy conservation more seriously, imposing a speed limit on motorways and main roads (100 and 80 km. per hr.) and prohibiting Sunday motoring (in fact the measures were short-lived and the ban on Sunday motoring was dropped after three weeks). On the other hand it accelerated its programme to build more nuclear power stations, believing that these would reduce dependency on oil and meet industry demands for rising energy consumption. Bowing to pressure from business and trade unions and concerned about rising unemployment, the government relaxed its environmental policy: a key meeting between the government, opposition parties and representatives of industry and labour at Gymnich castle in June 1975 decided to implement environmental measures already in the pipeline but to avoid further action that could endanger the economy. In the event parliament approved current measures but they were heavily watered down and no new initiatives were undertaken.

Despite the setback of the oil crisis and economic recession, in 1976 the government produced a report which established three principles of environmental policy. These have served as guidelines for administrations ever since. The first principle stressed the importance of prevention and allowed the state to act to forestall a potential threat to the environment even before incontrovertible scientific proof of one exists (*Vorsorgeprinzip*). The second principle laid down that the polluter pays for damage to the environment (*Verursacherprinzip*; this was implemented in the Environmental Liability Law or *Umwelthaftungsgesetz* of 1991). The third principle was based on co-operation between affected parties (*Kooperationsprinzip*): where possible, industrialists, trade unions, scientists and environmental groups would work together to achieve a consensus on drawing up and implementing environmental policy.

1978–1982: protest

The government's commitment to nuclear power met with growing protests from environmental groups and from a general public deeply concerned over the risks and long-term dangers associated with the industry. Thousands demonstrated against the policy, chanting the slogan 'Better active today than radio-active tomorrow' (Fritzler 1997: 45). Violent confrontations between police and demonstrators took place at the Gorleben and Brokdorf atomic power stations in northern Germany. Several new environmental groups emerged and took an active role in local and regional politics. The first political party created specifically to campaign on the single issue of the environment was the USP (*Umweltschutzpartei*, founded in 1977 in Niedersachsen). It was followed a year later by Green Action for the Future (*Grüne Aktion Zukunft* or GAZ), led by Herbert Gruhl, an expert on ecological affairs and author of a book entitled *A Planet is Being Plundered* (*Ein Planet wird geplündert*); Gruhl had been a CDU member of parliament before quitting the party in 1978 in protest over what he saw as its lukewarm environmental policies.

The protest groups of the 1970s appealed strongly to a younger generation of Germans, the children of the economic miracle, who had not experienced the material shortages of the post-war years and ranked social and environmental concerns above traditional views of economic progress. Of all the new ecological parties, the Greens proved the most active and successful in breaking the mould of the political establishment. Founded in 1980, the

Greens failed to win enough seats to enter the *Bundestag* in the general election of that year. Continuing public protests over atomic power, however, and extensive media coverage of a new concern – the threat to German forests from acid rain – helped sweep the Greens into the *Bundestag* with 5.6 per cent of the vote and 28 seats in March 1983. The Greens were a sharp reminder to the newly elected conservative–liberal government of 1983 of the need to inject fresh urgency into environmental policy.

1983–1986: a new urgency

The administration elected in 1983 acted promptly to reduce air pollution by large factories (*Großfeuerungsanlagen-Verordnung*, 1983) and took a leading role in persuading the EU to control harmful emissions from cars and to introduce lead-free petrol. Fearful of the powerful car users' lobby, however, it resisted pressure from the Greens and other groups to impose a national speed limit on motorways.

The government was heavily criticised over its response to the Chernobyl crisis of April 1986, when in the world's worst ever nuclear disaster, an atomic power station in the Ukraine bombarded much of Europe with radioactivity. In Germany the environmental authorities failed to keep the public adequately informed and it emerged that they were totally unprepared for such a catastrophe. Within two months of the crisis the Federal Chancellor had removed responsibility for atomic energy and the environment from the interior ministry and set up Germany's first fully-fledged Federal Ministry of the Environment (BMU), with Walter Wallmann as minister (the inexperienced Wallmann was soon replaced by Klaus Töpfer, who had been regional CDU environment minister for Rheinland-Pfalz).

1986– : new initiatives and setbacks

Apart from Chernobyl, which confirmed the public's worst fears about the dangers of the nuclear industry, a series of incidents – the most serious being a fire at the Sandoz chemical factory in Basel in November 1986 which highlighted the seriousness of industrial pollution in the River Rhine – kept the environment at the forefront of German politics. As scientists confirmed the reality of global warming and the loss of the ozone layer, Germans joined environmental groups in their tens of thousands (Fritzler 1997: 50). The greatest challenge of all, however, came soon after the fall of the Berlin Wall in November 1989, when the enormous scale of industrial pollution in the GDR and the threat to public health became known. The FRG and a reform GDR government acted swiftly. By February 1990 a joint East–West German commission on the environment was in place which agreed a framework law (*Umweltrahmengesetz*) that enabled the GDR, even before formal unification, to adopt West German environmental legislation and standards; the framework law came into force on 1 July 1990.

As had occurred in the early 1970s, however, a downturn in the economy – this time brought about in part by the unexpectedly high costs of unification – acted as a sudden brake on environmental policy. As before, businesses and trade unions saw compliance with environmental regulations as an additional burden just when industry was struggling to remain competitive. Environmental ministers Klaus Töpfer and, from 1994, Angela Merkel tried hard to persuade business leaders that ecological concerns should not be jettisoned whenever the economic going got tough; they also pointed out that companies could actually cut costs through saving energy and increase their competitiveness by developing environmentally friendly goods and production processes.

Tensions between meeting environmental objectives and rescuing the national economy characterised government policy during the 1990s. On the one hand, mindful of the need to alleviate unemployment, the government relaxed ecological standards for the approval of new factories and made it harder for members of the public to object to new industrial developments on environmental grounds. On the other hand it pledged the nation to meet the targets of Agenda 21: to this end it set up various regional and national bodies to draw up concrete plans and undertook to reduce emissions of carbon dioxide by 25 per cent between 2000 and 2005, although it was not clear in 2000 that this target could be met (*Der Tagesspiegel* 11 March 2000: 1). Three federal states, Bayern, Baden-Württemberg and Niedersachsen, began after 1995 to develop a formal response to the challenge of Agenda 21, which was reflected by a number of local initiatives (Fritzler 1997: 117). In 1994 the *Bundestag* also voted to include protection of the 'natural basis of life' (*natürliche Lebensgrundlagen*) as an official aim of the state (*Staatsziel*, article 20a). This measure, however, has not satisfied the environmental lobby, who argue that the right to a clean and safe environment should be included in the constitution as a fundamental human right. A consequence of such inclusion would be that citizens could take to court authorities and organisations that violate such a right. The election in 1998 of a national government with the Greens as coalition partners (and a Green as environment minister) encouraged many to believe that new life would be breathed into Germany's environmental policy. The government pledged, in particular, to shut down the nuclear industry and to introduce ecological taxes on non-renewable fuels. While making significant progress on these issues, it was criticised for neglecting broader aspects of environmental policy and experienced internal tensions between the SPD and the more radical Green Party members.

ENVIRONMENTAL LEGACY OF THE GDR

In 1968 the constitution of the GDR declared that the state, its organs and ordinary citizens had a duty to safeguard the natural environment, in particular the air, water, landscapes, fauna and flora (article 15). The GDR was one of the first countries to set up (in 1972) a ministry for the protection of the environment (*Ministerium für Umweltschutz und Wasserwirtschaft*). However, after the five-year plan for 1971–75 failed to achieve most of its ecological targets, the constitutional commitment to improving the environment was ignored. The state pursued economic and industrial growth at all costs. The results were immense damage to the natural environment and serious public health hazards; children in certain areas suffered a marked increase in respiratory and skin diseases. While emissions and pollution levels in western Germany consistently fell after 1980, they rose in the GDR. Regulations for energy saving and the control of pollution existed only on paper: they either were ignored or could not be implemented for lack of technology and expertise. Data on the condition of the environment became a state secret from at least 1982 and open discussion of ecological issues was discouraged. The state-controlled Society for Nature and the Environment (*Gesellschaft für Natur und Umwelt* or GNU) was set up in 1980 to pay lip-service to growing ecological concerns on the part of the population, who were well aware of deteriorating air quality and chemical pollution in industrial areas. Unofficial dissident groups, which led a precarious existence under the umbrella of the East German Protestant Church, collected information and data on the state of the environment, disseminated papers and held small seminars. Infiltrated and closely monitored by the authorities, they faced constant official harassment. The true extent of environmental damage in the GDR did not become known until after the collapse of the regime in November 1989.

Areas of the GDR most heavily affected by pollution were the coal- and energy-producing centres of the industrial south and east, especially the industrial cities of Halle, Leipzig, Bitterfeld, Dresden and Cottbus. Just before unification the GDR had the highest levels of air pollution in Europe. The intensive application of fertilisers and chemicals on huge farming collectives contaminated the soil and water supplies. Even after treatment, 50 per cent of rivers and streams were so poisoned by household and industrial waste that they could not be used for drinking water. Of factories 95 per cent pumped virtually untreated effluent into the natural water system. Opencast coal mining ruined whole landscapes, and the type of coal burned – brown coal (*Braunkohle*) – was not only inefficient in terms of energy production, it also generated considerable atmospheric waste; its large-scale extraction lowered the ground water level by up to 80 metres in parts of Sachsen, a problem exacerbated by east Germany's relatively low rainfall (Jones 1994: 115). Atomic power stations contributed little to the country's energy requirements and factories lacked facilities for cleaning gas emissions. Lead-free petrol and catalytic converters for road vehicles were unknown. West Germany also exported waste to the GDR (summarised in Fritzler 1997: 53).

Possibly the most dangerous single source of pollution in the GDR was the radioactive waste from the uranium mining concern SDAG Wismut in Thüringen and Sachsen. The plant was built after the Second World War in order to extract uranium for the Soviet atomic bomb programme. Not only did the miners have to work under criminally dangerous conditions, but from at least 1961 until the fall of the GDR about 109 billion tons of untreated radioactive waste were channelled across open land. The clean-up operation became the biggest ever environmental rescue operation in Germany's history, costing 13 billion DM and lasting into the twenty-first century.

The picture in the GDR was not entirely negative. Although two-thirds of woodland were damaged through air pollution, sparsely populated areas that were almost unaffected by human activity were able to support rare species of plant and animal life. The GDR also maintained a national network of depots for the reclamation of valuable raw materials (the SERO concern), although this was done for economic rather than environmental reasons.

APPARATUS OF ENVIRONMENTAL CONTROL

The most senior body responsible for environmental issues in Germany is the Federal Ministry for the Environment (BMU). With a staff of around 800 and several technical departments, the BMU supports and represents the Minister of the Environment in the various committees of the *Bundestag* (the *Bundestag* has its own special committee on the environment and since the late 1980s has held various commissions of enquiry on environmental concerns). The main tasks of the BMU are to prepare draft legislation, educate the public and to work closely with other government ministries (such as agriculture, transport and energy), whose responsibilities overlap with environmental matters. The BMU also concludes agreements with ministries of other states and exchanges information at international level. The BMU's own budget is relatively small; much more is spent by other ministries on environmental projects in their particular area (19.2 billion DM in 1996). Three departments or offices (*Ämter*) represent the ministry's main activities: the largest, the Office of the Environment (*Umweltbundesamt* or UBA) collects data, informs the public, monitors environmental programmes and is the main point of contact with the EU; the Office for the Protection of Nature (*Bundesamt für Naturschutz* or BfN), which is the successor of an institution founded in 1906, is responsible for protecting plant and animal species; the Office for Nuclear Safety (*Bundesamt für Strahlenschutz* or BfS) was set up in 1989 in the wake of the Chernobyl disaster to oversee the transport and storage of radioactive materials and to monitor levels of radioactivity in the environment. Established in 1971 and attached to the BfN since 1986, is the Council of Experts on Environmental Affairs (*Umweltrat*). The Council's seven members are independent of government and civil service and report every two years on progress on the environment: it chooses its own themes and makes recommendations.

From 1972 the environment ministers of the *Länder*, which are responsible for implementing environmental policy in their regions, have met twice yearly to exchange information and co-ordinate activities. Some *Länder*, such as Nordrhein-Westfalen and Baden-Württemberg, have set up research institutes of international standing (for a list of research foundations see Fritzler 1997: 79). At local level the municipalities (*Kommunen*), which attend to local public transport, utilities (gas and electricity), the water supply and waste disposal, play a key role in promoting, for instance, greater use of buses and trains or in financing energy-saving programmes.

INSTRUMENTS OF ENVIRONMENTAL CONTROL: ROLE OF BUSINESS AND CITIZENS

While Germany does not levy an environmental tax as such, the red–green coalition of 1998 came to power promising to close nuclear power stations and to introduce 'green taxes' on electricity, fuel oil and gas. The tax on electricity, for instance, was projected to double, while the less energy-efficient gas and coal power stations would be taxed accordingly (*Der Tagesspiegel* 6 January 1999: 4). The state already used taxation on petrol consumption as a lever to promote the production and use of non-polluting and lean-burn cars. Under international discussion (and so far used only in the USA), is the introduction of a trade in licences, by which companies whose emissions exceed or do not satisfy minimum standards are able to buy the right to pollute from those that do meet the targets. In Germany a business which discharges waste water directly into a river or stream pays a levy (*Abgabe*) to the regional state authorities which is calculated according to the volume and the harmful content of the permitted discharge; this acts as an incentive to avoid such practices (Fritzler 1997: 88–9).

During the late 1980s and early 1990s German citizens rated the environment as politically more important than even employment (Fritzler 1997: 69). After unification the public's enthusiasm waned as they rated unemployment, criminality or (especially in the east) the preservation of the welfare state as more pressing concerns. To some extent the change reflected the genuine improvements that were made to the environment in Germany after the media began reporting cases of pollution and their consequences: by 1991 over half the population were reporting that they were well satisfied with the state of the environment. At the same time individuals were reluctant to take positive action to improve the environment if it involved a threat to jobs, expense (such as dearer goods in the shops, higher taxes or dearer petrol) or personal inconvenience. To counter such perceptions the German authorities and ecological organisations have instituted a variety of measures to inform the public and change patterns of behaviour. These include around 350 local government-sponsored consumer centres (*Verbraucherzentralen* or VZ) which provide advice on purchasing ecological goods, the Blue Angel (*Blauer Engel*) mark of quality, awarded by jury since 1978 to biodegradable or environmentally friendly products, and a host of recycling and energy-saving schemes, including car-sharing.

Possibly the best known of these schemes is the 'green dot' mark on goods. Introduced in 1992, this obliges businesses to use recyclable packaging materials or to take them back from the customer. The Dual System Germany Ltd (*Duales System Deutschland GmbH* or DSD) was set up as a commercial concern to pre-process the packaging, which citizens deposit in distinctive yellow bins and sacks. To run the scheme businesses pay a levy to DSD that is lower for recyclable items; the levy thus acts as an incentive to industry to reduce the use of non-degradable or non-recyclable materials in their packaging.

ENVIRONMENTAL ORGANISATIONS

Around 4 million Germans belong to an environmental organisation, although only a small proportion are active members. Over 1 million are employed full time in some way in environmental protection (Fritzler 1997: 75). Four national organisations, all professionally run with full-time staff, dominate the scene.

The most recent and by far the most powerful is the German section of Greenpeace. Founded in 1980 and comprising over half a million members, Greenpeace has the largest annual income (73.7 million DM in 1996) and will campaign on any issue, from atomic energy to the protection of species. In Germany the organisation was especially active over the issue of acid rain and the threat to the alpine forests: its *Bergwelt* (Alpine Mountain Landscape) project was launched to protect the alpine forests as a barrier against avalanches. In 1992 Greenpeace helped promote the CFC-free refrigerator (CFC gases contribute to the loss of the ozone layer). The organisation has been criticised for its hierarchical structures, although regional groups have freedom to campaign on local issues. Young people are organised in so-called 'Greenteams' (Fritzler 1997: 74).

The German section of the World Wide Fund for Nature was founded in 1963. With a membership of 100 000 and an annual income of 28.7 million DM, WWF Germany concentrates on preserving threatened species and geographical areas (rivers, coasts, wetlands and forests). WWF Germany is based in Frankfurt but on unification opened an office in the east (Potsdam). The fund maintains a research institute in Rastatt and augments its income through marketing its famous panda bear logo. In 1990 it held a conference on the tiny island of Vilm, off Rügen on the Baltic coast, to draw attention to its concern for endangered natural landscapes in the former GDR.

The Bonn-based NABU (*Naturschutzbund Deutschland*) started life in 1899 as a bird protection society (*Deutscher Bund für Vogelschutz*). It changed its name in 1990 after merging with a sister organisation in the former GDR and extended its activities to include the protection of rare plants and the habitats of birds and animals. With 200 000 members and a budget of 27.3 million DM, NABU supports over 5000 projects. Like WWF Germany, it took on the challenge of rescuing endangered species in the former GDR, where it has regional branches. NABU also organises seminars and publishes a journal, *Naturschutz Heute*.

Founded in 1975 and affiliated since 1989 to the Friends of the Earth network is the *Bund für Umwelt und Naturschutz Deutschland* (BUND). The organisation's logo is a green and black 'hands around the earth' symbol. Although located in Bonn, over half of BUND's 230 000 members are in Bayern and it has a strong youth section. With an annual income of around 14.7 million DM, BUND does not allow commercial concerns to use its logo for money, although it works with the Hertie department store to promote ecological products. BUND works on a broad range of issues, from nature protection to acid rain, water pollution and energy conservation. It is a strong lobbier of regional and national government and has local groups in east and west Germany. Its campaigns include rescuing the streams (*Rettet die Bäche*) and a programme to protect European forests (*Europäische Forstwelt*, aimed mainly at young people). It publishes a journal, *Natur und die Umwelt*.

Other organisations include *Die Naturfreunde* (Friends of Nature, over 110 000 members), which maintains a chain of hostels for walkers and ramblers and *Der Deutsche Alpenverein* (DAV, the German Alpine Association, 440 000 members), which provides maps, guides and huts for visitors to the Alps and has lobbied intensively to protect the mountains and its forests from acid rain. A number of tourist organisations promote environmentally friendly activities such as cycling and walking and lobby for better bus and rail facilities.

After the heyday of public concern over the environment in the early 1980s, some organisations experienced a relative decline in income from individual members. To counter this they began to adopt techniques of commercial sponsoring. Although Greenpeace continued to eschew any form of dependence on commercial interests, many organisations found it fruitful to move away from confrontation with business, co-operating with firms as partners in joint projects.

ECO-AUDIT

Apart from saving energy and using ecologically friendly production processes, industry can help the environment in purchasing and recycling materials, transporting goods by rail instead of road and encouraging staff to be more environmentally conscious. Such an approach presupposes that the company is prepared to review all aspects of its operations as a first step towards adopting an environmental policy. Since 1993 firms have been able to undergo a voluntary 'eco-audit' (full title: Environmental Management and Audit Scheme or EMAS), which does just that. Successful firms are awarded a three-year 'eco-audit certificate'. When the EU agreed EMAS in early 1993, Germany was in fact the only member to resist it. The reason for the opposition from a country whose government had taken a lead in environmental issues was that German industry had hitherto focused on purely technological solutions to environmental problems (e.g. installing waste purifiers). As a consequence it was deeply suspicious of how the audit would also assess how a company's management monitored and responded to ecological issues. Moreover, businesses feared that the intense domestic concern over the environment would effectively make the audit compulsory for them. However, once the government accepted the scheme and German firms were reassured that their own industry organisations would be closely involved in implementing it, they adopted it with gusto. In April 1999, 75 per cent (2020) of the total 2704 EU companies registered were German. Businesses reported that the main benefits of conducting the audit lay in identifying potential improvements in management, legal security and company image. An outcome of the audit would be an 'eco-balance' of, for instance, the use of raw materials or energy in production.

German companies' exemplary participation in EMAS showed signs of declining in 1999. The reasons were two-fold. First, companies did not feel that either the public or the state gave the audit sufficient recognition. Second, the emergence of a newer international standard in October 1996 (ISO Norm 14001), with less stringent and more straightforward requirements, undermined the appeal of the EU scheme. During 1998 and 1999 the EU began reviewing EMAS with a view to increasing its attractiveness (Bültmann and Wätzold 1999). Although German industry remains sceptical of external controls and of the on-costs associated with improving the environment, studies show that a positive environmental policy actually creates more jobs than it destroys. There are also signs that German trade unions are beginning to view environmentalism with less suspicion. In 1996 the first trade union was formed which included the term 'environment' in its title (IG Bauen-Agrar-Umwelt); the organisation is committed to gaining its members a greater say in ecological issues in the workplace (Fritzler 1997: 77–8).

ACCESS TO INFORMATION

Access to information on the current state of the environment allows independent organisations to monitor progress; it also increases public awareness and confidence. Belatedly, following a 1990 directive of the EU Council of Ministers, Germany passed a law on environmental information (*Umwelt-Informationsgesetz* 1994) which obliges authorities to provide data on the environment to members of the public on request. In 1997, however, the EU Commission took the German government to the European Court of Justice for failure to properly implement certain provisions of the directive. The German authorities wished to levy fees for providing information and also to withhold data altogether if this was the object of legal proceedings. In its judgement (1999) the court held that the German authorities could levy reasonable fees for providing information but not when refusing such a request. It did, however, permit the withholding of information during certain types of court proceedings (Case C-217/97 Commission v. Germany).

STATE OF THE ENVIRONMENT

Building on legislation that had been in force since the 1980s but applied largely to air and water, the *Bundestag* passed a law in 1997 which for the first time lay down national standards for the use and protection of the land (*Bundes-Bodenschutzgesetz*). The main sources of land pollution are dangerous chemicals (in particular heavy metals, the by-products of production processes, waste discharges from factories and farm pesticides), acid rain (resulting from sulphurous and nitrous oxide emissions from factories and power stations) and ammonia-based and nitrate deposits in farmland (the end-product of intensive farming techniques; designed to increase yields of monocrops, these undermine the chemistry of the soil and displace other forms of plant and animal life). The law further aimed to remove legacy pollution (*Altlasten*). This consists mainly of disused industrial plants and in-fill sites but it also includes areas of former military production and army exercise ranges. In 1995, 170 000 such sites had been identified, with the polluters in many cases either untraceable or unable to be brought to account, especially in the former East Germany (the uranium extraction plant mentioned above is a case in point). To ensure that today's waste would not become tomorrow's legacy pollution, the German Environment Ministry set up a special programme in 1993 which aimed to pre-treat and render harmless all household and small-scale industrial waste by 2005; this would be achieved through the use of incinerators, specially constructed storage dumps and (for organic materials) composting plants. By 1995 legacy pollution was concentrated in Hamburg and Bremen in the west and Berlin and Sachsen in the east (Schäfers 1998: 21).

Building and roads

Apart from controlling pollution through chemicals and waste products, the 1997 law also encompassed the threat to the land posed by the encroachment of buildings and roads. Germany is a relatively 'green' country in terms of the distribution of urban and rural land; over 90 per cent of large areas in the east and south (Bayern) are given over to farming or natural landscape. Nevertheless the proportion of built-up area to nature in western Germany increased from 7.1 per cent in 1950 to 12.7 per cent in 1993 and is expected to continue rising in line with a growing demand for housing. At the same time, 50 per cent of the total built-up area is made up of open spaces in the form of parks, cemeteries and gardens. Naturally, the main 'concrete jungles' are large cities and urban conurbations such as the Ruhr area of Nordrhein-Westfalen, Hamburg, Berlin and the Frankfurt region. Any increase in building that covers a significant area of land heightens the risk of flooding as rainwater that is unable to drain away into the soil runs off into already overloaded rivers and streams. Land erosion, on the other hand, is a natural process and perhaps less of a problem. Nevertheless, erosion was accelerated in the post-war years as farmers removed hedges and trees in order to use machinery more effectively; this was especially true for the former collective farms in eastern Germany. Such practices are now discouraged.

Water

Germany has no shortage of water. The main consumers of water are atomic power stations (which use 59 per cent of the total water consumption for cooling before returning it to rivers or lakes) and industry (25 per cent). Relatively small consumers are human beings (13 per cent for drinking water, drawn mainly from underground aquifers) and agriculture (3 per cent for irrigation). To preserve the quality of drinking water, 10 per cent of Germany is designated as water-protection areas (*Wasserschutzgebiete*) where potentially polluting activities such as washing or re-fuelling the car or changing the oil are prohibited. Partly due to conservation measures and partly as a result of rising prices to cover the costs of extraction and purification, water consumption fell during the 1990s. Despite the abundance of water, one-third of ground water supplies are estimated to be affected by farm pesticides and a quarter by nitrates. In 1996 stricter controls were applied to waste water, although the principle by which consumers must meet the costs of purification will certainly mean higher water charges. The modernisation of waste treatment plants and the introduction of phosphate-free washing powders produced a marked improvement in the water quality of rivers and streams during the later 1980s and early 1990s. From being heavily polluted in 1975, the Rhine had moved to being only moderately polluted in 1995 and able to support fish and a variety of life forms. The east also began to recover from often catastrophic levels of pollution: the Elbe, for which a new category of 'ecologically destroyed' had to be introduced in 1990, improved to 'critically polluted' within five years. In 1995 the most polluted rivers in Germany were in the east (Elbe, Havel, Spree, Saale, Mulde, Oder, Peene); in the west the Weser and Werra were still critically polluted, as were stretches of the Ems, the Neckar and the Danube, to name a few (Fritzler 1997: 97–102). As pollution levels in the rivers feeding into the North German coast fell, the North Sea and the Baltic Sea began to recover ecologically.

Air pollution

Improvements in air quality are due mainly to the 1974 law on emissions (*Bundes-Immissionsschutzgesetz*). The law, which was extended and given more bite over the next two decades, obligates factories to obtain state permission to emit harmful substances and to appoint staff to ensure compliance with environmental standards; it also regulates noise levels of machinery, the use of appropriate fuels in the production process and requires authorities to draw up plans to combat atmospheric pollution in their area. During the 1980s power stations were equipped with purifiers (after unification several in the east were closed down altogether and replaced by modern plants) and cars began to run with catalytic converters. As a result, emissions of sulphur dioxide and nitrogen fell in West Germany by 66 per cent and 32 per cent respectively between 1984 and 1994, removing the immediate threat of the destruction of the forests (*Waldsterben*) which had attracted so much concern. Despite the dramatic fall in air pollution levels, sulphur dioxide emissions in the eastern states were still double those in the west in 1994, posing a challenge for Germany's commitment to reduce emissions by 87 per cent by 2005 (from 1980 levels). Germany also undertook to reduce nitrogen levels by 30 per cent (by 1998) and cut harmful substances generated by road traffic. In 1995 a law aimed at cutting ground-level ozone came into force. The law empowered authorities to prohibit heavily polluting vehicles during high levels of atmospheric ozone (which occur mainly during the summer in fine weather), although the measure was not particularly successful. Germany took a swift lead in the elimination of CFC gases, which contribute to the greenhouse effect: it brought down CFC emissions by 80 per cent during the four years after unification and has virtually prohibited its production and use. Carbon dioxide also contributes to global warming. Germany pledged a 25 per cent reduction in emissions over the period 1990–2005, achieving a fall of 11 per cent by 1994: the biggest producers of the gas remain power stations (40 per cent) and road traffic (18 per cent), the latter actually generating more carbon dioxide in 1994 than in 1990. A third contributor to global warming is methane gas, which is produced by waste dumps and in animal husbandry: emissions fell by 8 per cent in the period 1990–94 (Fritzler 1997: 105).

Noise pollution

The 1974 law on emissions also addressed noise pollution. Local laws regulate the use of noisy machinery (such as lawn mowers) and even the depositing of glass in recycling containers. More significantly, some motorway sections are equipped with sound deadening walls or screens, while many sections of road are subject to 30 km. per hr. speed restrictions, partly for reasons of safety and partly to reduce noise levels. At airports, landing charges for aircraft are pegged, among other things, to engine noise.

Radioactivity

Radioactivity has long been one of the most controversial environmental issues in Germany. Radioactivity occurs naturally in drinking water, in the atmosphere and in the ground (higher concentrations of the radioactive gas radon are found in the *Eifel* mountain range west of the Rhine, in the east in the *Fichtelgebirge* mountains and in the former uranium-mining regions of Sachsen and Thüringen). Natural levels of radioactivity, however, are supplemented by nuclear weapons tests, fall-out from the Chernobyl disaster and emissions from atomic power stations; it is, of course, the latter item over which Germans feel able to exert direct control. There have been a number of incidents involving atomic reactors, notably in 1980 in France and in 1979 at Three Mile Island in the USA; by far the most serious, however, was the explosion of the Chernobyl plant in April 1986 that bombarded much of Europe with radioactivity. The basis of the safe and peaceful use of nuclear power is the 1959 atomic energy law (*Atomgesetz*), which has been progressively updated in line with technical developments. The law regulates the industry and lays down maximum levels of exposure to radioactivity. The Chernobyl disaster exposed major deficiencies in Germany's ability to detect a nuclear accident and manage its effects. Within months the *Bundestag* passed a new law that by 1993 had led to the setting up of a national network of over 2000 monitoring stations designed to provide reliable data and inform prompt action in the event of a serious incident.

Atomic energy

Although Germany produces over half of its electrical power from coal (it extracts more lignite or brown coal than any other country in the world), approximately a third is generated by atomic reactors; gas and hydro-electric plants account for a mere 10 per cent. In Europe only France (78 per cent) and Belgium (60 per cent) are more reliant on atomic energy; Sweden (46 per cent) has opted for a complete nuclear shut-down spread over forty years. At the end of the twentieth century Germany was operating 19 reactors, most of which came on stream in the late 1970s and 1980s (the oldest was Obrigheim in northern Baden-Württemberg, which began operating in 1968; the newest reactor is Neckarswestheim 2, also in Baden-Württemberg, which started in 1989). After the closure of the Greifswald reactor on the Baltic coast in 1991, no plant operates in the east. Nuclear reactors employ uranium fuel elements as their source of energy and control rods to control the atomic reaction; when spent, these materials are radioactive to varying degrees and eventually require transportation to special facilities for permanent storage or reprocessing. Reprocessing is designed to extract reusable uranium and plutonium from the fuel elements but it also generates highly radioactive waste. During the 1980s the government earmarked a number of installations for the permanent or temporary storage of nuclear waste and for reprocessing. In 1991 the Mecklenburg-Vorpommern state government agreed to use the decommissioned Greifswald power station as a temporary store; a similar facility is located at Mitterteich in north-eastern Bayern. The industry also sends waste material to the UK (Sellafield) and France (La Hague) for reprocessing. In addition to operational nuclear plants, Germany has a number of disused reactors in both west and east (Fritzler 1997: 109–10; Rohlfs and Schäfer 1997: 94–8; Schäfers 1998: 72–3).

Public objections to the building and operation of nuclear reactors emerged in the late 1970s and 1980s. Opposition was led by environmentalists and the Green Party but it also attracted support from the SPD, especially after Chernobyl. Between 1976 and 1986 thousands demonstrated against the plants at Brokdorf (north of Hamburg and operational since 1986), at Grohnde (near Hannover, 1984) and at Kalkar near the Dutch border (although built, this station never entered service). A plan agreed in 1985 to construct a reprocessing plant at Wackersdorf in Bayern was finally abandoned in 1989 after objectors occupied the site. Proposals to store nuclear waste underground at Schacht Konrad and Gorleben (both Niedersachsen) ignited an intense debate about the risks of transporting radioactive material on the national rail and road network. Between 1995 and 1997 demonstrators disrupted the movement of three large rail consignments of waste material (known as Castor-transports; Castor = Cask for the Storage and Transport of Waste Material) from the Philippsburg plant near Karlsruhe to Gorleben in the north; a further transport in March 1998 saw well-publicised confrontations between police and demonstrators. By 1997 the only permanent storage facility to enter service was at Morsleben (Sachsen-Anhalt), which was originally commissioned in 1986 by the government of the former GDR.

Despite the public protests the conservative-liberal coalition under Helmut Kohl remained committed to atomic energy: the government passed a new law in 1997 safeguarding the future of the nuclear industry in Germany and giving it greater legal security. However, when the red–green coalition, which had campaigned for a swift and irreversible withdrawal from atomic energy, was elected in September 1998, the future of Germany's nuclear power industry was sealed. In early 1999 the government announced plans to make reprocessing nuclear waste in Germany illegal. Although the Green Party insisted on an immediate nuclear shut-down, commercial and technical obstacles made this unrealistic. A compromise reached with the industry in the summer of 2000 provided for a phased closure based on an average operational life of 32 years for each reactor; the power companies would receive no compensation. Since the newest reactor came on stream in 1989, the agreement implied complete closure by 2021. Castor movements of nuclear waste, generated in Germany, reprocessed in France and destined for storage at Gorleben, resumed in March 2001, attracting renewed demonstrations and dividing the Green Party; the environment minister Jürgen Trittin, a leader of the Greens, had once protested against nuclear dumping but acquiesced to the resumption of transports. The thorny issue of storage and reprocessing remains unresolved. It is likely that Gorleben and Schacht Konrad will be mothballed and a decision on a permanent national storage facility postponed, possibly until 2020 or 2025. Germany will continue to send material for reprocessing to France and the UK in the medium term (probably until 2005).

THE FUTURE: A CONCEPT OF SUSTAINABILITY

The future of the environment in Germany, including the likelihood of the country meeting the targets of Agenda 21, depends heavily on the means by which primary energy is produced, its rate of consumption and the ability to move away from non-renewable resources. In 1997 a parliamentary commission of enquiry on environmental protection presented its conclusions in the form of a study whose title focused on the concept of sustainability (*Konzept Nachhaltigkeit – Fundamente für die Gesellschaft von morgen*, or 'The concept of sustainability – the basis for the society of the future'). While environmental policy had so far achieved success in repairing damage to the environment and in removing harmful substances at the very end of the industrial process (in the form of gas purifiers, catalytic converters, or water treatment plants), the study called for an integrated approach. The essence of such an approach is to avoid the production of harmful substances to start with, to recycle as far as possible materials used in the production process and to reduce the current dependency on fossil fuels, which are non-renewable. Between 1950 and 1992 Germany's consumption of primary energy (i.e. the generation of energy from natural resources, mainly coal, oil and gas) more than tripled, although it fell slightly at times of economic crisis (e.g. the oil crisis of 1973, in 1980 and after unification).

An important target must be to maximise the efficiency of generators of primary energy. Conventional coal-fired power stations, for instance, are only 35 per cent energy efficient, since 65 per cent of the energy content of the coal consumed to generate the electricity is lost in unused heat. Power stations that store heat and deliver it to nearby housing estates or factories can increase their efficiency to 90 per cent. The main consumers of primary energy in Germany are households (consumption rose by 13 per cent between 1990 and 1995), followed by transport (whose consumption rose by 8 per cent) and industry (which registered a fall of 17 per cent, although this was due largely to the post-unification economic downturn). The above mentioned study envisages a reduction in the role of atomic energy and a significant increase in the contribution of energy from wind, water, the sun and biological sources (*Biomasse*). Whether consumption can indeed be reduced and the largely untapped potential of these alternative sources be realised remains to be seen. A report by the Council of Experts on Environmental Affairs published in 2000 was critical of government policy. While supporting the red–green coalition's basic policies on atomic energy and ecological taxes, it regretted the government's neglect of the issue of sustainability and felt that greater progress was needed on the protection of the land, air and nature, and on waste disposal and recycling (Birnbaum 2000).

PROTECTION OF NATURAL SITES

Designated sites of natural beauty and significance have enjoyed legal protection in Germany since 1935. The first significant change came in

1976 when the social–liberal coalition, responding to the environmental movement, introduced a new law for the protection of nature (*Bundesnaturschutzgesetz*). The law established various categories of protected areas to be designated and managed by the federal states. As a result of the law, over 25 per cent of Germany is now subject to some form of environmental protection. The categories are described below.

Nature reserves (*Naturschutzgebiete*) enjoy the most stringent protection, generally aimed at preserving particular species of plants or wild animals. Their symbol is a green and white triangle enclosing a bird on a yellow background. There are over 5300 reserves throughout Germany, covering 2.4 per cent of the country; their size varies, but one-third are smaller than 50 hectares. Public access (*Betretungsrecht*) may be restricted or even prohibited, but in many cases footpaths and viewing points are provided for visitors. Activities that change or damage the reserve are forbidden, but this does not necessarily preclude farming or leisure.

A little over 2 per cent of Germany's surface area is devoted to national parks (*Nationalparks*). These are large tracts of mainly state-owned countryside (at least 1000 hectares). Parks are typically divided into zones. The central or core zone (*Kernzone*) enjoys the maximum level of protection for flora and wildlife habitats; it is usually surrounded by an intermediate or buffer zone. In these zones only pedestrian access is allowed. A third zone may be designated for leisure activities and there may also be a fourth, regeneration zone, in which a damaged landscape is in the process of being reclaimed. The priority in all zones is nature conservation, although this is not incompatible with a limited level of commercial and leisure activity in the less strictly protected zones. Bayern led the way in designating two national parks: the Bavarian Forest (*Nationalpark Bayerischer Wald*, designated in 1970, i.e. before the federal act) and the Alpine/Berchtesgaden Park (*Alpen- und Nationalpark Berchtesgaden*, 1978). National parks need not be land-based: three parks are coastal mudflats (*Wattenmeere*) off the North Sea coast and one is an area of coastal shallows bordering the Baltic (*Vorpommersche Boddenlandschaft*).

Landscape protection areas (*Landschaftsschutzgebiete*) are areas of outstanding natural beauty in which agriculture and forestry are often permitted but building and industrial development are strictly prohibited. The public enjoys recreational access to these so-called *Kulturlandschaften*, which may be translated as 'traditional heritage landscapes' (Speakman and Speakman 1992: 27). Germany boasts 5900 such areas, covering about 25 per cent of the total land area.

More recent creations are the 70 or so nature parks (*Naturparks*) which account for 20 per cent of the total area of Germany. Nature parks are generally privately owned and permit levels of agriculture and controlled tourism (including roads, accommodation and campsites) that can sustain quite large communities. The parks may also contain nature reserves and landscape protection areas where more stringent rules of protection apply. Debates have arisen over the permissible scales of new development in nature parks (such as road building) and the effectiveness of the conservation work that is being carried out there. Where parks straddle national boundaries (as between Germany and Belgium, Luxemburg and the Netherlands), they are called Europa parks.

Inspired by a UNESCO initiative, a 1997 amendment to the 1996 law for the protection of nature created a new category of landscape. Biosphere reserves (*Biosphärenreservate*) are designed, not just to conserve the natural ecology, but also to enable researchers and environmentalists to develop new concepts of land use by human beings. In many ways the concepts are very traditional: historical forms of agriculture and local industries are encouraged, as are communities living and working alongside nature. There are currently around a dozen such reserves, both privately and state-owned, accounting for 3 per cent of the total land area.

A very small proportion of German forests (0.2 per cent) is designated as nature forest reserves (*Naturwaldreservate*), although the term varies from state to state. Any form of human intervention or harvesting in these areas is prohibited and nature is allowed free reign. There are over 600 such reserves.

Right of access in Germany means that members of the public can usually walk along tracks, paths and farm roads in forests, mountains and along the coast. The right does not extend to cultivated farmland. Unlike the UK there is no system of designated public rights of way or bridleways in Germany, although conflicts of access between private landowners and members of the public wanting recreational access rarely arise in practice (Speakman and Speakman 1992: 28).

Red lists

Since the early 1970s the Federal Office for Nature Protection (*Bundesamt für Naturschutz*) has published at irregular intervals red lists (*Rote Listen*) of endangered plants and animals in Germany. By 1996 scientists had investigated about half of the total 28 000 or so plant species in Germany and identified 30 per cent as under threat. Most endangered were plants that thrived in nutrient-free water and whose natural habitats, such as still-water lakes, ponds or streams, had disappeared. A red list for animals and fishes compiled in 1984 (for western Germany only) revealed that up to 64 per cent of fish species investigated and 75 per cent of reptiles were significantly endangered. A list for species of birds (compiled in 1991) placed 39 per cent of the 273 native nesting birds into this category. In 1994 the Federal Office published for the first time a list of biotopes (ecological micro-environments). The list identified about 500 different biotopes, ranging from high alpine meadows to various kinds of water environments, and classified 60 per cent of them as endangered (including wetlands, moors, streams, rivers and heathland). The figure for biotopes gives some cause for concern since, while fauna and flora may recover fairly rapidly in the right conditions, the destruction of micro-environments is often irreversible (Fritzler 1997: 113–14).

FURTHER READING

Fritzler (1997) and Malunat (1994) gives comprehensive pictures of the development of German environmental policy. The journal *Praxis Geographie* contains numerous articles relevant to environmental issues. For further reports and up-to-date information, see the website for the Federal Office of Environmental Protection (*Bundesamt für Naturschutz*), which also contains links to the regions. All the leading environmental protection organisations mentioned in the chapter maintain internet sites in Germany. Rüdig (2000) considers the genesis and development of the phasing out of nuclear energy, in particular the dilemma faced by the Green Party and the role played by the powerful German electricity industry.

11

LANGUAGE ISSUES: COMMUNICATION PROBLEMS BETWEEN EAST AND WEST GERMANS

Johannes Schwitalla

INTRODUCTION

When, during the night of 9–10 November 1989, East Berliners could drive their East German Trabi cars unhindered across the border into West Berlin and young people danced on the Berlin Wall, the Germans were, in the words of Chancellor Helmut Kohl, 'the happiest people in the world'. But the euphoria did not last long. Like the hangover after a party, disillusionment set in after the initial enthusiasm. West Germans saw the former GDR as a ramshackle structure needing large sums of money to restore. East Germans saw themselves deprived of many of the things that had contributed to their former security and well-being: free childcare and day nurseries, state-subsidised housing, a guaranteed workplace and an assured financial future. When the former GDR suddenly adopted the social, economic and political structures of West Germany, its citizens also came under pressure to acquire western forms of communication and patterns of linguistic behaviour. West Germans could carry on speaking and writing as before, but east Germans were obliged to adapt to western norms of communication if they did not want to see themselves relegated to a sub-culture (Eroms 1997: 7). In the words of Peter von Polenz:

> After the transitory phase of spontaneous, linguistically creative liberation from a highly ideological, institutionalised and ritualised language, the new citizens of the Federal Republic found themselves, linguistically and politically, in an unparalleled situation: very rapidly they had to acquire total mastery of a system of public communication to which they had had only superficial exposure or had

imitated only to a limited extent; and it was a process to which they could not bring very much of their own experience.

(Polenz 1993: 139)

The following chapter analyses the extent of the communication problems encountered between east and west Germans after unification. The reader will require some knowledge of the German language, although, where possible, items have been translated into or explained in English.

NEW COMMUNICATION DEMANDS ON EAST GERMANS

Unlearning old words

Overnight words and phrases that belonged to official political life of the GDR and to Marxist–Leninist ideology became redundant. The first to disappear were terms for state institutions, although designations for jobs, professions and social roles were also discarded. Examples include: *der Dispatcher* (project controller), *der Ferienhelfer* (holiday helper), *die Frauen-Sonderaspirantin* (female Ph.D. scholarship student), *der Kandidat* (candidate member for the SED), *der Kulturobermann* (functionary responsible for culture in a trade union group) and *der Neuerer* (working methods innovator). To the list may be added the many types of cadre or cells of party activists that were found in all walks of life in the GDR (*Führungskader, Nachwuchskader, Nomenklaturkader, Reisekader, Spezialkader, Wirtschaftskader, Kaderleiter, Kadersachbearbeiterin*). Terms for events, such as *die Dorffestspiele* (village fair), for crimes designated by the state, such as *die Republikflucht* (leaving the GDR without an exit visa) and *der landesverräterische Treuebruch* (literally treason, but used to persecute political opponents), and for official awards, flags and other symbols or icons simply disappeared. Throughout the country streets and squares were renamed.

Many words that had associations with everyday life in the GDR suddenly became tainted. An applicant for a job, for instance, had to decide whether to write that he had been *werktätig* (GDR usage for employed) or *erwerbstätig* (western usage; see Kühn and Almstädt 1997: 90). Should he refer to his national service as *Armeezeit* (east) or as *Wehrdienst* (west)? Even quite innocent words became suspect simply because by using them speakers immediately betrayed that they came from the new eastern states: examples include *Fahrerlaubnis* (for *Führerschein*, driving licence), *Drei-Raum-Wohnung* (for *Dreizimmerwohnung*, a three-room flat) and *werter Herr!* (for *meine Damen und Herren*).

Inhabitants of the eastern state of Sachsen also have to cope with the fact that their dialect sounds comical to many Germans. Among the German dialects, Sächsisch is fairly low down in the scale of popularity. Indeed, nowhere are courses for learning how to speak in standard high German more heavily subscribed than in Sachsen (Heinemann 1995: 393; practising high German is also a theme of Uwe Timms' novel *Kopfjäger*).

Learning new words and phrases

Although east Germans were always better informed about conditions in the Federal Republic than west Germans were about the GDR, they had to bear the burden of linguistic reorientation. Along with a new political system, the complete political and economic lexicon of the FRG entered the eastern states. Words such as *Talsohle* (in the doldrums), *Produktivität* (productivity), *Konjunktur* (conjuncture), *Arbeitsamt* (employment office), *Umweltverträglichkeit* (compatibility with the environment), *Sozialhilfe* (welfare benefit), *Subventionen* (subventions) and *Randgruppen* (fringe groups) had to be learned from scratch (Polenz 1993: 137).

The new language began with the basics of greetings and addresses. There was widespread uncertainty in the east about how to address strangers (Good 1993: 251; Kühn and Almstädt 1997: 92). In the former GDR you addressed someone you did not know personally in a letter as *Sehr geehrter Herr X!* or as *Werter Herr X!* (for a woman the address was: *Sehr geehrte/verehrte/werte Frau X!*). In any case it was unusual to write to a total stranger, and the need to draw up a job application never arose. Many east Germans found the customary western address of *Sehr geehrte Damen und Herren* (followed by a comma instead of an exclamation mark) highly unusual. Even odder, possibly insincere, for them was the closing formula *mit freundlichen Grüßen*. All easterners knew that the final greeting *mit sozialistischem Gruß* was archaic, but they were unsure whether to write *Freundliche Grüße, Mit freundlichen Grüßen, Mit bester Empfehlung* or *Ihr sehr ergebener*. According to Ingrid Kühn and Klaus Almstädt, who run a free telephone advisory service in Halle, there is still considerable uncertainty as to the correct usage (Kühn and Almstädt 1997: 92).

Also new for east Germans are the many Anglicisms used in the Federal Republic. These include not only everyday words from computing (*hotline, online, homepage*) but also terms such as *City-Shuttle, Hair-Stylist, der Hot-dog, das Handy* (for hand-held telephone or mobile) and *das Team*. Now fashionable throughout Germany, *Team* used to be a taboo word in the GDR (Fix 1997: 38). It is replacing the east German *Kollektiv* (collective), although *Kollektiv* continues to appear in compounds such as *Arbeits-, Ärzte-, Stations-, Lehrer-, Klassen-* and *Schülerkollektiv* (Kühn and Almstädt 1997: 93; Reiher 1997: 45). As in the west, the widespread use of anglicisms generates protests, especially from people who have not learned English. Thus in a letter to the east German newspaper *Mitteldeutsche Zeitung* a reader wrote: 'I don't at all see why I must say *cash* when we have the perfectly good German word *bar* which everyone here understands' (Kühn and Almstädt 1997: 91).

Re-learning old words

Words which referred to aspects of life in the Federal Republic and which from the Marxist point of view were therefore bourgeois suddenly lost their negative connotations after unification. There are a number of examples of this. The word *Gymnasium* (grammar school) is no longer a type of school which produces class inequality but the most desirable institution in which to have one's own children educated. Similarly a *Privatpatient* (private patient) who can afford to pay for medical treatment outside the state health service is demonstrating his or her high professional status. The *Beamte* (civil servant), who is in many respects the western counterpart of the *Kader*, is looked up to as having a dream job at a time of high unemployment. Easterners who are able to set up their own firms and become self-employed have the prestige of joining the ranks of the *Mittelstand* (the sector of small to medium-sized independent businesses).

New modes of communication and text types

The changes in political and economic circumstances that took place in the east after unification led to a demand for new kinds of texts. In the old GDR there was no market for buying and selling houses and apartments. Apartments were allocated by a special commission (*Wohnraumkommission*) run by the local state authorities (Hellmann 1991: 23). Anyone who wanted to move into a more suitable flat normally advertised for an exchange. Such advertisements or notices were restricted to purely informative descriptions of the kind of apartment that was being offered and what was being sought: e.g. *Biete gr. 3-Raum-Whg., 96 m². Dimi str. VH. 1 Tr., Balkon, gefl. Dusche, IWC, verkehrsg. Suche 2-Raum-Komf.-Whg., auch Altneubau, mit mod. Hzg. Tel. 449 75 29, ab 18 Uhr* (Reiher 1997: 42). For west Germans such an advertisement and the terms it uses are hard to understand. An *IWC*, for instance, is an *Innen-WC* or inside toilet. An *Altneubau* is an old building or property (*Altbau*) that has been renovated. *Gefl.* is an abbreviation for *gefliest* (tiled). A *Komfortwohnung* has a bath and toilet. *Dreiraum-Wohnung* would be *Dreizimmerwohnung* in the west.

In a capitalist economy most apartments are not let by the state or by city authorities but by private persons or organisations. This means that prospective tenants have to introduce themselves personally in an advertisement and make a good impression on the landlord. It is important to stress that he or she has permanent employment (and can therefore pay the rent regularly) and enjoys the highest possible social status. An advertisement in a Dresden newspaper (*Dresdner Neueste Nachrichten*) that appeared as early as 1990, the year of unification, reads as follows:

> Jg., christl. Familie (Dipl.-Ing, Musikpäd.) mit kleinem Clown (6 Monate) sucht dringend eine 3-Raum-Wohnung o. größere mit Bad. Zahle Miete auf westdeutsch. Niveau. Auch Kaufangebote angenehm.

> (Reiher 1997: 48)

Easterners are unaccustomed to interview situations in which they have to introduce themselves or apply for a position. There are considerable differences in the way in which east and west Germans present themselves. In interviews east Germans avoid referring to themselves in direct, open terms, preferring to talk about their biographical circumstances rather than their personal wishes, interests and capabilities. This is reflected in the syntax of their language, which employs the subjunctive more frequently in order to soften or qualify ideas, contains more passive constructions and uses the impersonal pronoun *man* (one) more often instead of the self-referring *ich*-form. East Germans also make an effort to strike a more formal tone in interviews: they use words that are stylistically marked as more formal (*Besiegelung* instead of *Unterschrift* for 'signature'), speak in a more round-about manner, and draw on phraseology that is characteristic of official speeches and pronouncements; they also use more rhetorical dual forms (*ständig und fortwährend*), more noun formations and functional verbs (thus *prüfen* is reformulated as *prüfende Tätigkeiten aufnehmen*; see Birkner and Kern 1996; Auer 1998, 2000).

It is also interesting to note that the German maxim 'work is fun' (*Arbeit macht Spaß*) makes sense to west Germans but at first meant little to easterners. When asked in 1992 what makes being a salesperson 'fun', an east German became very confused and said: 'I can't just go and say to people . . . I'm doing this just for fun'. When asked the same question, a west German on the other hand simply replied: 'It's fun if someone doesn't plan to buy anything but ends up buying something anyway' (Birkner and Kern 1996: 9). This picture changed, however, from the mid-1990s onwards. Now east Germans claim as often as west Germans that work is enjoyable (ascribing to it words such as *Spaß* or *Reiz*; Birkner and Kern 2000: 59). Furthermore, in a comparison of job interviews carried out in 1992 and 1995 Auer (2000) found that east Germans were adapting to western linguistic usage: in 1995 they were using more frequently the *-in* suffix for female job titles and avoiding synonymous dual forms and other manifestations of officialese, although the pronoun *man* still occurred more often than *ich*. On the other hand, modal particles such as the southern German *halt*, which is advancing steadily northwards and is also encountered more often in west Berlin than the east of the city, are acquiring a certain prestige among east Germans (Dittmar 2000: 225ff.).

Partially identical expressions with different meanings

That east and west Germany share the same language should not lead us to overlook the fact that people from the old and the new states to some extent associate different concepts or connotations with the same expression. At a conference of sociologists in 1993 in Düsseldorf, at which the role of intellectuals in the GDR was discussed, a west German delegate closed his paper with the words: 'Intellectuals – but you didn't have any in East Germany' (reported in *Die Zeit* (15) 1993: 67; see also Fraas 1994: 89f.). Apart from simple ignorance the speaker revealed a particularly west German understanding of the term 'intellectual'. In the west to be an intellectual implies adopting a critical attitude to prevailing social and political conditions. An intellectual is likely to be an independent author or artist rather than, as was the case in the east, a paid civil servant of the state (see also Fraas 1994: 88f. for concepts such as *Mutter* (mother), *Sicherheit* (security); and Polenz 1993: 142f. for 'false friends' such as *planen, Markt, Bilanz, rationalisieren, sanieren, kalkulieren, Fond, persönlich, individuell, Eigentum, privat, gesellschaftlich, Partei, Freiheit, Pluralismus, russisch*).

The unpleasant experiences that many east Germans had with the new economic system (unemployment, short-time working, loss of income) reinforced the negative connotations of words such as *Konkurrenz* (competition), *Team, Unternehmer* (entrepreneur) (Good 1993: 254f.). Likewise west German trade unionists had to learn to handle with care words which were highly valued in the east: examples include *Solidarität* (solidarity), *Bewusstsein* (consciousness), *Einheit* (unity), *Fortschritt* (progress), *die Massen* (the masses) and even *Partei* (party). Many citizens of the former GDR could no longer bear to hear these words because they had been so grossly overworked by their politicians.

Serious misunderstandings arise even in everyday life because the same expression is partly interpreted in a different way. Manfred Hellmann (1994: 132f.) reports from his own experience how an estate agent in a west German town tried to arrange an apartment for a young couple from the east. At first the couple was very reserved (*schüchtern*) and appeared 'almost as supplicants' (*fast wie Bittsteller*); the properties offered were generally too expensive. The agent then offered them an *Altbauwohnung* (literally, a flat in an old building). The couple were outraged and said something along the following lines: 'No flat in an old building for us! You can't do that with us any more!' As a result the agent considered the east Germans to be 'demanding' (*anspruchsvoll*) and 'ungrateful' (*undankbar*). The couple presumed that the agent was trying to fob them off with the worst of all possible properties. What had happened? Simply, west and east Germans understand different things by the term *Altbau*. In the GDR it was a flat that had not been properly renovated since the Second World War. In the west it is a house about 20 years old which has all the facilities that an *Altbau* lacked in the GDR: central heating, running hot water and its own toilet.

REACTIONS IN THE EAST: EXCESSIVE CONFORMITY V. OUTRIGHT RESISTANCE

Excessive conformity

If you travel by car through the eastern states of Germany you are struck by how often English words appear in advertisements or in public notices. One advertisement, for instance, contained the following: *Bestellen Sie über unsere Hotline das Frühstückscenter für Kids* (Kühn and Almstädt 1997: 91). A *Frühstückscenter* denotes a breakfast box or tin (normally: *Frühstücksdose* or *Frühstücksbüchse*). Elements of advertising copy are even adopted in spoken German. Thus, in a store (*Kaufhalle*, itself an eastern term for *Kaufhaus*) in the Prenzlauer Berg district of Berlin, a 'rustic woman' asked for *krispi Röggli* and *beste Bohnen* instead of what would normally be *Schrippen* (the Berlin word for a bread roll) and simply *Kaffee* (coffee) (Good 1993: 253).

Office secretaries complain that their bosses take great care to adopt western linguistic usage. One said:

> All my life I have been writing the word *Stenographie* (typing) with an 'f'. Now I am supposed to write it with 'ph'. Just because, unlike the GDR-Duden, the new all-German dictionary lists the version with 'ph' first, my boss considers it to be the correct usage.
>
> (Kühn and Almstädt 1997: 87)

Outright resistance

Recordings of family conversations in Thüringen (Grötsch 1994) show how citizens of the former GDR compare themselves with their new western compatriots, and in particular how they set up contrasts between 'us' and 'them' (*wir* and *sie*), 'here' and 'there' (*hier* and *drüben*), 'the east' and 'the west' (*Osten* and *Westen*) and 'as it was in the GDR' and 'now in the Federal Republic' (*damals in der DDR* and *jetzt in der Bundesrepublik*) (Hausendorf 2000: 87ff.). Disillusioned easterners, especially old people, defend everything associated with the east and find nothing good in things western. Typical remarks include: 'In the GDR all types of salt had iodine added – not so in the west'; 'I don't like the taste of sausage from the west'; 'We used to be able to get sheep's cheese and it was dirt cheap' (compared to the present); 'Over there they're much more inhibited' (about bathing in the nude) (Grötsch 1994: 16, 27, 43, 18).

East Germans also express a stubborn adherence to former patterns of living by continuing to use words that were characteristic of the GDR. Not all words which have a west German synonym have been abandoned. East Germans (including journalists writing in eastern newspapers) still say *Broiler* instead of *Brathähnchen* (roast chicken), *Lehrling* for *Auszubildender* (apprentice), *Zielstellung* for *Zielsetzung* (goal or objective), *Kaufhalle* for *Kaufhaus* (department store), *Plaste* for *Plastik* (plastic), *vorfristig* for *vorzeitig* (before the deadline) and *Altstoffhandel* for *Recyclingbetrieb* (recycling unit) (for lists of east–west synonyms see Kühn and Almstädt 1997: 90; Reiher 1997: 44). Above all, the words *Plaste, Kaufhalle* and *Broiler* have acquired the status of symbols of east German resistance to the west (Eroms 1997: 8: Hellmann 1997: 19; Kühn and Almstädt 1997: 93; Reiher 1997: 45). An east German wrote to the language advice centre in Halle:

> In a school with imported (!) teachers from the west we find it hard to maintain our language usage. For us a *Broiler* (*Grillhähnchen*) is just that and a *Plastebeutel* (plastic bag) is not the same as a *Plastikbeutel*. But, if you please, when we use these words it doesn't mean we are making a mistake and have to be corrected. To correct us is being small-minded.
>
> (Kühn and Almstädt 1997: 93)

In school, east German pupils continue to address their teacher as *Fräulein*, although this form has completely disappeared in the west as a result of feminist criticism of sexist language (Gansel and Gansel 1997: 62). The east German woman will still refer to her job or title without the (feminine) -in suffix: thus she is an *Arzt* (doctor), *Lehrer* (teacher), *Rentner* (pensioner) or *Anwalt* (lawyer), whereas the west German will call herself *Ärztin, Lehrerin, Rentnerin* or *Anwältin* (Eroms 1997: 12).

On unification many east Germans were shattered to discover that their apartment block was suddenly owned by a west German. As soon as renovation work had been carried out they were faced with rent increases, or the building was sold to a wealthy buyer from the west; attempts were also made to evict tenants of several years' standing. Experiences with unscrupulous and money-grabbing western landlords are reflected in accusing words such as *Raffke, Miethai* and *Entmietkommando* (Eroms 1997: 12). Easterners also voiced their discontent through jokes. The following joke was at first censored in a broadcast by the east German radio station *Mitteldeutscher Rundfunk*:

Mrs Bähnert, how do you know when unification is complete?

When the name of the last east German is taken off the land register.

(Eroms 1997: 9)

COMMUNICATION CONFLICTS IN DISCOURSE BETWEEN EAST AND WEST GERMANS

Most studies of differences in linguistic behaviour between east and west Germans are based on public or formal situations, such as radio and television broadcasts, discussions and debates held in institutional surroundings, or job interviews. Little research has been undertaken into differences that may arise in private communicative contexts (Grötsch 1994).

Besserwessi

Probably sooner rather than later after unification west Germans began to treat the east Germans as inferiors. Such behaviour served only to reinforce the stereotype of the *Besserwessi*, a pejorative word for the know-all, superior westerner. During the Leipzig Trade Fair of 1990 Sabine Ylönen (1991) made a video recording of a discussion between a west German supplier of prefabricated homes and a potential east German customer enquiring about a possible business relationship. The west German behaves in an authoritative, almost schoolmasterly manner. He explains fundamental principles of the market economy, talks for much longer than the easterner whose concerns he ignores; curtly stating his demands ('you have to pay'), he displays no signs of uncertainty or any inhibitions and sets down all the conditions, using expressions such as *Sie müssen* (you must), *das muß also* (it has to), *Sie könn nich* (you can't) and *das Unternehmen hier in der DDR muß* (the company here in the GDR must). He even moves to a higher step on the exhibition stand in order quite literally to 'talk down' to his interlocutor.

West Germans often find themselves in situations in which they have to explain things to east Germans. As representatives of a triumphant political and economic system they are projected into the interactive role of the expert adviser, although this in turn reinforces the stereotype of the *Besserwessi* (Fiehler 1995: 337, 340f.; Paul 2000: 133).

East Germans: insecurity and provocation

Complementing demonstrations of west German superiority, east Germans conform willingly to the role of novices who have much to learn. During the above conversation analysed by Ylönen, the representative of the east German company listens patiently and shows that he is paying close attention by giving the appropriate signals of assent. He avoids using his native dialect (Sächsisch) and speaks in hyper-correct standard German. He uses the subjunctive and the modal verb *können* (can) to qualify his statements.

The easterner's feeling that he is swimming in uncertain communicative waters produces insecurity in his own speech. Kühn and Almstädt (1997: 88) report that west Germans have no inhibitions about calling up the language advice centre, in contrast to east Germans, who are hesitant and proffer excuses. While west Germans conceal their lack of knowledge, easterners openly admit it:

> Can I possibly approach you with a language problem? I'm not sure whether . . .

> I can't find an explanation in the reference books for . . . I don't have the latest editions.

> I hesitated for a long time before calling you. Please help me.

East Germans need to be reminded that they should not be too modest in a job application when they are describing their personal abilities and the state of their knowledge (Kühn and Almstädt 1997: 92). In conversations with westerners, east Germans freely acknowledge the inferiority of the political and economic system of the old GDR. They make excuses and offer explanations for their lack of expertise and skills ('we didn't have that', 'we couldn't do that', or 'we weren't allowed that'). They try to evoke sympathy and to adopt the standard German of the westerner (Heinemann 1995: 393). On the other hand, the expert or superior tone adopted by westerners generates annoyance in both east and west Germans. Easterners respond by interrupting, objecting very strongly and defending highly valued terms and expressions from the former GDR (for an example, see Paul 2000: 125ff.). They refer to their industriousness and thus assert a common sense of identity *vis-à-vis* west Germans.

Problems of self-presentation

For a west German it can be a problem asking someone from the east about what he or she did before unification. If the easterner had an exceptionally high position in society, it raises the question of how he or she stood in relation to the political system. As a result east Germans do not find it as easy as westerners to present themselves. Nor do they see their previously high social status in a positive light (Wolf 1995). If someone was a school headteacher, a senior doctor, a manager in a state-run industrial organisation, the natural presumption is that he or she was a member of the SED or might even have worked for the secret service or *Stasi*. Even showing pride in having visited the west is hazardous: membership of the privileged travel cadres (*Reisekader*), who were permitted to travel outside the socialist bloc, suggests a particularly high degree of loyalty to the state.

In any case, east Germans find it much harder than westerners to present themselves personally. Whereas west Germans can relax in being citizens of a successful, model democracy, easterners are compelled to explain their attitude towards the former GDR state. In terms of attitude we can – very broadly – distinguish three categories of east German: the declared opponent to the regime; those who stayed on the sidelines (rather like those who went into 'inner emigration' during the Nazi period); and those who supported the GDR state out of idealism. The third type tends to explain the fall of the GDR by claiming that he or she was let down by the regime and that the calcified party apparatus was no longer capable of carrying out reforms.

Differences in proximity and distance

A very important reason for communication problems lies in the varying interpretation of interpersonal proximity and distance – as often occurs in encounters between members of different cultures. East Germans were accustomed to working in groups (collectives) which fostered the formation of diverse and intensive interpersonal contacts. People had more time during their work to talk to each other than in the west. They spoke more about personal problems and knew more about the living circumstances of their colleagues. They were also more likely to go for a beer together in the pub after work.

When *Ossis* (or east Germans) criticise *Wessis* (west Germans) as *kalt* (cold), *unpersönlich* (impersonal) or even *herzlos* (unfeeling), they are also expressing their disappointment at having lost the close interpersonal proximity that they enjoyed in the old GDR. Difficult situations arise if east Germans assume that their new western colleagues want to establish a close relationship of this kind. When asked *Wie geht es Ihnen*? (How are you?), easterners will answer at length and in detail until they notice that the question was meant only as a polite and rather empty phrase (rather like Anglo-Saxon usage), not as an enquiry after one's personal health. They are likely to encounter distrust or rejection if they suggest doing something privately outside work, such as going for an excursion. They give small presents to persons with whom, from a western point of view, they do not have a close enough relationship to merit such gifts. They begin a telephone conversation by launching into the first topic as though they had just seen the interlocutor.

They go to social events organised by colleagues which west Germans in a similar professional position would never attend. They speak more openly about personal problems that westerners would be more likely to keep to themselves and they offer people insights into aspects of their private lives that west Germans would share only with a few close friends.

East Germans have realised very quickly that this way of close, trusting communication is not approved of in the west and have adapted to the new customs. At the same time they have retained the stereotype of the 'superficial' and 'cold' *Wessi*, which they explain as a product of capitalism and its culture of competitiveness.

Ideological differences

In conversations between east and west Germans phrases repeatedly occur that are characteristic of one side or the other. In a discussion about success in school a woman from west Berlin referred generally to 'sociocultural' (*soziokulturell*) and 'social' (*gesellschaftlich*) circumstances that affect the individual: 'Well, it's not the state that controls things, it's more, really, how shall I say, sociocultural, social factors, and things like that, isn't it?' Her east German interlocutor answers: 'Yes, and it's also a question of how much money you've got' (Streeck 1995: 432). The east German draws on a different explanatory model for social phenomena: instead of trying to see things in some vague 'sociocultural' context she refers to economic conditions, which are in turn interpreted in terms of a Marxian theory of a base (*Basis*) and a superstructure (*Überbau*); in other words, rich parents can afford better schools (also see Paul 2000: 128ff.).

Opposing stereotypes

East and west Germans have formed clear and mutually opposing images (stereotypes) of themselves and of each other. Seen from the east, west Germans are hard-working but ruthless and pushy (Germans refer to this as the *Ellenbogenmentalität or* 'elbow mentality'). As *Besserwessis* they are arrogant, boastful, egoistic and avaricious. Everything in the west is sparkling clean but lacks a homely feeling. In 1994 a young east German said in a television broadcast:

> If, for example, a *Wessi* says to me, 'Do you feel at home in these run-down houses?', I tell him, 'Yes, I prefer that to when I go to the west, where everything looks tip top, the streets look wiped clean and the grass is cut perfectly'. I feel at home here. It's cosy and has a nice atmosphere.

From a western perspective the east Germans are too subservient, have an authoritarian streak in their character and are anti-foreigner. They are not very creative and tend to hide away in the group. Everything in the east looks a bit shabby, if not dirty. The landscape is polluted and the staff on public transport are very unfriendly. Since the *Wende* they like to feel sorry for themselves (Moeller and Maaz 1995; Auer 2000: 171; Hausendorf 2000: 89; for changes in stereotypes see Pohl 1997: 67).

These mutually held stereotypes are well known. As a result, when west and east Germans communicate with each other, each side protects itself against the prejudices that they presume the other side is nurturing. In a discussion between east and west German members of a political party, a western woman made it clear that she shared the 'prejudice' that creativity was not valued in the GDR. An east German pretended not to hear the self-characterisation as a 'prejudice' and began to present herself as a creative woman who, frustrated by the rigid structures of the GDR, simply gave up rebelling: 'All my life I can say I was actually creative. But I couldn't succeed. In the end I was totally deadened' (Wolf 1995).

It is unfortunate that, by admitting she had given in to her resignation, the east German women confirms another western stereotype: namely that her compatriots – with the honourable exception of the 1953 uprising – kowtowed to the regime for 40 years. Both east and west Germans feel compelled to put themselves forward as people who do not conform to the established stereotypes. In a television chat show about the consequences of unification, the west German host (Michael Jungbluth) said: 'We will just **advise**, because I don't believe that we should go around everywhere saying we **know exactly what should be done'** (Fiehler 1995: 345). This statement can only be understood as an attempt by the speaker to distance himself from the stereotype of the *Besserwessi*.

Similarly, in a television debate, an east German woman distanced herself from the stereotype that easterners feel themselves only to be victims of the new conditions:

> The *Wende* did not do me much good. Like many others I lost my job. The reason was the children. I have two small children. **But I have never complained** because I am one of those who say 'we never want the (Berlin) Wall back again'.
> (Televised debate *Deutsche Einheit*, broadcast in Leipzig, 1994)

In the same debate young east and west Germans repeatedly drew attention to a known stereotype and then questioned it. A common device for this was the phrase, 'There are some types and there are others' (*Es gibt solche und solche*). A young east German from Berlin said:

> There are certain situations where I say, 'OK, I'll put three kilometres between me and the *Wessi* if he comes along with his arrogant behaviour' . . . **on the other hand** I must also say I've known *Wessis* who have helped me.

A young west German woman said: 'But it's really **not** true that **all** *Wessis* **are know-alls** and **all** *Ossis* – er – **are just after the money.'**

Often, however, speakers actually confirmed the stereotype that the other side had of them. A young west German estate agent who rejected the stereotype that all *Wessis* were egoistic displayed those very features of boastfulness, superficiality and materialism by the way in which he himself talked:

> If you look at all the *Ossis* who have made a lot of money, yes, who have cottoned on to how to make a fortune, yes? They don't live any differently from

the *Wessi* . . . that every *Wessi* who goes to the east for the first time wants to show off for the first couple of weeks and – er – prove to the *Ossi* how fast his car is and so on, that's obvious, isn't it? But I reckon none of that will last for long.

CONCLUSION

It is not surprising that for some years now east Germans have been experiencing a certain nostalgia towards the former GDR: the German word for this is *Ostalgie*, a play on *Ost* (east) and *Nostalgie* (nostalgia). *Ostalgie* can go as far as denying how the regime suppressed freedom of thought, especially on the part of *Andersdenkende* (people who dared to 'think differently'), and trivialising the Berlin Wall. It appears in expressions such as 'not everything was bad in the GDR', or 'we had children's nurseries, a job and a home', 'life was a lot more peaceful' or 'we didn't have to make so many decisions as we do today'. To counter such whitewashing it is necessary to recall how the regime used techniques of spying, blackmail, unlawful imprisonment and even violence to maintain its authority.

Forty years of diametrically opposed political and economic structures, conflicting ideologies, different living conditions, the intimidation of a whole people and the brutal suppression of dissidents necessarily leave their mark. Difficulties in communication will remain as long as differences in living conditions persist. I should like to conclude with two hopeful observations and a comparison.

First, in the summer of 1996 my wife and I spent our holiday in Vorpommern, in a small village on the Baltic Sea. A couple from Thüringen was staying in the same guest house. We talked almost every evening and struck up a good relationship. When the holiday was over my wife and I wondered whether we had experienced any communication difficulties because we came from east and west Germany. We found none.

Second, if you ask west German professors teaching at an east German university what strikes them about their students they will reply that those who were still at university during the GDR period behave in a totally different way from west German students. Younger east German students, however, are no different from west Germans.

Finally, if you say that communication between east and west Germans is difficult, you have to remember how much more difficult it was when the country was still divided by the Wall. Most west Germans never visited the GDR, so there was virtually no communication at all. And when citizens of the Federal Republic conversed with strangers from the GDR, they encountered many more problems than they would now: east Germans who actively supported the GDR were ideologically immune and could muster a Marxist–Leninist response to any democratic argument. At the same time, critics of the GDR did not dare to speak openly because of the fear of being denounced.

12

BERLIN SINCE 1989: POLITICS AND CULTURE IN THE CAPITAL

Ulrike Zitzlsperger

Since reunification Berlin has become a renewed focus of national and international interest, although this interest is no longer due to the city's former status as a symbol of the division between the major power blocs of East and West. While Berlin's situation is unique, the city mirrors cultural trends which to some extent are representative of developments in the country as a whole. For this reason this chapter will use Berlin as a case study for analysing contemporary German culture. It will emphasise broad trends and developments and, where relevant, draw on aspects which are not specifically Berlin-based. The chapter will provide a brief survey of the city's history, explain its role for post-unification Germany and outline how a metropolis deals with its past, present and future. It will then examine how literature, film and theatre are responding to new parameters that have been set since the fall of the Wall.

BERLIN IN THE TWENTIETH CENTURY: A BRIEF HISTORICAL SURVEY

The impact of the fall of the Berlin Wall in 1989 and the subsequent *Wende* in German political, social, economic and cultural life has been felt most strongly in the newly reunified Berlin. More than ten years later, at the beginning of the twenty-first century, this process still has no obvious end in sight. In fact this is not the first time that Berlin has had to adapt itself to new circumstances. In the last 130 years the city has been shaped by many changes in its appearance and image. After the First World War, the magnificent imperial city of the late nineteenth and early twentieth century was inextricably linked with the culturally vibrant but politically doomed Weimar Republic. Under the National Socialist dictatorship of 1933–45, Berlin became the headquarters of a reign of terror. During these years the forced emigration of those who disagreed with the politics and ideology of National Socialism and the brutal persecution of the Jews and many others drained Germany, and particularly Berlin, of its most notable cultural resources.

With sufficient time, Hitler would have ruthlessly transformed the city centre: in the summer of 1937, he commissioned the architect Albert Speer to prepare plans for the construction of a new Berlin, to be called *Germania*. Only the Second World War (1939–45) brought these plans, which were gross in terms of their monumental scale and the cultural message they conveyed, to a halt.

By 1945, aerial and artillery bombardment had reduced Berlin to rubble. After the destruction that the war had brought to Europe, Germany had to make a completely fresh start: the expression *Stunde Null* (zero hour) given to the period immediately after Germany's capitulation on 8 May 1945 epitomises the amount of destruction and the conscious desire to break with the past. The destruction of Berlin – like that of most German towns and cities – was on a vast scale: there were 75 million cubic metres of debris, a seventh of the volume of rubble in the whole of Germany. As in other cities the dumping of this rubble led to the construction of artificial hills, one of the most famous in Berlin being the *Teufelsberg*. The women who cleared away the remains were dubbed *Trümmerfrauen* (rubble women); their work was back-breaking, since most of it had to be done by hand or with very simple tools. The immediate post-war street scene was dominated by these women, since many men had been killed or wounded or else remained in foreign captivity as prisoners of war. It took months until electricity, gas, water and food supplies, mail and telephone services were restored, even if only on an *ad hoc* basis. Raw materials, whole factories and railway rolling stock were commandeered by the occupying Soviet troops, who had reached Berlin before the other allied forces; the entire electrified railway system was dismantled and transported to the USSR.

Like the rest of Germany, Berlin was divided by the victorious allies into four zones of occupation. The eastern sector, which included the historic city centre, fell under Soviet occupation, while the western half of the city was occupied by the Americans, the British and the French. Inevitably, the diametrically opposed political and ideological views held by the western allies and the USSR soon led to disagreements and tension. When a new currency, the *Deutsche Mark* (DM) was introduced in the West – including West Berlin – Stalin reacted by blockading the city, virtually taking its inhabitants hostage and cutting off all supplies from the West. Road, rail and shipping traffic were all interrupted. This apparently hopeless situation led to one of history's logistically most impressive airborne operations. From 24 June 1948 until 12 May 1949 the western allies supplied West Berlin with all its essential needs by air. Despite Soviet harassment some 277 000 flights brought food (mostly in dried or powdered form, to reduce its weight), medicine, coal and even spare parts for a new power station.

By the time the blockade was eventually lifted, the Soviet Union had suffered considerable loss of face. Furthermore, western help had turned former enemies – notably the Americans – into friends, and the West Berliners' stamina during these trying times provided them with international recognition and admiration. The number of West Berliners who took up the communist authorities' invitation to avoid the impact of the blockade of the western sectors by shopping in the east had been insignificant: only about 5000 out of approximately 2 million people chose to give in to the deprivations imposed on them. In 1998 Berlin celebrated the 50th anniversary of the Airlift, recognising the astounding achievement both of the pilots and of the Berliners. Today, the Berlin Airlift – the *Berliner Luftbrücke* – has acquired mythical status: it has become one of the glorious legends that contributed – and still contributes – to the self-confidence of a city whose political and physical division rendered it unique.

During the Cold War Berlin became a playground of the superpowers. In 1961 the construction of the Wall, which split Berlin in two, appeared to make the division of both the city and Germany as a whole permanent. Berlin had become two separate entities – two cities, two countries within one; within each half, people's lives were determined by radically different systems of government. Over the years the Wall – a man-made structure visible from the moon – was refined into a more and more sophisticated system that became virtually impregnable. The long-term impact of such a tangible symbol of demarcation can also be seen in literature. Before 1989 novels, stories and poems tried to come to terms with the division by analysing the effects that it had on the lives of the population and on the city itself. However, even literature written after the fall of the Wall continues to record the scar across the middle of Berlin and to acknowledge the persisting differences between people who had been living in a city that had been divided not just geographically but also politically, economically and culturally.

After the establishment of the two German states in 1949, East Berlin became the capital of the German Democratic Republic (GDR) while Bonn was chosen as the provisional capital for the Federal Republic of Germany (FRG). It was intended that Bonn, as capital, should be replaced by Berlin if circumstances permitted (in other words, if Germany were to be reunited), although in most people's minds this became more and more unlikely. Although West Berlin was part of the FRG, it retained a unique status: it did not enjoy the same political position as a federal state such as Bayern or Baden-Württemberg.

After 1961 the authorities in East Berlin were keener than ever to promote its role as a model communist capital within the Warsaw alliance. The communist government concentrated considerable resources on this still war-damaged showpiece, while other parts of the GDR were deprived of much-needed investment; such preferential treatment became a source of irritation to East Germans. West Berlin, meanwhile, faced challenges on a different scale. Its particular geographical position as an outpost of West Germany within the GDR made it strategically important – it was still occupied by the western allies – but this isolated shop window of western wares and western ways was highly dependent on subsidies from the FRG. The political situation in West Berlin led to a quite different development from that of other West German cities such as Frankfurt, München or Stuttgart. Geographical isolation and the latent threat from the East made West Berlin unattractive to potential investors. Eventually the city became demographically unbalanced: it consisted of more than the average number of pensioners and of people under 30, many of the latter eventually leaving for the West to take up a more promising career.

At the height of the student movement of 1968–69, it was the young who began to shape the cultural image of a city whose very lack of normality meant that it could be turned into something creative, something unconventional. During the 1970s and 1980s young people, including students, those avoiding conscription in the FRG by living in Berlin and politically aware lateral thinkers, established several movements calling for an alternative society. These alternative groups had a considerable and enduring impact on the cultural scene; indeed, some of Berlin's fringe groups survived the changes of 1989. These movements are closely associated with one district in particular, Kreuzberg. After 1961 Kreuzberg found itself right next to the Wall and became the place to go for cheap living or to express certain views. Its vibrant and multicultural creativeness and sporadic outbursts of political extremism turned it into another Berlin 'myth'. With the fall of the Wall Kreuzberg lost its exceptional geographical status and many of its former activists moved on to the nearby fashionable eastern districts *Mitte*, *Friedrichshain* and *Prenzlauer Berg*; now attracting more affluent residents, these central areas are beginning to display interesting shifts in their demographic structure.

In 1987 Berlin celebrated its 750th anniversary (the first reference to the city appears in a document dated 1237). As ever, co-operation between East and West proved impossible; both halves of the city celebrated the event separately – a powerful expression of its divided status. In the year preceding the anniversary a serious debate on German historical issues (the *Historikerstreit* or 'historians' dispute') had begun in the press and had some impact on the celebrations. On 6 June 1986 the right-wing historian Ernst Nolte triggered the debate in the West German daily newspaper *Frankfurter Allgemeine Zeitung*. Nolte focused attention on contemporary Germany's responsibility for the nation's National Socialist past. Some participants in the ensuing controversy argued for a balanced judgement of twentieth-century Germany that took account of the many other crimes against humanity committed during the course of the century. The debate rages on: in a public speech given in 1998 when awarded the Peace Prize of the German Book Trade, the prominent author Martin Walser fanned the flames by calling for a considered end to the long-established practice of *Vergangenheitsbewältigung*, the Germans' 'coming to terms' with their own past. Controversially, Walser characterised Auschwitz, the central symbol of the horror of the Holocaust, as a 'means of intimidation or moral bludgeon which can be used on any occasion' (*'jederzeit einsetzbares Einschüchterungsmittel oder Moralkeule'*).

While some Germans debated their past, others looked forward. One of the international special guests who visited West Berlin in 1987 was the American President Ronald Reagan. In a speech delivered at the Berlin Wall he challenged the Soviet Union by demanding: 'Mr Gorbachev, tear down this Wall.' To most people this call simply appeared as empty rhetoric; few thought that such a demand would soon be fulfilled. In East Berlin the celebrations for the city's anniversary went ahead – ostentatiously and according to the government's plans. How worn out the GDR had actually become only fully emerged two years later. The ageing governing élite was unable to react to the people's increasingly vocal demands for democracy. Following several months of political unrest, the Wall was finally breached: East and West Berliners came together on the night of 9 November 1989 after nearly three decades of separation. Images of the fall of the Wall and the subsequent outburst of enthusiasm were televised live all over the world. Thanks to technological innovations each and every aspect and development of this peaceful 'revolution' could be recorded and presented to an international public who were avidly following events. Berlin, which had in truth only been one of a number of cities where protesters demanded changes in East Germany, once again became a focal point of international attention – this time for purely positive reasons.

A decade later, the unification of Germany (which officially took place on 3 October 1990) was viewed somewhat more soberly. The process proved to be far more complicated than most expected, embracing politics, economics and culture and necessitating careful management of the legacy of the immediate past. While some European countries initially displayed marked reservations over the rapid developments of 1989–90, a new generation of foreign journalists reporting from Berlin expressed surprise that so many Germans continued to worry about the country's image. When Germany took stock on the two anniversaries – 9 November 1999 and 3 October 2000 – it was clear that for those generations whose lives had been shaped by the divide, one of the unfinished tasks that still needed to be addressed was the removal of the Wall in people's minds. But throughout the first decade of reunification Berlin was a hotbed of creative experiments – a forum for new definitions of the city, of Germany and of the future role of both within a European and international context. The fact that up to 1999 there have been more than 17 000 recorded publications on 'reunification' shows just how controversial the topic has remained.

THE LEGACY OF REUNIFICATION

Reunification meant that Berlin suddenly became the natural focal point of the newly constituted Germany: historically, since up to 1945 it had been the capital of the German Reich; culturally, because throughout the years of division it had benefited from substantial subsidies for all kinds of cultural events, simultaneously profiting from an active alternative scene; and symbolically, for when viewed from abroad, the reunification of the city represented the process in the whole of Germany. Descriptions such as 'bridge', 'workshop' and 'building site of unity' demonstrate Berlin's particular role. As Germany is federally organised, Berlin's role is not comparable to that of Paris or London. On the contrary, the Federal Republic has several cities which are cultural centres with a vibrant and creative life of their own. München, Stuttgart, Leipzig, Dresden, Frankfurt, Köln, Hannover and Hamburg all have a distinct cultural identity. But Berlin's cultural importance also fulfils a representative function: as the capital city, where east and west come into direct contact, and as a modern metropolis whose inhabitants are drawn from over 180 nationalities – including 130 000 Turks, 30 000 Poles and 23 000 Russians – Berlin offers a veritable kaleidoscope of cultural possibilities.

Once Berlin was reunified and had become the focus of international attention, it appeared to be the obvious candidate for the seat of government. However, in the early 1990s a debate began about whether Bonn or Berlin was the more appropriate choice. Partly due to the anticipated international response, the German Parliament (*Bundestag*) discussed the issue with care. Indeed, it was a highly sensitive issue, one that had to take account of Germany's history, its strong economy and central position within Europe. While the provincial town of Bonn had represented 40 years of sensible and efficient democracy, several political commentators placed great weight on Berlin's geographical position within the former GDR. A successful Berlin would, they hoped, also present an opportunity to the new federal states (*neue Bundesländer*), as the regions in the former GDR became known. The then Chancellor, Helmut Kohl, had rashly promised *blühende Landschaften* (blossoming landscapes) in the new states. Others portrayed Berlin as a bridge between eastern and western Europe, and stressed its vital position at the heart of the continent. Some advanced the argument that the historical handicap of the National Socialist past had to be considered as a special factor; others, however, pointed out that the burden of the National Socialist past applied throughout Germany and not only to Berlin.

There were further powerful issues to consider. In 1949 Bonn, a pleasantly modest town on the Rhine, had represented a fresh start and had symbolised West Germany's commitment to the western powers. In contrast to this, the sheer number of Berlin's inhabitants (about 3.5 million), its much-praised multicultural atmosphere and its diverse social problems made it a genuinely lively and modern political centre.

Another argument also had a historical dimension. Since the late 1940s politicians had stressed Berlin's role as the capital-in-waiting when reunification would eventually be achieved. To ignore this article of faith would have been to question a historical commitment and to ignore the fact that for 50 years Berlin had officially symbolised the determination of the German people that their country would one day be reunited. One point made by supporters of Bonn has proved to be accurate: the cost of reorganisation and reconstruction in Berlin has turned out to be higher than had been forecast.

On the other hand apprehension that a government based in Berlin might undermine Germany's well-established federal tradition appears to have been unfounded. However, although the official transfer of the German government's work to Berlin (1999) did not banish Bonn to obscurity, the town underwent a dramatic change. The political functions that remain cannot compensate for what it has lost. At the same time the life and infrastructure of Berlin have been transformed dramatically by the move.

On 20 June 1991, after an emotional debate, parliament voted on Berlin as the capital and seat of government (*Hauptstadt- und Regierungssitz*). The result was a close call, with only 337 votes for and 320 against. Prominent supporters of Berlin included the then Chancellor, Helmut Kohl, and the former mayor of West Berlin and ex-Chancellor, Willy Brandt. Party loyalties played little part in the outcome – certainly less than local allegiances or where members of parliament came from. Representatives from the west and south of Germany tended to vote for Bonn, those from the north and the east for Berlin. Older members of parliament also seemed to be more inclined to approve the relocation than their younger colleagues. Whatever such trends, the first democratically elected German Chancellor to work in Berlin since 1933 was Gerhard Schröder (SPD), who entered government in coalition with the Green Party (*die Grünen*) in 1998.

Already in the mid-1990s some, including the German media, had coined a new term for the Federal Republic, dubbing it the *Berliner Republik*. This provoked further heated debate. For some the term is all-too reminiscent of the ill-fated *Weimarer Republik*. Others are concerned that the constitutional continuity in the Republic's politics may become blurred if this new name gains currency. On the other hand the term *Berliner Republik* epitomises the changes in social and cultural conditions taking place throughout the Federal Republic of Germany and emphasises the fact that the capital serves as a sign-post for new trends in the twenty-first century.

Arguably, Berlin's most important government building is now the *Reichstag*, originally completed in 1894. The interior was completely redesigned by the British architect Norman Foster. Central to Foster's design is an enormous glass dome. This much-debated feature has proved to be a huge success, especially since the general public is able to ascend the glass structure and have a panoramic view not only of Berlin but also of parliament at work. As an institution, the *Reichstag* played a central role in the downfall of the Weimar Republic: when the building was destroyed on 27 February 1933, a young communist, Marinus van der Lubbe, was found guilty of arson. This gave the National Socialists a welcome opportunity to persecute, torture and imprison anyone who disagreed with their regime. During the Third Reich the building, which had briefly stood as a symbol of German democracy, was put to use as a venue for Nazi propaganda exhibitions such as 'Bolshevism without its mask' (*Bolschewismus ohne Maske*) or anti-Semitic events such as the exhibition of 'The Wandering Jew' (*Der ewige Jude*). Against this background it is hardly surprising that the *Reichstag* was one of the buildings most fiercely fought over in 1945:

more than a million bullets hit its walls. Thanks to careful renovation work, the scribbles and doodles left behind by the victorious Soviet soldiers can be seen again. After the Wall divided the city in 1961 the *Reichstag* was only used occasionally: though situated in the western part of the city it was next to what the GDR referred to as the 'bulwark against fascism' (*antifaschistischer Schutzwall*). Attempts by the *Bundestag* to meet in the *Reichstag* building during the Cold War years were interrupted by low-flying Soviet aircraft. The exhibition *Fragen an die Deutsche Geschichte* (Questions on German History), organised by the German *Bundestag* and opened in 1971, turned out to be a long-term success. When reconstruction work began on the *Reichstag* the exhibition moved into the *Deutsche Dom* in the *Gendarmenmarkt*, one of Berlin's most beautiful squares and situated in the former eastern half of the city.

In 1995 a unique event captured both public and media attention alike for two weeks. The artist Christo, his wife and their team 'wrapped' the *Reichstag* in iridescent fabric. His view was that

> The use of fabric on the *Reichstag* follows [a] classical tradition. Fabric like cloth-ing and skin, is fragile. It expresses the unique quality of impermanence. For a period of two weeks, the richness of the silvery fabric, shaped by the blue ropes, created a sumptuous flow of vertical folds highlighting the features and propor-tions of the imposing structure, revealing the essence of the *Reichstag*.
>
> (Christo and Jeanne-Claude 1995: 93)

The visual impact of Christo's undertaking was no doubt overwhelming. The special atmosphere surrounding the area during those weeks drew com-parisons with the American 1969 Woodstock Festival. The magazine *Stern* wrote:

> It is quiet. Thousands of people move respectfully round the building; the silvery cover is like a halo. Visibly moved, these people touch the heavy cloth and take small pieces back as relics. Berlin has a new holy shrine for pilgrims, one that offers unity to everyone.
>
> (*Stern* 1995: 21)

To stage this unique event Christo had had to battle with the authorities for some 24 years. And only after a 70-minute debate in the *Bundestag* and a close vote (292 to 223 with nine abstentions) was he allowed to proceed.

With the resumption of parliamentary business in the reconstructed *Reichstag* the building has been open to the public on a number of occasions – not simply the dome and the surrounding terrace with its view over Berlin but also the main building itself. This has established the *Reichstag* as one of the city's new landmarks. The American publicist Michael Z. Wise com-ments that the choice of the British architect Foster was in itself symbolic. It is hard to disagree with his point that it would be difficult to imagine France, Britain or the United States appointing a foreigner to draw up plans for their parliament buildings (Wise 1998: 126).

The controversial wrapping of the *Reichstag* was an important cultural phenomenon in its own right, proving that, given a new historical situation, culture can follow new paths. As well as attracting tourism, this condition of

Figure 12.1   Many streets, in particular in the city centre, were renamed after unification

flux in a metropolis caught between past and future has also provided authors with interesting topics and resonant metaphors. It is through cultural activities that the inhabitants of Berlin have regained possession of their city during the post-1989 transitional years. The public's acceptance of all the large-scale rebuilding of Berlin's city centre has been decisive; for nearly a decade the building sites have replaced the Wall as a major tourist attraction. In 2000 alone around 10 million tourists stayed in Berlin for at least one night (55 per cent more than in 1993), overtaking München and Hamburg for the first time. This figure still does not compare favourably with the 25 million overnight stays in Paris and the 60 million in London, but the 1999–2000 millennium celebration with its 'light show' around the Victory Column (*Siegessäule*) attracted a further 1.5 million visitors to Berlin from all over the world. Besides the usual tourist sites, young people in particular are attracted by the less 'mainstream' parts of the city and its receptiveness to different cultures.

During the 1990s wholesale reconstruction of derelict land left over from the Second World War or resulting from the removal of the Wall gave rise to further public debate. In particular this focused on the necessary integration of the infrastructure left over from the divided city and the redevelopment of the government quarter. The discussion concentrated on the architectural, town-planning and historical dimension of each scheme. In part this was due to the *Schaustellen-Sommer* (Showcase Berlin, a series of cultural and architectural events staged at building sites throughout the summer from the mid-1990s) organised by the Berlin Senate in co-operation with the agency

Figure 12.2   *Potsdamer Platz*

Partner für Berlin, but it also reflected the sheer immensity of the building work and its importance for the future of the city. *Potsdamer Platz* – during the 1990s Europe's largest urban building site – is without doubt the most remarkable example.

Potsdamer Platz, a square originally just outside the city's western gates, was at its liveliest and most famous during the 1920s, when it was a busy centre day and night and legendary for its provision of all manner of entertainment. One of the few nostalgic remnants of this period is a replica of Europe's first traffic-light, which was installed to control the increasing urban traffic of the 1920s. After the Nazis' accession to power in 1933 *Potsdamer Platz* changed. Hitler and Speer's architectural plans for *Germania* would have made the square obsolete. Their fantasies, however, were overtaken by events: wartime bombardment and defeat transformed it into yet another expanse of rubble. After 1945 three of the allied sectors had their boundaries here, which made it an ideal site for the burgeoning black market. Ingeborg Wendt's post-war novel *Notopfer Berlin* describes the atmosphere thus:

> The sun is shining above the Potsdamer Platz, a neutral sun overlooking parties and nations, the righteous and those who are not. Three sector boundaries converge here and though you cannot see them that makes them all the more noticeable: the Russian, the English and the American border. The Potsdamer Platz is in the East, the Potsdamer Strasse in the West and in between there is the dark ruin of Potsdamer Bahnhof, a burnt out shell, empty and redundant. In West Berlin they build flats, department stores, night-clubs and palaces for insurance companies. In East Berlin they build new housing estates, theatres, nationalised shops

and government buildings. The local governments in East and West are building, but Berlin is divided.

(Wendt 1956; reprinted 1990: 40)

The few buildings to survive the War intact – such as the *Columbus-Haus* – were destroyed on 17 June 1953 when East German workers demonstrated against the communist government in a futile attempt to change its policies. Throughout the 1950s *Potsdamer Platz* served both as a crossing point within the city and a border between the Eastern and Western zones. Absurdly, Western tram-drivers had to disembark here to be replaced by their Eastern colleagues at the boundary. Day and night, political information flooded the square: news and propaganda via loudspeakers, films and banners constantly delivered the ideological soundbites of the day. With the construction of the Wall the square was turned overnight into an empty wasteland, through which ran an increasingly sophisticated death strip. The memory of the square's former glory was revived in a short scene in the film *Der Himmel über Berlin* (*Wings of Desire*, directed by Wim Wenders, 1987).

A few months before November 1989, the Daimler-Benz company (now Daimler-Chrysler) purchased part of the land where the former square had been from the West Berlin Senate. With the fall of the Wall on 9 November the former no man's land became the centre of the city again: the new owners turned what once might have appeared as a peripheral building venture into a centre-piece of the new Berlin. In 1992 an international architectural competition was held to decide how the square should be rebuilt. Building work started in 1995 and 'Daimler-City' was opened on 2 October 1998. Meanwhile other plots of land, such as that owned by Sony, have also been completed, and *Potsdamer Platz* is now one of the most prominent landmarks of the unified city. Though it has prompted some adverse criticism its success with Berliners and tourists (70 000 visitors per day) seems to justify the choice of design.

Throughout the redevelopment of the square the public have been kept deliberately involved. The history and the 'myth' of *Potsdamer Platz* were carefully nurtured, the meaning of each architectural decision was explained, so that for an increasingly aware citizenry the process of building could be turned into yet another – this time long-term – 'Berlin event'. Ballet companies danced on newly laid foundations; during the night the countless cranes were artistically illuminated and a temporary information centre – the *Info Box* (1995–2000) – explained what was happening on the building sites. It is significant that the *Info Box* became one of Berlin's most popular destinations for tourists and locals alike. 'Needless to say', Werner Sewering reminds us, 'this welling-up of spirit is more directly concerned with the production of images than with the real Berlin' (Sewering 2000: 47).

The link between building work and cultural events, which shaped the life of the city throughout the 1990s, has been labelled *Architainment* and has helped Berliners to accept the numerous changes to the face of the city while simultaneously making many cultural events more public and accessible. In the literature of the 1990s – for example in the novels *Allerseelen* by the Dutch author Cees Nooteboom and Peter Schneider's *Eduards Heimkehr* (both published in 1999) – *Potsdamer Platz* features as a metaphor for Berlin's history, the city's wounds and the current process of 'healing'. It is also a focal point for the protagonists' observations of the new Berlin. But the square symbolises far more than the anticipation of a completely new city centre, because the past is totally unavoidable here: Hitler's bunker, although not open to the public, lies nearby, as do the Gestapo's torture chambers, which are now part of the museum and memorial, *Topographie des Terrors*. The very question of Germany's past and how individuals and the nation may best try to come to terms with it has been another literary theme since the early 1990s.

One building that has stimulated public awareness does not even exist any longer: the former *Berliner Stadtschloß*. Here too, the practical questions confronting Berlin after reunification cannot be separated from the historical dimension. The *Schloß*, once the Berlin residence of the Hohenzollern monarchs, was badly damaged during the Second World War. Situated in the old city centre, it became part of the Soviet sector after 1945. Six years later, Walter Ulbricht, the East German head of state ordered its destruction, regarding it as a symbol of a 'reactionary way of thinking'. International protest, even from Moscow itself, could not save the building. It was razed to the ground – apart from the balcony where in 1918 Karl Liebknecht had proclaimed a Soviet-style republic, only two hours after the Social Democrat Philipp Scheidemann announced the establishment of the democratic republic from the *Reichstag*. The balcony was later integrated into the nearby *Staatsratsgebäude*. The demolition of this *Schloß* posed difficult questions in the 1990s: how was the newly unified Federal Republic to deal with the heritage of communism – in this case a huge, barren parade ground and the so-called *Palast der Republik*, which had been nicknamed 'ballast of the republic' by citizens of the GDR? As far as the architecture that had been shaped by communist ideology was concerned, this question had far wider implications: was this heritage to be accepted as part of history and therefore to be integrated into the new Republic, or was the *Berliner Republik* to wipe out all traces of a widely despised past – comparable to the clean sweep which took place in both parts of the country after 1945? That the 'clean sweep' approach could go too far became obvious in the early 1990s when a small minority demanded the demolition of the East Berlin TV Tower on *Alexanderplatz* – one of the highest and most frequently visited constructions of its kind in Europe. Along with a host of political and town-planning considerations there is also a strong need for preservation of Berlin's cultural heritage. Those who feel nostalgic (or, to use one of the popular neologisms, *ostalgisch*) indulge in the opportunity to invoke the past: shops selling GDR goods (*Ostalgie-Läden*), parties with old GDR music (and, as a high point, another 9 November to finish off the night) and, although outside Berlin, even a hotel run in the style and manner of the

GDR – all are in demand, at least from those whose lives were shaped by the period between 1949 and 1989.

One reason put forward for rebuilding the *Schloß* is that there is now an unattractive gap at its former site on the boulevard *Unter den Linden*. On the other hand, the undertaking seems irresponsibly expensive when compared with more urgent tasks. The original building had well over a thousand rooms, posing an interesting question as to what to do with a building of this size. To make the debate more comprehensible to the public, Wilhelm von Boddien, a businessman from Hamburg, started a private initiative in 1993. He instructed the Parisian artist Catherine Fess to cover scaffolding with painted strips imitating the original façade of the building. For several weeks this folly gave Berliners and visitors an impression of what the area would look like if it were properly restored. After the elections for the Berlin Senate in 1999, the SPD and CDU accepted the rebuilding option as part of their coalition agreement.

The physical removal of the Wall changed the appearance of Berlin fundamentally. While it stood, 155 kilometres of the Wall surrounded the western enclave; it had 302 watchtowers and 43 kilometres were driven right through the heart of the city. Districts which previously had been on the periphery of one or the other half of the city suddenly became central. What had been the centre of West Berlin, the area around the *Breitscheidplatz* with the ruin of the *Kaiser Wilhelm-Gedächtniskirche*, is now located to the west of the city. The *Kurfürstendamm*, during the Cold War the West's principal shop window, was soon faced with serious competition from the rebuilt *Friedrichstraße* and the world famous boulevard *Unter den Linden*. An even stronger potential threat to West Berlin's shopping centre is the stylish new shopping mall at *Potsdamer Platz*, the *Arkaden*, which is advertised as an urban entertainment centre and 'invites' Berliners to feel like tourists. While these competing projects are new, others have a longer history. As a result of Cold War divisions, Berlin is a city of mirror images, with all the most important structural components duplicated. It soon became clear that some rationalisation of the duplication would be needed. There are, for instance, three large universities: the *Freie Universität* which was founded in the West during the *Berlin Blockade*, the *Technische Universität* and the long-established *Humboldt-Universität* on *Unter den Linden* in the former East. There are 14 specialist colleges, over 200 state-owned or private research establishments, numerous large district libraries and three opera houses: overall, Berlin has about 2300 permanent cultural institutions. Even a decade after reunification some of these issues still triggered heated arguments about the perceived preferential treatment of institutions in the western or eastern half of the city.

Throughout the 1990s an increasing number of 'new areas' established themselves as points of attraction. Before 1989 people had met in the western districts of *Schöneberg* and *Kreuzberg* to spend the small hours in the countless modern, old-fashioned and unconventional pubs which were open 24 hours a day; this licensing allowance was a conscious attempt to make West Berlin, geographically isolated as it was, more attractive. Now the new magnets are the former eastern districts *Mitte*, *Friedrichshain* and *Prenzlauer Berg*. *Prenzlauer Berg* had established itself before 1989 as a haven for disaffected people who were out of sympathy with the GDR and tried to lead an alternative life-style.

One of the most heavily promoted streets in the old city centre is the *Oranienburger Straße*. The rebuilt synagogue at the south-eastern end of this street is a new focus of Jewish life in Berlin and its golden cupola constitutes one of the most important landmarks of 'the new Berlin' (*das Neue Berlin*, as it was widely advertised during the 1990s) skyline. The street, which once belonged to the *Scheunenviertel*, a rather poor district inhabited by Jewish immigrants from the east, ends at *Hackescher Markt* with a development called *Hackesche Höfe*. Renovated in the early 1990s, the complex of courtyards, typical of the layout of many once densely populated poorer districts of Berlin, is now dominated by a mixture of cinemas, cabarets, cafés, bookshops and studios. At the other end of *Oranienburger Straße* is the *Tacheles*, formerly the *Friedrichstraßen-Passage*. In the first decade of the twentieth century, this was one of Berlin's first shopping arcades; now home to alternative culture, the ruin was occupied in the early 1990s by young artists who combined cultural activity with their characteristic life-style. The ruin has now been renovated, and in the year 2000 its inhabitants were able to secure the future of their project. Their occupation of the historical building had, in fact, contributed to its fame. Houses occupied by squatters were first found in West Berlin during the early 1980s when young people tried to save empty buildings from being demolished by speculators. The evictions that followed often led to violence between the police and the occupants. The author Ingo Schramm dealt with this topic in *Fitchers Blau* (Berlin 1996); his novel is set in the early 1990s when blocks of flats in East Berlin were repossessed by their pre-GDR owners.

A wide variety of clubs contribute to the vibrant culture; here young Berlin's contribution, techno music, took off. Many of these clubs thrive in unusual locations such as the *E-Werk*, a former power station. The well-established cultural scene has since adopted a similar strategy – with huge successes, such as the staging of Mozart's *Don Giovanni* in the *E-Werk*. In 2001, one of the leading 'institutions' is *Maria am Ostbahnhof*, but the club culture is subject to rapid change. The very nature of the clubs has fostered a proliferation of posters and leaflets (flyers) – often the only reliable source of information about what's on. Since 1989 the *Love Parade* – originally a genuinely spontaneous political demonstration – has taken over the city centre for a day each summer. Up to a million people participate in this music and dance spectacular; though this event is subject to increasing criticism, it is very successful – not least financially (indeed, since 2000 it has been copied in other cities too). Smaller projects such as the *Schultheiss-Brauerei*, which uses a former brewery for various cultural activities, are looking for public–private partnerships in order to stay solvent.

REMEMBERING THE PAST

Berlin's past is omnidirectional, but there is no agreement as to the nature of its significance or how best to commemorate it. When on 3 August 1998 a memorial to the Wall was erected in the *Bernauer Strasse* many of those who had lived with the real divide were distressed by its lack of authenticity. Among the few original sections of the wall that have been preserved is the *Eastside Gallery*, a 1.3 km stretch that separated East Berlin from the death strip between *Oberbaumbrücke* and *Ostbahnhof*. Artists from all over the world painted their impressions, memories and interpretations of the Wall on it. One of the most famous paintings on the now listed remains is *The Kiss* between Erich Honecker and Leonid Brezhnev, the former Soviet leader, by the Russian artist Dimitry Vrubel. Some critics object that this memorial detracts from the quality of a nearby canal bank, but both the artwork itself and its communication of what the Wall was really like – however imprecise – fully justify its continued preservation. There are many literary reflections on the East–West divide and the danger of forgetting – the Wall has gone and only the 'Wall in people's minds' (*die Mauer in den Köpfen*) remains, as Peter Schneider anticipated in his 1983 narrative *Der Mauerspringer*. More and more documentaries are now reviewing the recent past, but the importance of such authentic evidence increases with the passing of time; lines on the road indicating where the Wall once stood are not enough.

A bitter debate arose over the Holocaust Memorial to be located just south of the Brandenburg Gate in the very heart of Berlin. First proposed in 1988,

Figure 12.3   Artwork on the Berlin *Eastside Gallery*

Figure 12.4   *Eastside Gallery: The Kiss* and a fond memorial to the '*Trabi*'

more than 500 artists and architects took part in a competition in April 1994, followed by a second competition only open to invited participants. After lengthy discussions and much revision, a design by the American architect Peter Eisenman was finally accepted. Some concern was raised that the central position and high profile status of this memorial might threaten the status of other existing memorials. Some felt memorials to Jewish victims of the National Socialist regime should not take pride of place over all the others who were persecuted and perished, for example gypsies, homosexuals and members of certain religious groups. In time, a general consensus developed in favour of Eisenman's memorial, and in June 1999 it was approved by Parliament. It will consist of 2700 concrete columns intended to convey the impression of a gigantic swaying cornfield.

In the same year, the Jewish Museum was opened as an extension built on to the *Berlin Museum* and designed by the architect Daniel Libeskind. The

Figure 12.5 Site for the Holocaust Memorial

architectural features of this building have proved to be so eye-catching and thought-provoking, that even when empty of exhibits, the museum has become a major attraction; during the first six months of 1999 alone 70 000 visitors came to see it. The new museum has no entrance of its own, the purpose being that the *new* should only be accessible via the *old*. The building is clad with a metallic façade and designed like a flash of lightning in zigzag form – one that is intended to signal the juxtaposition of German and Jewish culture, a concept that is repeated throughout the museum. The intentionally integrated empty spaces, the so-called *voids*, symbolise Jewish life destroyed by the Holocaust. Three paths lead the visitor through the museum: the first represents the Holocaust, a cul-de-sac ending in the oppressive *Tower of Silence*; the second is the path of exile which leads into a garden of columns, suggesting the sense of being lost and the helplessness felt by many exiled Jews who ended up in countries where they were not necessarily welcome or whose language they did not speak; the third is the path of continuity which takes the visitor through the museum and cultural achievements of Jewish history.

A memorial illustrating the reactionary cultural tendencies of the Third Reich can be found on the *Opernplatz* opposite the Humboldt University. At the very place where in May 1933 allegedly 'immoral' and 'subversive' books were destroyed by the National Socialists, a glass plate set in the pavement affords a chilling view into a bare white room, its walls lined with empty bookshelves. The authors whose works were burnt included Albert Einstein, Thomas and Heinrich Mann, Carl Zuckmayer and Stefan Zweig. That even very popular memorials need to be protected is shown by a development in 2001: the Berlin Senate was considering turning the site into an underground car park.

ART IN POST-WALL BERLIN

Both fine art and the various cultural events benefited from the renewed historical awareness and curiosity of a general public experiencing change on all sides. In the 1990s a new awareness of the physical location of a cultural event emerged. The *lange Nacht der Museen* (literally, 'the long night of the museums'), which is part of *Schaustelle Museum*, exemplifies this. It is not just the opening hours that break with the normal routine of museum-visiting. The idea is that one can go to various museums on a particular night. During the event these museums are linked by shuttle buses and offer music, readings and food. In the year 2000, when this took place for the seventh time, 50 institutions took part.

This new receptiveness, as well as the increased awareness of locations, can be observed outside Berlin too. In the industrial district of the Ruhr, for example, the *IBA Emscher Park* (International Building Exhibition Emscher Park) – which was open from 1989 to 1999 and spread over 120 different sites – displayed exhibits featuring aspects on ecology, regional planning, infrastructure and (mainly industrial) culture. This aimed to give fresh stimulus to the whole region; the central theme was the need to reshape the appearance of the area by paying special attention to the strengths and requirements of its physical location.

In Berlin, new museum and exhibition space also brought private collectors to the fore. The *Sammlung Berggruen* (Berggruen collection), which includes exhibits by Picasso, Braque, Klee and Giacometti, and *Sammlung Marx* (Marx collection) with its contemporary art in the decommissioned and renovated *Hamburger Bahnhof*, both opened in 1996. They have remained successful despite the fact that the main area of interest is concentrated increasingly on the old centre further east.

It was not until the fall of the Wall that Berlin's public art collections, separated since the War, could be reorganised. In 1998, for example, the new Picture Gallery opened at the *Kulturforum*, close to *Potsdamer Platz*. Not least because of Germany's renewed collaboration with countries in eastern Europe and increased transparency in international relations, art illegally commandeered during and after the Second World War has become a prominent issue.

In 1999 the Federal Republic celebrated both the 50th anniversary of its foundation and the 10th year of the *Wende*. Among the many events that were held, one in Berlin stood out in particular: the exhibition *Einigkeit und Recht und Freiheit. Wege der Deutschen 1949–1999* (Unity and Justice and Freedom. German Paths 1949–1999). As in other exhibitions examining the once separated Germanys, the question arose as to how the GDR could be best represented only ten years after its demise. Commenting on this particular exhibition in the German weekly *Die Zeit*, Jeannette Otto criticised perceptions of the GDR that focused solely on its repressive measures; these, she argued, did not necessarily shape everybody's daily life. She maintained that a major reason for the many misunderstandings between the two halves of the country lay in their lack of interest in each other: 'Ten years are a long time to talk and to listen. Few have achieved this. After 1989, 40 per cent of all West Germans have never been to the East, 12 per cent of the East Germans have never been to the West' (Otto 1999).

More often than not, the history of the GDR has been represented as a historical accident, and there has been a notable tendency to lump art and culture together as if they had been directed solely by the state. This is actually an unjustified generalisation, devaluing what was achieved. On the other hand, in recent years there have also been attempts to reconstruct and compare the histories of the two halves of Germany, two remarkable examples being *aufbau west aufbau ost* (construction in the west and construction in the east, 1997) and *deutschlandbilder* (images of Germany, 1998). In addition, a number of retrospective exhibitions have reflected art in the light of the outgoing twentieth century: *Die Epoche der Moderne. Kunst im 20. Jahrhundert* (The Epoch of Modernity. Art in the 20th Century, 1997) and *das xx. jahrhundert. ein jahrhundert kunst in deutschland* (the 20th century: a century of art in Germany). The latter was a particularly ambitious project comprising numerous exhibitions mounted in 1999–2000 in various parts of Berlin and exploring the central theme from differing angles.

Since the *Wende* many new galleries (there are some 350 private galleries in the city) have been established – nowhere more so than in the *Mitte* district of Berlin. Here the influx of eastern European artists has proved especially beneficial. In particular, video art and new trends using communications media (*Kommunikationskunst*) look promising, although by the end of the century no clear direction for their future development had emerged. This is true of the so-called 'New Berlin' in general. A wealth of 'experiments' and 'beginnings' can be observed, dealing with the past and anticipating the future. This very diversity has become characteristic of the years of transition.

ECHOES OF THE *WENDE* IN LITERATURE, FILM AND THEATRE

The fall of the Wall created substantial interest in new novels dealing with the *Wende*. The word *Wenderoman* implies a novel intended to explore feelings in east and west, to make the whole process more understandable and perhaps even to offer a point of reference amid the confusion. Curiosity and expectations ran high, and when the well-known author Günter Grass announced his intention of writing a novel observing recent developments with a critical eye, the anticipation became tangible. *Ein weites Feld* (*Too Far Afield*, 1995) attempts to respond to recent events through a panorama of German history. Here the year 1989 and the early 1990s are just part of a long process, with Berlin set centre stage. The focus of attention, the ageing office-boy Theo Wuttke, alias Fonty, is both a modern figure and also a recreation of one of the most famous German authors of the nineteenth century, Theodor Fontane. Fonty's constant companion is Hoftaller, the eternal informer, whose behaviour reminds the reader that spying by the state was not just a phenomenon unique to the GDR. When *Ein weites Feld* first appeared, reviews were rather unfavourable. Some complained that it was too clever by half, others dismissed it as plain boring. Such fierce reactions, not least in the television discussion programme *Das literarische Quartett*, were the result of exaggerated expectations and it became equally obvious how institutionalised and bound by the mass media literary criticism had become.

Helden wie wir (*Heroes like us*, 1995) by a hitherto unknown east German writer, Thomas Brussig, takes a more light-hearted approach to the recent past and is free of such historical digressions. The central figure is an anti-hero, the involuntary joker Klaus Uhltzscht. When the book was published it was hailed as another 'definitive' *Wenderoman*. Uhltzscht experiences a GDR childhood with all its subtle repressive measures, as a result of which he ends up as an informer for the secret police. Brussig describes the methods of the *Stasi* in a tragi-comic way. Guided by the illustrations of women in glossy catalogues, Klaus perceives the West as a mixture of a forbidden territory and promised land. The discoveries and failures of his sexual experiences constitute one of Brussig's main themes and are the reason why critics described the novel as 'adolescent'. In the final chapters the action becomes farcical: Klaus rescues the GDR party leader Erich Honecker, and the ensuing medical treatment accidentally leaves the protagonist with an enormous penis which subsequently causes the fall of the Berlin Wall. Brussig does not indulge in nostalgia but adds a comic touch to the past. One of the novel's strengths is that its casual approach to serious matters opened up some new perspectives in terms of its orientation to recent history.

Brussig's next publication, *Am kürzeren Ende der Sonnenallee*, makes it clear that in 1999 the absurdity of a divided Berlin is still a rich source for narrative fiction. The main theme of the novel is not simply an attempt to come to terms with the more recent past but to provide an ironic, at times grotesque, reflection on everyday experiences with the Wall. While some critics complained that the book and the film, which appeared in the same year, played down the reality of GDR life, others, who were more favourable to Brussig's approach, felt that it was about time to point out that people in the GDR had led normal lives too. Brussig, by now well known, was given the prestigious project of working as a co-author with the director Edgar Reitz. Reitz gained fame with the film *Heimat*, a chronicle of German life in the twentieth century. In fact *Heimat* comprised three films. The first (and most famous) appeared in 1989 and the second in 1993. The third, *Heimat 2000 – Die Erben* covers the period from the fall of the Wall to the end of 1999.

The label *Wenderoman*, by now a dubious accolade, was also applied to the work of another east German author, Ingo Schulze, whose *Simple Storys* have been translated into 13 languages and comprise American-style short stories. All more or less interconnected, they describe life in the east German provinces. In the aftermath of 1989 some of the characters experience a total change in their way of life, but others live on as if nothing had happened. The authenticity of *Simple Storys* derives from the way in which reunification does not feature merely as a historical backdrop but forms an integral part of the lives described.

Grass and Brussig, by contrast, refer far more to contemporary history, locations, events and public life. Brussig in particular attacks one of the GDR's outstanding literary figures, the novelist Christa Wolf. She achieved notoriety due to conflicts between literary aspiration, political obligations and the writer's responsibility to society – which were all fiercely discussed during the early 1990s. The debate, which became known as the *Literaturstreit*, was ultimately more far-reaching than it might first have appeared. Not only was the focus of debate on Wolf's influential role before and after 1989, but specifically on how much collaboration with the ruling powers was considered legitimate. There were also confessions by other authors, members of the church and politicians. These were often greeted by irritation and accompanied by a media reaction that tended to be more sensationalist than reflective. The fact that the East German intelligentsia resisted the euphoric delights of being absorbed by West Germany only added to the tension. Many were overcome by disappointment when they considered what, given more time and opportunity, the GDR might have become. Early on the author Christoph Hein saw the writing on the wall: 'If we fail, we will be swallowed by McDonald's' (Glaser 1999: 550).

Although Christa Wolf's involvement with the *Stasi* was minor and lay well in the past, she was criticised for the way she handled the situation. Some felt that this hostile reaction was an attempt to drive one of the few authors who were known both in the East *and* the West, into the 'Eastern corner'. Wolf herself interpreted this as symptomatic of the destruction of leading GDR personalities, stating:

> German scholars have suddenly changed their assessment of GDR literature. This has happened not because of literary criteria but because of political and ideological judgement. We were used to this in the GDR and registered with surprise how

ideological West German criticism had become – in particular, when they were looking at East German authors.

(Interview in *Der Tagesspiegel*, 30 April 1996)

The debate had been triggered by one of Wolf's own publications. *Was bleibt* (*What remains*) had appeared in November 1989, although it had actually been written in 1979 and updated. *Was bleibt* describes an attempt by the *Stasi* to recruit her. Interesting though the subject matter is, the main significance of the work lies in the consequences of its publication. Wolf finally found support in the east where her stance against repressive measures was acknowledged and where she was known for standing up for those who had written without following the party line.

The sensitivities aroused by such events should not be played down. In Wolf's case it was relatively easy to separate – if one was willing – the practical possibilities and restrictions of an author's responsibility towards society and the state. When Alexander (Sascha) Anderson's background as a kind of literary double agent became known, the revelations were far more shocking. Anderson had been well known for initiating 'subversive' publications and meetings. For many years he was considered, even outside the GDR, to be one of the driving forces in East Berlin's dissident district *Prenzlauer Berg*. The discovery that for many years he had passed on information about friends and their plans to the *Stasi* came as a bombshell. The betrayal of his friends could not be justified by any claims of putative advantages which his collaboration may have provided for its victims. The close-knit group of artists and authors of *Prenzlauer Berg* were now overwhelmed with mistrust for one another, and what they had believed to be group opposition to the state in the years up to 1989 was now overshadowed by doubt. While everyone knew the *Stasi*'s influence was considerable, no one imagined it could reach that far. One indication of the extent of the *Stasi*'s infiltration of every aspect of life in the GDR is the extent of their records. If the organisation's meticulously kept files – not including the vast collection of photos, films and tapes – were laid out together, they would stretch for 180 kilometres.

At the same time as Sascha Anderson's double life was revealed, the singer-songwriter Wolf Biermann, commenting bitterly on the case, returned to prominence. In the 1950s Biermann had moved from Hamburg to East Berlin because of his political convictions; but persistent criticism of the regime eventually led to his East German citizenship being withdrawn while he was on tour in West Germany in 1976. Though East German cultural and educational politics had been tightened up with the result that Biermann's artistic freedom was curtailed, exile came as a complete shock. As an author, Biermann had become homeless overnight. The fall of the Wall changed all that yet again. Biermann's case typified the difficulties intellectual dissidents now faced: their insights had become obsolete. In 1999, however, Biermannn's *Paradies uff Erden. Ein Berliner Bilderbogen* (*Paradise on Earth. A Picture Book of Berlin*), a collection of songs and ballads was published; its theme is the new capital.

The year 1990 was marked by yet another cultural sensation when the two German literary associations (PEN) were merged. The fusion turned out to be far more laborious than had been expected. Discussions foundered once again on unresolved suspicions on the eastern side and what appeared as arrogant condescension from the west. An additional factor was the anger felt by those who had been forced to emigrate to the west before 1989; they felt embittered when meeting those who had either contributed to their plight or, at best, not helped them. It was not until 1995 that this unhappy situation was resolved when more than 60 authors from the west joined the eastern association.

Despite all the revelations and disappointments of the first years of reunification it soon became obvious that writers from the former GDR still had much to offer. Young authors, in particular, published novels and short stories which did not shy away from social criticism. Few of their western colleagues seemed able to live up to the same standard. Writers who now found critical recognition often had their roots in the (former eastern) alternative literary and artistic scene – for example the linguistic virtuoso Adolf Endler, Jens Sparschuh, the lyric poet Durs Grünbein and Peter Wawerzinek. Some of their publications contributed to a more open-minded, less romanticised view of the rebellious past of dissident writers in the GDR. Endler's diary notes from the early 1980s are particularly worthy of mention. They were published in 1996 under the title *Tarzan am Prenzlauer Berg*. Wawerzinek describes life in the same district in *Mein Babylon* (1994), which draws an impressive picture of the price to be paid for living as part of an alternative culture. His novel *Café Komplott* (1998) deals with contemporary united Berlin: a bank robbery at *Potsdamer Platz* is the setting for the observations of protagonists trying to come to terms with the recent past.

Volker Braun, Helga Königsdorf, Brigitte Burmeister, Monika Maron and Irina Liebmann, to name but a few, published throughout the 1990s. Some of their novels and essays view the past of individual East German citizens; others, such as Ingo Schulze, concentrate on the 1990s and the type of life that people lived after the fall of the Wall. In addition to recent writing, new editions of established literature also flourished after the *Wende*: Theodor Fontane's novels, for example, enjoyed renewed popularity now that it was again possible to trace his footsteps in the former GDR. Furthermore, some novels formerly proscribed by the East German censors now found a wider readership – for example Manfred Bieler's *Maria Worzeck oder das Kaninchen bin ich*, which was written in 1963 and appeared in the west in 1969.

One of the most impressive literary documents to be published in the 1990s was the anthology *Berliner Geschichten*, edited in 1995 by Klaus Schlesinger, Martin Stade and Ulrich Plenzdorf – the latter best known for his novel *Die neuen Leiden des Jungen W.* (*The New Sufferings of Young W.*, 1973). The anthology had originally been put together in the 1970s during the brief period when it was hoped that the GDR's cultural policy might become more lenient. Contributors included well-known authors such as Günter de Bruyn, Stefan Heym and Günter Kunert. However, all attempts to get the book published failed, so the illusion that the government had become more open-minded was shattered:

> Sometime in spring 1976 we called the attempts off and sent the texts back to the authors. Those willing to recognise the reality of the cultural principles established by the Eighth Party Conference were now able to do so. For us it was a morality play on the double standards of power.
>
> (Plenzdorf *et al.* 1995: 14)

What makes the 1995 edition of particular interest is a documentary introduction which includes the files of the *Stasi*, then unknown to the authors, from the years 1975–76. 'On 16 November 1976, the day on which Biermann was deprived of his citizenship, the authority of the state spoke openly; one might say it put its foot down. The echo of that was to stay with us until they finally lost power' (Plenzdorf *et al.* 1995: 19). From publications such as *Berliner Geschichten* it is clear that the past remains integral to future cultural developments. To acknowledge that the legacy of the past lives on is important for understanding how each part of the country lived and why reunification is such a slow and at times painful process.

Looking beyond the critics' dogged search for the archetypal German *Wenderoman*, one is struck by the huge increase in other forms of literary production. A number of authors have attempted to write a new *Großstadtroman* – a novel concerning itself with the phenomenon of the metropolis – as Alfred Döblin did in *Berlin Alexanderplatz* in 1929. The new curiosity about Berlin manifested itself in numerous anthologies, crime novels and biographies which deal with life in Berlin during the Weimar Republic and the Second World War. The creation of huge building sites and the all-pervasive mood of change sparked off a boom in photographic documentaries. Popular novelists profited from a new range of topics that offered themselves in the Berlin of the 1990s. A comment such as 'the first real novel about unification' (*der erste echte Vereinigungsroman*), referring to Marcia Zuckermann's *Das vereinigte Paradies* (1999), is indicative of the need for a more light-hearted approach to the theme of reunification. By the end of the 1990s a number of books had appeared evoking the former West Berlin – Bodo Morshäuser's *Der weiße Wannsee* (1997) being one example.

More than any other city in Germany, Berlin captures the imagination and arouses the curiosity of authors and journalists. The *Feuilleton* – the cultural section found in German newspapers – became a growth industry, and by now most of the major newspapers and magazines have an office in the capital with specialist commentators reporting regularly about political, cultural and architectural developments. At present there are about 200 publishing houses in Berlin; only München has more. A recent survey listed 347 recognised authors in the capital. In March 2001, when the French *Salon du Livre* focused on Germany, it not only confirmed that German literature now tends to be associated principally with its capital but also that the metropolis in particular nurtures young talent. The new interest in media has promoted the establishment of *Kulturkaufhäuser*, department stores which not only offer traditional cultural products but also contain cafés and small cinemas and have stage readings and exhibitions. Meeting places for both unknown and famous authors include the *Literarische Colloquium am Wannsee* in the south-west of Berlin, the *Literaturhaus* in *Fasanenstrasse*, the *LiteraturWERKstatt* and the *Literaturforum* in the *Brechthaus*.

The constantly shifting political scene has, not surprisingly, also rejuvenated German satire. Two controversial publications in particular have attracted public interest: *Der Barbier von Bebra* (*The Barber from Bebra*, 1996) by Wiglaf Droste and Gerhard Henschel, and *Adolf, die Nazisau* (*Adolf the Nazi Pig*, 1998) by the cartoonist Walter Moers. Droste and Henschel's protagonist operates as a crudely explicit serial killer who targets well-known contemporary German figures. Its controversial comic tone is comparable to that of the *endgültige Satiremagazin* ('the ultimate satirical magazine') *Titanic*, which has been both delighting and annoying readers with its irreverent treatment of social taboos since 1979. *Adolf, die Nazisau* resurrects Hitler as a ridiculous modern loser-figure. Commentators from abroad have interpreted this publication as an indication that the Germans may be learning to dissociate themselves from their country's past.

All these new publications cannot disguise the fact that German writers account for only 20 per cent of the domestic market in literature. German works are sparsely represented abroad, although translations are increasingly popular in some former Eastern bloc countries such as Poland. Authors are often accused of being too inaccessible, and since the end of the 1980s there have been regular complaints about a dearth of talent or a lack of life-experience reflected in literature. This is frequently attributed to the fact that cultural activities in Germany are accustomed to being cushioned by subsidies. Neither concepts, such as 'literary postmodernism', invoked to explain the depressed mood, nor comparisons to the heyday of German literature in the 1920s and 1960s have helped to make the environment more encouraging for young writers. Nevertheless, authors such as Judith Hermann (*Sommerhaus, später*, 1998), Felicitas Hoppe (*Picknick der Frisöre*, 1997) or Inka Parei (*Die Schattenboxerin*, 1999) – again, to name but a few – have come to the fore in recent years. Acclaimed as 'the sound of a new generation' they are renowned for their novels and short stories which deal predominantly with individual rather than social topics. Other bestsellers in recent years were the internationally praised *Der Vorleser* (*The Reader*, 1995, translated into 29 languages) by Bernhard Schlink and *Schlafes Bruder* (*Brother of Sleep*, 1992) by Rolf Schneider; the latter followed by a Josef Vilsmaier film adaptation in 1994.

It is also worth observing the remarkable durability of the authors of the post-war literary scene. They continue to prompt intellectual debate, mainly in the former West. Prominent examples were Martin Walser's speech at an award ceremony in 1998, and the publications of Peter Handke with his *Würde des serbischen Eigensinns* (*The Dignity of Serbian Obstinacy*) in 1996 and Günter Grass with *Ein weites Feld* in 1995. Younger authors cause less sensational debates and scandals, but successful sales in the year 1999 indicate – as the magazine *Der Spiegel* ((41) 1999: 245) puts it – that 'the grandchildren of post-war literature are lining up'. They write about recognisably new topics, they have no experience of the National Socialist past and they take obvious pleasure in story-telling. Well-known authors who anticipated this development were, for example, Patrick Süskind with *Das Parfüm* (*The Perfume*, 1985) and Sten Nadolny with *Die Entdeckung der Langsamkeit* (*The Discovery of Slowness*, 1983). The revival of the literary *Salon*, no longer so exclusive, consciously refers to oral traditions of literature; so too do new trends such as 'Open Mike Events' where all those present are invited to present their literary efforts. The immediate contact with an audience is taken as a genuine challenge. Furthermore, a formal platform for new talent is provided at regular intervals by competitions for young authors.

In 1999 Günter Grass was awarded the Nobel Prize for literature, the first German author to win the accolade since Heinrich Böll in 1972. In his acceptance speech Grass, speaking for his generation, acknowledged that,

> Immediately after the war, literature was struggling with the German language, which had been corrupted by the National Socialists' rule. Böll's generation, but also younger authors like myself, were constantly reminded of a sentence that had the power of a prohibitive sign. Theodor Adorno had declared: 'It is barbarous to write a poem after Auschwitz . . .' [*Berliner Morgenpost* 8 December 1999]. Well, we wrote nevertheless. But we had to regard Auschwitz as a rupture, an irreparable break with the history of civilisation.

Grass's latest book, *Mein Jahrhundert* (*My Century*, 1999) has been translated into 30 languages; his novel *Die Blechtrommel* (*The Tin Drum*, 1959), which contributed to his winning the prize, has been translated into 33 languages.

Ten years after the fall of the Wall only a limited number of films deal with the *Wende* and the succeeding years (for example, the comedy *Go, Trabi, Go* by Peter Timm in 1991; the tragic *Wege in die Nacht* by Andreas Kleinert, 1999; while *Die Unberührbare* by Oskar Roehler, 1999, and *Die Stille nach dem Schuß* by Volker Schlöndorff, 1999, explore contemporary German history in the light of the past). However, the 10th anniversary in 1999 stimulated a remarkable number of documentaries (for example *Nach dem Fall* by Eric Black and Frauke Sandig, 1999). Distance over time also allows irony in recording the past. The film *Sonnenallee* (1999) – followed on 9 November 1999 by Sebastian Peterson's film adaptation of *Helden wie wir* – was advertised as a 'birthday present' for the fictional 50th anniversary of the GDR. The director of *Sonnenallee* is Leander Haußmann, the former manager and artistic director of a leading West German theatre (Bochum). In typical GDR jargon the press announcement declared: 'The film-makers of the GDR have joined forces to present the Republic with this birthday present' (*Die Filmschaffenden der DDR bündeln ihre Kräfte und präsentieren der Republik dieses Geburtstagsgeschenk*). Reviewers were hostile: they quickly found fault with the rose-tinted view of the GDR as an apolitical Republic of Hippies, full of amiable citizens. Haußmann was actually sued for allegedly denigrating victims of the Wall – another indication of how widely diverging views of the past and the way in which it ought to be treated are still prevalent.

One of the actors in *Sonnenallee*, Detlev Buck, is also one of the younger generation of directors who have made a number of successful low-budget films (for example *Wir können auch anders*, 1993). These films often feature minor social figures, as do several more recent films about Berlin: *Nachtgestalten (People of the Night*, Andreas Dresen, 1999) studies people who lost their way in the Berlin of the 1990s. Two films with a similar theme are Esther Gronenborn's *alaska.de* (2000) and Uli Schüppel's *planet.alex* (2001). Wolfgang Becker's *Das Leben ist eine Baustelle* (*Life is a Building Site*, 1997) focuses on the daily life of young Berliners, while *Lola rennt* (Tom Twyker, 1998) portrays the same story but in three significantly different versions. The techno soundtrack of the latter contributed to its international success.

Films dealing with the past have usually gone down well with the critics, for example Helmut Dietl's 1991 *Schtonk!*, a satire based on the forged Hitler diaries. In 1997–98, *Comedian Harmonists* (Joseph Vilsmaier), based on the rise and fall of the musical group of the same name, led to a revival of *a cappella* music. The group was internationally famous from 1927 to 1935, after which its Jewish members were excluded. Contemporary interest in 1920s' culture is an additional factor which contributed to the film's huge success. Within a few weeks it had been seen by more than 2 million people in Germany and subsequently enjoyed considerable popularity in the United States. Romuald Karmakar's *Der Totmacher* (1995) is also based on an authentic case that took place during the Weimar era. It tells the story of the mass murderer Fritz Haarmann, impressively portrayed by the actor Goetz George. The persecution of the Jews and intellectuals is treated in two films produced in 1999: *Aimée und Jaguar* (Max Faerberboeck), based on the novel of the same name by Erica Fischer (1994), reminds today's audience of the tragic love story between the Jewish journalist Felice Schragenheim and the German housewife Lilly Wust during the Second World War; *Der Vulkan* (Ottokar Runze, 1999), adapted from the novel by Klaus Mann, portrays the desperate situation of German and Jewish emigrants in other European countries during the Third Reich. In 1993 a sequel to Wim Wenders' 1987 film *Wings of Desire* – which had so accurately captured the divided Berlin of the post-1961 years – was released: *In weiter Ferne, so nah!* is set in the vibrant city of the 1990s.

After 1989 the director Volker Schlöndorff attempted to revive the fortunes of the traditional film studios in Babelsberg, close to Berlin, but here, too, co-operation between East and West proved complicated. At about the same time a new generation of directors had emerged, eager to break away from everything to do with the cinematically unimportant 1980s.

Berlin-based events which support the film industry are film awards and film festivals. They take place every year. One of the most prestigious is the *Bundesfilmpreis*, founded in 1951. Since 2000 the festival preceding the award takes place at *Potsdamer Platz*, where the *Filmhaus* is now housed. Films that are not accepted for general distribution are, for example, shown during the *BerlinBeta Medienfestival*.

Attempts to restore Berlin's former role as an internationally acclaimed centre of film-making cannot conceal the decline in independent cinemas: respected smaller film houses are increasingly being driven out of business by the huge multiplex centres. This commercialisation and centralisation represent a considerable cultural loss to Berlin, since the existing hundred or so establishments have traditionally made an important contribution to the artistic life of the city. Unlike Köln, München and Hamburg, Berlin only gives limited financial support to new films. Nevertheless the number of film production companies is impressive: out of approximately 700 film and production firms the largest is in Berlin-Adlershof. Berlin is also increasingly popular as a location for TV films and series.

As for the theatre, East Berlin was on equal terms with its western counterpart. Years of censorship made the stage an important instrument for subtle political comment. Before the *Wende*, in particular, theatres functioned as a mouthpiece for the concerns of East Germans – with the *Deutsches Theater* leading the way. By the end of September 1989 the stage had more than ever become a political instrument. The director and playwright Heiner Müller remarked at the end of 1989 that:

> It is decisive that those who were silent are finally speaking up . . . The resistance of intellectuals and artists, who have been privileged for decades, to the current sell-out will achieve precious little, unless a dialogue is established with the underprivileged silent majority, who have been underprivileged for decades and who have been deprived of their rights in the name of Socialism.
>
> (*Neues Deutschland* 14 December 1989)

One reason East German theatres were able to assert themselves even amid the fundamental changes after 1989 – notably at the prolific *Volksbühne*, directed by Frank Castorf – was the fact that many eastern directors had worked in the West before the Wall came down. Nevertheless, financial and intellectual problems eventually began to emerge:

> What can art achieve once it does not function as an outlet any more? What kind of new aesthetics and structures will develop?. . . [There are] difficulties of communication: with West Germans. Even people from the theatre do not speak the same language. We talk in different tongues. Our motivation to make theatre is totally different.
>
> (Ingeborg Pietzsch, *Theater der Zeit* (6), 1990: 12–13)

By the end of the 1989–90 season GDR theatres had lost about 5 million of their audience.

In the process of reunification it became increasingly obvious that theatres – apart from seasonal highlights like the annual *Berliner Theatertreffen* – had entered a time of crisis. This had already begun in West Germany in the 1980s. Theatres that were solely dependent on box-office revenue were forced to close. Once again, institutional duplication between east and west Berlin made matters worse. In 1993 the renowned *Schillertheater* in west Berlin finally closed its doors despite widespread prostests. In this particular area of cultural production the process of rationalisation and 'liquidation' (*Abwicklung*) hit the west harder than the east (see also Patterson 1995).

In 1999, Germany had 152 publicly-owned theatres. Berlin had eight, about

30 privately-owned houses and numerous temporary venues. One of the new establishments is André Heller's variety theatre *Wintergarten* in *Potsdamer Strasse*. Alternative groups stage plays in the *Tacheles*, in *Podewil*, which in GDR times used to be the 'house of young talent', in the *Kulturbrauerei* in *Prenzlauer Berg*, in the *Bar jeder Vernunft* or in the well-established *UFA-Fabrik*. The *Tempodrom* with its variety performances and musical events had to leave its traditionally relaxed site in the *Tiergarten* when the government relocated to Berlin: its tents would have been within the officially designated area surrounding the government buildings, in which no public meetings or marches may be held. Since the end of 2001 it is housed in a new building at *Anhalter Bahnhof*.

Until his death in 1995, Heiner Müller ran the *Berliner Ensemble*, which was formerly Bertolt Brecht's theatre. A fixation with the past, closely linked to an admiration of Brecht carefully nurtured by the GDR government, had previously limited the potential of this theatre. After years of discussion and argument the *Berliner Ensemble* was finally taken over by Claus Peymann, who moved from the *Burgtheater* in Vienna in 1999. The beginning of his first season after a complex – and again carefully stage-managed – renovation of the building itself saw a programme that made a gesture of respect to Austro-German theatrical tradition: *Die Brecht-Akte* by George Tabori, Thomas Bernhard's *Der Ignorant und der Wahnsinnige* and Franz Xaver Kroetz's play *Das Ende der Paarung*. Kroetz's work is a dramatisation of the life and death of Petra Kelly, a leading Green Party politician who was shot by her partner Gert Bastian in the early 1990s. By 2000 the first high expectations had given way to wariness in critical reactions.

The most remarkable change of all happened in the West Berlin *Schaubühne*, when in 2000 a promising young team including Thomas Ostermeier and Sasha Waltz took over. The plan is to revive the features that in the 1970s contributed to the international reputation of this theatre – in particular, performing works by contemporary authors and involving the whole company in a democratic management structure. As well as staging the world premieres of new plays, the *Schaubühne* offers a programme of highly praised dance productions – modern dance being one of Berlin's most important cultural exports today. Coming after a period of stagnation, this venture marks the transfer of initiative in the theatre to a new generation.

The tradition of political provocation on stage has been revived by the controversial Christoph Schlingensief, who originally belonged to the *Volksbühne*. He has initiated sensational and topical campaigns (*Partei, Chance 2000*); the effect of his work can be described as being somewhere in between avant-garde and trash, between itinerant theatre and 'happening'.

As a result of these developments there has been a tangible revival of the theatrical scene. In 1999, the Berliner *Akademie der Künste* took stock and organised an exhibition comparing East and West German theatre since the end of the Second World War. Their aim was to stimulate productive comparisons and dispel dogmatic judgements.

CONCLUSION

More than a decade after reunification the cultural life of Berlin, which has been described as the European metropolis of the future, is still shaped by political, economic and intellectual change. The ten years since the *Wende* can be considered as a transitional period. For Berlin, as for Germany, reviewing past and present has been a demanding process and the culture in the city has adapted – an increase in the number of *events* being one of the dominant features. Many impulses of the 1990s have grown into longer-term trends, which may eventually turn out to be peculiar to Berlin. Others reflect cultural issues that may also be observed in Germany as a whole. One of the few things that can be stated with any certainty is that while the fall of the Wall has triggered cultural developments, writers and producers will not be able to capitalise on the events of 1989–90 for ever.

FURTHER READING

The bookshop Kiepert (Ernst-Reuter-Platz, 19587 Berlin) offers a yearly update of publications on Berlin. Links to relevant internet websites are available at: *http://www.berlin.de, http://www.BerlinOnline.de, www.berlinet.de/_ frame/start.htm* and *www.statistik-berlin.de*. A publication by the Berlin Senate (Senatsverwaltung für Stadtentwicklung, 2000) is worth consulting for developments in the 1990s. Overviews of the history of Berlin include Fisher and Read (1994), Richie (1999) and Large (2001); see also *Presse- und Informationsamt des Landes Berlin* (1992). Wise (1998) and Ladd (1997) cover the architecture of the city. For Berlin's cultural development and topics of the 1990s, see Süß and Rytlewski (1999), Siebenhaar (2000), Krüger (1998) and Taylor (1997). Glaser (1999), Kolinsky and Will (1999) and Flanagan and Taberner (2000) provide useful introductions to German culture in general. For literature in Berlin see Bienert (1999) and Schütz (1999). Hughes and Brady (1995) and Patterson (1995) contain relevant material for film and theatre just after the *Wende*. Sontheimer (1999) provides a critical account of the German government's move from Bonn to Berlin. Garton Ash (1997) offers a personal view on the methods and legacy of the *Stasi*. A selection of literary material may also be found in the magazine *Grand Street* ((69) 1999).

CONCLUSION:
SOME OBSERVATIONS
ON GERMAN CULTURAL
IDENTITY TODAY

By way of conclusion the following section looks briefly at some of the ways in which German language, life, customs and behaviour may be said to contribute towards a distinctive German cultural identity. Previous chapters have provided enough historical, political and social evidence for readers to judge for themselves the extent to which the national institutions and political, economic and social structures of modern Germany differ from their home country. Many institutions and aspects of life in Germany are, of course, increasingly subject to processes of Europeanisation and economic globalisation. Such processes may be expected to erode any narrow sense of cultural identity that is based on historical nationalism or traditional state boundaries. At the same time there is ample evidence of significant cultural diversity within Germany itself. We have seen in particular how Germany's regions, which have considerable autonomy in politics and educational policy, differ in terms of employment patterns, their economic strengths, the distribution of the population and many other aspects of human and physical geography. We should also note that globalisation at a supra-national level tends to strengthen feelings of social and cultural identity at the local level and may actually even reinforce awareness of more parochial cultural differences (Müller 1991b: 30). The observations below focus on western Germany, although differences in social values and styles of communication persist between east and west Germany (see, for example, Chapter 11).

DIALECTS

Germany's cultural diversity is reflected, among other things, in its dialects. Although the standard language is a powerful centralising force, dialects remain strong in Germany and continue to reinforce self-perceptions of local and regional identity. The main historical difference is between the Low

German dialects of the north and the High German dialects of the south. The division between the two areas is represented by a line extending from just north of Köln in the west to south of Berlin in the east. High German is further divided into Central German (a relatively narrow belt stretching from the Rhineland in the west to Leipzig in the east) and Upper German, which comprises mainly Alemannic (Swiss and Swabian) and Austro-Bavarian; the German-speaking area and its dialects extend, of course, beyond the national boundaries of the Federal Republic. A dialect is characterised by distinctive features of phonology, vocabulary, syntax and style, which mark it off significantly from other dialects and the standard (for overviews of the German dialects see Barbour and Stevenson 1990; Russ 1994). Both Upper and Central German have contributed to the national standard language spoken today. The influence of Central German owes much to Martin Luther's translation of the Bible, the first German version of the complete scriptures, which appeared between 1522 and 1534. The translation, disseminated in book form throughout Germany during the Reformation (the moveable-type printing press was developed at the same time), incorporated many features of Luther's native East Central German dialect and acted as a powerful model for the standard language that was to emerge during the seventeenth and eighteenth centuries.

By using a dialect, its speakers reinforce their sense of cultural and social distinctiveness. Purely linguistic features play a role in this perception. Thus the Berlin dialect (Berlinisch) has a preponderance of high front vowels (for example, *keen* for standard German *kein*), tends to be spoken very rapidly, and employs a rather harsh-sounding expiration or breathiness to express emphasis. These features are widely associated with the Berliners' typical attitude of disrespectfulness, pithiness, even rudeness (known as *Berliner Schnauze*, which may be politely translated as 'Berlin cheek'). The vocabulary of Berlin as a city dialect has also been influenced by immigrant populations of French and Jews, who have contributed many distinctive words, some of which have entered standard colloquial German (for instance, *meschugge* for 'crazy') and which have enriched the dialect's original Low German base. Berlin dialect retains a small number of Slav words that survived from the period when the area was colonised by German settlers during the early medieval period. The high frequency of place names ending in -*ow* in the surrounding area and the non-standard pronunciation of -*in* of 'Berlin' also reflect Slav influence. Witty turns of phrase and colourful metaphors (including nicknames for buildings) are a particular feature of Berlin style. The sharp, outwardly aggressive character of the Berlin urban dialect contrasts markedly with the softer, musical tones of Bavarian, which uses darker-sounding back vowels (*do* and *hob* instead of *da* and *hab*(e)) and employs many vocalic glides (diphthongs, such as *guat* for *gut*) where standard German has simple monovowels (monophthongs). Bavarian speech is more tonal than Berlin dialect, which lends it a more musical character.

It would be misleading to suggest that there is an inherent link between the linguistic features of a dialect and the social characteristics of its speakers. Nor do all of Germany's dialects exhibit the strong contrasts that we have noted between Berlinisch and Bavarian. Nevertheless, rather like religious customs, food and drink, holidays and festivals, dialect is part and parcel of a community's identity and Germans continue to regard regional language as an important element of their linguistic heritage. Between 1966 and 1992 four major surveys of dialect usage were conducted in Germany in order to establish where dialects were most widely spoken and which social groups employed them most often. Since the former GDR undertook no significant research into dialect usage, the eastern *Länder* could only be included in surveys after unification (Niebaum and Macha 1999: 144–52). The surveys, spanning a quarter of a century, confirmed the relative stability of dialect usage in relation to standard German, with over 58 per cent of the population (up to 8 per cent more men than women) claiming to be competent dialect speakers. There were, however, significant social and regional differences. Competence in dialect was strongest among older people, manual workers and in smaller, rural communities. It is also well known that actual usage of dialect depends on situation and interlocutor: it tends to be employed more with tradesmen and in the family, say, rather than more formal contexts such as in official institutions, the bank or at the doctor's (Russ 1994: 36). Overall the 1966–92 surveys showed dialects to be more firmly established in the southern states of western Germany (Bayern, Baden-Württemberg, Rheinland-Pfalz and the Saarland) than the central and northern *Länder*. Data on dialect usage in the eastern *Länder* remain sparse, although limited surveys suggest that the dialect base is considerably stronger here than in the old FRG. Interestingly, the correlation between competence in dialect and age, education and job is not as clearly defined as in the west. This is probably a legacy of the GDR's policy of overcoming traditional class differences and establishing a more uniform social structure.

CULTURAL STEREOTYPES

While dialects provide evidence of local diversity, some observers, often writing popular guides for visitors (especially businesspeople), draw attention to what they see as general characteristics of the German people. One such guide, for instance, sees Germans as possessing an 'innate romanticism' which makes them 'long for the beyond' and indulge in 'relentless tourism' (Flamini 1997: 18). According to the guide, the roots of this trait lie in the artistic and philosophical movement of romanticism, which arose in the early nineteenth century. It points to the fact that the German word 'Wanderlust' has entered the English language and reminds us how Germans pioneered the environmental movement at the turn of the century; further evidence of a fundamentally romantic character is alleged to be found in Germans' fascination with exotic cultures. While such observations may be valid, it should also be recognised that tourism and travel are largely a function of material affluence. Once again, readers must judge for themselves whether those Germans that they encounter in real life conform to such stereotypes or whether particular characteristics belong to individual social groups that attract more attention than they deserve. It is also salutary to consider whether, alongside nineteenth-century romanticism, we could point to other cultural movements (such as naturalism or expressionism) which support the construction of quite different stereotypes.

Although the existence of stereotypes should be approached with caution, there are many areas in which Germans are held to exhibit national cultural characteristics. These include an excessive love of rules and prescriptions designed to regulate social life, such as the prohibition against mowing the lawn on Sunday afternoons or the requirement not to deposit glass in recycling containers during quiet hours. On the other hand, Germans value very highly their personal freedom in certain areas and activities which are elsewhere regarded as unsocial: these include the right to smoke in public places and to travel at unrestricted speeds on the motorway.

Germans are widely perceived to take things literally and be very frank. They will, for instance, voice their opinions in conversation and are relatively uninhibited in matters of sexuality. Another alleged national trait is an unwillingness to take risks. Some observers see the fear of risk-taking as a positive factor contributing to Germany's post-war economic success. It is manifested, for instance, in the concord or 'social partnership' (*soziale Partnerschaft*) struck between trade unions, the workforce and employers. Related to risk-avoidance is the high premium most Germans attach to stability and dependability, which may explain why German investors traditionally prefer lower-interest accounts providing reliable financial returns over a longer period (Flamini 1997: 24). On the other hand, we have already noted signs of value change in younger Germans and the mounting pressure on German banks and managers to become more entrepreneurial and risk-taking.

Finally, Germans are supposed to be lacking in humour. In fact Germany has a long tradition, not only of burlesque and slapstick but also of wit and political satire, which comes to the fore in *Fasching* carnivals preceding Lent and has long been part of the Berlin cabaret scene. As for humour which is based on the manipulation of language, it has been suggested that Germans see their language in too serious a light to promote the development of purely verbal humour (such as irony or word-play) in anything but creative and artistic writing. Possible reasons for this are the German fondness for prescribing rules of language usage and a tradition of perceiving close links between language, ideology and philosophy (Clyne 1995: 129). As is probably the case in other cultures, humour in Germany is more acceptable in certain contexts than it is in others. In promotional advertising, for instance, while humour has been demonstrated to capture the attention of a German audience and amuse it, it will not persuade individuals to buy a product. While this is understandable for expensive and technical items such as motor cars, it also applies to toothbrushes and cigarettes (Staunton 1999).

STYLES OF INTERCULTURAL COMMUNICATION

Some of the following observations are drawn from guidelines that are readily available for business people who need to negotiate with Germans and for whom it is important not to offend their interlocutors through ignorance of cultural norms of communication. Most such advice is based on the need to conform to the high degree of formality that governs business meetings in Germany. Thus, when arriving for a meeting, visitors are expected to observe a fairly strict protocol: they will shake hands with all present and in order of seniority (introductions are accompanied with brief descriptions of responsibilities), and will exchange business cards before starting the meeting proper. Unlike their Anglo-Saxon counterparts, Germans will not use first names and will expect to be addressed by their formal titles, such as *Herr*, *Frau* (used for a married or unmarried female aged over eighteen or even younger) or *Doktor*. In formal situations Germans may insist on their academic titles (in contrast to the UK, academically and technically qualified staff are much more likely to be encountered in senior positions in German companies). In formal conversation Germans also tend to place more physical distance between their interlocutors than, say, Asians or North Americans and will avoid introductory small talk. While Americans, for instance, will readily talk (and enquire) about family and personal life, Germans separate the private and professional spheres. They will make direct eye contact, avoid demonstrative body language, and not be afraid to criticise or state their views and opinions openly and directly; in return, they will expect responses to be equally clear and will not easily pick up on messages conveyed indirectly through subtle hints ('reading between the lines').

As a rule business meetings will be based on facts and figures and will rely on a fairly open exchange of factual information presented in an objective, low-key manner. Gossip, digressions or unfounded criticisms of a competitor, for instance, will not impress a German business audience. Meetings in German clubs and similar organisations, however, appear to be run along less formal lines than businesses, allowing for more digressions and variations in speed (Clyne 1995: 138). Incidentally, it is worth noting that the widespread custom in the United Kingdom of attempting to combine social events with work (notably in the form of 'working lunches' or even 'working breakfasts') has not spread to Germany, where such practices will more probably be seen as inefficient and as violating the unwritten rule that work and leisure are kept apart. Germans are likely to regard the UK culture of regularly working beyond normal office hours as demonstrating a rather unhealthy imbalance between the spheres of work and home. Whether the growth of new media-based industries (for instance in Berlin) will undermine such conventions, including the formality associated with business meetings, remains to be seen,

Outside the business context, some of the features noted above have been observed in more general communication patterns among German-speakers (Clyne 1995: 121–5). Research suggests that Germans use more direct language in formulating complaints and requests and, compared with English-speakers, employ more modal markers that intensify the impact of an utterance (so-called upgraders, such as 'absolutely', 'I'm sure', 'you must understand'). In terms of inter-personal directness Germans rank somewhere below Argentineans and Israelis (who are more direct) and above Australians and French-Canadians (who are more indirect). German discussions may appear argumentative and contain stronger expressions of disagreement compared with, say, similar situations in English, Finnish or Spanish. Contrasts in communication routines have also been noted between (north) Germans and Austrians. Among other things the latter tend to use overstate-ments, more subjunctives and produce longer utterances as part of a central European style of discourse which employs justifications and explanations to support elaborate politeness routines. Austrians will take longer over intro-ductions while Germans will produce more but shorter statements and will move more rapidly to the point of the conversation; Germans will also close a conversation more quickly and employ fewer expressions of politeness (such as 'It was nice meeting you'; Stevenson 1997: 195).

From the mid-1980s various studies of intercultural communication between native German speakers and Germany's large immigrant population appeared (Rost-Roth 1997: 184). While focusing on the problems experienced by foreigners in communicative situations, these studies have also revealed something of the cultural expectations of Germans and of Europeans in general. Thus a German being interviewed for a job will draw attention to his or her abilities and previous experience, while a Turkish person is more likely to stress that he or she is aware of the difficulty of the task but is nevertheless willing to tackle it. It has also been observed that Germans, in common with other Europeans and white Americans, display more overt signs of listening (by nodding the head and maintaining eye contact) than other ethnic groups and are less tolerant of silences during conversation. Intercultural differences have been noted in rituals of greeting and departure, in forms of address, in talking about emotions and in styles of argument. Thus Germans make com-pliments less often than Americans, are more ready to criticise, and make less of an effort to entertain or amuse an audience.

Regional styles of communication

Regional differences in styles of communication have also been noted within Germany. Thus Germans from the Rhineland will more readily accept com-pliments than Swabians, while Bavarians, Berliners and Rhinelanders tend to be more expansive in verbal communication than northerners. The infor-mal pronoun *du* (you) is used more widely in South Germany and Austria than in the north and more in rural districts than in cities; it can also pre-dominate in areas with a strong left-wing tradition, such as Nordrhein-Westfalen, and in communities with a strong sense of political and social solidarity, such as university students (Clyne 1995: 125–6, 136). Patterns of maintaining physical distance (so-called proxemic rules) are also supposed to vary. Thus Bavarians and Rhinelanders are more likely than Germans from other regions to sit next to or directly opposite each other when entering a train (Clyne 1995: 127).

Styles of writing

Intercultural studies of writing have suggested that German academic texts are more excursive, digressive and provide fewer definitions than linearly structured English texts. The difference has been explained in terms of the Germans' preoccupation with content and their interest in providing a thorough treatment of the historical or theoretical background of a topic (Clyne 1995: 138). Germans will also rate incomprehensibility in a text positively as a sign of its serious and scientific nature, while English authors will feel a greater obligation to ensure that their readers understand the content (Clyne 1995: 138; Stevenson 1997: 193–4). The ability to express oneself orally is rated highly in Germany, whereas written language skills are considered more important in, say, Australia and within certain social groups in the UK. Such intercultural variations are probably due to different systems and patterns of education. At the same time, there is no shortage in Germany of books and guides on good style and on both written and oral communication, generally aimed at promoting success in business and work. German business letters and formal correspondence with institutions are subject to quite strict conventions in terms of layout and formulation. Many of these conventions have their origin in the *Kaufmannsbrief* (business letter) of the nineteenth century, whose formal style and phraseology were widely imitated and taught in schools and colleges and whose mastery was seen as a mark of commercial expertise and was rewarded with promotion.

The general spelling reform (*Rechtschreibreform*), debated since the 1950s, agreed in 1996, and introduced from 1 August 1998, has spawned a plethora of guides and dictionaries as well as generating a fierce and ongoing controversy about how or even whether German spelling and its complex rules of punctuation should be simplified (for overviews of the history of the reform and the issues raised see Stevenson 1995: 87–92; Clyne 1995: 180–5). Overall, Germans appear to attach far greater importance to the issue of standards and norms in their language than, say, English-speakers, who are possibly more accustomed to accepting international variations in the use of their language.

CONCLUSION

The above observations suggest that Germany combines internal cultural diversity with features that continue to mark its inhabitants and their traditions as distinctive from other peoples. Such features are, however, likely to change over the coming decades as Germany both becomes more integrated into Europe and reinforces its national political identity after unification.

INTERNET RESOURCES ON GERMANY

Since internet links on Germany are too numerous to list, only a small selection of sites relevant to the topics covered in this book is included here. For many more links and an annotated directory of internet resources see the website *Surfin' Germany – Germany on the Web*, maintained by the School of Modern Languages at the University of Exeter (author: Paul Joyce). Created primarily for undergraduate students, the site contains over 400 useful German websites in 22 areas of research which have been gathered here for easy reference. An assessment of each homepage tells you what you can expect to find and how to access the different resources. The site's address is: *http://www.exeter.ac.uk/flc/germtips/*. The School of Modern Languages also maintains the *German Media Index*, a collection of over 730 pages of links to German newspapers, magazines, news services, television and radio stations: *http://www.ex.ac.uk/german/media/*. All the following links and many more besides are included in the Exeter site.

Internet directories and search engines
http://www.dino-online.de/
http://web.de/
http://www.fireball.de/
http://www.suchindex.de/
http://www.metaspinner.de/

General reference and statistics
http://www.wissen.de/
http://www.xipolis.net/
http://userpage.chemie.fu-berlin.de/adressen/brd.html
http://194.94.238.74/tatsachen_ueber_deutschland/
http://www.statistik-bund.de/

German history
http://www.phil.uni-erlangen.de/~p1ges/vl-dtld-e.html
http://library.byu.edu/~rdh/wess/germ/hist.html
http://www.dwelle.de/d50/deutsch/

GDR and the *Wende*
http://www.ddr-im-www.de/
http://www.ddr-suche.de/
http://www.chronik-der-wende.de/

Federal states
http://www.bundesrat.de/ (with links to all the *Länder*)

Politics
http://www.politische-bildung-online.de/
http://de.yahoo.com/r/dh
http://www.gksoft.com/govt/en/de.html
http://www.bundestag.de/ (the *Bundestag* home page)
http://www.bundesregierung.de/ (the home page of the Federal Government)

Economy
http://www.deutsche-wirtschaft.de/
http://www.diw.de/
http://www.german-way.com/german/privat.html

Education
http://www.bildungsserver.de/
http://www.kmk.org/ (for schools)
http://www.hrk.de/ (for universities)

Social affairs
http://www.bmfsfj.de/ (general)
http://de.dir.yahoo.com/Gesellschaft_und_Soziales/ (general)
http://www.bundesauslaenderbeauftragte.de/ (foreigners)
http://www.uni-marburg.de/dir/ (foreigners)
http://www.isoplan.de/aid/ (foreigners)

Environment
http://www.bmu.de/ (Federal Ministry of the Environment)
http://www.gein.de/ (general)
http://www.bund.net/

Language issues
http://www.neue-rechtschreibung.de/ (spelling reform)
http://www.ids-mannheim.de/ (Institute for German Language)
http://nosferatu.cas.usf.edu/german/dialects/ (dialects)
http://focus.de/D/DI/DI08/DI08F/di08f.htm (east–west differences)

Berlin and cultural events
http://www.berlinonline.de/
http://www.berlin.de/
http://www.kultur-netz.de/
http://www.kulturportal-deutschland.de/

Cultural perceptions of Germans
http://rcswww.urz.tu-dresden.de/~english3/Jana/cultpage.htm

BIBLIOGRAPHY

Albrecht, G., Albrecht, W. and Bütow, M. 1996: Vorpommern – Stiefkind der Entwicklung? *Geographische Rundschau* **48** (9), 494–500.

Auer, P. 1998: Learning how to play the game. An investigation of role-played jobs in interviews in East Germany. *Text* **18**, 7–38.

Auer, P. 2000: Was sich ändert und was bleibt: Vorläufiges zu stilistischen Konvergenzen Ost → West am Beispiel von Interviews. In Auer, P. and Hausendorf, H. (eds), 151–76.

Auer, P. and Hausendorf, H. (eds) 2000: *Kommunikation in gesellschaftlichen Umbruchsituationen. Mikroanalytische Aspekte des sprachlichen und gesellschaftlichen Wandels in den Neuen Bundesländern*. Tübingen: Niemeyer.

Barbour, S. and Stevenson, P. 1990: *Variation in German: A Critical Approach to German Sociolinguistics*. Cambridge: Cambridge University Press.

Bedürftig, F. 1998: *Taschenlexikon Deutschland nach 1945*. München: Piper Verlag.

Behnke, K. and Wolf, J. (eds) 1998: *Stasi auf dem Schulhof. Der Mißbrauch von Kindern und Jugendlichen durch das Ministerium für Staatssicherheit*. Berlin: Ullstein.

Behrend, H. (ed.) 1995: *German Unification: The Destruction of an Economy*. London: Pluto Press.

Benz, W. 1989: Die Bundesrepublik Deutschland 1949–1989. In Weidenfeld, H. and Zimmermann, H. (eds), 35–47.

Bienert, M. 1999: *Berlin. Wege durch den Text der Stadt*. Stuttgart: Klett-Cotta.

Birkner, K. and Kern, F. 1996: Frictional encounters. German-German communication in job interviews. Lecture given at the 11th Sociolinguistic Symposium, Cardiff.

Birkner, K. and Kern, F. 2000: Ost- und Westdeutsche in Bewerbungsgesprächen. In Auer, P. and Hausendorf, H. (eds), 45–81.

Birnbaum, R. 2000: Vom Weg abgekommen. *Der Tagesspiegel* 11 March, 2.

Black, I. 2000: Internet giving race-hate groups new lease of life, EU watchdog says. *Guardian* 24 November, 17.

Black, I. and White, M. 2000: Nervous Britain rejects call to elect EU president. *Guardian* 15 November, 15.

Blacksell, M. 1995: Germany as a European power. In Lewis, D. and McKenzie, J. (eds), 77–100.

Blanke, B. and Perschke-Hartmann, C. 1994: The 1992 health reform victory over pressure group politics. *German Politics* **3**(2), 233–48.

Böltken, F. 1997: Einstellungen zu Ausländern. Ein Vergleich zwischen den neuen und den alten Bundesländern. *Geographische Rundschau* **49**(7–8), 432–7.

Boothroyd, S. 1998: The media landscape. In James, P. (ed.), 141–58.

Bricks, W. 1997: Thüringen –Tradition und Wandel. *Praxis Geographie* **6**, 4–11.

Bricks, W. and Gans, P. 1996: Thüringen. Regionale Vielfalt im Zentrum Deutschlands. *Geographische Rundschau* **48**(1), 4–11.

Brummer, A. and Elliott, L. 1999: Sailing into choppy water. *Guardian* 18 February, 17.

Buck, T. 2000: German minister gives academics a lesson in reform. *Financial Times* 26 October, 8.

Bültmann, A. and Wätzold, F. 1999: Die EG-Öko-Audit-Verordnung im verflixten siebten Jahr. *Aus Politik und Zeitgeschichte* B48/99, 30–8.

Bunting, M. 2000: Confronting the perils of global warming in a vanishing landscape. *Guardian* 14 November, 1.

Busch, E., Handschuh, E., Kretschmer, G. and Zeh, W. 1990: *Wegweiser Parlament.* Bonn: Bundeszentrale für politische Bildung.

Carlin, W. 1998: The new east German economy: problems of transition, unification and institutional mismatch. *German Politics* **7**(3), 14–32.

Cesarani, D. 2000: Need to know. *Guardian* 7 October, 8 (review section).

Christo and Jeanne-Claude 1995: *Verhüllter/Wrapped Reichstag.* Köln: Taschen.

Clemens, C. and Paterson, W.E. 1998: Special issue on the Kohl Chancellorship. *German Politics* **7**(1).

Clyne, M.C. 1995: *The German Language in a Changing Europe.* Cambridge: Cambridge University Press.

Czyzewski, M., Gülich, E., Hausendorf, H. and Kastner, M. (eds) 1995: *Nationale Selbst- und Fremdbilder im Gespräch.* Opladen: Leske + Budrich.

Dahrendorf, R. 1966: *Bildung ist Bürgerrecht.* Hamburg: Wegner Verlag.

Davies, P. and Dombrowski, P. 1997: Appetite of the wolf: German foreign assistance for central and eastern europe. *German Politics* **6**(1), 2–22.

Derbyshire, I. 1991: *Politics in Germany: From Division to Unification.* Edinburgh: Chambers.

Deutscher Bundestag (Referat Öffentlichkeitsarbeit) (ed.) 1991: *Berlin Bonn, die Debatte: alle Bundestagsreden vom 20. Juni 1991.* Köln: Kiepenheuer & Witsch.

Dittberner, J. 2000: Routine ist tödlich. *Der Tagesspiegel* 6 June, 30.

Dittmar, N. 2000: Sozialer Umbruch und Sprachwandel am Beispiel der Modalpartikeln *halt* und *eben* in der Berliner Kommunikationsgemeinschaft nach der Wende. In Auer, P. and Hausendorf, H. (eds), 199–234.

Duckenfield, M. 1999: The Goldkrieg: revaluing the Bundesbank's reserves and the politics of the EMU. *German Politics* **8**(1), 106–30.

Eich-Born, M. 1996: Industriestandort Mecklenburg-Vorpommern. Dominanz der Werftindustrie. *Geographische Rundschau* **48**(9), 517–24.

Enzyklopädie der DDR. 2000: Berlin: Directmedia Publishing GmbH.

Eroms, H.-W. 1997: Sprachliche 'Befindlichkeiten' der Deutschen in Ost und West. *Der Deutschunterricht* (1), 6–16.

Fest, J. 1999: Das Böse als reale Macht. *Der Spiegel* (43), 25 October, 182–97.

Fiehler, R. 1995: Die Wiedervereinigung als Kulturberührung. Ausarbeitung von wechselseitigen Kategorisierungen und von Beziehungsmodellen im massenmedialen deutsch-deutschen Diskurs. In Czykewski *et al.* (eds), 328–47.

Fischer, E. 1994: *Aimée und Jaguar. Eine Liebesgeschichte, Berlin 1943.* Köln: Kiepenheuer & Witsch.

Fisher, D. and Read, A. 1994: *Berlin. The Biography of a City.* London: Pimlico.

Fix, U. 1997: Die Sicht der Betroffenen. Beobachtungen zum Kommunikationswandel in den neuen Bundesländern. *Der Deutschunterricht* (1), 42–9.

Flamini, R. 1997: *Passport Germany.* San Rafael, CA: World Trade Press.

Flanagan, C. and Taberner, S. (eds) 2000: 1949/1989: Cultural perspectives on division and unity in East and West. *German Monitor* **50**, Amsterdam/Atlanta: Rodopi.

Flockton, C. 1998: Employment, welfare support and income distribution in east Germany. *German Politics* **7**(3), 33–51.

Flockton, C. and Kolinsky, E. 1998: Recasting east Germany: an introduction. *German Politics* **7**(3), 1–13.

Fraas, C. 1994: Kommunikationskonflikte vor dem Hintergrund unterschiedlicher Erfahrungswelten. *Zeitschrift für Germanistische Linguistik* **22**, 87–90.

Frey-Vor, G. 1999: Sehen Ostdeutsche anders fern? Über Unterschiede in der Nutzung von Fernsehangeboten. In Probst, L. (ed.), 163–76.

Fricke, K.-W. 1991: *MfS intern. Macht, Strukturen, Auflösung der DDR-Staatssicherheit. Analyse und Dokumentation.* Köln: Verlag Wissenschaft.

Fritzler, M. 1997: *Ökologie und Umweltpolitik.* Bonn: Bundeszentrale für politische Bildung.

Fulbrook, M. 1995: *Anatomy of a Dictatorship: Inside the GDR 1949–1989.* Oxford: Oxford University Press.

Gabriel, K. 1998: Kirchen/Religionsgemeinschaften. In Schäfers, B. and Zapf, W. (eds), 371–81.

Gabriel, O. W. and Holtmann, E. (eds) 1997: *Handbuch politisches System der Bundesrepublik Deutschland.* München: Oldenbourg Verlag.

Gabriel, O. W., Kunz, V. and Ahlstich, K. 1997: Die kommunale Selbstverwaltung. In Gabriel, O.W. and Holtman, E. (eds), 325–54.

Gansel, C. and Gansel, C. 1997: Zwischen Karrierefrau und Hausmann. Aspekte geschlechterdifferenzierenden Sprachgebrauchs in Ost und West. *Der Deutschunterricht* (1), 59–69.

Garton Ash, T. 1997: *The File: A Personal History.* London: Vintage Books.

Gaus, G. 1983: *Wo Deutschland liegt.* Hamburg: Hoffmann and Campe.

Geiger, H. 1993: Zur Entstehung der Behörde des Bundesbeauftragten und des Stasi-Unterlagen-Gesetzes. In Henke, K.-D. (ed.), 35–48.

Geißler, R. 1998: Sozialstruktur. In Schäfers, B. and Zapf, W. (eds), 643–52.

Gensicke, T. 1992: Mentalitätswandel und Revolution. *Deutschland Archiv* **25**(12), 1266–83.

Germis, C. 2000: Zwiespältig. Warum die PDS beobachtet wird. *Der Tagesspiegel* 4 April, 2.

Giersch, H., Pacqué, K.-H. and Schmieding, H. 1992: *The Fading Miracle: Four Decades of Market Economy in Germany.* Cambridge: Cambridge University Press.

Gill, D. and Schröter, U. 1993: *Das Ministerium für Staatssicherheit. Anatomie des Mielke-Imperiums.* Hamburg and Berlin: Rowohlt.

Glaser, H. 1999: *Deutsche Kultur 1945–2000.* Berlin: Ullstein.

Goldhagen, D.J. 1996: *Hitler's Willing Executioners: Ordinary Germans and the Holocaust.* New York: Vintage Books.

Good, C. 1993: Über die 'Kultur der Mißverständnisses' im vereinten Deutschland. *Muttersprache* **103**, 249–59.

Graf, W.D. (ed.) 1992: *The Internationalization of the German Political Economy.* London: Macmillan.

Grammes, T. and Riedel, R. 1997: Bildungs- und Wissenschaftspolitik. In Gabriel, O.W. and Holtman, E. (eds), 729–50.

Grieder, P. 1999: *The East German Leadership 1946–73.* Manchester: Manchester University Press.

Grötsch, V. 1994: 'Damals, zu DDR-Zeiten, . . .' Zur moralischen Kontamination von Vergleichselementen in ostdeutschen Familientischgesprächen. Arbeitspapier Nr. 13 des Projekts Moral. Konstanz: Gießen.

Grünewalder, K.-W. and Manthey, H. 1986: Niedersachsen und Bremen. *Praxis Geographie* **5**, 6–13.

Gukenbiehl, H. 1998: Bildung und Bildungssystem. In Schäfers, B. and Zapf, W. (eds), 85–100.

Hahlen, J. 1999: Statement von Präsident Johann Hahlen zum Pressegespräch Hochschulstandort Deutschland. *Statistisches Bundesamt* 25 November. *http:www. statistik-bund-de/presse/deutsch/pm/st_hs99.htm*

Hancock, M.D. and Welsh, H.A. (eds) 1994: *German Unification: Processes and Outcomes.* Boulder, CO, San Francisco, CA and Oxford: Westview Press.

Harding, R. 1999: Standort Deutschland in the globalising economy: an end to the economic miracle? *German Politics* 8(1), 66–88.

Hausendorf, H. 2000: Ost- und Westgehörigkeit als soziale Kategorien im wiedervereinigten Deutschland. In Auer, P. and Hausendorf, H. (eds), 83–111.

Heinemann, M. 1995: Vorher war alles irgendwie organisiert: Verhaltensmuster im deutsch-deutschen Dialog. In Czyzewski *et al.* (eds), 389–95.

Hellmann, M. 1991: 'Ich suche eine Wohnung.' Zur vergleichenden Untersuchung alltagssprachlichen Handelns in den beiden deutschen Staaten. *Beiträge zur Sprachwissenschaft 5. Kommunikationsbedingungen und Alltagssprache in der ehemaligen DDR,* Hamburg, 19–32.

Hellmann, M. 1994: Ostdeutsch – Westdeutsch im Kontakt. Brücke oder Schranke der Verständigung? *Terminologie et Traduction* (1), 105–38.

Hellmann, M. 1997: Tendenzen der sprachlichen Entwicklung seit 1989 im Spiegel der Forschung. *Der Deutschunterricht* (1), 17–32.

Henke, K.-D. (ed.) 1993: *Wann bricht schon mal ein Staat zusammen! Die Debatte über die Stasi-Akten auf dem 39. Historikertag 1992.* München: dtv.

Henkys, R. 1989: Die Evangelische Kirche in der DDR. In Weidenfeld, W. and Zimmermann, H. (eds), 193–202.

Heringer, H-J. (ed.) 1994: *Tendenzen der deutschen Gegenwartssprache.* Tübingen: Niemeyer.

Hettlage, R. 1995: Integrationsleistungen des Rechts im Prozeß der deutschen Einheit. In Hettlage, R. and Lenz, K. (eds), 22–67.

Hettlage, R. and Lenz, K. (eds) 1995: *Deutschland nach der Wende. Eine Bilanz.* München: Verlag C.H. Beck.

Hitchens, D.M., Wagner, K. and Birnie, J.F. 1993: *East German Productivity and the Transition to the Market Economy.* Aldershot: Avebury Publishing.

Hoffmann, R. 1995: Brandenburg an der Schwelle ins 21. Jahrhundert. *Praxis Geographie* 10, 5–9.

Höllen, M. 1989: Die Katholische Kirche in der DDR. In Weidenfeld, W. and Zimmermann, H. (eds), 174–84.

Hooper, J. 2000a: Gleaming dome belies a dark reality for Germany's Jews. *Guardian* 7 October, 18.

Hooper, J. 2000b: Germany says welcome, but for how long? *Guardian* 31 October, 16.

Hooper J. and Connolly, K. 2001: Germany wants EU integrated in 10 years. *Guardian* 1 May, 15.

Hughes, H. and Brady, M. 1995: German film after the *Wende.* In Lewis, D. and McKenzie, J. (eds), 276–96.

Jakobs, H.-J. 1999: Alles unter einem Dach. *Der Spiegel* (41) 11 October, 162–4.

James, P. (ed.) 1998: *Modern Germany: Politics, Society and Culture.* London: Routledge.

Jansen, F. 2000a: Skins sind Mainstream. *Der Tagesspiegel* 21 December, 8.

Jansen, F. 2000b: Von rechts wegen. *Der Tagesspiegel* 22 December, 2.

Jansen, F. 2000c: Und es werden immer mehr. *Der Tagesspiegel* 22 December, 2.

Jarausch, K. 1994: *The Rush to German Unity.* Oxford: Oxford University Press.

Jeffery, C. (ed.) 1999: *Recasting German Federalism: The Legacies of Unification.* London and New York: Pinter.

Jeffery, C. and Whittle, R. 1997: *Germany Today.* London: Arnold.

Jones, A. 1994: *The New Germany: A Human Geography.* Chichester: Wiley.

Kaase, M. 1998: Massenkommunikation und Massenmedien. In Schäfers, B. and Zapf, W. (eds), 452–61.

Kaufman, D. 1998: The Nazi legacy. Coming to terms with the past. In James, P. (ed.), 124–40.

Kaufman, F.-X. 1989: Die soziale Sicherheit in der Bundesrepublik Deutschland. In Weidenfeld, W. and Zimmermann, H. (eds), 308–25.

Kershaw, I. 1999: Historian to the hollow man. *Guardian* 16 October 11.

Kettenacker, L. 1997: *Germany since 1945.* Oxford: Oxford University Press.

Klages, H. 1998: Werte und Wertewandel. In Schäfers, B. and Zapf, W. (eds), 698–709.

Kleßmann, C. and Sabrow, M. 1996: Zeitgeschichte in Deutschland nach 1989. *Aus Politik und Zeitgeschichte* B39/96 3–14.

Klimsa, P. 1997: *Multimedia. Anwendungen, Tools und Techniken.* Hamburg: Rowohlt.

Knapp, U. 1999: Verfassungsgericht verlangt von den Ländern die Neuregelung des Finanzausgleichs. *Der Tagesspiegel* 12 November, 1.

Koch, K. 1995: The German economy: decline or stability. In Lewis, D. and McKenzie, J. (eds), 127–47.

Koch, K. 1998: The impact of German unification on the German industrial relations system. *German Politics* 7(3), 52–68.

Kolinsky, E. and Will, W.v.d. (eds) 1999: *The Cambridge Companion to Modern German Culture.* Cambridge: Cambridge University Press.

Kopka, F.J. 2000: Pastor Allwissend. *Die Woche: Wirtschaft* 29 September, 3.

Kowakle, H. 1994: Der Freistaat Sachsen – ein geographischer Überblick. *Praxis Geographie* 9, 4–11.

Kowalski, M., Schuster, J. and Schwab, F. 2000: Risiken und Nebenwirkungen. *Focus* (2) 10 January, 165–8.

Krechtig, M. 2001: First women join combat units. *Guardian* 3 January, 14.

Kropp, S. 1997: Die Länder in der bundesstaatlichen Ordnung. In Gabriel, O.W. and Holtmann, E. (eds), 245–88.

Krüger, T. (ed.) 1998: *Die bewegte Stadt. Berlin am Ende der Neunziger.* Berlin: FAB Verlag.

Krupa, M. 2000: Die Angst der Politiker vor dem heiklen Thema Einwanderung. *Textarchiv Berliner Zeitung* 18 May. *http://www.BerlinOnline.de*

Kühn, I. and Almstädt K. 1997: Deutsch-deutsche Verständigungsprobleme. Erfahrungen aus der Sprachberatung. *Der Deutschunterricht* (1), 86–94.

Laabs, D. and Meyer, C. 2001: Ökolust statt Körnerfrust. *Der Spiegel* (3) 15 January, 25–34.

Ladd, B. 1997: *The Ghosts of Berlin: Confronting German History in the Urban Landscape.* Chicago, IL: University of Chicago Press.

Large, D.C. 2001: *Berlin: A Modern History.* Harmondsworth: Penguin.

Larres, K. and Panayi, P. (eds) 1996: *The Federal Republic of Germany since 1949: Politics, Society and Economy before and after Unification.* London and New York: Longman.

Lehmann, H-G. 1996: *Deutschland-Chronik 1945 bis 1995.* Bonn: Bundeszentrale für politische Bildung.

Leonardy, U. 1999: The institutional structures of German federalism. In Jeffery, C. (ed.), 3–22.

Lewis, D. 1995: The GDR. *Wende* and legacy. In Lewis, D. and McKenzie, J. (eds), 52–73.

Lewis, D. and McKenzie, J. (eds) 1995: *The New Germany: Social, Political and Cultural Challenges of Unification.* Exeter: University of Exeter Press.

Ludz, P.C. and Kuppe, J. 1975: *DDR Handbuch.* Köln: Wissenschaft und Politik.

Lütz, S. 2000: From managed to market capitalism? German finance in transition. *German Politics* **9**(2), 149–70.

McElvoy, A. 1992: *The Saddled Cow: East Germany's Life and Legacy.* London: Faber and Faber.

Maier, H. 1989: Die Katholische Kirche in der Bundesrepublik Deutschland. In Weidenfeld, W. and Zimmermann, H. (eds), 165–73.

Malunat, B.M. 1994: Die Umweltpolitik der Bundesrepublik Deutschland. *Aus Politik und Zeitgeschichte* B49/94, 3–12.

Maretzke, S. and Irmen, E. 1999: Die ostdeutschen Regionen im Wandel. Regionale Aspekte des Transformationsprozesses. *Aus Politik und Zeitgeschichte,* B5/99, 3–99.

Maull, H. 2000: German foreign policy, post-Kosovo: still a civilian power? *German Politics* **9**(2), 1–24.

Menze, C. 1996: Zur Geschichte der Universität 1945–1996. *Pädagogische Rundschau* **50**, 379–406.

Meyn, H. 1992: *Massenmedien in der Bundesrepublik Deutschland.* Berlin: Colloquium Verlag.

Moeller, M.L. and Maaz, H-J. 1995: *Die Einheit beginnt zu zweit. Ein deutsch-deutsches Zwiegespräch.* Reinbek: Rowohlt.

Mönch, R. 1998: Zwei von drei Häusern wurden korrekt erworben. *Der Tagesspiegel* 16 December.

Müller, B.-D. (ed.) 1991a: *Interkulturelle Wirtschaftskommunikation.* München: iudicium verlag.

Müller, B.-D. 1991b: Die Bedeutung der interkulturellen Kommunikation für die Wirtschaft. In Müller, B.-D. (ed.), 27–52.

Müller-Heidelberg, T., Finckh, U., Narr, W.-D. and Pelzer, M. (eds) 1998: *Grundrechte-Report. Zur Lage der Bürger- und Menschenrechte in Deutschland.* Hamburg: Rowohlt.

Müller-Schneider, T. 1998: Freizeit und Erholung. In Schäfers, B. and Zapf, W. (eds), 221–31.

Nave-Herz, R. 1998: Familie und Verwandschaft. In Schäfers, B. and Zapf, W. (eds), 201–10.

Neather, E. 1995: Education in the new Germany. In Lewis, D. and McKenzie, J. (eds), 148–72.

Neubacher, A. 2000: Abschied vom Monopol. *Der Spiegel* (6) 7 February, 72–3.

Neuweiler, G. 1994: Das gesamtdeutsche Haus für Forschung und Lehre. *Aus Politik und Zeitgeschichte* B25/94, 3–11.

Niebaum, H. and Macha, J. 1999: *Einführung in die Dialektologie des Deutschen.* Tübingen: Max Niemeyer Verlag.

Nissen, S. 1997: Soziale Sicherung. In Gabriel, O.W. and Holtmann, E. (eds), 681–96.

Noelle-Neumann, E., Schulz, W. and Wilke, J. (eds) 2000: *Publizistik. Massenkommunikation.* Frankfurt am Main: Fischer.

Nooteboom, C. 1999: *Allerseelen*. Frankfurt am Main: Suhrkamp.

Nowak, K. 1995: Evangelische Kirche in der DDR. *Geschichte in Wissenschaft und Unterricht* **46**(1), 142–52.

Oppermann, C. 2000: Vereint in Armut und Reichtum. *Die Woche: Wirtschaft* 29 September, 14–15.

Osborn, A. 2000: Official calls for public vote on enlarging EU. *Guardian* 4 September, 12.

Otto, J. 1999: Winners and losers. *Die Zeit* 9 September.

Paterson, T. 2000a: East Germans revive red rite of passage. *Guardian* 1 April, 15.

Paterson, T. 2000b: Row as Holocaust defender wins prize. *Guardian* 1 June, 16.

Paterson, T. 2000c: Schröder condition on EU entry. *Guardian* 19 December, 14

Paterson, W.E. and Southern, D. 1991: *Governing Germany*. Oxford: Blackwell.

Patterson, M. 1995: The German theatre. In Lewis, D. and McKenzie, J. (eds), 259–75.

Patzelt, W.J. 1997: Der Bundesrat. In Gabriel, O.W. and Holtmann, E. (eds), 207–28.

Paul, I. 2000: Gerahmte Kommunikation. Die Inszenierung ost- und westdeutscher Kommunikationserfahrungen im Mediendiskurs. In Auer, P. and Hausendorf, H. (eds), 113–50.

Peacock, A. and Willgerodt, H. (eds) 1989: *Germany's Social Market Economy: Origins and Evolution*. London: Macmillan.

Pfahl-Traughber, A. 1999: *Rechtextremismus in der Bundesrepublik*. München: Verlag C.H. Beck.

Picht, G. 1964: *Die Deutsche Bildungskatastrophe*. Freiburg: Walter.

Plenzdorf, U., Schlesinger, K. and Stade, M. 1995: *Berliner Geschichten*. Frankfurt am Main: Suhrkamp.

Plöhn J. 1997: Die Gerichtsbarkeit. In Gabriel, O.W. and Holtmann, E. (eds), 355–77.

Pogunkte, T. 1997: Politische Parteien. In Gabriel, O.W. and Holtmann, E. (eds), 501–23.

Pohl, I. 1997: Bedeutung sprachlicher Ausdrücke im Wandel. *Der Deutschunterricht* (1), 50–8.

Polenz, P. v. 1993: Die Sprachrevolte in der DDR im Herbst 1989. Ein Forschungsbericht nach drei Jahren vereinter germanistischer Linguistik. *Zeitschrift für germanistische Linguistik* (21), 127–49.

Pötzsch, H. 1998: *Deutsche Geschichte von 1945 bis zur Gegenwart. Die Entwicklung der beiden deutschen Staaten*. München: Olzog.

Presse- und Informationsamt des Landes Berlin 1992: *Berlin Handbuch. Das Lexikon der Bundeshauptstadt*. Berlin: FAB Verlag.

Pritchard, R. 1998: Education transformed? The east German school system since the *Wende*. *German Politics* **7**(3), 126–46.

Probst, L. (ed.) 1999: *Differenz in der Einheit*. Berlin: Christoph Links Verlag.

Prützel-Thomas, M. 1993: The abortion issue and the Federal Constitutional Court. *German Politics* **2**(3), 467–84.

Raff, D. 1985: *Deutsche Geschichte vom Alten Reich zur Zweiten Republik*. München: Max Hueber Verlag.

Rauch, Y. v. and Visscher, J. (eds) 2000: *Der Potsdamer Platz. Urbane Architektur für das neue Berlin*. Berlin: Jovis.

Reiher, R. 1997: Dreiraum- versus Dreizimmerwohnung. Zum Sprachgebrauch der Ostdeutschen. *Der Deutschunterricht* (1), 42–9.

Richie, A. 1999: *Faust's Metropolis: A History of Berlin*. London: HarperCollins.

Richter, G. 1999: Enttäuschte Erwartungen? Liebesbeziehungen zwischen Ost und West. In Probst, L. (ed.), 152–62.

Richter, M.W. 1994: Exiting the GDR: political movements and parties between democratization and westernization. In Hancock, M.D. and Welsh, H.A. (eds), 93–138.

Roberts, G.K. 1997: *Party Politics in the New Germany*. London: Pinter.

Rohlfs, H.-H. and Schäfer, U. (eds) 1997: *Jahrbuch der Bundesrepublik Deutschland 1997*, 12th edn. München: Deutscher Taschenbuch Verlag.

Rost-Roth, M. 1997: Language in intercultural communication. In Stevenson, P. (ed.), 171–206.

Roth, A. and Frajman, M. 1998: *The Goldapple Guide to Jewish Berlin*. Berlin: Goldapple.

Rother, K. 1994: Gedanken zur Gliederung und Terminologie Deutschlands. Das Beispiel 'Mitteldeutschland'. *Geographische Rundschau* **46**(12), 728–30.

Rüdig, W. 2000: Phasing out nuclear energy in Germany. *German Politics* **9**(3), 43–80.

Russ, C.V. 1994: *The German Language Today: A Linguistic Introduction*. London and New York: Routledge.

Salzen, C. von 2000: Erschreckende Ahnungslosigkeit über Holocaust. *Der Tagesspiegel* 18 February, 5.

Sandford, J. 1995: The German media. In Lewis, D. and McKenzie, J. (eds), 199–219.

Schäfers, B. 1998: *Politischer Atlas Deutschland. Gesellschaft, Wirtschaft, Staat*. Bonn: Dietz Verlag.

Schäfers, B. and Zapf, W. (eds) 1998: *Handwörterbuch zur Gesellschaft Deutschlands*. Opladen: Leske + Budrich.

Schlicht, U. 2000: Hotel Mama begünstigt das Studium zu Hause. *Der Tagesspiegel* 27 September, 36.

Schlicht, U. and Törne, L.v. 1999: Eine Frage der Scheine. *Der Tagesspiegel*. 30 October, 2.

Schluchter, W. 1994: Die Hochschulen in Ostdeutschland vor und nach der Einigung. *Aus Politik und Zeitgeschichte* B25/94, 12–22.

Schneider, H.-P. 1999: German unification and the federal system: the challenge of reform. In Jeffery, C. (ed.), 58–84.

Schneider, P. 1999: *Eduards Heimkehr*. Berlin: Rowohlt.

Schröder, U. 1996: Corporate governance in Germany: the changing role of the banks. *German Politics* **5**(3), 356–70.

Schroeder, K. 1998: *Der SED-Staat: Partei, Staat und Gesellschaft 1949–1990*. München: Propyläen Taschenbuch/Carl Hanser Verlag.

Schuster, F. 2000: Den Standort Thüringen stärken. Regierungserklärung des Ministers für Wirtschaft, Arbeit und Infrastruktur vom 16. März 2000. *http://www.thueringen.de/pm/pm2–1603.htm*

Schütz, E. (ed.) 1999: *Text der Stadt. Reden von Berlin. Literatur und Metropole seit 1989*. Berlin: Weidler.

Schwehn, K.J. 1998: Der FDP fehlen die Frauen. *Der Tagesspiegel* 28 August, 2.

Seifert, W. 1997: Integration von Ausländern. *Statistisches Bundesamt*, 579–89.

Seils, C. 2000: Die Birthler-Behörde. *Die Woche: Wirtschaft* 29 September, 10.

Senatsverwaltung für Stadtentwicklung (ed.) 2000: *Berlin. Zehn Jahre Transformation und Modernisierung*. Berlin.

Sewering, W. 2000: Herz, Kunstherz oder Themenpark? In Rauch *et al.* (eds), 47–58.

Sharp, I. and Flinspach, D. 1995: Women in Germany from division to unification. In Lewis, D. and McKenzie, J. (eds), 173–95.

Siebenhaar, K. (ed.) 2000: *Kulturhandbuch Berlin. Geschichte und Gegenwart von A-Z.* Berlin: Bastelmann und Sieben.

Smith, E.O. 1994: *The German Economy.* London and New York: Routledge.

Smith, G., Paterson, W.E. and Merkl, P.H. (eds) 1989: *Developments in West German Politics.* London: Macmillan.

Smyser, W.R. 1993: *The German Economy: Colossus at the Crossroads*, 2nd edn. Harlow: Longman.

Sontheimer, M. 1999: *Berlin, Berlin. Der Umzug in die Hauptstadt.* Hamburg: Hoffmann und Campe.

Speakman, F. and Speakman, C. 1992: *The Green Guide to Germany.* London: Green Print.

Staritz, D. 1996: *Geschichte der DDR.* Frankfurt am Main: Suhrkamp.

Statistisches Bundesamt (ed.) 1997: *Datenreport 1997.* Bonn: Bundeszentrale für politische Bildung.

Statistisches Jahrbuch (ed.) 1999: Statistisches Jahrbuch für die Bundesrepublik Deutschland und für das Ausland. Wiesbaden and Stuttgart: Statistisches Bundesamt/Metzler-Poeschel Verlag. Published as CD-ROM.

Staunton, D. 1999: No jokes please we're German, advertising students told. *Guardian* 20 June, 16.

Steele, J. 2000: Fortress Europe confronts the unthinkable. *Guardian* 30 October 17.

Stern 1995: In Hülle und Fülle. *Stern* (27), 21.

Stevenson, P. (ed.) 1997: *The German Language and the Real World: Sociolinguistic, Cultural, and Pragmatic Perspectives on Contemporary German*, revised edn. Oxford: Clarendon Press.

Steyer, C-D. 2000: Der Konflikt mit den Bauern ist im Nationalpark vertagt. *Der Tagesspiegel* 7 April, 18.

Story, J. 1996: Finanzplatz Deutschland: national or European response to internationalisation? *German Politics* 5(3), 371–94.

Streeck, J. 1995: Ethnomethodologische Differenzen im Ost-West-Verhältnis. In Czyzewski *et al.* (eds), 430–6.

Strohschneider, S. 1997: Eine Nation, zwei Arten des Denkens. *Psychologie Heute* March, 30–5.

Sturm, R. 1997a: Aufgabenstrukturen, Kompetenzen und Finanzierung. In Gabriel, O.W. and Holtmann, E. (eds), 619–58.

Sturm, R. 1997b: Arbeit und Wirtschaft. In Gabriel, O.W. and Holtmann, E. (eds) 659–79.

Süß, W. and Rytlewski, R. (eds) 1999: *Berlin. Die Hauptstadt. Vergangenheit und Zukunft einer europäischen Metropole.* Berlin: Nicolai.

Taylor, R. 1997: *Berlin and its Culture: A Historical Portrait.* New Haven, CT and London: Yale University Press.

Traynor, I. 1998a: Pornography test case for internet providers. *Guardian*, 13 May, 14.

Traynor, I. 1998b: Disaffected east turning its back on Kohl the unifier. *Guardian* 23 September, 17.

Traynor, I. 1999a: Germany champions women in the home. *Guardian* 19 June, 16.

Traynor, I. 1999b: German Catholics in uproar at Pope's ban on abortion advice. *Guardian* 19 June, 16.